The Cambridge Companion to
Modern Japanese Culture

This Companion provides a comprehensive overview of the influences
that have shaped modern-day Japan. Covering topics such as technology,
food, nationalism and the rise of anime and manga in the visual arts, this
book traces the cultural transformation that took place over the course of
the 20th century, and paints a picture of a nation rich in cultural diversity.
With contributions from some of the most prominent scholars in the field,
The Cambridge Companion to Modern Japanese Culture is an
authoritative introduction to this subject.

YOSHIO SUGIMOTO is Professor Emeritus in the School of Social Sciences,
La Trobe University, Melbourne, Australia.

Cambridge Companions to Culture

The Cambridge Companion to
Modern Japanese Culture

Edited by
YOSHIO SUGIMOTO

CAMBRIDGE
UNIVERSITY PRESS

CAMBRIDGE UNIVERSITY PRESS
Cambridge, New York, Melbourne, Madrid, Cape Town, Singapore, São Paulo, Delhi

Cambridge University Press
477 Williamstown Road, Port Melbourne, VIC 3207, Australia

www.cambridge.edu.au
Information on this title: www.cambridge.org/9780521706636

First published 2009
Reprinted 2010

Cover design by Mary Mason
Typeset by Aptara Corp.
Maps by Tony Fankhauser
Printed in China by Printplus

National Library of Australia Cataloguing in Publication data
   The Cambridge companion to modern Japanese culture / Yoshio Sugimoto.
   9780521880473 (hbk.)
   9780521706636 (pbk.)
   Includes index.
   Bibliography.
   Japan—Civilization—1945–
   Japan—Social conditions—1945–
   Sugimoto, Yoshio, 1939–
   Cambridge University
952.04

ISBN 978-0-521-70663-6 paperback
ISBN 978-0-521-88047-3 hardback

Contents

Figures

Tables

Contributors

HIDEO AOKI, Institute on Social Theory and Dynamics, Hiroshima, is a sociologist who specialises in studies of urban middle classes and homelessness in Japan and the Philippines. He has published *Japan's Underclass: Day Laborers and the Homeless* (Trans Pacific Press 2006) and 'Homelessness in Osaka: Globalization, *yoseba* and disemployment,' *Urban Studies*, 40(2), 2003, pp. 361–78.

HARUMI BEFU, Stanford University, is currently working in the areas of globalisation, diaspora, kinship and community. His publications include *Hegemony of Homogeneity: An Anthropological Analysis of* Nihonjinron (Trans Pacific Press 2001) and *Ideorogī to Shite no Nihon Bunkaron* (*Cultural Theories of Japan as Ideology*), third edition (Shisō no Kagakusha 1997).

HUGH CLARKE, University of Sydney and Waseda University, researches Japanese language and literature as well as Okinawan studies. He co-authored *Colloquial Japanese* (Routledge 2003) and published 'The great dialect debate' in Elise Tipton (ed.), *Society and State in Interwar Japan* (Routledge 1997), pp. 193–217.

STEPHEN COVELL, Western Michigan University, is a specialist in modern and contemporary Japanese Buddhism. He has published *Japanese Temple Buddhism: Worldliness in a Religion of Renunciation* (University of Hawai'i Press 2005) and co-edited a special issue on 'Traditional Buddhism in contemporary Japan' for the *Japanese Journal of Religious Studies*, 21(2), 2004.

TOSHIKO ELLIS, University of Tokyo, specialises in modern Japanese literature in the context of modernism and modernity. Her publications include *Hagiwara Sakutarō: Shiteki Imēji no Kōsei* (*The Poetic Imagery of Hagiwara Sakutarō*) (Chūsekisha, 1986) and 'The topography of Dalian and the cartography of Fantastic Asia in

Anzai Fuyue's poetry', *Comparative Literature Studies*, Special Issue: East-West, Penn State University Press, 41(4), 2004, pp. 482–500.

ANNE E IMAMURA, Georgetown University, specialises in urban community, gender and family in Japan. She has published *Urban Japanese Housewives: At Home and in the Community* (University of Hawai'i Press 1987) and edited *Re-imaging Japanese Women* (University of California Press 1996).

TAKASHI INOGUCHI, President, University of Niigata Prefecture, and a political scientist formerly with the University of Tokyo, has authored, among other titles, *Japanese Politics: An Introduction* (Trans Pacific Press 2005), and co-authored *Citizens and the State: Attitudes in Western Europe and East and Southeast Asia* (Routledge 2008) and co-edited *Globalization, Public Opinion, and the State* (Routledge 2008).

NAOMICHI ISHIGE, National Museum of Ethnology, Japan, is an expert on comparative studies of food culture and has published *The History and Culture of Japanese Food* (Kegan Paul International 2001) and co-authored *Fermented Fish Products in East Asia* (International Resources Management Institute 2005).

JUNKO KITAGAWA, Osaka Kyoiku University, is an expert in the sociology of music and has published *Oto no Uchi Soto* (*Inside and Outside of Sound*) (Keisō Shobō 1993) and 'Some aspects of Japanese popular music,' *Popular Music*, 10(3), 1991, pp. 317–26, and co-edited *Gendai Nihon Shakai ni Okeru Ongaku* (*Music in Modern Japanese Society*) (Hōsō Daigaku Kyōiku Shinkōkai 2008).

MIHO KOISHIHARA, Kokushikan University, specialises in historical studies of sports and the literature on sports. She authored *Coubertin to Montherlant: 20-Seiki Shotō ni Okeru France no Sports Shisō* (*Coubertin and Montherlant: The French Philosophy of Sports in the Early Twentieth Century*) (Fumaidō 1995).

TAKAMI KUWAYAMA, Hokkaidō University, Japan, is a cultural anthropologist who has authored *Native Anthropology: The Japanese Challenge to Western Academic Hegemony* (Trans Pacific Press 2004) and co-edited *Yokuwakaru Bunka Jinruigaku* (*Accessible Cultural Anthropology*) (Minerva Shobō 2006).

SEPP LINHART, University of Vienna, a sociologist who specialises in work and leisure, old age and popular culture in Japan, has co-edited *The Culture of Japan as Seen through its Leisure* (State University of New York Press 1998) and *Written Texts – Visual*

Texts: Woodblock-printed Media in Early Modern Japan (Hotei Publishing 2005).

MORRIS LOW, University of Queensland and Johns Hopkins University, researches the history of Japanese science and technology and Japanese visual culture. He has authored *Japan on Display: Photography and the Emperor* (Routledge 2006) and *Science and the Building of a New Japan* (Palgrave Macmillan 2005) and edited *Building a Modern Japan: Science, Technology, and Medicine in the Meiji Era and Beyond* (Palgrave Macmillan 2005).

ROSS MOUER, Monash University, is a comparative sociologist who specialises in the sociology of work in Japan. He co-authored *A Sociology of Work in Japan* (Cambridge University Press 2006) and *Images of Japanese Society* (Kegan Paul International 1986).

CRAIG NORRIS, University of Tasmania, specialises in new media and new knowledge economies and has published 'Girl power: the female cyborg in Japanese anime,' in Haslem, Ndalianis and Mackie (eds), *Super/Heroes: From Hercules to Superman*, (New Academia Publishing 2007), pp. 347–61 and 'Australian fandom of Japanese anime (Animation),' in Ang (ed.), *Alter/Asians: Asian-Australian Identities in Art, Media and Popular Culture* (Pluto Press 2000), pp. 218–31.

KAORI H OKANO, La Trobe University, specialises in studies of education and social inequality and researches minorities and ethnicity in Japan and Asia. Her publications include *Education in Contemporary Japan* (co-author, Cambridge University Press 1999) and she has edited *Language and Schools in Asia: Globalization and Local Forces* (Multilingual Matters 2006).

YOSHIO SUGIMOTO, La Trobe University, studies Japanese society and comparative sociology. His books include *An Introduction to Japanese Society*, second edition (Cambridge University Press 2003), *Images of Japanese Society* (co-authored, Kegan Paul International 1986) and *Japanese Encounters with Postmodernity* (co-edited, Kegan Paul International 1995).

ANN WASWO, Nissan Institute of Japanese Studies and St Antony's College, Oxford, specialises in social change in modern Japan and has published *Housing in Postwar Japan: A Social History* (RoutledgeCurzon 2002) and *Modern Japanese Society* (Oxford University Press 1996).

Acknowledgements

I would like to express my gratitude to all the contributors for their cooperation throughout the project in response to my persistent suggestions and queries. My foremost thanks are due to Helena Bond and Miriam Riley who assisted me at different stages in editing the volume – a multicultural work that involved eighteen authors from five countries with different language backgrounds. Without their thorough, intelligent and perceptive work in text editing, we would not have been able to bring the book to the present level.

Yoshio Sugimoto
October 2008

Chronology

1868	Meiji Restoration, the collapse of the feudal system and the establishment of the imperial system.
1870	The government allows commoners to assume surnames.
1871	The Ministry of Education is established.
1872	The Solar calendar system is adopted.
1874–90	Movements for civil rights and freedom gather strength in opposition to the Meiji regime.
1877	Tokyo Imperial University is established.
1879	The *Asahi Shimbun* starts publication in Osaka.
1879	The Okinawa Kingdom is incorporated as Japan's Okinawa prefecture.
1889	The Imperial Constitution is promulgated.
1894–5	The Sino-Japanese War. China surrenders.
1895	Colonisation of Taiwan. The Government-General of Taiwan is established.
1899	The *Law to Protect the Former Savage in Hokkaidō* is promulgated to deal with the Ainu.
1902	The Anglo-Japanese Alliance Agreement is concluded.
1903	The system of government-approved school textbooks begins.
1904–05	The Russo-Japanese War.
1910–45	Annexation of Korea.
1915	The first national middle-school baseball championship is held.
1918	Rice riots spread throughout the nation.
1925	Public radio broadcasting commences in Tokyo, Osaka and Nagoya.

1931   The Mukden incident marks the beginning of Japan's invasion of Manchuria and the start of the Fifteen Year War, which ends in 1945.

1932   The state of Manchukuo is established in Manchuria under Japan's puppet government.

1936   The Japan Professional Baseball League is established.

1937   The Japanese military occupies the Chinese city of Nanking and carries out the Nanking massacre.

1940   The Imperial Rule Association is established to organise the entire nation to support the government's war policies.

1941   Japan attacks Pearl Harbor. The Pacific War begins.

1945   Atomic bombs are dropped on Hiroshima and Nagasaki.

1945   Japan surrenders to the Allied Forces.

1945–52   The Occupation by the Allied Forces. Labour, land and educational reforms are implemented.

1946   The first national elections held with universal suffrage.

1946–48   The Tokyo War Tribunal.

1946   Japan's new Constitution is promulgated.

1947   The new compulsory education system is introduced, with six years at primary school and three at middle school.

1949   Professor Hideki Yukawa of Kyoto University is awarded the Nobel Prize in Physics and becomes Japan's first Nobel Laureate.

1951   Commercial radio stations start broadcasting.

1952   The Peace Treaty comes into effect. Japan regains independence.

1952–68   Osamu Tezuka's *Tetsuwan Atomu* (Astro Boy) is published as a serial in the magazine *Shōnen*.

1953   Public and commercial TV networks commence transmission.

1960   Social movements against the ratification of the US–Japan Security Treaty sweep the nation.

1960   The Mitsui Coal miners' strike in Kyūshū, the largest industrial action in postwar Japan.

1964   The Tokyo Olympics.

1964   The Shinkansen Bullet Train system starts operation between Tokyo and Osaka.

1965   Ratification of the Basic Treaty between Japan and South Korea.

1968–70   New Left student movements spread on university campuses.

1970s	The heyday of *Nihonjinron* (theories on the Japanese) and the rise of cultural nationalism.
1972	The US returns Okinawa to Japan, which becomes the nation's 47th prefecture.
1978	Narita International Airport opens.
1980s	The decade of the so-called 'bubble economy'. The peak of the postwar economic boom.
1985	The Equal Opportunity Law comes into effect.
1990s	The so-called 'lost decade'. The Japanese economy enters into stagnation and recession.
1991	*Zainichi* Korean residents given special permanent residency status.
1993	The Liberal Democratic Party loses government after four decades of uninterrupted reign. The coalition government of opposition parties gains power.
1994	The first Ainu parliamentarian attends the House of Councillors.
1996	The Liberal Democratic Party regains power.
2000s	The intensification of the campaign to establish Japan as a 'soft power' nation based on the export of manga and animation.
2001	Prime Minister Junichirō Koizumi commences large-scale deregulation and privatisation programs.
2002	Hayao Miyazaki's animation *Spirited Away* wins the Academy Award for Best Animated Feature.

Map of Japan

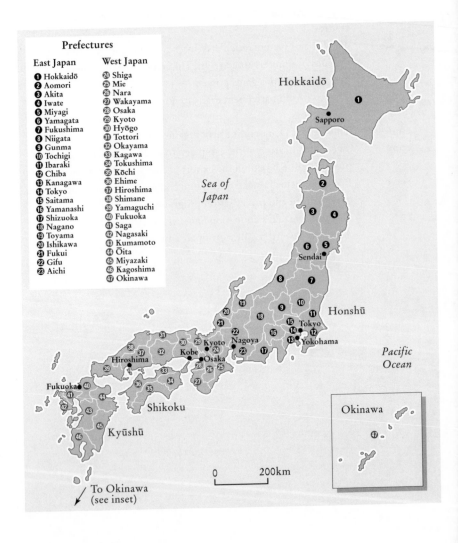

Prefectures

East Japan	West Japan
❶ Hokkaidō	㉔ Shiga
❷ Aomori	㉕ Mie
❸ Akita	㉖ Nara
❹ Iwate	㉗ Wakayama
❺ Miyagi	㉘ Osaka
❻ Yamagata	㉙ Kyoto
❼ Fukushima	㉚ Hyōgo
❽ Niigata	㉛ Tottori
❾ Gunma	㉜ Okayama
❿ Tochigi	㉝ Kagawa
⓫ Ibaraki	㉞ Tokushima
⓬ Chiba	㉟ Kōchi
⓭ Kanagawa	㊱ Ehime
⓮ Tokyo	㊲ Hiroshima
⓯ Saitama	㊳ Shimane
⓰ Yamanashi	㊴ Yamaguchi
⓱ Shizuoka	㊵ Fukuoka
⓲ Nagano	㊶ Saga
⓳ Toyama	㊷ Nagasaki
⓴ Ishikawa	㊸ Kumamoto
㉑ Fukui	㊹ Ōita
㉒ Gifu	㊺ Miyazaki
㉓ Aichi	㊻ Kagoshima
	㊼ Okinawa

YOSHIO SUGIMOTO

'Japanese culture': An overview

Paradigm conflict over Japanese culture

An unacknowledged paradigm shift appears to be underway in contemporary Japanese culture, with public discourse suddenly focusing upon internal divisions and variations in the population. At the beginning of the 21st century, the nation has observed a dramatic shift in its characterisation from a unique and homogeneous society to one of domestic diversity, class differentiation and other multidimensional forms. The view that Japan is a monocultural society with little internal cultural divergence and stratification, which was once taken for granted, is now losing monopoly over the way Japanese culture is portrayed. This transformation has resulted not so much from intellectual criticisms levelled at the once dominant model as from public perceptions of structural changes that have been in progress since the late 20th century.

Part of the perceptual shift results from the accumulation of observations that point to the notion that Japan is a multi-ethnic society, comprising a considerable range of ethnic groups.[1] Ethnic diversity has rapidly expanded and formed a seemingly irreversible trend, with the influx of an increasing number of foreign migrants into Japanese society. As of 2008, their officially documented numbers exceed two million – approximately 2 per cent of the total population. Some 6 per cent of new marriages in Japan today are between Japanese and non-Japanese nationals. Further, the increase in activities and movements of minority groups such as Korean residents and the indigenous Ainu have contributed to the articulation of the image of a multi-ethnic Japan. The upsurge of ethnic consciousness around the world has also sharpened the focus on ethnic diversity in Japan. The confluence of these factors has given rise to what one might call the *ethnic turn* of the definition of Japanese culture.

The second abrupt transformation of public perceptions concerns the way in which Japan's class structure is defined. The prevailing majority view of Japan as an egalitarian, equitable and relatively classless society swiftly collapsed in the early 2000s with many influential publications[2] asserting that Japan is now a highly stratified, inequitable and class-based society with significantly unequal distributions of socioeconomic resources and rewards. The label *kakusa shakai* (disparate society or socially divided society) is now frequently attached to Japanese society. The rise of such discourse reflects the growing splits in the labour force between the privileged minority of full-time regular employees with occupational security and the deprived majority of part-timers, casuals and day labourers with little job protection.[3] Though applicable to only a quarter of the workforce at its peak, the three treasures of Japan's corporate culture – lifetime employment, seniority-based wage structure and enterprise unionism – which once were celebrated as the cornerstone of Japan's rise to economic superpower status are now under threat. Organised labour based mainly on the advantaged sector tends to prioritise its own interests at the expense of temporary, irregular and outsourced workers. In this milieu, the image that Japan is a society of sharp class distinction has taken root and will not easily fade away.

Not only have occupational classes received serious public attention but regional, gender-based, generational and other forms of inequality are also under the spotlight. The growing economic gap between urban and rural areas, between the relatively prosperous metropolitan centres and the underperforming periphery in particular, has exasperated the electorates in the countryside and generated inter-prefectural political confrontation. The discrepancy between the facade of gender equality and the reality of discrimination against women is increasingly obvious. The twin trends of the decline in birthrate and the prolongation of life expectancy have led to a pension crisis involving a long-term public debate over the extent to which the younger generation in the workforce should support the older generation after retirement. To the extent that the notion of Japan as a multidimensional class society is now acknowledged more broadly than ever, Japan's public opinion climate has made, as it were, a *class turn*, that appears to be irreversible.

Once Japan is defined as a multi-ethnic and multi-class society, Japanese culture emerges as a mosaic of diverse beliefs, practices, artefacts and

Table o.1 *Two competing models of Japanese culture*

Criteria	Monocultural model	Multicultural model
Number of Japanese cultures	One/single	Many/plural
Major theme	Homogeneous, uniform	Heterogeneous, hybrid
Extent of cultural integration	Japanese culture as a consensual and harmonious whole	Japanese cultures deriving from rival groups with different demographic characteristics
Definition of the Japanese	Exclusive, restrictive	Inclusive, liberal
Minority population	Exceptionally small	Of considerable size
Class structure	Egalitarian, almost classless	Competing class groups, much class division
Regional differences	Minimal	Significant
Holders of high literacy in Japanese culture	*Ware ware Nihonjin* (We the Japanese)	Depends upon which Japanese culture

symbols, produced and consumed by ethnic and class groups with different levels of access to privilege, power and prestige. With the convergence of the ethnic and class turns, Japanese public discourse has achieved a *cultural turn*: a paradigm transformation that has inspired many recent studies on Japanese culture. The present volume reflects the new framework, the 'multicultural model' of Japanese society, and highlights the ways in which Japanese culture is diversified and stratified along class, regional, generational and gender lines, among others. Table o.1 contrasts the two orientations – monocultural versus multicultural.

These developments must be observed with caution. The two models coexist in rivalry rather than one completely overwhelming the other. The monocultural model is still firmly entrenched and thriving in some parts of the social science community in Japan. Moreover, whether or not Japanese society recorded a *sudden* increase in social variation and stratification is a moot point. Some analysts argue that Japan has always been a diversified and stratified society, that there is no evidence of abrupt mutation in this regard.[4] Others maintain that it is public perception rather than empirical reality that has undergone drastic changes. Either way, the Japanese perception of 'Japanese culture' has lost the stability that it enjoyed during the heyday of monoculturalism a few decades ago.

As Harumi Befu elaborates in chapter 1 of this volume, the monocultural paradigm is based on the so-called *Nihonjinron* (the theories on the

Japanese), which have attracted a large audience captivated by portrayals of Japan and the Japanese as being exceptionally unique and fundamentally different from Western societies and Westerners. The genre has produced a number of best-selling books that variously describe Japanese culture as essentially shame-based,[5] group-oriented,[6] founded on a vertically structured society,[7] built on a dependency-oriented personality-type,[8] focused on interpersonal relations[9] and so forth.

The irony of *Nihonjinron* is that most analysts in this area have failed to identify who the *Nihonjin*, the Japanese, are – the very population that is supposed to demonstrate the traits attributed to it. A few key examples will demonstrate the point. First, a majority of Japanese work in small companies with fewer than 300 employees and do not possess four-year university degrees, yet the world of large-company employees with high education is often used as the empirical base to characterise Japanese culture.[10] Second, while the cultural differences between the residents of eastern Japan (whose centres are Tokyo and Yokohama) and those of western Japan (Osaka, Kyoto and Kobe) are widely acknowledged, this does not appear to have had a significant impact on *Nihonjinron*. Finally, and more concretely, though the promoters of Japan's whaling activities in the Antarctic Ocean attribute them to Japan's food culture, one out of three Japanese are against eating whale meat, and only about half of the population are in favour of the practice at all.[11] This means that Japan has two competing cultural groups, though only one is acknowledged to exist in that country. Given that Japanese culture is what the Japanese produce and consume, who the Japanese are ought to be spelt out prior to the examination of the qualities of Japanese culture. The formulation of the Japanese necessarily precedes that of Japanese culture. To put it technically, the definition of the Japanese is the independent variable; that of Japanese culture the dependent.

The criteria for judging who the Japanese are can range from citizenship, 'biological pedigree', language competence and cultural literacy, to subjective identification.[12] We can use a restrictive and exclusive yardstick and define the Japanese, for instance, as only those persons who possess Japanese passports, have 'Japanese blood' and are native speakers of the Japanese language. Using a more liberal and inclusive benchmark, we can designate as Japanese those individuals possessing at least one of these attributes. It is possible to identify a middle position between the two frameworks, where certain attributes – for instance, citizenship and 'pedigree' – are seen as indispensable criteria for someone to be classified as Japanese.

In a nutshell, there are two rival frameworks governing the way the relationship between the Japanese and Japanese culture is defined: the deductive approach in which Japanese culture is defined *a priori* and the Japanese are those who embody it; and the inductive approach which assumes that there are a variety of Japanese who generate various kinds of culture, with the demographic base of each cultural formation being a crucial factor. Within the latter framework, on which this book is based, *cultural demography* constitutes a key field of linkage between cultural agents and cultural goods; Japan's culture is multiple, not singular, and comprises a variety of orientations, practices and artefacts developed by manifold demographic groups. For example, the socioeconomic differences between older and younger Japanese condition their cultural distinctions. The culture of company executives and that of temporary blue-collar workers differ because of their class bases. Junko Kitagawa, author of chapter 14, is explicit in identifying the demographic foundations of Japan's music culture. In chapter 13, Craig Norris presents the demographic underpinnings of consumers of various types of *manga* cartoons.

These cultural variations suggest that no one can claim to be totally culturally literate about Japanese culture.[13] Most assembly-line workers in Japanese car firms are more familiar with the culture of total quality control than upper-class ladies who enjoy playing golf and tennis.[14] Tokyoites who cannot speak any local dialect would be less knowledgeable about Japan's linguistic culture than many Japanese who can handle both the so-called standard Japanese language and their own regional vernacular, as Hugh Clarke's chapter 3 implies.

Since Japanese culture is a problematical construct rather than a given reality, it should not be taken to refer to any bounded entity.[15] Instead of a short summary of each chapter of this volume, the ensuing discussion presents a brief schematic sketch of three dimensions: (1) a few unresolved debates over concept and theory formation in studies of modern Japanese culture; (2) the two dominant forces – the state and the market – that shape the realm of Japanese culture; and (3) how various demographic groups consume Japanese culture in response to these two constraints. In short, this volume considers both the conceptual and theoretical issues of Japan's modern culture and the substantive configurations of its shapers and consumers, recognising that modern Japanese culture is not only diverse and hybrid but also subject to constraints that are global and internal, material and immaterial, socioeconomic and geo-political. In this sense, we will not move away 'from class to culture' but attempt to sharpen our focus on the importance of broadly defined, multiple class variables in the investigation of culture.

Dilemmas of cultural relativism

While the monocultural model has been roundly criticised in the last few decades, such critique raises some intriguing issues. In particular, questions about the extent to which the culture of each individual ethnic minority group within Japanese society tends to be constructed as a uniform entity in a monocultural way. The generations of Korean residents in Japan, for example, have attempted to defend and maintain what they regard as Korean culture within the mainstream culture of Japan. But 'Korean culture' is neither uniform nor homogeneous. Which Koreans are taken here as the demographic basis of Korean culture? Is the argument about the preservation of the Korean tradition within Japan based on a kind of *Kankokujinron* (theories on the Koreans) – a Korean counterpart of *Nihonjinron*? Similar issues arise when considering the largest minority group in Japan, *burakumin*. Despite being Japanese both in terms of nationality and race, they are discriminated against due to the widely held prejudice that their blood is contaminated because their ancestors engaged in livestock slaughter during the feudal period, a job regarded as filthy at the time. But as Hideo Aoki's contribution on *buraku* culture (chapter 10) elucidates, the increasing diversification of *buraku* communities makes it difficult to define a single unified *buraku* culture.

There is an analogous dilemma in placing Japanese culture in a global context. Takami Kuwayama argues that Japan remains on the periphery of the 'academic world system' (chapter 2) and, more widely the modern world system of knowledge, in which the dominant centres – the United States, the United Kingdom and other Western countries – wield overall international cultural power. This is of course partially contested and mediated, as demonstrated by the recent inroads of Japanese animation (see chapter 19) and food culture (chapter 16) into the global sphere. Nonetheless, on the whole, Hollywood, CNN and McDonalds globally define what is beautiful, newsworthy and tasty. English is the *lingua franca* that the Japanese have to learn. In tracing the historical transformations of Japanese housing in chapter 15, Ann Waswo shows how the culture of sitting, eating and sleeping on the floor has been modified in line with Western housing models to make Japanese housing look more 'civilised'. As Morris Low vividly demonstrates in his analysis of *wakon yōsai* (Japanese spirit and Western technology) in chapter 7, the 'significant other' for modern Japanese culture has invariably been the imagined culture of the West. One wonders what the cultural orientations of many Japanese would look like if the centres of news media were in Latin America, the internationally prestigious universities were clustered in Africa and the language of international communication were Hindi or Thai.

These considerations for cultural relativity draw attention to two types of cultural relativism. On one hand, one has to be mindful of cultural diversity and stratification *within* Japanese society: domestic multicultural realities that are relative to each other. On the other hand, one must also be conscious of cultural relativity *between* Japan and other societies and consider the extent to which Japan is peripheral in the global cultural system. However, these two dimensions of cultural relativism pose a thorny dilemma. If one overemphasises *intra*-cultural relativism, *inter*-societal cultural relativity tends to be diluted. If one underscores *inter*-societal cultural relativism, one is often trapped in a pitfall where *intra*-societal diversity is attenuated and national stereotypes are apt to prevail. There appears to be an unavoidable *negative* correlation between the two types of cultural relativism.

Social science concepts and theories produced in the West are disseminated and studied in Japanese academia, not the other way around. Little is known outside Japan about the concepts or cultural categories that have been developed in the Japanese context and that cannot be translated into Western languages in a straightforward manner. One such notion, *seikatsu*, illustrates this point.

Seikatsu generally means livelihood, everyday life or a wide range of life activities.[16] The agents of *seikatsu* are *seikatsusha*, the ordinary, nameless and common men and women who actively construct their living conditions. *Seikatsusha* constitute the core of Japan's civil society, independent of powers of the state and the market. The narrow definition of *seikatsu* focuses upon the world of consumption, in which *seikatsusha* consciously carve their independent life activities, not simply as passive and submissive consumers. The broad definition of *seikatsu* includes almost every sphere of life, including clothing, food, housing, folk customs, language, recreation and entertainment, not to mention work and consumption. In activist usage, *seikatsu* denotes various autonomous areas of life culture in which *seikatsusha* attempt to improve their standard of living and quality of life by developing lifestyles that counter the forces of capitalist consumerism and government regulation. Based on life culture at the grassroots and linked with everyday usage of the term, the notion of *seikatsusha* tends to be more reality-focused than the terms like *shimin* (citizens) and *kokumin* (members of the nation). In the world of social movements, Japan has had strong reformist organisations as the networks of *seikatsu kyōdō kumiai* (literally 'everyday life cooperative associations'). In social sciences, the discipline of *seikatsu-gaku*, 'lifology', occupies an area of inter-disciplinary study.

The notion of *seikatsu* that has been developed in Japan as an analytical concept deserves attention in relation to such Western sociological concepts as Schütz's 'world of everyday life', Habermas's 'life-world' and Dahrendorf's 'life chances'. In its ambiguity and inclusiveness, the concept of *seikatsu* intersects and overlaps with that of culture too. Many chapters of the present volume draw inspiration from the Japanese studies of *seikatsu* and *seikatsusha*, though without explicitly referring to them. In chapter 12, for example, Sepp Linhart refers to Japan's recent national policy to strive to be *seikatsu taikoku* (a lifestyle superpower), while, in chapter 16, Naomichi Ishige derives much of his analysis of food culture from the work he has done in the above-mentioned field of *seikatsu-gaku*. Further, Okano's chapter on school culture (chapter 5) details aspects of *gakkō seikatsu* (school life). There are many other cultural categories that require attention not only for the interpretation of Japanese culture but also as tools of comparative analysis. In chapter 4, for instance, Anne Imamura analyses the notion of *ie* (household), while in chapter 6 Ross Mouer discusses the concept of *shūshoku* (obtaining lifetime full-time employment). In chapter 8, Covell points to the disparity between the Japanese notion of *shūkyō* and the English term 'religion' and the importance of cultural sensitivity in comparative studies of spiritual life.

These conceptual concerns stem from Japan's perceived duality in the international community: as an economic centre and technological superpower; yet as culturally peripheral and a part of Asia. With Japanese culture viewed in relative and comparative terms, one might have to revisit the 'convergence' debate over the extent to which all industrial societies tend to demonstrate analogous characteristics due to the imperatives of industrialisation, not only in social structures and institutions but also in value orientations and lifestyles. Japan has been the prime testing ground for the debate because it is the foremost industrial power outside the Western cultural framework. While discussing a number of Japan-specific styles of leisure consumption, Linhart declares that he supports the notion that such convergence does tend to occur in Japanese leisure consumption practices. Mouer's study on work culture (chapter 6) suggests that there are considerable similarities in the patterns of employment and the values of workers due to the added momentum of the globalisation of work. Yet Stephen Covell's chapter on Japan's religions (chapter 8) and Miho Koishihara's chapter on sports culture (chapter 17) call the convergence thesis into question, pointing to the possibility that Japan's distinctive cultural forces may be so robust that Japan has been taking a distinctly unique path, or that Japan's situation may demonstrate that the pattern of global convergence is more complex than initially thought.

Whether postmodern or neo-modern, the Japanese culture today that faces issues of cultural relativism, linguistic gap problems and the convergence debate sensitises analysts of Japan to the ambivalence and duality that derive from its specific historical and geo-political circumstances.

The dilemma of cultural relativism manifests itself in the 'name order debate': which way should the Japanese order their surnames and given names in Western languages? Since the early Meiji years and until recently, most Japanese have followed the Western system of placing their given name first and their surname second when identifying themselves in Western languages, although the convention in the Japanese language is the other way around – the surname first followed by the given name. More recently, from the perspective of cultural relativism, some Japanese intellectuals have started using the Japanese system when writing in Western languages, a position that is gaining ground among Japan specialists in Western countries. However, there is a strong, competing argument in favour of using the Western system to facilitate smooth international communications and to avoid unnecessary confusion and needless misunderstanding. This volume reflects the controversy to the extent that each contributor chose their preferred style in referring to Japan's historical figures and citing Japanese authors. We exercised no editorial control over this matter, though the contributor's name order at the beginning of each chapter follows the given name–surname sequence to avoid confusion in citations. When uncertain, readers are requested to refer to the bibliography and the index at the end of the book. Though ostensibly trivial, this issue reflects Japan's dual identity in international communication media in a concrete and tangible fashion.

Table 0.2 *Four types of culture by the agents of production and appreciation*

	Producers	
Appreciators	Specialists	Amateurs
Specialists	Elite culture	Populist culture
Amateurs	Mass culture	*Seikatsu* culture

Cultural agents and culture shaping forces

Broadly defined, culture is an all-embracing and equivocal concept. It includes all forms and processes that produce meanings to human beings. These include categories, symbols, artefacts, practices, rituals, value orientations, worldviews and even paradigms. The present volume does not confine itself to any particular definition of culture. Aside from the concerns outlined above regarding the need to avoid essentialised statements about culture, some chapters deal primarily with the institutional contexts, constraints and circumstances in which culture is produced and the ways in which organisations and networks influence the meaning systems of schools (chapter 5), work (chapter 6) and science and technology (chapter 7). Others address textual contents focusing, for example, upon literature (chapter 11) and visual arts (chapter 13). Still others investigate such artefacts as housing (chapter 15) and food (chapter 16).

A typology of culture

Turning to focus upon the agents of Japanese culture and the cultural products they yield and consume, one can identify two categories – producers and appreciators. These can be either specialists or amateurs in each cultural field. As Table 0.2 shows, these considerations pinpoint four types of Japanese culture.

In *elite* culture both producers and appreciators are specialists. Cases in point would include Japanese tea ceremony, flower arrangements, *noh* play, *koto*, symphonies, operas, museum exhibitions and calligraphy, in which consumers, listeners or viewers are well versed and share the relevant knowledge with the performers.

Mass culture represents the sort in which specialists present their products to an amateur audience who are not expected to have a professional understanding of these products and the processes involved in their production. Movies, animation, manga, most literature, TV shows, popular songs, fashion and advertisements would all fall into this category.

The type of culture in which the amateur public create messages to be received by professional cultural producers may be called *populist* culture. This takes place in such outlets as popularity contests, readers' letters, TV ratings, street protest demonstrations and fan letters. The rise of 'online activism' is expanding this area of cultural democracy, though it sometimes turns into political demagogue. Populist culture often goes beyond communications from amateurs to professionals and overlaps with the amateur-to-amateur interactions that form the final category.

This is a realm of *seikatsu* culture where both producers and receivers of culture are amateurs.[17] In this domain, laymen's everyday life intersects with cultural expressions in the form of meanings, symbols, values and artefacts. Examples of *seikatsu* culture would include: origami, bonsai, private gardening, *bon* festival dancing, graffiti art, New Year's card writing, kite painting, local folk songs, community festivals and tomb arrangements. Even the ways of bowing, gesturing in conversation, chanting choruses in street demonstrations, blogging in cyberspace, preparing meals and taking a bath would also fall into this category.

In competition with state and market hegemony, *seikatsu* culture forms a realm in which voluntary and informal groups and networks actively pursue liberal and democratic principles, thereby producing innovative and creative culture for individuals' self-actualisation. Many cultural activities in Japan have ample elements of this momentum. Volunteer groups and non-governmental organisations that have mushroomed around the country since the late 20th century embody the spirit of civil society. Japan has many voluntary hobby groups and networks formed and maintained by those who share interests, for instance, in bonsai, haiku, *senryū* (ironical haiku), *shodō* (calligraphy), *kanshi* (Chinese poetry) and *shōgi* (Japanese chess). Those who enjoy creative writing contribute novels and poems to small private magazines, called *dōjinshi*, published by a group of like-minded people. Some local festivals and community folk practices are also relatively shielded from the powers of the state and the market and promote the meaning systems of voluntary groups. Feminists, ecologists, ethnic and sexual minorities, and other networks of dissenters against state and commercial interests form distinctive cultural groupings that contribute to the expansion of Japan's civil society and *seikatsu* culture.[18]

Superimposed on these cultural spheres are the influences of the state and the market, the two dominant forces that shape the cultural orientations of the Japanese. The government machinery actively intervenes in the cultural realm to promote national cohesion, while the business world uses the market's consumption of culture as major profit-making opportunities. Meanwhile, some cultural pursuits spread without effective involvement of the state and the market, with civil society being their major driving force. Within this overall context, both the Japanese state and Japan's capitalist market are undergoing radical transformation. The state is adapting to the increasing variations within the nation, preserving its unity while accommodating diversity. At the same time, the market is shifting from industrial capitalism to cultural capitalism where knowledge, information and other cultural goods take the centre stage.

State transition from imposing uniformity to accommodating diversity

It is almost trite to suggest that the power of the state manifests itself not only in governmental institutions but also in the processes of classification and social interactions. Maps that show Japan's national boundaries as being made up of an archipelago of 47 prefectures are based upon categories formulated by the Japanese state. It organises, controls and manipulates symbols, knowledge, information and other immaterial forms, including: defining the correct standard Japanese language (see chapter 3); describing the traditional authentic Japanese family (chapter 4); prescribing Shintoism as the indigenous national religion (chapter 8); promoting sumo as the national sport (chapter 17); and portraying the Emperor as the embodiment of national unity. The list of concrete instances would be virtually endless.

The state machinery that engages specifically in fostering what it regards as Japan's national culture includes the Ministry of Education, Culture, Sports and Science and Technology, the Agency for Cultural Affairs, the Japan Art Academy, the National Institute for Japanese Language, the Japan Foundation and many others. The state screens the contents of school textbooks and curricula, defines national treasures, ranks tourist spots, controls the official Japanese language and confers decorations on eminent individuals every spring and autumn ... again a comprehensive list would be almost endless. Through a huge budget, the state manages to establish, maintain and expand national unity and togetherness in its interests, often selectively mobilising the historical memories, mythologies and symbols, which are crystallised most sharply in the national anthem (*Kimigayo*) and the national flag (*Hinomaru*). The promotion of Japanese national culture is an indispensable component of the Japanese national community.

The state also has a major stake in the way Japanese culture is presented abroad, because Japan's cultural export products – from *manga* to animation, from sushi to Sudoku – form a major economic and political tool for 'soft domination' in worldwide competition. As these cultural goods entertain and excite, they elevate the image of Japan, making it possible not only for Japan's cultural industry to achieve material gains but for Japanese interests abroad to be seen in a favourable light. With the enactment of the *Basic Law of Intellectual Properties* in 2002, the government regards the foundation of a nation based on highly marketable cultural commodities as its strategy to enhance the nation's position in the international hierarchy.

The paradigm conflict in the formulation of Japanese culture, discussed at the beginning of this overview, reflects the emerging division of the state into two views of how Japanese culture should be defined.[19] The first is based on Japan's conventional political economy dominated by the leadership and intervention of the state bureaucracy. This group represents the ancient cultural regime, so to speak, that presses for the adoration of the nation's unique history, the maintenance of lifetime employment and seniority-based wage structures in the corporate world, the preservation of gender role differences, the expansion of Japanese 'traditional family values', discipline and order in school life and the extension of state-led nationhood throughout the country.

The second view is a product of the increased globalisation of Japan's economy and technology and shares the values of deregulation and privatisation, seeking less state involvement and more private-sector initiatives in business affairs. Those in this sector have benefited from growing internationalisation in various spheres of life and have much at stake in the successful integration of Japanese society with the global community. An increasing number of politicians, high-ranking bureaucrats and business leaders either enthusiastically or reluctantly accept the possibility that it would be more cost-effective and less conflicting to manage the nation on the assumption that it is fraught with internal variation and class competition. The growth of this group in Japan's political establishment indicates that the Japanese nation state is now in the process of cultural adaptation in the face of globalisation and other shifting circumstances, a form of defence rather than collapse.

From industrial to cultural capitalism

Market forces, the second major influence that shapes contemporary Japanese culture, are also transforming themselves. Some 80 per cent of Japan's national domestic production is now in the service sector, and a large proportion of the manufacturing industry has moved offshore in pursuit of cheap labour. In place of industrial capitalism, which relies on mass-produced and cost-effective industrial goods for mass consumption, the Japanese economy is increasingly dependent upon the production and sales of cultural goods, which now form its lifeline both domestically and internationally.

'Japanesy' cultural products are increasingly visible around the world, ranging from Japanese anime, manga, karaoke, sushi, and fashion to marshal arts. So are such knowledge commodities as Sudoku games, the Kumon methods of education and the Suzuki methods of teaching music. For Japan's trade business, these cultural goods are as important as 'physical' commodities like cars and electronic appliances. As the Japanese state attempts to establish itself as a leading 'soft power' in the world, Japanese capitalism finds its largest market in the so-called 'Japan cool' products. It has been claimed[20] that though Japan may not be an industrial superpower anymore in terms of Gross National Product it has developed into a powerhouse in terms of what might be called Gross Cultural Cool, an index that measures the overall level of 'cool' pop culture products. In chapter 19, at the very end of the present volume, Mouer and Norris explore this recent development.

The externally exported cultural images of Japan have undergone transformation over the last few decades and now appear to be built upon three co-existing layers. At its base are the pre-modern symbols of cherry blossoms, samurai spirit, *ukiyoe*, geisha, *shamisen*, Mt Fuji and other exotic entities that have dominated since before the Second World War. The middle layer is made up of representations associated with Japan's corporate culture: cars, electronic appliances, total quality control and other economic goods that reflected the nation's rise as an economic superpower during the 1970s and 80s, exhibiting such hallmarks of a modern industrial Japan as industriousness, formality and perseverance. This layer includes portrayals of the workaholic Japanese loyal to their companies, willing to live in small condominiums and keen to let their children study madly hard to gain admission to prestigious universities. On top of these, there is a new layer of images in which the elements of Japaneseness are absent and Japan is described as almost 'non-Japanese'. Conspicuous since the 1990s, this trend is visible in the novels of internationally acclaimed Japanese writers such as Haruki Murakami and Banana Yoshimoto, whose storylines can take place anywhere in the world and place no emphasis on uniquely Japanese attributes, as detailed in Toshiko Ellis's analysis in chapter 11. Manga and animation made in Japan also tend to avoid stereotypical Japanese cultural ingredients and sell images that are hybrid and transnational (see chapter 19).[21] Japanese computer games, some of which are eccentric and bizarre, reinforce the notion that Japan is a land of playfulness, casualness and unpredictability, with no significant differences with other countries.

Meanwhile, it has become trendy in some areas outside of Japan to consume these contemporary ideas of Japan, wearing T-shirts with Japanese-like characters, exchanging DVDs of Japanese films or dining at Japanese restaurants. In Taiwan there is a new social phenomenon of Japanophile groups, called *harizu*, that are obsessed with Japanese films, food, comics and music. Japanese anime is estimated to constitute some 60 per cent of all animation programs broadcast on television in the US. In Australia, large-scale costume parties attended by hundreds of youngsters in the guise of anime characters are annual events. Some sort of cultural Japanisation appears to be in progress in many parts of the world. There is no doubt that the positive images of Japan's cars and electronic appliances as high-quality and advanced have been helpful in spreading similar images about Japanese cultural commodities. If *sushi* were a delicacy of a country without industrial might or *sashimi* a health food of a remote village in a technologically disadvantaged region, it is doubtful that the cultural diffusion of these foodstuffs around the world would have been possible.

These developments, however, must be observed with caution and in perspective. Not all Japanese cultural products are well received abroad. Pachinko (Japan's pinball) parlours, so pervasive within the country, have never had an international presence. The number of active practitioners of sumo is very small. *Nattō* (fermented sticky soybeans), which enjoy a large market within Japan, have never been popular in Japanese restaurants overseas. Unlike Chinese noodles, Japanese counterparts like *udon* and *soba* have not received broad acceptance. Nor has Japanese green tea. The thought of eating whale meat, though a delicacy to many Japanese, would sicken many Westerners. Some Japanese manga, particularly of a violent and sexist nature,[22] have triggered a great deal of antipathy. With these reservations, however, the value-added cultural goods 'made in Japan' now form both the domestic and international faces of Japanese culture.

Macro-demography of value orientations

Value orientations are at the heart of culture. And the values of various groups in Japan are shaped in response to the two most powerful forces – the market and the state. On one hand, the market operates under international capitalism and fluctuates in a 'global village', cutting across national boundaries. On the other hand, while changing its form of authority, the state remains strong and keeps moulding national culture despite the increasing globalisation of the economy and technology. As Inoguchi explains in chapter 18, the spread of globalisation and the rise of cultural nationalism undergo an interactive process.

Four different cultural orientations are discernible as different sections of Japanese society respond to these two dimensions. The first dimension concerns the extent to which a given group accepts or rejects the penetration of global, multinational market forces into their domestic environment, be they the influences of industrial or cultural capitalist nature. The second dimension relates to the extent to which a given group accepts or rejects national unity under the state apparatus, whether such unity is achieved through the ideology of homogeneity or diversity.

Crisscrossing these two dimensions, Figure o.1 demonstrates four rival orientaions that prevail in different sectors of Japan: (1) *cosmopolitans* who regard the process of globalisation as civilising and the erosion of both the state and nationhood as desirable; (2) *multiculturalists* who accept Japan's multicultural reality and promote interactions and intercommunications with other nation states while defending domestic national unity and state-based integration; (3) *monoculturalists* who advocate a strong state and the essence of 'Japaneseness' and criticise international market capitalism as Americanisation and Westernisation; and (4) *communitarians,* who see the penetration of the global market into the community as destructive, while favouring the reduction of state control and the disintegration of national identity. These four competing views are ideal types and distributed unevenly among different socioeconomic groups.[23]

As in other developed countries, cosmopolitans abound in the sectors that have reaped the benefits of globalisation. High ranking employees of Japan's multinational enterprises travel the world and often, for a short period, become business expatriates in foreign countries and thereby acquire a global market-oriented perspective that rejoices in consumerism and detests the interventions of national government agencies and officials.[24] These cosmopolitans are generally well educated, enjoy high incomes and

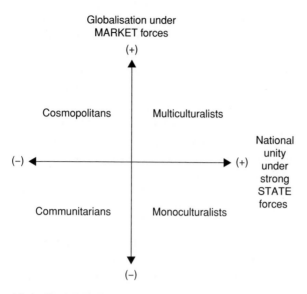

Figure 0.1 Four-fold typology of competing cultural orientations to the state and the market.

communicate well in English. Some have extravagant lifestyles at home and abroad and engage in fraternal conversations with their overseas counterparts, with whom they share analogous educational backgrounds and similar hobbies such as golf and tennis. Cosmopolitans promote global arrangements designed to weaken the control of national bureaucrats over the affairs of sovereign states. Those in the IT industry and in import and export businesses also tend to develop this type of value orientation because of their daily exposure to the world beyond their national boundaries. As Ellis describes in chapter 11, many contemporary Japanese novelists have little Japanese consciousness and are distinctly cosmopolitan.

Multiculturalists differ from cosmopolitans in defending, sometimes even wishing to expand, the integrative power of the state and Japan's sense of national unity. They do this, however, while accepting the necessity for Japan to increase cross-border economic transactions and cross-cultural interactions more generally. On this basis, the Japanese parliament classified the Ainu in 2008 as the indigenous people of Japan for the first time, a position which it had rejected for a long time. Further highlighting the multiculturalist perspective, some conservatives estimate that it will be necessary to accept some 10 million foreigners into Japan in the next five decades.[25]

This paradigm of multiculturalism differs from that of the globalisation promoted by cosmopolitans in that it envisions a future in which mutually exclusive and internally cohesive nation states interact with each other. Hence, in this discourse it is assumed that the governance structure of the international system of competing nation states will remain unchallenged, with the internal regulatory power of each state remaining intact. The collaboration of the main agents of consumer capitalism and the machinery of the state would, in that model, be ensured. If profit motives are predominant amongst cosmopolitans, 'national interests' remain uppermost in the minds of multiculturalists.

'Adaptive' politicians and 'enlightened' bureaucrats in Japan tend to take a multiculturalist stance. As the guardians of the Japanese nation state, they seek to adjust the state structure in response to changing external economic circumstances without undermining their governing control over it. The 'enlightened' urban middle class, employed mainly by large corporations, also tend to adopt the multiculturalist position. They are all too aware that Japan's economy is firmly intertwined with the outside world, a situation that requires smooth international relations. Even so, their lives are so intricately connected with the national systems of employment, welfare, education and taxation that they never dream of abandoning their commitment to Japan's nationhood.

Monocultural sentiments, analysed in some detail by Befu in chapter 1, are most prevalent among the agricultural and small, independent business sectors, both of which find it necessary to safeguard their vested interests against the penetration of international market forces. In one public opinion survey after another, farmers and self-employed small business people demonstrate strong nationalist leanings of this type. Like their counterparts elsewhere, Japanese farmers and their families feel vulnerable to changes in production costs of agricultural produce, meat products, dairy commodities and other cost-competitive imports. Obviously it is in the interest of these farmers for the Japanese government to adopt protectionist policies, to provide them with farm subsidies and to further raise import taxes on agricultural goods. For small self-supporting businesses, globalisation represents the threat of multinationals and big business organisations making inroads into, and eventually taking over, the limited markets that they serve. In Japan, small shop managers, subsidiary and subcontracting manufacturers, family business owners and other small, independent, self-supporting proprietors have networks of self-protection. Shops at *shōten-gai* (shopping streets) provide solid voting blocs of support for particular politicians and thereby exercise considerable political clout.

Communitarians comprise a variety of community groups that have found themselves subjected to the adverse effects of global market forces, yet remain opposed to an expansion of government power. Many of these groups take part in what are broadly called citizens' movements, which are organised by individual volunteers concerned about specific issues in their local community. Such issues include environmental destruction, residential degradation, ethnic prejudice, gender discrimination and many others that impact upon the everyday lives of citizens at the community level. These citizen groups emphasise quality of life, voluntary cooperation and the spontaneity of grassroots activities. Okano suggests in chapter 5 that there is a growing emphasis on multicultural education that is sensitive to ethnic and other dimensions of diversity. Inoguchi's empirical finding (chapter 9) that the Japanese neither strongly identify themselves with nor trust their nation appears to point to the possibility that civil society in Japan today might be much more pervasive than is widely believed. Civic, localist thinking permeates students, housewives, senior citizens and some sections of the casual workforce – groups that are distant from the power centres of the state and are not directly connected with the capitalist order of production and distribution. They tend to view the activities of both market-oriented companies and power-oriented state machineries as detrimental to human communities and natural environments alike.

The tug of war between these cultural value orientations continues to escalate with the intensification of globalisation within Japanese society. The changing socioeconomic conditions and *seikatsu* of the competing groups involved will inevitably determine the shifting equilibrium of Japanese culture in the coming decades.

Notes

1 See Komai (2001); Denoon, McCormack, Hudson and Morris-Suzuki (2001); Lie (2004); Weiner (1997).
2 See, for example, Toshiaki Satō (2000); Kenji Hashimoto (2003); Tachibanaki (1998, 2005 and 2006); Miura (2007); Iwata and Nishizawa (2008).
3 See Kosugi (2007); Mouer and Kawanishi (2005).
4 Hara and Seiyama (2006) and Chiavacci (2008) tend to be cautious as to the degree to which the transformation in question is abrupt.

5 Benedict (1946).

6 Reischauer (1978).

7 Nakane (1967b; 1970).

8 Takeo Doi (1973).

9 Hamaguchi (1985).

10 Sugimoto (2003: 1–2).

11 A national survey conducted by the *Asahi Shimbun*, published on 8 February 2008. Among the respondents, 56 per cent favoured eating whale meat and 26 per cent disagreed with the practice. Among females in their 20s and 30s, those who opposed the practice exceeded those who agreed.

12 See Mouer and Sugimoto (1995: 242–8); Fukuoka (2000: xxx); Sugimoto (2003: 185–8).

13 From this perspective, one can see the worldview of some of Japan's elite bureaucrats in their abortive scheme – developed by the Japan's Ministry of Agriculture, Forestry and Fishery – to provide certificates of 'authentic' Japanese meal providers to a limited number of overseas Japanese food restaurants.

14 Ihara (2007).

15 Strictly speaking, 'Japanese culture' should be surrounded with quotation marks, a system which we have not followed in this volume because that would unnecessarily obstruct the flow of sentences. For the same reason, wherever possible, we have avoided using the term 'cultures' although, rigorously speaking, the plural form would be appropriate in many places.

16 For a concise and articulate discussion of these concepts, see Seifert (2007).

17 This idea derives from Shunsuke Tsurumi's formulation of marginal art, a brief description of which can be found in Sugimoto (2003: 259–60 and 2008).

18 For studies of civil society in Japan, see Schwartz and Pharr (2003); Mouer and Sugimoto (2003); Iwai and Miura (2007); Fujita (2000).

19 See, for example, Pempel (1998).

20 McGray (2002).

21 This is the point made by Iwabuchi (2002a; 2002b).

22 See Kuniko Funabashi (1995); Kinko Ito (1995).

23 This section is based on Sugimoto (2006: 483–6) and a variety of analysis reports in 2005 SSM Chōsa Kenkyūkai (2008), especially vol. 7, which focuses upon 'publicness and economic inequality in contemporary Japan'.

24 See Ohmae (1999).

25 Proposal made in June 2008 by the League for the Exchange Facilitation of Talented Foreigners, a group formed by influential parliamentarians of the LDP.

I

Concepts of Japan, Japanese culture and the Japanese

Introduction

Reams have been written to question, explore and define 'Japan', 'Japanese culture' and 'the Japanese', both by Japanese scholars and by foreign observers of Japan. Most of it is based on an unwitting existential assumption that 'Japan', 'Japanese culture' and 'the Japanese' are 'things' out there, whose objectively verifiable forms need only be ascertained. Much of the discussion has centred on the specificities of these forms. I submit that this is not a productive approach: that at best, all these discussions and pronouncements of what 'Japan' is, what 'Japanese culture' constitutes, and who 'the Japanese' are, vary in accordance with innumerable and variegated experiences in changing historical circumstances.

In mid-20th century sociology and anthropology, facile assumptions were made that society, culture, people, polity and territory were coterminous such that their respective boundaries perfectly coincided.[1] This assumption was created and reaffirmed by structural-functionalist theory which pervaded social sciences of the time. It was thought that each society possesses a unique culture and that society and culture are contained in the political boundaries of the state. Japan was described and analysed on the basis of such a static theory in the early days of postwar Japanese studies.

Entirely new paradigms developed from the 1960s to account for the ever-changing and globalising world order which characterised the second half of the 20th century. How is Japan to be described in this new theoretical regime? In this chapter we explore this new approach to understanding Japan, appreciating the fact that the isomorphism of land = people = culture = society = polity is no longer tenable in Japan, if it ever was.

'Japan'

'Japan' cannot be dissociated from Japanese culture, since Japan is not just a physical entity. Japan as a chain of islands is meaningful only when culturally interpreted. Current conventional thinking is that Japan consists of the four major islands of Honshū, Kyūshū, Shikoku and Hokkaidō, plus the Ryūkyū Islands (Okinawa) and some small islands surrounding the four major islands. While Japan has such a physical reality, the perception of it is culturally elaborated and interpreted. Moreover, as culture is historically constructed, the meaning of 'Japan' changes with time.

Stratified Japan

Cultural interpretations of 'Japan' clearly emphasise the socially and politically stratified nature of this country. For example, cultural narratives of 'Japan' evoke a country of four seasons: spring with cherry blossoms, a summer of sweltering heat, autumn with beautiful foliage colours and a bitterly cold winter. But these evocations are biased in favour of central Japan – a region from Kansai (Kyoto–Osaka) to Kantō (Tokyo) – where the power to create such cultural narratives has historically resided. These images are a creation of the intellectuals based at the centre of Japan, and it is only from this vantage point that these evocations ring true.

From the peripheries of Japan, these seasonal changes are only partially true at best. As celebrated in the literature for eons, the famed cherry blossoms are supposed to be viewed from late March to mid-April. But school children in Naha, Okinawa, where the cherry trees blossom in January, simply have to memorise what they do not experience as prescribed in textbooks: namely that cherry blossoms are viewed in March–April. So do children in Hokkaidō, where they blossom well into May. The sweltering, hot and humid summer is unknown in Hokkaidō, as is the phenomenon of *tsuyu*, or 'plum rain' (the drizzly rainy season from June to July), so central to Japan's culturally defined seasonality, which covers Kanto and the south, but is decreasingly real and meaningful in Tohoku – the northern-most part of Honshū – and not at all real or meaningful in Hokkaidō, where *tsuyu* is non-existent. Similarly, autumn colours, celebrated in haiku and *waka* poetry, are unknown or diminished in Okinawa. The bitter cold of central Japan is foreign to Okinawans. Hokkaidō and Okinawa – territories that were added to Japan in the 19th century – simply do not feature in Japanese central narratives of seasonality. They are forever condemned to the peripheries, not only literally at the southern and northern ends of the island chain, but also figuratively in the culturally constructed seasonality of Japan.

The so-called 'standard' Japanese language, while not exactly the same as Tokyo dialect, resembles it more than any other dialect. Ever since the establishment of the modern government in 1868, the state has defined 'proper' Japaneseness, including the language, and tried to mould the Japanese in peripheral regions and non-ethnic Japanese into this state-defined form. School children are expected to speak 'standard Japanese' – the language of the power centre – disregarding the dialects they feel so at home in. Ainu and Okinawan school children were prohibited from using their native tongues, which are totally different languages from Japanese, and were forced to learn the 'standard Japanese', a practice still continuing to this date.

This culturally defined geographic hierarchy was also manifested sociologically in open discrimination against the Ainu and Okinawans. The Ainu suffered discrimination in their own land of Hokkaidō, where increasing immigration of Japanese from southern islands, quickly made them a numerical as well as a social and political minority, with their culture being treated simply as a relic of the past. Okinawans have remained the majority numerically in Okinawa, but when they migrate to foreign countries and to the northern islands of Honshū, Kyūshū and Shikoku, they are still subject to discrimination.

As Hokkaidō was colonised by Japan in the 19th century, its agriculture was much influenced by American farming methods introduced by the Japanese government from the start of the modern period. Its landscape is dotted with American-style silos, grain elevators, and farm buildings often painted in primary colours that one does not see in Japan to the south. But when the Japanese nostalgically evoke their homeland (*kokyō*) in terms of countryside, such as in *enka* songs,[2] Hokkaidō is seldom featured. It is, rather, rural scenes with small rice paddies, grass-thatched houses, and fishing villages in core Japan that are quintessentially evoked.[3] This conspicuous absence of Hokkaidō in the cultural imagination of Japan emphasises its peripheral status.

Hokkaidō's absence from the mainstream cultural imagination of Japan is not surprising, since it was officially added to Japan only in modern times. Except for its southern tip, which had been controlled by the Matsumae clan since the Tokugawa period, the island was not colonised by Japan until the Meiji era.

During its most expansive time, lasting from 1895 until 1945, 'Japan' included Taiwan, the southern half of Sakhalin, the Kuriles, the Korean

Peninsula, and Micronesia. The 'Japan' of that time was probably the most multi-ethnic and multicultural in Japanese history as it included numerous ethnic and racial groups in these territories. This fact, however, did not stop Japanese politicians and intellectuals from proclaiming a Japan of homogeneous culture and people. That is, 'Japanese' in the core area, and their culture, were considered to embody the essence of Japan. Those in other territories were considered second-class Japanese at best, not only because they did not speak Japanese, but also because of their lack of other core Japanese cultural accoutrements, and further, because of their colonial status. This distinction was expressed in the dichotomy of *naichi* and *gaichi*, *naichi* meaning Japan proper and *gaichi* signifying colonial territories. Tai[4] lucidly discusses this hierarchical subjectivity in imperial Japan.

Colonial peripheries were expected to emulate the 'real' Japan as much as possible. School classes in imperial colonies were given in Japanese, and Japanese was the language of colonial administration. Shinto shrines were exported to *gaichi* territories in an effort to 'Japanise' them. Volcanic mountains in *gaichi*, too, were nicknamed this or that Fuji as a way of emulating the 'real' Mt Fuji in central Japan. Colonials were 'Japanese', but they were inferior Japanese in the eyes of the 'pure' Japanese. This class system in the meaning of 'Japan' persisted throughout the pre-1945 imperial period.

Othernesses of Japan

We have seen that 'what Japan is' is not necessarily what Japan is in an absolute, objective and metaphysical sense. Images of what Japan is are rendered not only by the Japanese, but also by foreigners in comparison with their own countries. As I have elaborated in *Othernesses of Japan*,[5] outsiders' images of Japan are very much coloured by the historical relationship their countries have had with Japan.

Let us examine what Japan has been for the United States, and to some extent, the rest of the West. Before the Second World War, on the one hand, Japan was seen as a quaint, exotic country. The image of Japan as *Exotica japonica* was prevalent throughout the Western world, due in large part to the 'japonisme' craze that swept the Western art world, especially among French impressionists.[6] Also, as portrayed in the Orientalised *Madame Butterfly*, Japan was seen as a frail, feminine country of which the masculine West was able to take unfair advantage with impunity, as the US did in 1853–54 when Japan succumbed to the threat of the West's military might through 'gunboat diplomacy'.[7] On the other hand, Japan's image was coloured in the

US by American attitudes toward Japanese immigrants, which increasingly grew hostile due to racism accentuated by the rumoured 'yellow peril'. Japan reacted against this attitude with equal hostility, eventually leading to the Pacific War.

During the Second World War, as John Dower has ably shown in *War without Mercy*,[8] Japan was portrayed as being 'treacherous' and 'sneaky'. A monkey was the favourite animalistic representation of the Japanese. Yet the same Japan was envisioned during the postwar Allied Occupation – largely consisting of US personnel – as a backward country badly needing reform in all aspects of life. The Occupation's image of backward Japan was supported by US scholarship, in which political scientists, for example, tendentiously characterised postwar Japan as having 'a half-baked democracy' or a 'one-and-a-half party system', as if the US two-party system is superior to Japan's 'one-and-a-half' party system only because the US system allows alternation of controlling parties whereas Japan's 'one-and-a-half' party system does not. In the Soviet Union, predictably, the image of a backward Japan was given a Marxist twist, characterising Japan on the basis of the Marxist evolutionary scheme.[9]

Another biased US view of Japan positions Japan as an opposite of itself. Thus Americans are supposed to be individualistic, while the Japanese are said to be groupist – where Japanese groupism is definitely given a lower value status than US individualism.

From this single example it is easy to see how different the 'Japan' imagined by the West would be from the 'Japan' that the Chinese or Koreans, for example, would envisage, given their tortuous relationship with Japan in modern times. Japan is inevitably many things to many nations.

'Japanese culture'

Essentialism

The conventional understanding of Japanese culture is shrouded with the notion of *Nihonjinron* (discourses on Japaneseness).[10] *Nihonjinron* basically asserts the uniqueness of Japanese culture and people, and spells out the ways in which they are unique. The discourse on exceptionality covers the whole gamut: from the biological make-up of the Japanese,[11] prehistoric cultural development,[12] language,[13] literary and aesthetic qualities,[14] human relations,[15] and social organisation[16] to philosophy[17] and personal character[18] . In some formulations of *Nihonjinron* these features are interrelated. For example, Watsuji Tetsurō[19] argues that Japan's monsoon-impacted ecology influences Japan's agriculture, settlement pattern, family system, and even personal character. These qualities are assumed to have persisted throughout the history of Japan from time immemorial.

Numerous scholars have criticised *Nihonjinron*[20] for not admitting to the ethnic and cultural heterogeneity of Japan. Yet another important flaw, which these critics have failed to argue, is that features of the essentialised Japan propounded in *Nihonjinron* do not account for some of the most important events in Japanese history. Japan's first major transformation took place when Chinese culture was introduced from Korea. This transformation involved the introduction of elaborate political structures in government, a Buddhism rivalling the native Shintō, a writing system which allowed recording of history and literary accomplishments for the first time, and continental art and architecture in the form of magnificent edifices and refined Buddhist sculpture. None of these achievements are registered as part of the essentialised Japanese culture.

Second, the long period of Chinese influence from the 4th to the mid-19th century was replaced in the Meiji period by influence from the West as strong as, if not stronger than, the previous Chinese influence. As a result, Japan became heavily Westernised practically overnight. Strangely, the essentialised Japan of the *Nihonjinron* is one that is stripped of Chinese and Western influence. The injustice of this essentialised characterisation is that it disregards what made Japanese culture into a civilisation through the largesse of the Koreans, and ignores what made Japan an industrial powerhouse in the 19th and 20th centuries through Western borrowing. A characterisation of Japan that cannot account for these major events in Japanese history has to be defective.

Furthermore, an essentialist Japan that emphasises homogeneity does not recognise ordinary people's varied daily patterns of living, such as cultivation of yam, taro, all sorts of fruits and vegetables, and cereal crops other than rice, like barley, wheat and millet. Even fishing as a rural lifestyle is ignored in favour of rice growing, in spite of the vital importance of marine products in the Japanese diet. Also disregarded in the essentialism of Japan are regional cultural variations of all sorts, such as architectural style, clothing, rituals including weddings and funerals, food and culinary art, and dialect variations. Linguistic differences from region to region are enormous even now, let alone during the Meiji past. Such variations are totally ignored in favour of the 'standard Japanese', or *hyōjungo* (now replaced by 'kyōtsūgo', meaning 'common language'), which is supposed to be common to all Japanese. But in reality *kyōtsūgo* is a veneer over dialects that are still vibrant and are the preferred speech form used to express intimacy and local pride.

Thus the essentialised Japan is a standardised Japan with uniform characteristics disallowing internal variation. This Japan is largely the making of the central government since the Meiji period, bent on creating a unified, uniform, and homogeneous nation. This essentialised Japan is an imagined community far from the reality the country presents.[21]

De-territorialisation/re-territorialisation

Japanese culture has spread to all corners of the world over the years. This dispersion has taken two separate routes, one through Japanese emigration and the other through independent diffusion. The earliest emigration in modern times took place in 1868 when Japanese plantation workers went to Hawai'i. This was followed by emigration to North America and then to South America. While emigration to the Americas was going on, other Japanese citizens left for Micronesia, Australia, the Asiatic continent, and South-East Asia.[22] As Japanese emigrated, they necessarily took their culture with them. Over a million Japanese were living abroad before Japan's defeat in 1945. The largest overseas Japanese communities were in East Asia – China, Singapore and the Philippines – and the west coast of North America. Virtually all of them except those in North and South American, however, were repatriated with Japan's defeat in World War II. These communities had Japanese schools, Buddhist temples, Shintō shrines, retail shops selling Japanese consumer goods, business corporations, civil organisations, hobby groups, etc. Their language of communication was Japanese in all these instances. Here were transplanted Japanese communities: extensions of Japan.

After the war, the Japanese government continued its emigration program in order to alleviate population and economic problems. This time emigrants, by and large, went to South America. As this wave of emigration was winding down in the 1960s, Japan's postwar economic globalisation began in earnest, exporting its products and establishing corporate offices around the world. Businessmen were dispatched to staff the overseas offices, and their families accompanied them. As travel and living abroad became easier, other Japanese began to move to different parts of the world, notably to areas where Japanese corporate offices were concentrated, and settled there. By 2006, the number of Japanese residing overseas had once again exceeded one million.[23] In these areas, new Japanese migrants began businesses catering to business families and fellow Japanese. Here, again, in the postwar setting as in prewar times, Japanese communities sprang up, complete with Japanese establishments such as schools, restaurants, grocery shops, medical clinics, garages, real estate businesses and travel agents. In 2006, 16 cities abroad each were home to more than 10 000 Japanese people, including Bangkok, Hong Kong,[24] London,[25] Los Angeles,[26] New York, Paris,[27] Shanghai, and Singapore.[28,29] Japanese language is again the common means of communication in all these communities.

These prewar and postwar communities are extensions of Japan. The 'Japan' in the conventional sense was de-territorialised and re-territorialised to incorporate these numerous overseas extensions. Japanese culture is reproduced in these communities, with varying degrees of modification in adaptation to the local scene.

Aside from the spread of culture through emigration, cultural diffusion also takes place through another, independent means, motivated by the interest and desire of people abroad for things Japanese. As noted above, from the late 19th century we are familiar with French impressionists' interest in Japanese art, especially *ukiyoe*, or woodcut prints from the Edo period. Japanese pottery also was exported to Europe in large quantities about this time. Japanese manufactured goods began to be sold abroad in the latter half of Meiji period. They were reputed to be cheap and of inferior quality in the early days. But gradually, after the war they were replaced by industrial products of superior quality – from automobiles to electronic goods – establishing Japan's reputation for technological excellence. Also in the 1950s and '60s Japan enjoyed a streak of well known, innovative films, such as those by Kurosawa and Ozu. Although this trend did not last long, it established Japan's reputation in the field of popular culture. This was a precursor to the interest in Japanese pop culture that has arisen in Asia and the Americas since the 1990s, centring on manga and anime,[30] karaoke,[31] cuisine – especially sushi and instant ramen[32] – computer games, flower arrangement and tea ceremony.

The spread of Japanese religions, especially Zen, is also noteworthy. Most Japanese religions have basically followed emigrating Japanese, establishing themselves in overseas Japanese communities. But Zen and several so-called 'new religions', such as Sukyo Mahikari, Sekai Kyusei Kyo, and Soka Gakkai International, additionally took a different route, spreading largely to non-Japanese communities abroad though sometimes with the initial help of Japanese immigrants or gurus from Japan.[33]

What we see here is a breakdown of the formula: Japanese culture = Japanese territory. The isomorphism assumed in the homogeneity theory of Japanese culture is no longer, if it ever was, maintained. Since the Meiji era, Japan's culture has been de-territorialised and spread throughout the world. This new distribution of Japanese culture has re-territorialised the domain of Japanese culture.

'The Japanese'

The conventional approach to the question of who the Japanese are is to identify them in terms of a number of objective criteria, such as state affiliation,[34] language and cultural competence. A person who was born in Japan of Japanese parents, is a native speaker of Japanese, and embodies Japanese culture through enculturation and socialisation processes from birth is considered 'pure' or 'typical' Japanese; those who lack one or more of these features to the full extent is considered 'suspect' to varying degrees. But many categories of people are Japanese in one sense and not in another. Ruling all of them out is arbitrary and does injustice to many who consider themselves Japanese. Let us examine some of these cases.

Koreans and Chinese in Japan

The pre-1945 *naichi/gaichi* hierarchy has persisted metaphorically after the war by appropriating the distinction between 'the Japanese' and others, who may be discriminated against. More than a million people of Korean and Chinese descent were living in *naichi* (Japan 'proper') at the end of the war. These people were Japanese by legal definition as long as they came from Taiwan or the Korean peninsula. Although many of them repatriated at the conclusion of the war, most remained in Japan. Legally they retained the same status as any other Japanese after the war, however, the pre-defeat attitude of prejudice against them continued. This limbo state of having Japanese legal status and yet having a foreign (*gaichi*) social status lasted until the peace treaty was signed in 1952, at which time those of Korean and Chinese descent were stripped of their legal status as Japanese. Did they completely cease to be Japanese at this point? Not quite so. Let us examine some particular cases.

Passing as Japanese: During the colonial period, and into the latter part of the 20th century, many Koreans in Japan were assuming Japanese names. Since their appearance did not betray their ethnic origin, by using a Japanese name they could 'pass' as Japanese in day-to-day affairs, such as shopping, schooling, or banking, thus avoiding discrimination by the Japanese in most daily situations. Some were quite successful, effectively submerging into the sea of ethnic Japanese, not to be found and not wanting to be found. They continue to live in an uncomfortable situation of not necessarily wanting to be Japanese, but trying to appear Japanese, sometimes while retaining their Korean legal status. How are we to treat these individuals when considering the meaning of being 'Japanese'? To the extent that they are treated as if they are Japanese, at least in some situations, they are Japanese to others in these situations.

Japanese women married to Koreans: When, in 1952, the Japanese government stripped Koreans residing in Japan of their legal status as Japanese, Japanese women married to these Koreans automatically lost their legal status as Japanese.[35] These Japanese are biologically Japanese, born of Japanese parents, speak Japanese natively, and possess Japanese culture. Can they truly be said to be 'not Japanese' only because their marriage has made them not so in the legal sense?

Children of Koreans living in Japan: As time passed, children of inter-marriages and also of Korean couples have grown up with varying degrees of Korean cultural input and competence. Some have retained no Korean cultural heritage – no linguistic competence and no cultural knowledge of Korea – especially if their parents are 'passing' as Japanese. Their lifestyle is totally Japanese. Only their names, if they retained them, betray their Korean heritage. Tokyo Metropolitan University's Chung Daekyun[36] has maintained that these Koreans should naturalise and legally become Japanese since they are already 'all but Japanese' anyway except for their legal status, and possibly their names.

Dual citizenship: When the former Peruvian president, Alberto Fujimori, defected and resigned his post while he was in Japan, the Japanese government allowed him to stay. The Japanese government defended its actions by demonstrating Fujimori's Japanese citizenship, in addition to his Peruvian citizenship. Is Fujimori Japanese? In his defection to Japan, he was conveniently Japanese in spite of the legal stipulation that any Japanese with dual citizenships is required, before age 22, to give up one or the other legal status. Hence Fujimori should have been required to give up his Peruvian citizenship before being allowed to seek refuge in Japan as a Japanese citizen.

Conventionally, a Japanese is not a foreigner and a foreigner is not a Japanese. These are mutually exclusive categories. But before the war, it was common for Japanese immigrants in North and South America to register their children with the local Japanese diplomatic mission, so that the children would have Japanese state affiliation through the Japanese law of *jus sanguinis* (citizenship according to descent or blood) in addition to the local citizenship of the country of immigration through *jus solis* (citizenship according to birthplace). Also, after the war, tens of thousands of Japanese businessmen and their families were dispatched abroad, creating a legal anomaly for thousands of children born to Japanese parents who happened to be in countries that follow *jus solis*, such as the US.

These individuals with dual citizenship are definitely Japanese legally, although psychologically or culturally to what extent they feel they are Japanese is another question. Some, such as most prewar second-generation Japanese Americans (*Nisei*), have little identity as Japanese, while others, like the children of Japanese businessmen born abroad in recent decades, are likely to claim Japanese identity as fervently as any other Japanese. In-between, some are unable to decide, while others enjoy being both in varying degrees. During the war, many Japanese Americans holding dual citizenship were living in Japan, and were even conscripted by the Japanese military as Japanese citizens to fight the country of which they were also citizens.

Naturalisation, de-naturalisation: As noted, persons having dual citizenship are required by the Japanese government to give up the citizenship of one or the other country at age 22. However, since there is no way that the Japanese government can keep track of who has dual citizenship, this law is a dead letter. Also, some 500 Japanese abandon their Japanese citizenship every year and become naturalised citizens of other countries. They are totally Japanese culturally and linguistically but in terms of state affiliation, overnight they become non-Japanese. Their neighbours, say in Australia, would continue to refer to them as 'Japanese', even though legally they are not.

While some Japanese are thus 'defecting' from Japan, around 15 000 foreigners become naturalised Japanese citizens every year. While most of them have at least some smattering of cultural competence on Japan, the degree of such competence covers the full spectrum. Here are people who may look Caucasian and possess little Japanese cultural and linguistic competence, yet overnight they become legally 'Japanese'.

Japanese orphans and women in and from China: Near the end of the Second World War, the Soviet Union invaded north-eastern China, where hundreds of thousands of Japanese civilians had settled. Abandoned by the Japanese army, they had to rely on their own meagre resources to flee the country and repatriate. Most of them were women and children, since virtually all men had been conscripted into the military. With hunger, malnutrition, and sickness, many children, unless they died, were given up to Chinese families for adoption, sold to them, or abandoned to be picked up by the Chinese. Some women, unable to cope with the difficulties, gave themselves up to the Chinese and remarried. No one knows exactly how many of them remained there, or how many are still living. Some are said to be passing as Chinese, completely concealing their Japanese background because of the discrimination levelled against them. Still, they know they are Japanese. In contrast, children who were taken into Chinese families in their infancy are unaware of their Japanese origin, unless their adoptive parents revealed their background. Most of the orphaned children by now are married and have children of their own or even grandchildren, and most of the women are in old age. The slow and tortuous repatriation process of these Japanese left in China began only after the diplomatic relationship between China and Japan was restored in 1972.[37]

When these repatriates arrived in Japan, a good 30 or 40 years later, many no longer knew any Japanese and had lost most of their Japanese cultural knowledge. Many of them did not have, or could not find legal documents to show their legal status as Japanese, but claimed their Japaneseness. Without definite proof, however, the Japanese government has been reluctant to grant them Japanese citizenship. So they are Japanese in one sense and not in another. And what about the children of these orphaned Japanese children who eventually married Chinese men or women, and came to Japan with their parents? They do have legal status as Japanese in so far as one parent can establish their legal status as Japanese, but biologically they are only half Japanese, and culturally they are totally Chinese. Their Japanese neighbours would call them *zanryū koji* (orphans who stayed behind) or *zanryū fujin* (women who stayed behind), rather than 'ordinary Japanese'. As Kimiko Yamada, a woman who remained in China, puts it, 'In China, they call us "Japanese"; in Japan, they call us "Chinese"'.[38]

The same issue remains with those who are still in China. Without the language marker, and without cultural markers, their claim to Japaneseness rests only on their word or that of their adoptive parents. The Japanese government does not admit their Japanese legal status unless they can produce proof. But deep inside, legal proof or not, they know they are Japanese.

Bi-national parentage: Until recently, whether a child was legally Japanese or not depended on his or her parentage. If the father was Japanese, the child was also Japanese; if the father was not, the child could not be Japanese. A child born to a Japanese mother who grew up in Japan, spoke

Japanese natively, and was totally enculturated in Japanese culture was still a foreigner (or stateless, if the biological father did not admit parentage), whereas another child, born to a Japanese father, growing up in a foreign country with no Japanese language and cultural competence, would be nonetheless legally Japanese. With recent legal changes, regardless of the gender of the Japanese parent, the child of a bi-national marriage can acquire Japanese citizenship. That is, a child who could not be Japanese due to the father's foreign citizenship is now Japanese simply because of changes in the law.

Thus the fluke of legal arrangements can result in full entitlements (such as social welfare and health insurance) in Japan by the Japanese government for one child and none for another. Neighbours would treat a person fully socialised in Japanese culture as a fellow Japanese, and a person not so socialised as a foreigner, regardless of his/her legal status.

Similarly, regardless of the Japanese state affiliation, children of international marriages, especially of marriage with non-Asians, stand out in the crowd and have suffered prejudice and discrimination because of their foreign appearance.[39] Epithets with undesirable connotations such as *ainoko* (mixed blood), *gaijin* (foreigner) and *amerikajin* were hurled at them.[40] Here one is confronted with the issues of xenophobic Japanese who cannot accept those who do not 'look like us' as fellow Japanese, even though they may be legally Japanese.

To conclude this section on 'the Japanese', whether or not a person is Japanese is not a question that yields a facile 'yes' or 'no' answer. Depending on a variety of circumstances, the answer may be a clear-cut 'yes', a clear-cut 'no', an ambivalent 'yes and no', an ambiguous 'maybe yes or maybe no', or an uncertain 'somewhat . . .', 'more yes than no', 'more no than yes,' or finally 'it depends'. Also, self-perception (self-identity) may or may not coincide with the perception of others. Self-identity is a variable not to be taken for granted.

As Japan's territory expanded and shrank, those residing in the territories thus acquired and lost were made Japanese and then abandoned. The hierarchy of the Japanese people has always been a salient feature in this context: some are considered more Japanese than others. 'Lesser' Japanese are expected to emulate and acquire, if possible, features of the 'pure Japanese'. Those who cannot, whether it be for biological (mixed blood) or cultural (inability to speak 'standard' Japanese) reasons, are forever condemned to the second class.

Conclusion

Whether the issue is 'Japan', 'Japanese culture', or 'the Japanese', one is always confronted with the problem of essentialism, standardisation, homogeneity, on the one hand, and stratification, variation, relativism and de-territorialisation/re-territorialisation, on the other.

As we have seen, essentialism is the core of the conventional definition of these concepts, which are presented as if they are true and *a priori* representations. They define 'Japan', 'Japanese culture', and 'the Japanese people' in a simplified and standardised way, doing injustice to the reality of variation, and set up standards by which 'variants' are judged as inferior and made to conform to the established standard. Thus we have a definition of Japan which is based on events as known in central Japan (the Kansai–Kanto belt). 'Japanese culture' is defined in terms of a series of cultural traits said to be found in Japanese tradition from time immemorial, and ignoring the significant influences absorbed and indigenised into Japanese culture from China and the West. The complexity of who 'the Japanese' are is simplified in the essentialised conception of citizenship, parentage, and cultural/linguistic competence.

Essentialised conceptions privilege certain regions of Japan, certain linguistic patterns, and individuals with certain character traits, creating a stratified structure in which those who are not so privileged – those who metaphorically live in the 'peripheries' of Japan, those who speak dialects and languages different from the 'standard' Japanese, and those who do not fulfil all of the criteria of essentialised Japanese – are relegated to lower rungs on the social ladder.

Moreover, such conceptions assume that the essentialised qualities are an unchanging concrete reality. The position taken in this chapter is, rather, that 'Japan', 'Japanese culture', and 'the Japanese' are relativistic, fluid, mutable and multifaceted concepts. These concepts are in part born out of comparison of Japan, Japanese culture, and the Japanese people with those of other countries.[41] This means that how these concepts are to be defined is a function of who/what 'the other' is. Japan is many things to many peoples. The fluidity and mutability of these concepts are seen in historical vicissitudes, government policy, cultural competency and other factors.

To explore the social and political ramifications of these alternative conceptions, we might envision, in extreme forms, two sets of definitions: conservative-traditional versus liberal-progressive. Conservative definitions are restrictive and essentialist. They espouse the isomorphism of land = people = culture = polity, and tend to uphold a nationalistic and patriotic political stance.

This view of isomorphism continues to be embraced by a number of influential politicians and intellectuals, and forms the ideological basis of their political stance. It clings to the idea that there are 'pure' Japanese and non-pure Japanese, who are ranked accordingly. These definitions emphasise the homogeneity of the Japanese in a genetic and cultural sense, ignoring the reality of heterogeneity, and end up being xenophobic, patronising and discriminating against those who are not 'pure'. At the same time they assert a claim that Japan belongs properly only to 'pure Japanese', excluding those who do not fit its narrowest definition. These xenophobic definitions foster a narrow, ethnocentric nationalism that creates uneasy relationships not only with those reduced to second class status, but also with neighbouring countries. They foster, for instance, an environment in which mixed-blood Japanese are looked down on, and the unfortunate Japanese who could not repatriate from China immediately after Japan's defeat, through no fault of their own, are regarded as unwelcome foreigners.

Conversely, liberal-progressive definitions takes an inclusive position admitting the heterogeneity and multifacetedness of 'Japan', 'Japanese culture', and 'the Japanese', where all variants of these concepts have equal value, rather than privileging 'the pure' over 'the impure'. This cosmopolitan position admits Japan as a home to 'the Japanese' of all shades and colours, whatever their state affiliation, language and cultural competence, colour of skin or biological descent.

These differing interpretations obviously have far-ranging political and social implications. Conservative definitions of Japaneseness are supported by conservative politics, which is still very much alive, and in fact dominates Japan. Witness the unwillingness of the government to allow refugees to remain in Japan, and its reluctance to accept foreign workers in spite of the massive labour shortage.[42] But the empirical reality flies in the face of the conservative image of what Japan should be, and foretells an eventual shift to the liberal-progressive definitions.

Notes

1. Sugimoto (1999).
2. Yano (2002).
3. Ivy (1995).

4. Tai (2005).
5. Befu (1992).
6. Society for the Study of Japonisme (1980).
7. Mouer (1983).
8. Dower (1986).
9. Kabanov (1992).
10. Befu (2001).
11. Hanihara (1995).
12. Ueyama, Sasaki and Nakao (1976).
13. Ōno (1974).
14. Kuki (1930).
15. Hamaguchi (1985).
16. Nakane (1970).
17. Watsuji (1935).
18. Takeo Doi (1973).
19. Watsuji (1935).
20. See, for example, Dale (1981); Miller (1982); Mouer and Sugimoto (1986); Oguma (2002) and Weiner (1997).
21. Benedict Anderson (1983); Sugimoto (1996).
22. Befu (2000).
23. Ministry of Foreign Affairs (2007: 9).
24. Sakai (2003).
25. Paul White (2003).
26. Machimura (2003).
27. Yatabe (2001).
28. Ben-Ari (2003).
29. Ministry of Foreign Affairs (2007: 16).
30. Schodt (1996).
31. Shirahata (1996).
32. Cwiertka (2005).
33. Clarke (2000).
34. A word needs to be said on the terminology of the legal status of the Japanese and non-Japanese. The Japanese term is *kokuseki*, which is often translated as 'nationality' or 'citizenship', neither of which is accurate. The former is often used to reflect national or ethnic origins, as when an American might ask another, 'What is your nationality?', expecting an answer such as 'German' or 'French', meaning 'I am of German (or French) descent', which has nothing to do with citizenship. Thus using 'nationality' to refer to the legal affiliation can be misleading. 'Citizenship' has the strong connotation of individual rights and duties in a democratic political system. Japan, especially before 1945, did not have such a political institution. Use of 'citizenship' in such a context is misleading. Thus *kokuseki* will be translated as 'state affiliation' or 'legal status' in most contexts, and 'citizenship' will be used only in unambiguous contexts. When the term 'citizenship' is used, it is used only to convey the technical status of state affiliation.
35. Fukuoka (1993: xxxi; 2000: 11–12).
36. Chung (2001).
37. Tsuneko Ogawa (1995); Saijō (1978; 1980); Wu (2004); Yamamura (1981).
38. In Tsuneko Ogawa (1995: 219).

39. Shigematsu-Murphy (2002).
40. All these terms are pejorative in certain contexts. 'Mixed blood' implies impurity. 'Foreigner' and 'Amerikajin' imply 'you are not Japanese' to those whose self-identity is Japanese.
41. Befu (1992).
42. Kantō Bengoshi-kai Rengōkai (Federation of Bar Associations in the Kantō Area) (1990).

Further reading

Mouer, Ross and Yoshio Sugimoto (1986), *Images of Japanese Society*, London: Kegan Paul International.

Oguma, Eiji (2002), *A Genealogy of 'Japanese' Self-images*, Melbourne: Trans Pacific Press.

Weiner, Michael (ed.) (1997), *Japan's Minorities: The Illusion of Homogeneity*, London: Routledge.

2

Japan's emic conceptions

Emic and etic

The distinction between emic and etic was first proposed in the mid-1950s by the linguist Kenneth Pike. The term 'emic' derives from phonemics, which studies the sound system of a particular language that is meaningful for native speakers. The term 'etic', conversely, derives from phonetics, which studies the physical properties of speech sounds independently of the speaker's perception. The following examples illustrate this distinction. To most English-speaking people, the *p* sounds of *pike* and *spike* probably sound the same, but phonetically speaking, they are actually different because the former is 'aspirated' whereas the latter is 'unaspirated'. Such differences are, however, irrelevant in terms of meaning production, and are therefore ordinarily ignored by native speakers. By contrast, the *p* sound of *pike* is immediately understood as different from the *b* sound of *bike* because, even though they are articulated in almost the same way, the subtle distinction between 'voiceless' and 'voiced' that separates the two sounds produces decisive differences in meaning. Technically symbolised as /p/ and /b/, they form parts of the phonemic system of the English language. Simply put, phonetic differences are revealed when measured precisely by some sort of objective methods and standards, but seldom come to the attention of speakers themselves, whereas phonemic differences are not only perceived to be real, but also essential in their speech behaviour.

The anthropological debate
Drawing on the linguistic insight above, anthropologists have applied the emic/etic distinction in cultural analysis. Historically speaking, however, the anthropological discussion developed in ways that often departed from

the original linguistic formulation, which eventually resulted in the identification of emic with inside, subjective, mental, culture-specific, relative, etc., and of etic with outside, objective, behavioural, cross-cultural, absolute, etc.

The emic approach is represented by Ward Goodenough,[1] who devised a method called 'componential analysis'. This method, like the phonemic distinction between /p/ and /b/ explained above, contrasts pairs of related words, especially culturally significant ones, according to the 'components' that distinguish one from the other, in an attempt to show the cognitive map (i.e. classification system) of a people under study. Among English-speaking people, for example, a male family member who is lineal and of the same generation as the ego is *brother*, whereas a female family member with the same attributes is *sister*. In Japanese, another criterion – the relative age – is used in identifying whether the brother is *ani* (elder brother) or *otōto* (younger brother), and whether the sister is *ane* (elder sister) or *imōto* (younger sister). Goodenough and his associates[2] claimed that such analyses would help reveal the logic behind speech and, ultimately, the native mind.

The etic approach is well represented by Marvin Harris,[3] the contentious founder of cultural materialism. Major objections raised by Harris and by other critics of the emic approach may be summed up as follows. (1) The study of emics results in purely relativistic descriptions of particular cases, thus making cross-cultural comparisons difficult, to say nothing of generalisations that are expected to arise from such comparisons. The emic approach is anti-science. (2) Actual life is far more ambiguous and diverse than the linguistic analyses have made it out to be. By and large, linguistic models of cultural analysis, including the structuralism of Claude Lévi-Strauss, are too formal to explain the complexity of human behaviour. They are also a-historical because time as a factor is effectively eliminated. (3) Language analysis is ordinarily based on the data obtained from a small number of knowledgeable informants. It is unclear to what extent the results actually apply to the whole of the people described. (4) Componential analysis is only effective in the study of a limited number of subjects, such as kinship terminology and folk taxonomy of plants and animals, which are considered by the critics to be rather trivial.

The relevance for Japanese studies

The etic approach has its own shortcomings,[4] but the above criticisms of the emic approach are relevant to the study of Japan. The first point, namely, that the emic approach results in relativistic descriptions that are difficult to validate cross-culturally is parallel to the long-lasting criticism that Japanese studies are so self-contained that they have produced few, if any, insights into the study of other countries. In the end, this criticism is directed toward the prevailing belief in the uniqueness of Japan, which has given rise to 'Japanese exceptionalism'. The second and third points, namely, the failure to accommodate ambiguity and diversity and the problem of representativeness, together challenge one of the most dominant views of Japan – the idea that Japan is homogeneous, or, as Harumi Befu argued,[5] that homogeneity is hegemonic in Japan.

Whether emic or etic, most concepts used in anthropology have been made by anthropologists themselves. Certainly, emic concepts are frequently derived from native words or ideas, but it is, after all, anthropologists who determine their values and take them up for scholarly discussion. Inasmuch as the majority of these scholars are outsiders to the community under discussion, anthropological emics are actually etics. At least, little consideration has thus far been given to the possibility that explanations anthropologists claim to be emic may not, ironically, be recognised as such by the people who have been described. This oversight probably derives from the fact that until recently many of the communities studied by anthropologists have been small-scale, illiterate societies without scholars of their own. In this regard, Japan is almost exceptional: it has been thoroughly investigated by Westerners, but at the same time it has the world's second largest professional society of anthropologists.[6] Indeed, many of the emic concepts proposed by Japanese scholars have stemmed from their dissatisfaction with Western discourse on Japan.

Critical appraisals of Japan's emic concepts

In this section, Japan's emic concepts are critically examined. Particular attention is paid to four of the best-known works on the Japanese character: Takeo Doi's *The Anatomy of Dependence*,[7] Esyun Hamaguchi's 'A Contextual Model of the Japanese',[8] Chie Nakane's *Japanese Society*,[9] and Tetsurō Watsuji's classic, *Climate and Culture*.[10] All of these have been either translated into English or re-written based on the Japanese originals.

The use of native terms
'Native' is used throughout to mean people born and brought up in a particular place, or things related to such people. No pejorative sense is implied. Among the four works mentioned above, that of Doi on dependence or

amae stands out for its heavy reliance on Japanese words as keys to under-standing the Japanese mind. This is only expected, for Doi is a practitioner of psychiatry, which is often called a 'medicine of words'. The following episode illuminates this point. When Doi treated a patient of mixed parent-age, he questioned her English mother about her upbringing. The mother was born in Japan and fluent in Japanese, but spoke in English until she came to what Doi thought was a critical moment: she suddenly switched to Japanese and said, '*Kono ko wa amari amaemasen deshita*' (This child did not *amaeru* or depend much). Having been dimly aware of the importance of *amae*, Doi asked why she had said that in Japanese. The English woman thought for a while and replied, 'There is no way of expressing *amae* in English'.[11] From this and other similar clinical experiences, Doi became convinced of the critical importance of *amae* in analysing the psychology of his patients and, more generally, that of the Japanese.

Doi confessed that, at a relatively early stage of his career, he started writing patient histories in Japanese, paying close attention to the words actually used by his patients. This practice was unusual in his time because Japanese doctors, regardless of their specialty, customarily wrote in either German or English as some of them still do today. Doi felt that only by recording symptoms in the patients' language could physicians provide an effective cure. From this perspective, he was attracted to the Sapir-Whorf hypothesis, which holds that language is closely related to thought – a major assumption on which emic research rests.

Some additional comments are necessary concerning language. First, the use of native terms does not automatically make cultural analysis emic. Ruth Benedict, for example, in her book *The Chrysanthemum and the Sword*, used the phrase '*giri* to one's name' in order to explain the Japanese sense of honour. There is, however, no such expression in Japanese, although the word '*giri*' itself exists and is used in everyday life to refer to 'obligation', 'debt', 'duty', and so on. Benedict in fact stated: 'The Japanese do not have a separate term for what I call "*giri* to one's name"'.[12] This statement demonstrates that etic, rather than emic, concepts are occasionally invented by using native words.[13]

Second, within the native community, there are different interpretations for the same word. For Doi, the essence of *amae* lies in the desire to seek identity or a sense of oneness (*ittaikan*) with another person, particularly that between mother and child. He thus defined *amae* as the 'attempt to deny the fact of separation that is such an inseparable part of human existence and to obliterate the pain of separation'.[14] This interpretation was met with an objection from Bin Kimura, a psychiatrist and the author of *Hito to Hito no Aida (Between Person and Person)*. In this influential book, Kimura praised Doi for having discovered the scholarly significance of *amae*, but rejected Doi's definition, arguing that *amae* refers to the indulgence observable in a relationship in which identity has already been established between benefactor and beneficiary, rather than the desire to seek identity as Doi contended.[15]

And third, when native words are strictly defined for technical purposes, as has been the case with Doi's *amae*, they tend to depart from everyday usage, thus causing confusion. Doi pointed out that many concepts used in Western scholarship were originally ordinary words, and contended that common Japanese words, such as *amae*, could similarly be used as technical terms if defined precisely.[16] Although this is a legitimate claim, the problem is that in ordinary speech we cannot say that the mother feels or offers *amae* toward her son or daughter, except when the parent-child relationship is reversed in old age or under similar circumstances. Doi's definition contradicts this common usage, for it highlights emotional identification between parent and child, which can occur on both sides.

In a recent book, Elisabeth Young-Bruehl and Faith Bethelard[17] rendered *amae* as 'cherishment' and gave a detailed account of it. Because Doi had occasionally compared *amae* to nonsexual love, which in turn was compared to cherishment,[18] the authors' rendition is, in my view, appropriate. Nevertheless, the use of native terms almost always entails the problem of translation. Translation is not simply a matter of changing languages, but rather requires the understanding of the cultural logic working 'backstage'. In order to translate meaningfully, one must be familiar with the 'world views' concealed in both languages. In the United States, where Doi's theory has been widely accepted, the term 'dependence' carries negative nuances because independence is highly valued there. We may say, however, that his writing has impacted the American readership precisely because it has shown that in the faraway land of Japan, dependence is appreciated differently.

Anecdotes for evidence

From the perspective of anthropology, which is based on intensive fieldwork over a prolonged period of time, a major weakness of Japan's emic research is the paucity of the ethnographic data that supports the arguments being made. Furthermore, what little evidence is provided is generally no more than a collection of personal anecdotes of superficial nature.

This weakness is best exemplified by Hamaguchi's theory of *kanjin* (literally, 'between-person') as found in his book '*Nihonrashisa' no Saihakken* (*Rediscovering 'Japaneseness'*), which was first published in 1977. This book spawned the aforementioned English article, 'A Contextual Model of the Japanese', in which *kanjin* is rendered as 'the contextual'. The book begins with a brief comparison of Japanese and American public behaviours. In Wakayama, located south of Osaka, Japanese passengers on a packed bus ignored the notice 'Do not use auxiliary seats when the bus is full', and seated themselves as they liked, despite the driver's repeated warnings. For reasons not perfectly clear, Hamaguchi interpreted this behaviour as flexible and adaptive to the situation, and argued that it revealed the 'situational relativism' of the Japanese. In Honolulu, by contrast, where he spent a short time as a visiting researcher, American passengers got on a bus in an orderly manner, with men allowing women and children to go first, and, after getting on board, they seated themselves by always occupying the window side first. From these rather superficial observations, Hamaguchi jumped to the conclusion that Americans obey rules, regardless of the situation they are placed in, and that they respect behavioural consistency across situations. He even went one step further when he generalised 'Japanese' and 'Americans' into 'East Asians' and 'Westerners', respectively.[19] Putting aside the question of whether or not Hamaguchi's contention makes sense, it is surprising, to say the least, that the above episodes are among the few ethnographic cases given in his entire book, which exceeds 300 pages of *bunko* (small paperback) size.

The problem of insufficient evidence is also found in Chie Nakane's famous book *Tate Shakai no Ningen Kankei* (*Human Relationships in a Vertical Society*), on which her major English work *Japanese Society* is based. For example, she illustrated the 'peculiarity' of Japanese *joretsu* (hierarchy) using the following anecdote: during the time Nakane was at the University of London as a visiting scholar, an English professor of social anthropology came back from the US. Soon after his return, during the tea break, he said to his colleagues that he had met a Japanese scholar in the US who knew Nakane. Having heard that the Japanese were status conscious, the professor introduced the Japanese scholar's words and brought the house down when he said: 'The guy said Chie was his *kōhai* (junior). How Japanese he is!'[20] Such anecdotes are certainly effective in some types of cultural accounts intended for a general reading public, but they should not be substituted for ethnographic data, at least not in an academic treatise.

This last point deserves some related commentary. Many of Japan's emic concepts originally appeared in books and articles belonging to the *nihon-jinron* genre. As Befu[21] pointed out, they are for a general readership, rather than being purely academic works. As such, few people expect them to be subjected to rigorous scholarly analysis. Nakane seems to have been well aware of this, which probably explains why she completely re-wrote her book for the English version: it is in fact far more technical than the Japanese original. Also at issue here is the national background of the assumed audience. The degree to which a language is associated with a particular national or ethnic group differs, depending on how widely the language is spoken in the world. Obviously, the smaller the speech community, the stronger the connections between language and people. Japanese is on the strong side of this link, even though it is the native language spoken by more than 120 million people. Of course, no country is completely homogeneous, but it is safe to say that Japan has a stronger national unity than do multi-ethnic countries, especially those that are made up of comparatively new immigrants. The point is that under these circumstances, Japanese authors are able to communicate their ideas by drawing on a commonality among readers that is hardly expected in immigrant nations. In the terminology of Edward Hall,[22] in Japan's 'high context' culture, it is not necessary to say much to evoke sympathy among the audience/readership.

Misconceptions of 'the West'

Japanese scholarship has been strongly influenced by Western Europe and the US since the onset of modern times, that is, since the Meiji Restoration in the mid-19th century. The Japanese reaction to these countries, which are frequently collapsed into a single category called 'the West', has been both positive and negative. On the one hand, there is a strong attachment to Western theory and methodology because Japanese scholars have worked very hard to master them. On the other hand, there is deep-seated resistance, as well as resentment, against Westerners for having dominated Japan. In Japanese studies, these ambivalent feelings have often given rise to a categorical rejection of Western theory, followed by a bold, yet rather reckless, claim that only Japan-made theory – what Hamaguchi[23] called 'emics inherent to Japan's culture' – can fully explain Japan. There are, however, many misconceptions in such claims.

These misconceptions relate to the generalised notion of 'the West' which typically occurs on two levels – social and academic. First, on the social level, the many differences that exist between Europe and the US are practically ignored. To give just one example, the fact that many Europeans are multilingual has generated among them more respect for different styles of speaking and writing than among monolingual Americans. This difference is clearly observable at international academic meetings, but it is too often overlooked by the Japanese. Also, within Europe, there are obviously numerous regional variations between Western and Eastern Europe, between Northern and Southern Europe, as well as between Continental Europe and Great Britain/Ireland, all of which are characterised by different histories and cultures. Furthermore, although much of Europe is united by Christian faith, the distinction between Catholicism, Protestantism, and Orthodoxy has far-reaching consequences. This becomes obvious when we recall that Max Weber's *The Protestant Ethic and the Spirit of Capitalism* was an attempt to explain in religious terms the differences in economic development between the regions north and south of the Rhine. All of this is well known among Japanese intellectuals, but it is easily forgotten when Japan's emics are emphasised, as opposed to 'Western theory'.

On the academic level, the generalised West has been held responsible for its alleged failure to clarify the interpersonal quality of the Japanese character. A major paradigm in the study of this subject centres on the dichotomy between Western individualism (*kojinshugi*) and Japanese collectivism (*shūdanshugi*). Putting aside the confluence between Japanese and Western scholars in the formulation of this dichotomy,[24] many Japanese, most notably Hamaguchi, have argued that Western social theory has limitations because it is ultimately based on the view of each person as an individual, which, etymologically speaking, means 'not divisible'. This Western conception is alleged to have fatal errors in explaining the Japanese view of each human being as 'inter-person' – the kind of self that realises itself *between* person and person.

The validity of this argument is not the point here. Rather, it is the unquestioned *Japanese* belief in Western individualism, and the ensuing identification of Western social theory with individualistic theory alone, that is at issue. A careful review of the relevant literature unmistakably shows that the relationship between individual and society has been conceptualised by Western intellectuals in many different ways and that individualistic theory is only one of them, although it has certainly received much support. To give just a few of the most notable examples: Emile Durkheim, in *Division of Labor*, emphasised the collective nature of human groups, and was adamantly opposed to the utilitarian view of society put forth by Herbert Spencer. Similarly, Harry Stack Sullivan propounded an interpersonal theory of psychiatry, in contrast with Sigmund Freud's ego psychology. As Sullivan remarked, 'You will find that it makes no sense to think of ourselves as "individual", "separate", capable of anything like definitive description in isolation, that the notation is just beside the point... For all I know every human being has as many personalities as he has interpersonal relations'.[25] Similar opinions were expressed by George Herbert Mead, one of the founders of symbolic interactionism, who distinguished between two competing approaches to the study of self, one taking the social process as logically prior to the individual, and the other taking the individual as logically prior to the social process.[26] He supported the former approach.

To these observations should be added the historical transformation of concepts of individuality in the West. According to Peter Burke,[27] social historical study has shown that the 'mentality' of 16th century French farmers had many things in common with that of contemporary Chinese farmers. Particularly interesting in our context is the emphasis on collectivity over individuality among both populations. Comparable results are also reported by Antoine Prost, who studied the transformation of the French family. As Prost remarked, 'The individual once was an intrinsic part of his or her family. Private life was secondary, subordinate, and in many cases secret or marginal. Now the relation of individual to family has been reversed'.[28] These findings suggest that in societies with the same or similar subsistence basis, the self is conceptualised in similar ways, regardless of cultural differences. At least, we can reasonably suppose that the individualised self of the West had emerged in the process of modernisation, particularly in connection with the Enlightenment movement.

Considering the above, we must say that Japanese emicists, despite their contributions to the understanding of Japan from the native's point of view, have created a hypothetical enemy, a monstrous one at that, and they have fought a fierce war against it, while losing sight of their friends on the other side.

Whose emics?

One question that has seldom been raised in the voluminous anthropological literature on the issue of emic/etic is: 'Whose emics are they?' Earlier, I pointed out that many of the communities studied by anthropologists are small-scale, illiterate societies and that this explains why emicists have been spared confrontation with local scholars concerning the authenticity of their formulations.[29] The same fact explains why the internal diversity of a culture has seldom been considered in devising emic concepts: most of the communities that have been studied are too small to warrant a careful investigation into social stratification. Thus, whether or not there are different emics for different groups of age, gender, class, and region *within* the same culture, and, if so, what kinds of internal dynamics are working, have escaped the attention of most researchers. From the perspective of social diversity and variation emphasised in this book, one particularly interesting possibility is that the emics of dominant groups have been superimposed on those of other groups, thus having been elevated to the status of the etics for the entire culture, while having been presented as its emics in cross-cultural comparison. As Yoshio Sugimoto and Ross Mouer stated, 'The extent to which, and the processes by which, the emic concepts of one subgroup are superseded with the etic-cum-emic concepts of another subgroup, thereby elevating an emic term to serve as the standard medium for society-wide communication, would prove to be an interesting study.'[30]

In Japanese studies, little has been said on this subject, but the multiplicity of Japan's emics has long been recognised. Toshinao Yoneyama, for example, took issue with Nakane's characterisation of Japanese society as *tate* (vertical) by pointing out the widely acknowledged differences between north-eastern and south-western Japan in kinship and village structures.[31] In north-eastern Japan, particularly in the Tōhoku region examined in detail by Kizaemon Aruga,[32] human relationships are based on the *dōzoku*, a hierarchically organised group made up of one *honke* (main family) and a number of its *bunke* (branch families). This group is united by common ancestors, and the *honke* dominates its *bunke*, demanding both loyalty and labour, while providing protection in times of need. In south-western Japan, by contrast, the *dōzoku* hierarchy is surpassed by the egalitarianism of *kō*, a local association which originally developed as a religious group, but which began fulfilling economic functions at a later age, as was the case with *tanomoshi-kō*, the precursor of today's credit unions. Yoneyama maintained that Nakane's theory is a half truth that only applies to the mainstream of north-eastern Japan, centred on Tokyo. This scholarly discord partially stems from the differences in everyday practice between the two regions: Nakane is Tokyo-based, while Yoneyama is based in Kyoto, one of the centres of south-western Japan.

In terms of gender, study has shown that Hamaguchi's *kanjin* orientation is more strongly observed among women than among men.[33] This finding is parallel to the assertions of Carol Gilligan, author of *In a Different Voice*,[34] who criticised conventional theories of human development as male-centric. According to her, these theories highlighted independence to the neglect of interdependence. Generally speaking, before the postmodern turn in the 1980s, culture was conceptualised as an integrated whole possessing homogeneity and internal consistency. This coherent picture has been shattered by postmodernists who emphasise cultural multiplicity, fragmentation, dissonance, and so forth. It seems, however, that the pendulum has swung too far in one direction. Culture may not be shared as much as used to be thought, but it would be an exaggeration to say that there is no cultural sharing at all among members of the same group, be it a state, nation, or ethnic group. It is a matter of empirical research, rather than a particular *-ism*, to investigate what 'separates' people, as well as what 'connects' them, and to what extent.

Nationalism

A major paradigm in the study of Japanese character is, as noted earlier, the dichotomy between Western individualism and Japanese collectivism. In terms of intellectual history, its major source of influence has been the discourse of family state (*kazoku kokka*), which emerged at the end of the 19th century. From the beginning, Japan's 'familism' emphasised the welfare of the entire family over the wishes of its individual members. It was contrasted sharply with the stereotyped individualism of the West, which was frequently equated in Japan with selfishness. Before the end of the Second World War, this contrast was politically manipulated in Japan on numerous occasions in order to underscore Japan's 'spiritual superiority' over its Western rivals. The climax came when this perceived dichotomy was turned into a state ideology in *Kokutai no Hongi* (*Fundamentals of Our National Polity*), a booklet drafted and published by the Ministry of Education in 1937. It proclaimed, 'Our country is a great family nation, and the Imperial Household is the head family of the subjects and the nucleus of national life'.[35]

Two years before this pronouncement, the philosopher Tetsurō Watsuji wrote an influential book entitled *Fūdo*.[36] It was first translated into English as *Climate*, but was later re-titled *Climate and Culture*.[37] This book contains an archetypical analysis of Japanese collectivism in terms of *ie* (family or house) and its related emic concepts. First of all, Watsuji regarded the *ie* as signifying the totality of family, arguing that the *ie* takes precedence over its individual members. As was preached in the prewar moral education (*shūshin*), he maintained that *ie* members are both descendants of their ancestors and are themselves ancestors to those who are yet to come. Thus, the good name of the *ie* must be protected at any cost. Furthermore, Watsuji contended that the Japanese ideal of *aidagara* ('betweeness') is crystallised in the *ie*. This notion of *aidagara* was later elaborated by Hamaguchi in the 1970s when *nihonjinron* was booming. Watsuji went on to argue that in modern European capitalism each person is seen as an individual, and the family is no more than a gathering of individuals to meet economic interests, whereas in Japan the family has retained its strong solidarity even after the introduction of capitalism. Watsuji explained this difference by referring to a contrasting pair of terms now widely used in the study of Japan – *uchi* and *soto*. He maintained that the Japanese regard the *ie* as *uchi* (inside), a term synonymous with house, and that the world beyond it is considered *soto* (outside). Within the *ie/uchi*, said Watsuji, the distinction between individuals disappears, and the family is united as a whole, admitting 'no discriminating *aidagara*'. By contrast, this intimate world is strictly distinguished from *soto* – a distinction claimed by Watsuji to have no parallel in Europe. In this way, Watsuji both eulogised the Japanese spirit and emphasised its uniqueness.[38] For lack of space, no further details are provided here,[39] but there is no denying that Watsuji's discourse dovetailed with nationalist propaganda before and during the Second World War.

After the war, Watsuji was criticised on the grounds that he had fanned the flames of Japan's nationalism, but he was eventually awarded in 1955 an Order of Cultural Merit (*bunka kunshō*), the highest honour to be conferred on Japanese academics. Significantly, Watsuji was not alone in interpreting Japanese collectivism as having been derived from the ideal of *ie*. Similar views were presented by many other leading intellectuals, including Kunio Yanagita, who founded Japanese folklore studies in the 1930s.[40] Even today, their views are echoed in the works of many writers, including Nakane, who regards the *ie* as the archetype of Japanese organisations,[41] and the scholars who collaborated in the preparation of a governmental paper entitled 'The Age of Culture', which spelled out Japan's cultural policy in the early 1980s.[42]

Universality versus particularity

Japanese emicists are convinced that Western theory is incapable of fully explaining Japan. This conviction has led them to set about formulating alternative theory from the native's point of view. Such undertakings may, however, backfire when, for example, the Japanese attempt to apply their insights to the study of other countries: their theory may be dismissed for exactly the same reason as the Japanese have dismissed Western theory.

Since many Japanese emicists believe in the uniqueness of Japan, few such attempts have ever been made seriously. But as long as Japan's emic concepts contain theory or something comparable to it, there should be a universality that makes them applicable, however modestly, in non-Japanese contexts. Here we have come to a critical point – the perennial issue of universality versus particularity.

Japan's emic discourse typically starts, as does anthropological emic research, with language analysis. As a rule, this analysis employs one or both of the following two approaches. The first is to tap into native vocabulary in order to discover a distinctive word or a set of words that presumably expresses the 'essence' of the people being studied, as is illustrated by Doi's research into *amae*. Occasionally, terms like *uchi* and *soto* are used by non-Japanese scholars as keys to understanding Japan. A representative figure in this regard is Jane Bachnik, although her interpretations are influenced by the semiotics of Charles Peirce.[43] A second approach is to invent new terms for the question at issue. Hamaguchi's *kanjin* illustrates this approach. The term *'kanjin'* is made up of two characters, *kan* (between) and *jin* (person/people), which, if arranged in the opposite order, signify *ningen* (human being). Hamaguchi's theory has had wide appeal for Japanese readers because of the impact of this neologism. In just two characters, he has made his point that the Japanese conceive of human relationships as 'relational' or as being formed 'between' person and person.

A major pitfall into which this kind of study falls is the rash conclusion that because such and such words do not exist in other languages, they must be peculiar to the people being studied. In Japan, this conclusion has frequently been drawn from a casual comparison of Japanese with English and a few other European languages at most. Thus, despite the significance of Doi's discovery of *amae* psychology, the word *'amae'* has rather hastily been declared to be peculiar to Japanese. On this point, the Korean literary critic O-Young Lee cynically criticised Doi, saying that there are in Korean two equivalent terms for *amae*, *origwan* and *unsok*, which together convey the subtle nuances of dependence far more elegantly than does 'the simple Japanese term *amae*'. Lee's criticism partially stems from his dissatisfaction with the Japanese tendency to look to the West to the neglect of the East.[44] Whatever the truth may be, we should remember, first, that those Japanese words that have been considered peculiar may in fact have parallel words in languages not well known in Japan, and, second, that even if there are no equivalents, the ideas themselves may be present in concealed or disguised form, or indeed not verbalised at all.

This last point has been proven by Doi himself. While he struggled to overcome the difficulties of applying Freud's theory in the Japanese setting, Doi came across the British psychiatrist Michael Balint's writing on 'passive object love' or 'primary love'. Balint observed that 'in the final phase of the treatment patients begin to give expression to long-forgotten, infantile, instinctual wishes, and to demand their gratification from their environment'.[45] Doi interpreted this behaviour as 'none other than *amae*'. He became convinced of his interpretation when he found these words by Balint: 'All European languages are so poor that they cannot distinguish between the two kinds of object-love, active and passive'.[46] In a later work, Balint acknowledged the connection between primary love and *amae*.[47]

Similar supporting remarks are to be found elsewhere. Eric Fromm, for example, criticised Freud for having distorted his own discovery of the Oedipus complex by interpreting it in sexual terms. In Fromm's view, the little boy's attachment to his mother springs not from the desire to take her sexually, but rather from the child's desire for emotional protection, which is secretly carried into adult life. According to Fromm, this desire is found at the base of all neuroses.

> Is it surprising that he [the adult child] carries with him *the dream of finding a mother again or of finding a world in which he can be a child again*? The contradiction between *the loving of the paradisiacal child existence* and the necessities that follow from his adult existence can be rightly considered the nucleus of all neurotic developments.[48]

In this regard, I must mention that Doi overlooked the possible connection of *amae* with the Catholic belief in the Madonna. For lack of space, a detailed account is withheld here, but the 'Madonna Complex' as described by Anne Parsons[49] in her study of southern Italy shows some significant similarities to *amae*. Doi could have noticed this connection when the semanticist SF Hayakawa, a Canadian-born Nisei, asked him 'if the feeling of *amaeru* was similar to that experienced by a Catholic towards the Blessed Virgin'.[50] Unfortunately, Doi missed the importance of this question.

The foregoing argument suggests that *amae* is far from peculiar to the Japanese. It is, rather, a widely observed phenomenon, the existence of which has long been known even among Western psychiatrists. Until recently, however, it has not been recognised as such due to language differences. From this, we may generalise and say that the absence of a word in a particular language merely reflects the *relative* insignificance of the idea expressed by that word. It is by no means proof that the idea itself is non-existent in that culture.

This observation brings us back to the anthropological debate on emic/etic. Among the many different formulations of the *relationship* between the two concepts, that of Goodenough[51] is useful in considering the issue of universality versus particularity. He explained that when linguists embark on describing the phonemic system of a new language, they initially use etics, namely, the meaningful distinctions (e.g. whether or not consonants are aspirated) that are already known from previous research into other languages. And when unknown features are discovered, they make a new distinction with which to describe them. This new distinction is then added to the existing pool of etics. In this way, the emics of one language are explained, though incompletely, in terms of the etics of other languages, which in turn are enhanced by those newly discovered emics. As Goodenough maintained: 'Emic description requires etics, and by trying to do emic descriptions we add to our etic conceptual resources for subsequent description'.[52]

In sociocultural analysis, a major criticism of this kind of approach is that the emics of Western society have been elevated to the etics of the world's society to such an extent that they are now taken as the yardsticks by which to judge the non-Western world. Although this is a significant point, we must at the same time remember that there is no human group that is so different as to share nothing with other groups. As Befu aptly remarked, 'While our understanding of Japan increases as we engage in emic analysis and learn of its unique aspects, at the same time etic comparisons help us to discover how Japan is part of humanity'.[53] Instead of categorically rejecting Western theory, then, we should use it in the study of Japan as long as it is useful – with a full awareness that it has limitations, as does any other theory – while simultaneously endeavouring to find new insights that deserve to be added to the world's intellectual resources. In this way, we can at least avoid the mistake of throwing the baby out with the bath water.

Concluding remarks

In the modern world system, Japan has been subjected, as has almost every other non-Western nation, to domination by Western powers. This history has generated among Japanese intellectuals both admiration for and resentment against Western scholarship. On the one hand, they have voraciously studied the Western ideas they admire, and on the other, they have felt humiliated by not having received the respect they think they deserve from the West. These ambivalent feelings are observed in the intellectual community throughout the non-Western world, but are particularly strong in Japan because outside the West, Japan alone has had the power to create a modern empire of its own. The humiliation suffered by Japanese intellectuals has generated a reverse discrimination against Westerners, resulting in the tenuous contention that only the Japanese can understand Japan. Japan's emic concepts may therefore be seen as resulting from the attempt to reclaim the discourse on Japan.[54] Parenthetically, it is only recently that the presence of other Asian countries has been felt tangibly within Japan. Intellectual exchange with those countries has at last begun after a long interval of silence, but building sturdy bridges is a task for the future.

Placed outside the centre of the 'academic world system', in the humanities and social sciences at least, Japanese scholars have tried, whenever possible, to raise their status by claiming the originality of their research. The fact is, however, that many of Japan's emic concepts have emerged in response to, or out of struggle with, Western theory. Indeed, Doi's *amae*, Nakane's *tate*, and Hamaguchi's *kanjin* may be considered 'counter-discourses' against, respectively, Freudian psychology, modernisation theory (as opposed to the study of indigenous social structure), and generalised Western theory. Even Watsuji's *Fūdo*, which was presented before Japan's defeat in the Second World War, was stimulated by the philosophy of Martin Heidegger and by the 'climatology' of Johann Gottfried Herder. Put another way, they all engaged in dialogue with the intellectual giants of the West, instead of starting from scratch. Thus, we may say that the foundation on which modern Japanese theory is based has been provided by Westerners, however insufficient their theory may be when it comes to explaining Japan.

Considering the above, it would be appropriate to see the efforts of Japanese emicists as 'translation'. As already noted, translation is not simply a change of languages. Rather, it involves a creative process by which new possibilities of the existing ideas are explored through the laborious attempt to overcome the so-called 'incommensurability' between different languages. When successful, it is like transplanted plants growing in ways never imagined before. Similarly, to the extent that Japan's emic concepts have been stimulated, whether positively or negatively, by Western ideas, they are not completely original. They are, however, contributions in their own right, which should be commended for the new light they have thrown on the study of Japan, thus opening new horizons of research.

Notes

1. Goodenough (1968).
2. Tyler (1969).
3. Harris (1968).
4. Headland, Pike and Harris (1990).
5. Befu (2001).
6. The Japanese Society of Cultural Anthropology, formerly known as the Japanese Society of Ethnology, was founded in 1934. As of 2007, it had a membership of approximately 2000 people.
7. Takeo Doi (1973).
8. Hamaguchi (1985).
9. Nakane (1970).
10. Watsuji (1971).
11. Takeo Doi (1973: 18).
12. Benedict (1946: 145).
13. Kuwayama (2004: 89).
14. Takeo Doi (1973: 75).
15. Kimura (1972: 149).
16. Ōtsuka, Kawashima and Doi (1976: 27–33).
17. Young-Bruehl and Bethelard (2000).
18. Frank Johnson (1993: 197–200).
19. Hamaguchi (1988: 15–20). These remarks are based on Hamaguchi's Japanese-language book published in 1988. The book was originally published in 1977, then re-published in 1988 under the same title, but with a different publisher. Between the two editions, Hamaguchi summarised his ideas in a 1985 English-language article (1985).
20. Nakane (1967b: 86).
21. Befu (2001).
22. Hall (1966).
23. Hamaguchi (1985: 289).
24. See Kuwayama (2001) on how it developed in the study of *ie* or family.
25. Sullivan (1970: 392).
26. Mead (1934: 223).
27. Burke (1993: 94).
28. Prost (1991: 84).
29. See Kuwayama (2004: 15–17) for cross-cultural implications on this point.
30. Sugimoto and Mouer (1989: 15).
31. See Toshinao Yoneyama (1985) for a synoptic review.
32. Aruga (1954).
33. Sugimoto (2003: 23).
34. Gilligan (1982).
35. Tsunoda, de Bary and Keene (1964: 282).
36. Watsuji (1935).
37. See Berque (1996) for a review of the notion of *fūdo*.
38. Watsuji (1935: 141–5; 1971: 141–4).
39. See Bellah (2003) for an excellent critique.
40. Kuwayama (2001).

41. Nakane (1970: 10).
42. Kawamura (1989).
43. Bachnik and Quinn (1994).
44. Lee (1984: 10–13).
45. Quoted in Takeo Doi (1979: 267).
46. Quoted in Takeo Doi (1979: 267).
47. Balint (1992: 69).
48. Fromm (1980: 28–9), emphasis added.
49. Parsons (1969).
50. Takeo Doi (1973: 16).
51. Goodenough (1970).
52. Goodenough (1970: 112).
53. Befu (1989: 341).
54. This is best illustrated by Kunio Yanagita (1875–1962). His determination to create a distinctively Japanese approach to the study of folklore sprang from his intellectual nationalism. This in turn was aroused by his intense sense of rivalry against Western science, as well as by his resentment of self-appointed Western spokesmen for Japan, such as Lafcadio Hearn. For details, see Kuwayama (2005).

Further reading

Befu, Harumi (2001), *Hegemony of Homogeneity: An Anthropological Analysis of Nihon-jinron*, Melbourne: Trans Pacific Press.

Headland, Thomas N, Kenneth L Pike and Marvin Harris (eds) (1990), *Emics and Etics: The Insider/Outsider Debate*, Newbury Park: Sage.

Kuwayama, Takami (2004), *Native Anthropology: The Japanese Challenge to Western Academic Hegemony*, Melbourne: Trans Pacific Press.

3
_____

Language

Language reflects social change. This is perhaps nowhere better illustrated than in Japan, where massive upheavals in the use of language have occurred over the past two hundred years. These changes have affected not only the Japanese language itself, but also Japanese attitudes to their own and other languages. Neither are these attitudes constant. They fluctuate over time, reflecting the prevailing political or social climate, or the views, whether progressive or conservative, of the protagonists in the language debate. As with other aspects of Japanese culture, the story of language in modern Japan reverberates with the tensions between the centripetal forces of standardisation, unity and nationalism on the one hand and the centrifugal imperatives of diversity, regional identity and internationalism on the other.

This chapter aims to provide a broad overview of language in modern Japan, dealing not only with Japanese, but also with Ryukyuan, Ainu and English. Within each section the focus is on sociolinguistic matters, including language diversity, change, regulation, attitudes and controversy.[1] A secondary aim of the chapter is to provide readers with a guide to research resources accessible in English, both on the printed page and on the internet.

Historical overview

Contrary to long-held assumptions that language changes at a constant rate, recent research suggests that languages tend to go through cycles of relative stagnation followed by periods of rapid change.[2] The stimulus for change is often external pressure exerted through contact with different languages and cultures. The greatest changes we can observe in the history of the Japanese language have occurred after periods of major external impact. The first of these in the historical period was the introduction of Chinese language and culture with the advent of Buddhism in the middle of the 6th century.[3] The next major foreign influence on Japanese culture came through contact with Portuguese and Spanish missionaries in the 16th century. Then followed two centuries of isolation under the 'closed country' (*sakoku*) policy, in which the only window to the outside world was through limited contact with Dutch and Chinese traders at the tiny island outpost of Dejima in Nagasaki.[4] While these early European contacts contributed a few dozen words to the Japanese vocabulary (e.g. *pan* 'bread', *botan* 'button' and *tabako* 'tobacco' from Portuguese and *mesu* 'scalpel' and *korera* 'cholera' from Dutch),[5] their influence is negligible when compared with the next great wave of foreign contact that began pounding the shores of Japan from the mid-19th century. These early encounters with the English language acted as a catalyst for unprecedented change in Japanese language and society which, reinforced with the second impact of English after Japan's defeat in the Second World War, continues to exert a considerable influence to the present day.

In addition to these spontaneous changes triggered by contact with other languages and cultures, deliberate measures were debated from the last decades of the 19th century, and continued under successive Japanese governments, about how to 'modernise' the Japanese language. The major changes advocated fall roughly within the areas of simplification of the written language through the unification of written and spoken Japanese (*genbun'itchi*) and the establishment of a standard national language.

Characteristics of the Japanese language

The Japanese language is characterised by a simple phonetic system, SOV (subject, object, verb) word order, a highly developed respect language and a rich system of sound symbolism. It has a hybrid vocabulary made up of native Japanese words, loanwords from Chinese, English and other languages and a large number of Sino-Japanese neologisms, many created in Japan, fashioned to translate terms denoting Western ideas and technology. Japanese is unique in the sense that all languages are unique – it is their uniqueness that distinguishes them as discrete languages. Conversely, despite the claims to special status for the Japanese language often advocated by proponents of the *Nihonjinron*, Japanese is no more or less remarkable than most of the world's several thousand languages. In grammatical structure it is almost identical to Korean and it shares many features, such as the tendency to employ suffixes and particles (or postpositions), with other SOV languages, like Mongolian or Turkish. The simple consonant plus vowel sound system is similar to Polynesian and elaborate respect language is also found in Javanese, Hindi, Korean, Thai and many other languages.

Roy Andrew Miller has written at some length on what he sees as the irrational relationship many Japanese have to their language and how myths about Japanese are kindled and perpetuated in the popular writings of scholars of the Japanese language.[6] Indeed, since the end of the 1990s there has been a new boom in popular publications on the Japanese language. Saitō Takashi's *Koe ni dashite yomitai Nihongo* (Japanese to be read aloud), published in 2001, sold over a million copies and inspired ordinary citizens all over Japan to enrol in classes for the recitation of Japanese texts, *rōdoku*. This up-turn in interest in Japanese may be in response to embarrassment over Japan's poor international showing in English proficiency tests; or it may be through nostalgia and the psychological need to feel pride in Japanese language and culture at a time of economic recession.[7]

Debate over origins

Despite well over a century of conjecture and research regarding the genetic affiliation of Japanese, producing scores of books and hundreds of articles relating it to a large number of languages and language families as divergent as Hittite, Indo-European, Korean, Proto-Altaic,[8] Dravidian, Ainu and Austronesian, scholars have failed to reach a consensus on the origins of the language and many among them see it as a language isolate like Basque or Ainu.

It seems almost certain that there is a connection between Japanese and Korean, but it remains unclear whether this is the result of early borrowing or shared inheritance. The most likely candidates for relatives of Japanese seem to be the Altaic languages to the north and west or the Austronesian languages to the south. The only language that can be indisputably assigned to the same genealogy as Japanese is Ryukyuan, which, as we shall see below, Japanese linguists in general consider to be a group of Japanese dialects. One scholar at least, Murayama Shichirō, claimed that Japanese is a 'mixed language' with an Austronesian vocabulary and an Altaic grammar.[9]

Vocabulary

Japanese has drawn its vocabulary from a variety of sources. By far the largest outside contribution to the Japanese lexical stock has come from

Chinese. The Chinese language brought with it not only a large corpus of specialised abstract and technical vocabulary, much of it coined in China from Sanskrit originals to explain the practice and doctrine of Buddhism, but the writing system itself. Despite the semantic basis of the Chinese script, the characters are primarily representations of the sounds of the syllables of Chinese words.[10] Until modest changes in the shapes of some characters were introduced independently in Japan and China after the war, the shapes of the Chinese characters had changed very little in the 25 centuries since Confucius. The pronunciation of the characters, however, had changed considerably. As a result, the same Chinese character, borrowed into Japanese in different Chinese words at different times in history, may have two, three or more separate quasi-Chinese pronunciations (called *on* readings) in addition to the native Japanese translations (*kun* readings) representing the meaning of the character, rather than its original sound in Chinese.

The influence of English

The use of English loanwords in Japanese covers virtually all registers and genres of the language, ranging from *rippu sābisu* (lip service) – used to refer to former Prime Minister Abe Shinzō's responses to Western journalists – to the *chairudo rokku* (child lock) button on the simple washing machine in my Tokyo flat. In some cases, Japanese even makes distinctions in the use of loanwords that are not made in the original English. There are two words in Japanese that convey the English noun 'strike', *sutoraiki* for an industrial strike and *sutoraiku* for a strike in baseball. Similarly, glass, the substance from which windows and bottles are made, is *garasu* (an old loanword from Dutch), but the glass you drink from is *gurasu* or *koppu*. This latter term (also from Dutch) should not be confused with *kappu* (a cup), the china vessel with a handle from which one drinks Western, but not Japanese, tea.

Indeed, the influx of loans from English continues at such pace and volume that the National Institute for Japanese Language (*Kokuritsu Kokugo Kenkyūjo*) has felt the need to intervene. In 2003 the Institute established a foreign loanwords committee to survey the use of foreign loanwords in Japanese, issue guidelines and suggest substitutes for difficult or unnecessary borrowings from English and other languages. In four meetings up to March 2006 the committee suggested alternative Japanese translations for one hundred and seventy-six words.[11] The list of words targeted for remedial action includes two words from German, *torauma* (Trauma) and *biotōpu* (Biotop), and one from French, *komyunike* (communiqué). The remainder are from English, including well established, but apparently little understood, words like *aidentitii* (identity),[12] abbreviations like *infura* (infrastructure) and words coined in Japan from English roots like *nonsuteppubasu* (literally 'non-step bus', bus with wheel-chair access). The committee recommends that these be replaced respectively with the Sino-Japanese compounds, *dokujisei* (individuality) or *jiko ninshiki* (self awareness), *shakai kiban* (social foundation) and *mudansa basu* (level-floor bus).

The composition of the Japanese vocabulary, then, is a mix of native Japanese (*wago*), Chinese (*kango*), and other foreign, mainly English, components (*gairaigo*). Chinese character compounds, *kango*, frequently appear in written texts or in more formal spoken registers. Compare the usual native Japanese word for 'tomorrow', *ashita*, with its more formal *kango* equivalent, *myōnichi*, or the native colloquial word for cooked rice, *meshi*, with the more genteel *kango* word, *gohan*, or the *gairaigo* alternative, *raisu*. In practice this last term, derived from the English word rice, is restricted in meaning to designate rice served as an adjunct to a Western meal. Unlike *meshi* or *gohan*, which comes in a bowl and is eaten with chopsticks, *raisu* generally comes on a flat plate and is eaten with a fork.

Respect language

Like many societies with a history of hierarchical social structure, Japanese has an elaborate system of honorific language or *keigo*. Some consider *keigo* a feudal anachronism and fail to see how it can remain relevant to Japanese society in the 21st century, when virtually all Japanese consider themselves members of the middle class. Despite the younger generation's complaints about the system's complexity, it has survived by assuming the new functions of adding value to interaction between service providers and customers, smoothing social intercourse and maintaining harmony among equals of little acquaintance. The tendency nowadays seems to be towards reciprocity in the use of polite language and to confine the highest honorifics to customers and those generally perceived to be performing important roles in society, such as doctors, teachers and company presidents. Basically the system works at two levels: politeness and respect. Every Japanese sentence carries information about both categories. Politeness is directed towards the addressee, while respect is shown to the subject (subject honorifics), or direct or indirect object (object honorifics), of the verb. As the subject of object honorific sentences is invariably the first person, 'I', or someone closely associated with the speaker, traditionally the object honorifics were referred to as 'humble' or 'deferential language'. The older terms are still in general use, but specialists prefer 'object honorifics' as these forms show respect to a socially designated superior and carry no connotations of self-denigration on the part of the speaker.

While it is older Japanese who tend to have problems with the influx of foreign words, respect language is the bane of younger speakers. With the breakdown of extended families and the trend towards less formal school environments, Japanese today are not exposed to the hierarchical features of their society until they leave school and join the workforce. Consequently, the responsibility for training in respect language often falls on employers. Inevitably, variation creeps into the system and disagreements occur over what constitutes correct usage.

Language and gender

Japanese men and women speak differently. This remains true in spite of the protestations of older Japanese that young women these days speak more like men and young males are speaking more like women. The differences between men's and women's language are less apparent in the polite conversational style, though, even here, women tend to use more honorific expressions than men and many overuse the elegant noun prefix o-. Convention calls for the use of the prefix in words like *o-kane* (money) and *o-tsuri* (change); women often use it with traditional vocabulary like *o-sake* (sake), *o-kome* (rice) or *o-miai* (arranged marriage), but purists frown on its use with loanwords like *o-biiru* (beer) or *o-ninjin* (carrot). The typical sentence-final particles of female speech, *wa* (soft emphasis), *kashira* (mild speculation) and *no yo* (gentle assertion), are often heard in the informal style. Modern women don't seem to find the use of feminine language demeaning as they use it as much in the company of other women as in the presence of men, but in general they now show resistance to sexist terms from the past that suggest a lower social status for women. Consequently, activists insist that the neutral term *otto* (husband) be used in favour of the common term *shujin* that means master as well as husband. Similarly *tsuma* (wife) is preferred to *kanai* (literally, 'inside the house').[13]

Dialects

There is considerable regional variation in the Japanese language. Some of these variants, like the Tsugaru dialect of Aomori prefecture at the northern tip of Honshū and the Kagoshima dialect of southern Kyūshū, are mutually unintelligible and are of course incomprehensible to city dwellers of Tokyo or Osaka. The dialects of the Tōhoku region of northern Honshū, in particular, are characterised by the presence of the central vowels [ï] and [(ü)] and various sound combinations not found in the central dialects which provide the model for the so-called 'common language' (kyōtsūgo). In many of these northern dialects, for instance, words distinguished in the pronunciation of Tokyo, like sushi (sushi), shishi (lion), susu (soot), shushi (intention) and shishu (defending to the death) are all pronounced [sïsï] or [süsü]. This confusion often leaves Tōhoku dialect speakers the butt of jokes in Tokyo and Osaka, where their dialect is unkindly referred to as zuuzuuben (the zuuzuu dialect). Some northern dialect speakers, fewer nowadays than under the language assimilation policy of the past, develop a dialect inferiority complex because of their inability to modify their native vowel sounds. Conversely, the dialects of the kamigata region (Kyoto and Osaka) enjoy considerable prestige and are a source of pride to those who speak them. They are frequently heard on national television and radio, particularly in the traditional performing arts of manzai (comic dialogue) and kamigata rakugo (storytelling).

Leaving aside for the moment the dialects of Okinawa and the Amami Islands of Kagoshima prefecture, which I prefer to regard as dialects of Ryukyuan, a closely-related, sister-language of Japanese, the dialects of Japan can be divided into three broad groups on the basis of their phonological, grammatical and lexical features. These are the eastern dialects, the western dialects and the dialects of Kyūshū. The dialects of Hokkaidō are included in the eastern dialect group. As the island was largely settled in the Meiji period by immigrants from the Kantō region, the language is for the most part close to the language of Tokyo. Settlements on the coast, however, tend to share many features with the Tōhoku dialects, due to a long history of contact from the sea by fisherman from northern Honshū.

Within each of the Japanese dialect groups there are several subgroups, as set out in Figure 3.1. The major dividing line between the dialects of east and west Japan is a fuzzy bunching of isoglosses (the dividing line between different linguistic features) running through central Japan from the Pacific coast along the western border of Aichi prefecture, extending through Gifu prefecture to emerge on the Japan Sea coast between Toyama and Niigata prefectures. The position of the border varies according to whether the focus is placed on accent, other phonological features, vocabulary or grammar. The Kyūshū dialects preserve some features of the verb conjugations of Old

Japanese that have been lost in other areas of Japan. Kagoshima is famous for its impenetrability, due to the fact that many final syllables in the common language are reduced to a glottal stop in Kagoshima, and everybody knows that in Nagasaki *batten* means 'but' and the suffix *-ka* is added to adjectives, so the locals say *yoka* for 'good' in place of Tokyo *ii* (good) or Osaka *ee* (good).

The subgroups contain numerous closely related dialects, often differing from one village to the next, distinguished from one another by minor differences in pronunciation, grammar or vocabulary.

Japanese speakers on the whole seem to be keenly aware of minor differences in pronunciation, particularly in the pitch accent patterns, that are the most obvious distinguishing features of the regional dialects. For this reason, radio and television dramas often provide local colour or delineate characters by introducing regional accents.

Ryukyuan

Ryukyuan is used here in preference to the more common term, Okinawan, to describe those dialects spoken in the former Ryukyu kingdom; from the Amami Islands (annexed in 1609 by Satsuma, in present-day Kagoshima prefecture), to Yonaguni, a little over one hundred kilometres from Taiwan. There is a clear dialect division running south of the Satsunan and Tokara islands, separating Ryukyuan from the Japanese dialects. Further, the lack of mutual intelligibility between any Japanese and any Ryukyuan dialect, coupled with the traditional political authority of the language of Shuri as the *lingua franca* and literary language for the entire archipelago, is a strong argument against accepting the Japanese *teisetsu* (academic consensus) that these are all simply dialects of Japanese.

While there is a great deal of variation among the dialects of Ryukyuan, to the extent that virtually every community has its own dialect, the dialects fall together into two major divisions and several dialect groups as set out in Figure 3.1. There is debate over whether the Yonaguni dialect should be included with the Yaeyama dialects or whether it constitutes a separate dialect (or language). In Figure 3.1, for simplicity, I have arranged the northern Ryukyuan dialects into two groups, the Amami dialects and the Okinawa dialects. In fact, Uemura Yukio recognises six separate dialect groups for the Amami islands and two groups for the main island of Okinawa Island and its neighbouring islands.[14]

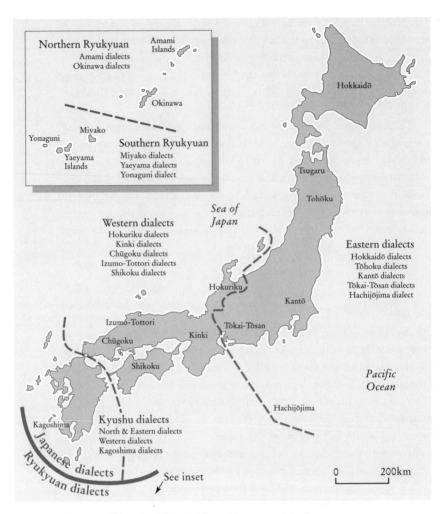

Figure 3.1 The major dialect divisions of Japanese and Ryukyuan.
Source: after Tōjō Misao and Uemura Yukio,[15] modified by the author.

It is not surprising, after nearly a hundred years of active suppression of local dialects and rigid enforcement of standard language education, that few communities in Okinawa now conduct their daily lives through the medium of their traditional dialect. Nor are local dialects being passed down from parent to child in the natural intergenerational transmission that occurs with healthy, robust languages. Consequently, many Ryukyuan dialects are in grave danger of disappearing within the next generation. Despite the loss of traditional dialects, however, Okinawans have, for the most part, managed to retain an identity distinct from that of other Japanese by drawing on their traditional music, ritual culture, food and subtropical natural environment; and over the past decade or so we have seen the emergence of a new *lingua franca* for the whole prefecture. Nicknamed *Uchinaa Yamatuguchi* (Okinawan Japanese) this new dialect incorporates features of Ryukyuan phonology, grammar and lexicon into modern Japanese, resulting in a means of communication which can be more or less understood anywhere in Japan, but clearly marks anyone speaking it as an Okinawan. In this respect, it goes some way toward filling the void caused by the loss of traditional dialects and contributes to the establishment of a new prefecture-wide Okinawan identity that has been lacking since the dialect of Shuri lost its role as the Ryukyuan *lingua franca* with the fall of the Ryukyuan kingdom in 1879.[16]

It is worth noting here that attempts to revitalise Ryukyuan, or at least *Uchinaaguchi*, could succeed even at this late hour if given adequate government support. The experience of Spain in moving from a policy of suppression of local languages and customs under the Franco regime to active government support for regional autonomy, including the use of the languages Basque, Catalan and Galician in the domains of local government and education, has shown that the process of language decline can be reversed.[17] But, despite recent signs that the Japanese government is moving towards acceptance, and even encouragement, of cultural diversity, it seems very unlikely that it will abandon its centralised education system in time to halt the demise of the Ryukyuan dialects.

The writing system

It is difficult to imagine a language with a more complicated writing system than Japanese. Chinese may employ a greater number of characters, but Japanese, with its two syllabaries, 3000 or so Chinese characters (*kanji*) in regular use, plus the Roman alphabet, must take the cake for complexity. The system is further complicated by the fact that each *kanji* generally has from two to as many as 10 or more pronunciations depending on the context. While, technically, either one of the syllabaries, the cursive *hiragana* or the more angular *katakana*, could adequately convey the sounds of the Japanese language, the Japanese penchant for incorporating elements from various sources and their reluctance to discard anything they have thus acquired has aided the retention of this unwieldy writing system.

Japanese is generally written without spaces between words, in vertical columns from right to left, or in horizontal lines running from left to right. Newspapers, magazines and most books are printed in vertical script, though there is an increasing tendency for books on technical topics to be written horizontally, as English is. This latter solution makes it easier to incorporate alpha-numeric data into the Japanese text. The lack of spaces between words does not impede comprehension, as the alternation of *kanji* and *kana* characters breaks the sentence into natural phrases or breath-groups (*bunsetsu*).

Put simply, the system works as follows. Most nouns and the stems of verbs and adjectives are written in *kanji*; grammatical particles, suffixes, adverbs and exclamations in *hiragana*; words borrowed from foreign languages other than Chinese, the names of less common animals and plants and onomatopoeia in *katakana*; and scientific names, numbers, dates etc. in Roman script.

The following sentence, taken from an article on the development of the next generation of high definition television sets (*Yomiuri Shimbun*, 14 Jan 2008, morning edn, p1), demonstrates the use of the four scripts – or five if we acknowledge the Arabic origin of Western numbers – used to write modern Japanese.

1990年代には、NHKなどがアナログ方式で日本のハイビジョン技術の国際標準化を目指した。

Transliterated into the Roman alphabet, with the original *kanji* in small capitals, *hiragana* in bold font and *katakana* in italics, the sentence would look like this.

1990NENDAI**niha**,NHK**nadoga***anarogu*HOUSIKI**de**NIHON**no***haibijon*-GIJUTU**nokoku**USAIHYOUJUNKA**wo**MEZA**sita**.

In standard Romanisation, with spaces added, the sentence becomes:

1990-nendai ni wa, NHK nado ga anarogu-hōshiki de Nihon no haibijon-gijutsu no kokusai-hyōjunka o mezashita

And in English:

In the 1990s NHK and others aimed to make Japanese analogue-type high-definition the international standard.

Table 3.1 illustrates the structure of the Japanese sentence. Here the *kanji* are used in their quasi-Chinese (*on*) readings in Sino-Japanese compounds

Table 3.1 *Structure of the Japanese sentence*

1990- nendai ni wa,	NHK nado ga	anarogu-hōshiki de	Nihon no	haibijon-gijutsu no	kokusaihyōjunka o	mezasita.
1990 year period in +TOP	NHK etc +SUB	analogue-type with	Japan of	high-definition (lit.'high vision') technology of	international standardisation +OBJ	aimed

+TOP = topic particle, +SUB = subject particle, +OBJ = object particle

(*kango*), except for the final verb, *mezashita*, meaning 'aimed at/for', written with the characters for 'eye' and 'to point', plus a suffix (written in *hiragana*) indicating the past tense, which is read in the Japanese (*kun*) pronunciation.

As complicated as the writing system is today, it is nevertheless a considerably simplified version of the script employed in the Tokugawa period, or even that in use up to the end of the Second World War. The move from historical spelling to a system based on the modern pronunciation was made in 1946, when most of the redundancy was removed from the system.

Language policy

While the new (1868) Meiji government delighted in denouncing as feudal anachronism all that the nation had inherited from the preceding 250 years of Tokugawa rule, it has become clear that the success of the government's language reforms can be attributed in large part to the relatively high levels of literacy achieved under the previous regime.[18] In addition, the use of the spoken language in the popular fiction (*gesaku*) of the Edo period helped pave the way for the introduction of the colloquial written style of modern Japanese.

In spite of an early consensus, achieved by the beginning of the 20th century among novelists, playwrights and, to a lesser extent, poets, that the colloquial style should provide the written norm, classical Japanese persisted in some genres until the end of the Second World War. The decision to write the new Constitution in the modern colloquial language sounded the death knell for classical Japanese, driving it out of its final stronghold as the vehicle of written legal discourse. Prewar attempts to simplify the Japanese script by restricting the number of characters or by replacing Sino-Japanese characters (*kanji*) altogether with one or other of the phonetic scripts fell foul of ultranationalist ideology which regarded any tampering with Japan's traditional writing system as tantamount to treason.

After Japan's defeat in the Second World War, those advocating reform of the script were able to exploit the tide of democracy and anti-militarist sentiment to finally achieve limited success in implementing their aims. In this task they had the encouragement of the Education Division of the Civil Education and Information Section of the SCAP (Supreme Command for the Allied Powers) Occupation that felt simplification of the writing system would raise levels of literacy and contribute to democracy by helping to create an informed electorate. It was well known that certain influential figures in the SCAP administration would have preferred a change to a Romanised writing system. Suzuki Takao, Professor Emeritus of Keio University and one of the doyens of the Japanese language establishment, has suggested that Japanese readiness to adopt limitations on the number of characters was driven in part by a fear that their traditional script might be replaced by *rōmaji* (Roman letters). But J Marshall Unger refutes this claim, maintaining that the modest progress achieved under the Allied Occupation was a natural consequence of plans for script reduction that had begun before the turn of the century and had continued even through the Second World War.[19]

Under the Allied Occupation, measures were introduced to limit to 1850 the number of Sino-Japanese characters (*kanji*) to be used in official documents and newspapers and to be taught in the nine years of compulsory education. These were called *Tōyō kanji* (Characters for Interim Use); the inference behind the term being that this was to be a first step towards further reduction in the number of *kanji* and possibly the eventual adoption of a phonetic script for Japanese.[20] In addition, a revised system of *kana*[21] spelling that, except for the spelling of three grammatical particles, followed the pronunciation of contemporary spoken Japanese, replaced the system of historical spelling that had reflected the pronunciation of the court language of Kyoto in the 11th century. In the post-Occupation years, continuing right up to the present, there has been a history of sporadic government intervention into language planning, with the introduction of a number of official regulations, some of which have had the effect of peeling back the reforms instigated during the Allied Occupation. Far from phasing out the use of *kanji*, the recent changes have actually increased the number of characters to be learnt in the years of compulsory education and established the principle of '*meyasu*' (a recommended guideline) in favour of the former mandatory restrictions on the number of *kanji* to be used.[22]

A number of researchers writing in English have examined the history of script reform in Japan.[23] They tend to emphasise the political machinations and government involvement in the debate between the traditionalists and the reformers. Often, they appear to lament the fact that some of the moderate reforms achieved in the immediate postwar years have been reversed and that the traditionalists have emerged as victors in the debate. Invariably, a win by the traditionalists is interpreted as a swing to the right in Japanese politics or even a dangerous re-emergence of Japanese nationalism. Even those reluctant to draw political conclusions from the language data see the defeat of the reformers as a lost opportunity. While it is true that it would be much easier for students of Japanese, both native speakers and foreign learners, to learn to read and write the language if it were written in a phonetic script, we cannot ignore the fact that many, perhaps most, Japanese actually quite like their complicated writing system and do not feel particularly hampered by it. The burden of remembering how to read and write a large number of characters has been made considerably lighter by the advent of electronic word processors and computers, which supply the correct characters in response to the user's Romanised input. The task of the writer then is simply to distinguish which of a number of homophones is appropriate in a given written context. Conversely, the number of characters available in computer generated fonts has swelled to over seven thousand.

Setting the standard

The celebrated modern novelist and playwright, Inoue Hisashi, has written a satirical drama for television entitled *Kokugo gannen* (National language – year one) dealing with the difficulties the new Meiji government faced in creating a standard language. This task was seen as a major priority in building national unity and introducing the universal system of education necessary for Japan's goal of 'catching up with the West'. The situation was exacerbated by the fact that many of the senior bureaucrats in the new government were from those areas distant from Edo (renamed Tokyo in 1868) that had been instrumental in the overthrow of the Shogun, and were themselves speakers of divergent dialects quite unlike the language of the new eastern capital. In Inoue's play we meet five-year old Nangō Jūtarō, born of a Satsuma (Kagoshima) mother and a Chōshū (Yamaguchi) father. In his childish innocence Jūtarō understands how delighted his father is when he hears the boy using Chōshū dialect and that his mother and grandfather love to hear him speaking in the language of Satsuma. But the poor child becomes confused and is at a loss to know which dialect to use in the presence of both his parents together.[24]

The Meiji government, however, felt the need for a common spoken language to facilitate the integration of a new national army and central bureaucracy based in Tokyo. With the introduction of compulsory education the need arose for textbooks written in 'correct national language' (*tadashii kokugo*), i.e. 'common colloquial language' (*kyōtsū kōgo*). The first edition of the *Journal of the Ministry of Education* (*Monbushō Zasshi*) published in January 1874, lamented the fact that communication was being hampered by the great number of dialects unintelligible to residents of the capital and called for the production of appropriate colloquial language teaching materials to be used in schools across the country. That year, a number of 'conversational readers' (*kaiwa tokuhon*) appeared, but suddenly in 1875 the attitude of government authorities changed and the production of these textbooks came to an end. The reasons behind this sudden about-face seem to have been a realisation among educationalists that there was as yet no 'correct national language' based on the common colloquial on the one hand, and a conservative backlash against the progressive policies of the Meiji enlightenment on the other. The emphasis moved back to the written word. Even the few magazines that had initially adopted a colloquial style reverted to the classical grammar with an abundance of Chinese characters (*kanji*) that characterised the writing of early Meiji.

It was only 10 years later that authorities again seriously considered the question of an appropriate common colloquial language.[25] This was largely the result of a good deal of prodding from the scholar Ueda Kazutoshi, who had studied philology under Basil Hall Chamberlain at Tokyo Imperial University and later in Germany under the dialect scholar, Wenker. In 1902, when Ueda was professor of linguistics at Tokyo Imperial University, he was seconded by the Ministry of Education to head the Kokugo Chōsa Iinkai (National Language Investigation Committee) established within the Ministry of Education and finally, in 1904, questionnaires on 29 points of pronunciation were sent out to city and prefectural offices, teachers' colleges and other educational establishments covering the seventy-odd old *kuni* divisions all over Japan. The reports were collated and published along with 29 distribution maps in 1905 under the title *On'in Chōsa Hōkokusho* (*Report of the Phonological Survey*). The validity of the findings is open to question as very few of the investigators had had any training in phonetics and many of the questionnaires were incomplete. Nevertheless, the report and particularly the maps represent a milestone in Japanese language research as the first attempt at a comprehensive survey of the Japanese dialects. (Interestingly, the dialects of Okinawa prefecture were not included in these original surveys.)

The standard language that emerged was based on the speech of the educated classes of Tokyo with a sprinkling of honorific expressions from western Japan to accommodate the relocation of the emperor and the aristocracy in the former Shogun's capital.

Ainu

Ainu (*Ainu itak*) is the language of the indigenous inhabitants of Hokkaidō. The Ainu homeland (*Ainu moshir*) previously also included southern Sakhalin, the Kurile Islands and parts of the Kamchatka Peninsula. Ainu place names in northern Honshū suggest that Ainu also lived in this area before they were driven out by, or absorbed into, the expanding Japanese population. The name Ainu, applied to both the ethnic group and their language, is simply the Ainu word for 'person' or 'human being' but excludes Japanese, who are called *sisam* and Westerners who are called *huresisam* (red[-haired] foreigners).

Ainu is generally considered to be a language isolate like Basque; that is to say, its genetic relationship with other languages cannot be demonstrated. Japanese has taken in a number of words from Ainu to describe the flora and fauna of Hokkaidō and the material culture of the Ainu. The ubiquitous salmon, now a major item in the Japanese diet, is known by its Ainu name *shake* (or *sake*). Other Ainu loanwords in Japanese include *rakko* (sea otter), *tonakai* (reindeer), *atsushi* (Ainu paper cloth), *konbu* (sea weed) and *shishamo* (smelt [fish]). Although Ainu seems not to be related to Japanese, the word order of the two languages is virtually identical. The major grammatical feature of Ainu not found in Japanese is that pronominal subjects and objects are incorporated into the verb in the manner of polysynthetic languages like Inuit.[26]

To assimilate the Ainu into the Japanese population the Meiji government banned the use of the Ainu language, outlawed hunting and traditional rituals and relocated many Ainu communities onto poorer land. As a result of this early disruption to the patterns of traditional Ainu life and the neglect of successive governments well into the final decades of the 20th century, Ainu has long ceased to be the first language of any group or individual. Yet we should not conclude that Ainu is on the verge of extinction. In fact, there are indications that the language is undergoing a modest revival. As long ago as 1987, STV Radio Hokkaidō began broadcasting Ainu lessons.[27] In addition, the 'Act for the Promotion of Ainu Culture & Dissemination of Knowledge Regarding Ainu Traditions' that came into effect in 1997 provided the necessary legislative framework for the revitalisation of the Ainu language and has led to an increase in the number of courses of instruction throughout Hokkaidō.

It is difficult to estimate the number of Ainu, let alone the number of speakers of the Ainu language. Because the definition of Ainu ethnicity is largely a matter of self-selection exhibiting a willingness to be identified with a stigmatised group, estimates vary widely, ranging from around 24 000 to as many as the 300 000 claimed by some activist groups.[28] DeChicchis identifies four categories of Ainu speakers: archive speakers, Ainu-Japanese bilinguals, token Ainu speakers and learners of Ainu as a foreign language.[29] The archive speakers, most of them long deceased, are those native speakers of Ainu who grew up using the language in its social context. They left behind the corpus of recordings and transcribed material that provides the basis for the revitalisation of the language. The Ainu-Japanese bilinguals use Japanese in their daily activities, but retain enough of the Ainu they learnt in their childhood to act as teachers and informants for others wishing to acquire a knowledge of the language. The token speakers identify themselves as Ainu, but generally know only a few words of the language in very limited contexts. The non-native learners include not only citizens with an interest in Ainu culture, but researchers and academics with a sophisticated practical command of the language. DeChicchis, writing in 1995, reports that the Ainu revitalisation effort has progressed to the stage where it is now possible to find enough teachers, judges and contestants to hold Ainu language speech contests.[30]

English

In addition to the national language, from the earliest years of the Meiji period, educated Japanese were expected to be well versed in English. In the early Taisho period, one third of the time in the middle school curriculum was devoted to the study of English. This proportion dropped off gradually into the 1920s and 1930s and the teaching of English was banned for a period during the war years. English was reintroduced into the middle school and high school syllabus in 1947 as an elective, but was taken by virtually all students, as it was inevitably a requirement of university entrance examinations. With the introduction of the five-day school week and the new syllabus in 2002, foreign language study, which usually meant English, became mandatory for all secondary school students. Since 1987, large numbers of native-speaking English teachers have been employed to teach practical communicative English in Japanese schools under the JET (Japan Exchange and Teaching) program, jointly run by the Ministry of Education and the Ministry of Foreign Affairs. Yet despite these efforts, Japan finished 180th of 189 United Nations member countries in the 1998 international Test of English as a Foreign Language (TOEFL) examinations. There has been considerable debate in Japan over the interpretation of the results, as far more Japanese students, many with low levels of proficiency in English, sit the exam than is the case in other Asian countries, where a higher proportion of elite students take the test. Nevertheless, as a result of the perception rather than the reality, the result was taken so seriously in Japan that an advisory group to Prime Minister Obuchi went so far as to suggest that English should be designated an official language in Japan.[31] Given the large number of English loanwords in the Japanese language and the continuing Japanese infatuation with North American culture, it is difficult to explain the low levels of attainment in English. Miller, writing in 1982, blamed the university entrance examination system and cramming colleges for perpetuating the abstract study of grammar and the rote learning of literary texts with little bearing on the practical use of English in the modern world.[32] Although the situation has improved considerably over the past 25 years, there is still a long way to go before ordinary Japanese function effectively on the world stage using English as an international *lingua franca*.

Conclusion

Language will continue to be a burning topic of debate in Japan. Government agencies, private think-tanks and TV panel discussions will continue to examine what constitutes 'beautiful Japanese', or suggest ways to arrest the decline in grammar and respect language. Nationalists will worry about the effect of English loanwords on the spirit of the Japanese language and those advocating respect for regional diversity will continue to argue for the need to foster local identity through the revitalisation of dialects and minority languages. Internationalists will lobby more strongly for better English language education and possibly add Chinese to the linguistic skills appropriate for Japanese in the 21st century. But the history of language in modern Japan has shown us that change comes slowly. The contest between progressive and conservative elements seems bound to continue.

Notes

1. For an excellent coverage of the linguistic aspects see Shibatani (1990).
2. The reference here is to Dixon's theory of 'punctuated equilibrium' (1997).
3. For a detailed account see Loveday (1996: 26–46).
4. This is not entirely true. The Satsuma fief (present-day Kagoshima prefecture) had access to foreign trade through the Ryukyuan kingdom, which had become its vassal state after Satsuma's invasion in 1609.
5. See Loveday (1996: 46–51).
6. Miller (1977; 1982).
7. Gottlieb (2005: 93).
8. See Miller (1975).
9. Murayama (1977: 14–21).
10. Unger (1996) claims that American misunderstanding of the nature of the Sino-Japanese writing system was one reason why change to a phonetic writing system, either *kana* or Romanisation, was rejected.
11. See http://www.kokken.go.jp/public/gairaigo/.
12. According to the Institute's survey on the reception of loanwords, not one in four Japanese understands the meaning of this word.
13. See also Gottlieb (2005: 13–15, 109).
14. The divisions of Northern Ryukyuan are; the Kikaijima dialects, the North Amami Oshima dialects, the South Amami Oshima dialects, the Tokunoshima dialects, the Okinoerabu dialects, the Yoron dialects, the North Okinawan dialects and the South Okinawan dialects. Uemura (2003: 23).
15. Uemura (2003)
16. Nagata (1996: 10–12).
17. For an excellent account of the success of the revitalisation of Catalan, see McRoberts (2001). For a report on success in the revival of Scottish Gaelic, see Carroll (2001: 231, n. 215).
18. Sadami Suzuki (2005: 303).
19. Unger (1996: 59).
20. Seeley translates the term as 'characters for current use', but endorses the interpretation given here (2000: 158).
21. The term *'kana'* is used to cover both the *hiragana* and *katakana* syllabaries.
22. In the words of Unger (1996: 121), the *'meyasu'* epithet has in effect changed what reformers had considered the 'ceiling' for the number of *kanji* to be used under the List of Characters for Interim Use (*tōyō kanji*) into the 'floor' for List of Characters for General Use (*jōyō kanji*). In other words, what had previously been seen as the maximum number of *kanji* required to read and write the language has become the minimum expected of an educated Japanese and people should now be encouraged to use *kanji* outside the *jōyō kanji* list if they so desire. The 20th meeting of the Kokugo Shingikai endorsed this principle in turning its attention to the form of characters outside the *jōyō kanji* list, giving its approval for the use of a range of non-standard abbreviations often used in computer-generated text.

23. See Twine (1991); Gottlieb (1994; 1995); Seeley (2000); Unger (1996); Carroll (1997; 2001).
24. Hisashi Inoue (2002: 11).
25. Hisashi Inoue (2002: 6–7).
26. For a linguistic description of Ainu see Tamura (2000); Shibatani (1990); and Kamei, Kōno and Chino (1997).
27. DeChicchis (1995: 115).
28. DeChicchis (1995: 109). This latter – hypothetical – figure includes those individuals who, it is claimed, would identify themselves as Ainu if only they were aware of their Ainu ancestry.
29. DeChicchis (1995: 110).
30. DeChicchis (1995: 115).
31. Gottlieb (2005: 70).
32. Miller (1982: 245).

Further reading

Gottlieb, Nanette (2005), *Language and Society in Japan*, Cambridge UK: Cambridge University Press.

Maher, John C and Kyōko Yashiro (eds) (1995), *Multilingual Japan*, Clevedon: Multilingual Matters.

Unger, J Marshall (1996), *Literacy and Script Reform in Occupation Japan: Reading Between the Lines*, New York: Oxford University Press.

4
_____

Family culture

All societies have a family system, but few are as consciously aware of their family system as the Japanese.[1]

Family *system* carries the image of components fitting into an organised whole; a sense of permanence and function. Family culture, in contrast, seems much less structured:

> a loose but identifiable set of assumptions and preferences that people use to make the critical decisions in their lives. Children absorb these preferences ... but they also may resist them, or rethink them ... they apply their assumptions and preferences to real problems ... Through the choices ... they create and re-create the institutions of society.[2]

Culture both shapes and is shaped by the choices and patterns of people. This chapter examines Japanese family culture from the Meiji period (1868–1912) to the present, as a living and developing culture, and will shed light on the decisions that have shaped and continue to shape the institution of the family in Japan.

Changes over time

The contemporary Japanese family exists in a framework of social expectations that stem from both the real and the imagined Japanese household or *ie* that provided the basis for the family system developed by the Meiji state.

Well aware that the Japanese family and the low status of women had been criticised by the West, the Meiji government enacted laws to produce a modern family that was based on values acceptable to the Japanese state. From the recent historical past, they drew from the household (*ie*) model that had previously applied to the samurai class.

The *ie* was a patriarchal/patrilineal household system geared to production and reproduction based on principles of cross-generational continuity, hierarchy by age and gender, duty and gender-based division of labour. The male head of the ie controlled the behaviour of the members. His wife (the *shufu*) had maintenance and managerial responsibilities related to the domestic resources of the *ie*, including training her successor, the bride of the heir, in the customs of the household. A single heir inherited the property, as well as the responsibility to care for aged members and improve or maintain the resources for the next generation. The heir was second only to the head in status. He earned this position not merely by birth order but by showing that he was capable of managing the *ie*. Eldest sons could be replaced as heirs by more capable younger sons. The heir had status, but not the freedom to develop other talents that might conflict with *ie* responsibility. His younger brothers might be given more education so that they could make their way outside the *ie*.

Women were subordinate to men and the in-marrying bride was the lowest member of the *ie*, under the training thumb of her mother-in-law; expected to be up first and go to bed last, to work hard and produce heirs. In the event that there were no suitable heirs, successors could be brought in by adoption, that is, a groom could be adopted for the most suitable daughter. Although as a male, his position was higher than a bride who joined the *ie*, in many ways his entire tenure was seen as a transition until his son could take charge: as in the case of the bride, he no longer belonged to his natal *ie*.

Marriage was a union of households decided by the heads of *ie*. Unsatisfactory brides were returned to their parents and a new bride sought. Children belonged to the *ie*, not to the mother.

In contrast, peasants and poorer townsfolk had a much more casual approach to marriage, and relatively free sexual relationships. Walthall's work on the mores of farm women suggests that even after marriage, there were variations in the control of sexual behaviour; importance of the conjugal relationship of the couple; and whether sexual indiscretions after marriage would automatically remove a woman from the household into which she married.[3] In addition Walthall found cases indicating that even when a woman produced a son and heir, she might be sent back for not being a good manager of the household. Thus, being a good manager was important to women's security.

Under the new Meiji Civil Code, select features of the *ie* became law and applied to all Japanese citizens. The term *kazoku* was coined to translate the term 'family'. The structure of the *kazoku* was defined administratively by family registries (*koseki*), civil documents certifying family membership. Each household head had the right and legal obligation to determine who was entered into his family registry, and to approve the marriage of his children until a son reached the age of 30 or a daughter the age of 25. Property was inherited by a single heir who was responsible to care for his parents and to maintain the household graves and honour the ancestors. Through these reforms, the legacy of the real or imagined *ie* applied to everyone in Japan.

Modern Japan required an educated citizenry and from Meiji on the state emphasised women's roles as mothers and educators of the next generation. Nolte and Hastings point out that the broader Meiji policy toward women was:

> ... based on two assumptions: that the family was an essential building block of the national structure and that the management of the household was increasingly in women's hands. The family relieved the state of responsibility for the old, young, and ill; taught acceptance of one's proper place in the social hierarchy; and performed as a more efficient economic and productive unit than the individual. The orthodox "goodwife" was one who pursued whatever employment and education would serve her family and the society.[4]

The family and the importance of women's domestic management role were now linked to the welfare of the state rather than 'just' the welfare of the household.

Although the economic role of the *ie* declined as Japan industrialised, the rural household provided both a source of young labour for industry and a place to which those labourers could return after several years to marry and start their own families. Through the Second World War and the Occupation, urban dwellers returned to their rural *ie* when they needed shelter from urban bombing, a place to live and/or food to eat. Thus the *ie* retained both cultural and economic significance. In Japan today, people know where their family came from, where the main house is located and where the family graves remain.

In developing the Japanese family system to meet the political and economic needs of the state, the Meiji government launched changes whose impact resonates today. Over time, the interaction of international influences, decisions by power brokers such as the state and/or economic institutions and choices by individual actors shaped and defined the institution of the family.

After the Second World War, the new Constitution gave women equality; universal suffrage gave women the vote, but protective labour legislation and gender-based employment limited women's economic potential. Their primary roles were housewife and mother and the family was still the basic unit of society. Even so, substantial changes occurred. The household head no longer controlled who was added or removed and individuals could establish their own *koseki*. However, to this day, the *koseki* system defines 'the Japanese family' because it requires that all family members, including married couples, have the same surname; individuals continue to move from their current *koseki* to that of the family they are entering at marriage or adoption; children are listed on the *koseki*, making their birth order and legitimacy apparent; and each household must have a head, who tends to be the male breadwinner. The concept of *seki* carries a sense of belonging that in turn carries a sense of responsibility to fulfil ones' roles both within the family and as a member of the family to the broader society. Thus, the *koseki* system both contributes to social stability and order and constrains choice.

The new Civil Code defined marriage as a union between individuals rather than families, and spouses as legal equals. Thus marriage became by law a horizontal rather than a hierarchical relationship. Property was to be divided among heirs and all children were responsible for the care of their parents. Although this was the legal principle, in practice daughters considered that they married 'out' and into their husband's family and that their male siblings (especially the eldest son) were responsible for the care of their parents. Thus when daughters married they could renounce both their right to inheritance and responsibility to care for their parents. This contributed to retaining a conservative view of family roles in spite of legal changes and is a good example of culture/people applying preferences and shaping or reshaping institutions. Legal change alone did not make all nuclear families equal. Eldest sons were still expected to be responsible for their parents, which lowered their desirability in the marriage market.

Another legal change was the Eugenics Protection Law that provided a very liberal basis to the right to obtain an abortion.[5] This was a direct contrast to the pro-natalist policy of the state during the war years and reflected a concern with overpopulation at a time when the economy was struggling to revive after the devastation of war.[6] It is both an example of the state shaping 'the Japanese family' by swinging from supporting high birthrates to encouraging limitation of births, and an increase in the opportunity for individual decisions (about abortion).

The structure of the postwar family was directly connected to economic growth. A new family form developed, composed of a salary-earning husband, his wife and their children. The salaryman family was numerically a minority, coexisting with other family types that continued to centre around an heir for the farm, fishing or small business household.[7] In addition, as discussed below, patterns of marriage and divorce varied by geographic region.

The salaryman lifestyle was modern, connected to the growing urban economy, and set the tone for the expectations of young Japanese men and women. Men wanted to be salarymen because their earnings and benefits were predictable and they had job security. Women wanted to marry salarymen because of this security and also because living near their husband's jobs meant they would not have to live under the roof of their mother-in-law. They could raise their two children in small modern apartments, and virtually did not see their hard-working husbands for six days a week. Women wanted to marry reliable providers, and salarymen wanted wives they could rely on to manage their homes and educate their children. Reflecting the fixed retirement age for men, the salaryman family developed a fairly standard pattern of marriage with two children born soon enough that they would be raised before their father retired. These expectations affected both the ideal age for marriage and women's opportunities outside the home.

The corporate world made use of the 'Japanese family model' to invent the 'corporation as family' based on the strict gendered division of labour. The company relied on the husband's ability to focus his entire attention on work and expected that his wife would manage all domestic aspects of their family. This gendered division of labour made the wife a member of the corporate family and while it provided her with the economic security that came from her husband's job stability, it constrained her from seeking full-time employment or engaging in any activity that would make her less available to manage the home. The allowances for dependent spouses that augment husbands' salaries and tax laws that provide economic disincentives if the dependent spouse exceeds a very low annual income ceiling reinforce the wife's domestic role. The wife was 'free' to take on economic activities that did not conflict with her managerial responsibilities. One such activity was piece work in the home, which gave her a source of income and provided corporations, and thus the national economy, with a source of cheap labour that became the foundation for Japan's economic growth.[8] Hamada, however, argues this model was actually anti-family.[9] The spouses operated in separate spheres and fathers had virtually no time to interact with their children because of their long hours at work.

By the 1970s, an adaptation of the salaryman family occurred. The 'new family' (as it was called in Japanese) developed both due to increased standards of living and to disillusionment with the salaryman lifestyle that had seemed ideal to the previous generation. Whereas marriage in the salaryman family was based upon finding a suitable partner with whom to build a household, marriage in the 'new family' should include 'companionship' and affection between the spouses. As a young family they tried to spend leisure time together. However, as the couple moved into their 30s their behaviour seemed to parallel that of the previous generation. The husband was gone long hours at work and the wife focused on educating their children. They were not entirely the same as the previous generation, however, for at least two reasons. Their hopes for companionship raised the level of expectation and today impacts on the divorce rate. The second reason is that the service sector developed, providing new opportunities for women to earn income.

International events and pressure continued to influence the Japanese family. As a result of Japan's signing the UN Declaration on Women, Japan's employment laws changed and although many hurdles remain, new opportunities became available to women. Women began to marry later and to indicate that marriage is not the only way for them to attain happiness. At the same time the economic bubble of the 1980s was accompanied by sharply rising housing costs. Competition to get into the best universities led to years of cram school preparation and mothers returned to the labour force, justifying their return by the cost of housing and children's education. Each of these decision patterns shaped the institution of the family. The male breadwinner was likely to be accompanied by a wife who worked until childbirth and returned to the (part-time/temporary) work force as soon as possible, depending on her childcare responsibilities. This pattern also fits well within Japanese family culture as women pursue whatever work serves their family. (Of course, individual women can use this rationalisation to obtain social approval for activities they wish to engage in for personal reasons.)

From the late 1980s, other family-related issues and trends have emerged. The mean age at first marriage continued to rise, the birthrate declined and it became difficult for men in some occupations (particularly eldest sons in the agricultural sector) to find Japanese wives, prompting them to seek spouses abroad. The Japanese government raised concerns about the declining birthrate that was leading to both a labour and a population shortage. By the 1990s the salaryman lifestyle was much less predictable. At least partially in response to international influence,[10] Japan enacted laws prohibiting domestic violence and child abuse, providing protections and at the same time allowing the state to intervene in what had previously been considered family matters. The economic bubble burst, and the security of a salaried position was shaken as major companies went bankrupt or hired new recruits without lifetime guarantees. Part-time and temporary workers now included young graduates and full-time 'permanent' work became difficult to obtain. Many young people became 'freeters', in temporary jobs that they quit when they wish and return to when they need more money. In contrast to their parents' generation or contemporaries who are tied to salaryman-like positions, freeters are not bound by commitment, but neither are their employers. It is unknown what percentage are freeters by choice, preferring freedom to security, and what percentage simply cannot find secure jobs in the post-bubble Japanese economy. Questions for the immediate future include the impact of freeters on marriage and family and the impact of the legacy of the family on this younger generation.

Debate and controversy

The underlying issue is whether the family is changing or breaking down and how that impacts Japanese society. Major debates include the effect of increased individualism on the family; how families balance work and domestic life; the causes and effects of the postponement of marriage and the significance of the rising divorce rate.

Increased individualism

As we enter the 21st century, delayed marriage and the low birthrate are viewed as indicators that increased individualism is diminishing the importance of the family. 'Selfish' women who reject traditional gender roles[11] have been blamed for the low birthrate and the state has been criticised for its inability to provide a climate in which young people may balance marriage, child rearing and paid work.[12]

A counter argument states that in the climate of new freedom and globalisation since the 1990s the family has become increasingly essential because it is the only institution that really values the existence of a particular individual, the only entity to which that individual is necessary.[13]

Balancing family and work

The good wife was expected to engage in whatever work suited her family (or the needs of the state). Today, some 20 years after the passage of the first Equal Employment Opportunity Law, the pattern of women's employment still graphs as an M-shaped curve relating to women's moving in and out of the labour force due to family obligations. The question is whether this pattern is an indication of the strength of the Japanese family or, as Ochiai[14] argues, the result of policies influenced by the economic and political spheres.

A major factor in balancing family and work is policy decisions concerning the connection between economic growth and social welfare.[15] In the early 1970s the social and environmental costs of the high rate of economic development became apparent and the Liberal Democratic Party (LDP) declared 1973 the 'first year of the welfare era' (*Fukushi Gannen*). However, by 1974 the growth of the Japanese economy slowed and policy emphasis changed to self help and relying on the family and local society rather than depending on the state. The state would only become involved if the family was unable to provide the necessary care. This policy relied on women as caretakers, and housewives working part time had that flexibility. Similarly, the 1980s focus on women's community participation was based on a breadwinning husband and a housewife who could and should participate in the local community as both a representative of her family and a contributor to society.[16] Thus political and economic institutions relied on the 'Japanese family' model.

Rising age at first marriage and declining birthrate

A notable feature of Japanese family culture is the strong belief that children should be born within marriage.[17] The percentage of births to unwed mothers is very low, only 1 per cent, in contrast to 33 per cent in the United States and 55 per cent in Sweden.[18] The *koseki* system that reveals whether or not a woman has a child outside of marriage, along with social stigma, work against an increase in such births.[19]

The birthrate for married couples according to the 2005 census was 2.15, above replacement, thus the way to increase the birthrate seems to be to encourage people to marry.[20] New permissiveness toward pre-marital sex is notable. One example is the Christmas Eve packages marketed by very respectable hotels that include overnight accommodations for couples, and another is wedding gowns designed for the approximately one in four brides who are pregnant. Perhaps we are seeing a new pattern in which a couple establishes a relationship and only makes the decision to marry if the woman becomes pregnant. In the future, increased acceptance of divorce may reduce the stigma against single-parent families, and the high percentage of pregnant brides leads one to ask whether there will be an increase in women who choose to be single mothers. The *koseki* system, women's earning power and the availability of childcare are likely to be major determinants in this decision.

Women's rising education levels and opportunities for employment were seen as producing selfish women who did not want to decrease their freedom to consume (and their standards of living) in order to marry and have children. However, the direct correlation between women's education and reason for postponing marriage is unclear. Educated women with a high commitment to career and a gender-egalitarian division of labour between spouses may find marriage increasingly unattractive and marry later if at all.[21] However, educated women with less commitment to work and to a gender-egalitarian division of labour between spouses may marry later because it is increasingly difficult to find a highly educated spouse who can support them. Women with lower levels of education also compete for highly educated men, which may reduce the number of such men who are available to be husbands for highly educated, gender-equal, career motivated women.

Men with low incomes are not attractive marriage partners. Full-time stable employment opportunities for both young men and young women are scarce, thus one of the main reasons for the rising age at marriage and decrease in birthrate is that young men cannot afford to marry.[22]

A contributing factor is that 'The current generation of parents is the first willing and economically able to support their children in perpetually dependent adulthood. Also, today's young women are the first to face downward mobility after marriage. Thus marriage offers fewer benefits, while society increasingly accepts their single lifestyle and sexual freedom.'[23] This also represents a change in family culture as parents continue to support their adult children.

Thus, there are several challenges, among them: to provide more opportunities for both men and women to have sources of steady income; to reduce young women's expectations that they will marry a husband who can support them as a full-time housewife; for young couples to consider both of their incomes as supporting the family; and for young people to develop more realistic expectations of a standard of living not funded by their parents.[24]

The stress placed on men both from economic insecurity and the gender role expectations of heads of households under the *koseki* system may also be a factor in postponing marriage. Gill[25] uses the image of *daikokubashira* (pillar) of the family to illustrate the importance of reliability and strength that is attributed to the male gender role and argues that the *koseki* system puts heavy stress on men due to the traditional and legal expectations that they will support both their parental and marital families. The stress is even greater due to the current decline in secure employment.

Today there are many hardworking young Japanese men who can find no one to marry them. They are too busy to look for wives and the system of introductions to potential marriage partners (*omiai*) is rapidly losing popularity. Modern dating and potential spouse introduction services have developed along with the recent phenomenon of *omiai* for parents seeking to meet other parents and if they get along, to introduce their children.

Divorce

The 'rising divorce rate' is seen as an indicator that the Japanese family system is falling apart. However, Japan was once a society with a very high divorce rate that was criticised by the West, which played some part in creating a new attitude toward marriage in the Meiji period.[26]

Since the Second World War, under the Civil Code, marriage and divorce have been considered matters between individuals. Japan's divorce rates fluctuated several times, began to climb since the 1990s and are now comparable to some European countries. Fuess argues that by returning to the divorce rates of its past, Japan has become a normal country in the present.[27]

In recent years, the length of time a couple lives together before divorce has increased. One result is that more children experience their parents' divorce and that child custody and support become issues. In contrast to the prewar family, in the majority of cases, the mother has custody. However, there is very little child support available.

A second effect is an increase in middle-aged divorces, perhaps as a result of the expectations of New Families. One of the images associated with divorce today is that of the middle-aged man abandoned by his wife just as he is about to retire. These men who have devoted their lives to their workplaces have neither domestic skills nor connections to the community in which they live. There are a range of programs and activities that aim to provide middle-aged men with these skills and some men's groups are trying to improve their ability to develop lives with their wives and avoid divorce. Each of these choices will impact family culture.

Finally, in recent years attitudes toward divorce have become more positive and saying that one is divorced is no longer a matter of shame.

Children of divorce and stepfamilies

Family culture is very apparent in issues relating to remarriage. At present, approximately one in four marriages includes a divorced partner.[28] Since the 1960s the trend has been for mothers to have custody of their children. Children used to have little if any contact with their father once they were removed from his *koseki*. Such contact was viewed as divisive and confusing to the child who would not know where he 'belonged'. However, very recently, recognition of the importance of the father in child rearing has increased and while there are still no joint custody rights, it is becoming increasingly common for fathers to maintain a relationship with their children after divorce.

The legal aspects of step-parenting have also changed. The prewar Civil Code viewed step-parents as legal parents with rights over their step-children who had inheritance rights. The current Civil Code views step-parent/step-child relations as relations by remarriage and in order to have parental rights and obligations the child must be adopted.[29] The current system, based on a horizontal structure in which both spouses have equal rights and obligations including parenting also raises issues about grandparents' rights.

Yet another issue related to divorce and remarriage is the current law stipulating that a baby born within 300 days of its mother's divorce will be considered the child of her former husband and thus registered on his *koseki* even if her current husband is the biological father. This law applies to premature babies as well as those delivered full term and legal procedures are required for either the former husband to testify the child is not his, or the current husband to recognise the baby. In at least one case a local government office issued such a baby a resident's certificate so the baby could get medical care and other administrative services, but it did not register the birth.[30]

Diversity

Class

There are major variations in family by socioeconomic class. From the Meiji period onwards, government policy aimed at making it possible for women of the middle class and above to concentrate on mothering and domesticity and for their lower class sisters to work outside the home. Farm families and family businesses must deal with the issue of succession if they are to survive. Women in these families and in blue collar families have had no economic option other than to struggle to balance 'work' and family.[31] In general, opportunities have increased for those married women who '*have*' to work and acceptance has been extended to those married women who '*want*' to work, but the ideal that can be lived out by those with the economic means to do so is still a family with a male breadwinner whose income permits his wife to '*choose*' whether to work after marriage or not.

Region

There are also regional differences. Eastern Japan was more hierarchical than western; Osaka business oriented; Kyoto elegant; Hokkaidō was Kyoto's direct opposite, known for a pioneer spirit and less concern with 'tradition'; and Okinawa for a combination of Chinese and Japanese influences. These differences were reflected in the family. Through the end of the 19th century the divorce rate in eastern Japan was higher than western Japan. However, in some respects this is an artefact of the acceptability of trial marriage in western Japan.

Today, higher rates of divorce are found in areas with higher rates of unemployment. Divorce rates are highest in Okinawa, followed by Hokkaidō and Osaka. Divorce rates are lowest in Niigata and the entire Sea of Japan area.[32]

The movement of young people from less prosperous rural to more prosperous urban areas is reflected in the greater decline in birthrate in the former regions than the latter.[33] Yet, (with the exception of Okinawa) the areas with the highest decline in birthrate have the highest percentage of marriages in which the bride is already pregnant.[34] These same areas have higher rates of abortion and are also losing their obstetricians, thus making it more difficult for those women who wish to have children.[35] Efforts to increase the birthrate also reflect regional differences and local level policies. One example is providing parents with discount cards that may be used at participating local merchants. The criteria for receiving such a card vary according to locality.[36]

Cross-cultural comparisons

Many societies face the issues of falling birthrates and the balance between work and family. Policies and decisions (individual or collective) reflect the cultural values of each society.

International data suggests that family policies have an impact on fertility rates. European countries that offer both generous maternity benefits and childcare services do much better at maintaining fertility rates than countries that do not offer both policies. Some countries supported dual earner career families and others eliminated most of the financial differences between part- and full-time work.[37] The former option enabled both parents to continue working and the latter secured employment and benefits for the parent who reduced working hours when children were young.

Work-life balance is the current focus in Japan, with the goal of dealing with several challenges: encouraging people to marry and have children; providing adequate financial support so that families can afford children; and allowing women to participate more fully in the labour force to offset the decline in male workers as the society ages. Japan has recently introduced a number of childcare and work-related policies that apply across socioeconomic classes.[38] In recent years, these policies have moved from advisory legislation for employers to providing various entitlements such as five days annual leave to care for a sick child. This move toward mandating compensated leave reflects a pattern observable elsewhere. For example, Norway and Sweden have policies that separate paternity leave from maternity leave and that mandate or strongly encourage paternity leave be taken. Japan has just started down this road. Recent government policies have attempted to deal with this by providing childcare leave for fathers and making it mandatory in some cases. The government is encouraging small and medium sized companies to provide employees the opportunity to take long childcare leaves, including providing cash incentives. Companies are developing a range of policies trying to determine the proper amount of paternity leave and dealing with the cost of such leave (both financial and in terms of human resources). Childcare leave still carries the image of a 'gift' to the men and a 'right' to women. Setting time limits may make it easier for men to take this leave, however if men and women are to be equal partners in child rearing is it just to provide men with shorter, paid leave and offer women longer unpaid leave?[39]

Family culture also impacts on childcare decisions. At one extreme are highly individualistic societies such as the United States in which childcare may be regulated by the government but is provided by the private sector. At the other end are societies such as Norway in which a great deal of childcare is government run and the majority of preschool children are in childcare. France provides a third model in which childcare in the home and a short working week are the norm. Japan has yet to adequately deal with this challenge. Increased childcare facilities and childcare leave have not increased the percentage of mothers who remain in the work force and in contrast to countries such as Norway, France and the United States neither policy nor the culture of work in Japan has provided a way for those who leave the labour force to return to full-time employment with career advancement possibilities.

There is at least one other area of cross-cultural interest related to family policy and fertility in Japan: the question of surrogate mothers. At the time of this writing, Japanese law does not accept a child born from a surrogate mother as the child of the biological parents. On 24 March 2007, the Japanese Supreme Court overturned a lower court decision and ruled that according to the current Civil Code maternity is based on giving birth. Thus, children born to a surrogate mother are not legally the children of their biological parents. Surrogacy is illegal in Japan, but it has occurred. The Japan Society of Obstetrics and Gynecology prohibits surrogacy on the grounds of the children's welfare, physical and psychological risks to surrogate mothers, and complicated family relations, and has not been accepted as ethical by all of society.[40]

Elder care is also an important part of family culture. In the United States, with a nuclear family culture, the ideal is to remain independent of one's children as long as possible. In countries such as Norway and France, this independence is supported by entitlements. Japanese family culture, like that of other societies influenced by Confucian values, assumed that the elderly would be cared for within the family, and thus it would be shameful to seek care outside the family. However, Ochiai argues that in contrast to Japan, other Asian countries permit purchases of help from non-family members and that because Japan does not allow visas for foreign home helpers and caregivers, Japanese women are tied down with complete responsibility for childcare.[41] It will be useful to see the effect of the recent approval of nurses and caregivers from the Philippines.

Japan has also begun to move from family-based welfare toward entitlement by establishing mandatory long-term care insurance. This will increase facilities and services for the elderly and remove the element of shame from those who use them. According to the 2007 *White Paper on the National Lifestyle*[42] 60 per cent of respondents said that care for the aged was an issue for the state or for local government rather than for the family or the individual. Yet at present the responsibility for caregiving still falls primarily on women, particularly those married to an eldest son.

Conclusion

Although the concept of 'the Japanese family' has been employed by both power brokers and individual Japanese to explain patterns of behaviour and values, it is clear that rather than a single pattern, there have been variations by class, geographical region and historical period. Economic and political circumstances have also played a role and the family structure has become much less hierarchical.

Conversely, the concept of 'Japanese family culture' has been and continues to be strong. The patterns of decision making (articulated by Steinhoff) for the most part illustrated shared meaning and ideology as people accepted the system and the definitions that came with the continuation of the *koseki* system rather than articulate policies that would be effective in changing the system. A major factor in this acceptance was the financial security that came through succeeding in the system and the lack of options if one did not. Today, patterns of decision making take place in a less secure environment and include changing patterns of intergenerational relations, marriage, procreation, divorce and re-marriage as well as emerging issues such as 21st century step-parenting and surrogate mothers. As the Japanese family is shaped and re-shaped by both domestic needs and international input, the question remains as to what changes will take place in the gender-based division of labour, particularly in the nurturing and early childhood education roles that have long been assigned to women? How will changes at the individual level re-shape legal definitions of spousal roles and parenthood? In what way will Japanese family culture of this century build on values from the past to develop the family of the future?

Notes

1. Dore (1958: 91).
2. Steinhoff (1994: 31).
3. Walthall (1991: 42–70).
4. Nolte and Hastings (1991: 171).
5. For a detailed discussion of Japan's abortion policy see Norgen (2001).
6. See, for example, Gordon (2005).
7. See, for example, Bernstein (1972); Marra (1996); and Hamabata (1990).
8. See Brinton (1993).
9. Hamada (1997).
10. Gelb (2003: chapter 3).
11. Hamada (1997).
12. See for example, Ministry of Welfare (1998).

13. Yamada (2007: 41–51).
14. Ochiai (2006: 42).
15. The following discussion is drawn from Lambert (2007); Ochiai (2006: 42); Trifiletti (2006: 179).
16. These points are drawn from Meguro (2005: 20–23).
17. Meguro (2005: 2).
18. Chikako Usui (2005: 62).
19. Rindfuss, Bumpass, Choe and Tsuya (2004: 856–7).
20. See for example, Merry White (2002: 39).
21. Raymo and Iwasawa (2005: 818).
22. This argument is the focus of Yamada's book (2007). See also Rebick (2006: 81).
23. Chikako Usui (2005: 62).
24. Discussion drawn from Yamada (2006: 24).
25. Gill (2003).
26. Harald Fuess (2004: 141–2).
27. Harald Fuess (2004: 145).
28. Discussion based on Nozawa (2006: 26–31).
29. See Hayano (2006: 40–53) for a detailed discussion.
30. 'Help eyed for remarried moms', *The Daily Yomiuri Online* (2 March 2007). See also 'Baby in 1898 law limbo gets special residence', *The Japan Times* (1 March 2007).
31. See, for example, Roberts (1994).
32. Ministry of Public Management, Home Affairs, Posts and Telecommunications (2004).
33. See Yamada (2007: 26).
34. Yamada (2007: 191).
35. See for example Takeda and Kinoshita (2007: 26–7).
36. '*Ko sodate setai kaimono yūtai* (Welcome shoppers from families raising children)', *Nihon Keizai Shimbun* (13 January 2007).
37. Chikako Usui (2005: 64).
38. See Lambert (2007) for a detailed discussion.
39. '*Yūkyūka ga senaka osu: Dansei no ikukyū shutoku sorori mada tanki, shokuba ni enryo mo* (Pushed by paid leave men are slowly taking childcare leave but still for a short period and with hesitation toward their place of employment)', *Nihon Keizai Shimbun* (6 November 2006: 22).
40. 'Court sides with boys born via surrogate: Shinagawa Ward slapped with order to accept their birth registration', *The Japan Times* (1 October, 2006).
41. Ochiai (2006: 45–52).
42. Cabinet Office (2007: 49).

Further reading

Molony, Barbara and Kathleen Uno (eds) (2005), *Gendering Modern Japanese History*, Cambridge MA: Harvard University Asia Center.
Rebick, Marcus and Ayumi Takenaka (eds) (2006), *The Changing Japanese Family*, London: Routledge.
Rosenbluth, Frances McCall (ed.) (2007), *The Political Economy of Japan's Low Fertility*, Stanford: Stanford University Press.

5

School culture

The term 'school culture' can conjure memories of one's own school-ing, imbued with fond nostalgia for some and quite the opposite for others. One is likely to recall a different culture at preschool, primary school, sec-ondary school and tertiary institutions. A person who happened to move to another school mid-way through an academic year, may recall initial feelings of excitement or anxiety about facing a new school culture. Furthermore, people often comment that today's school culture differs from that of the past. This diversity of school culture is usually taken for granted. How-ever, in the English language literature, views of Japanese school culture emphasise distinctively 'Japanese' features, often oblivious of the varieties in school culture that are assumed in English-speaking society.

School culture, simply stated, is how people attach meaning to various aspects of the schooling routine. It is a system of meaning which guides daily activities and interpretations, such as what teachers and students value as desirable. As such, school culture is conceived of as inherently existing in plural forms; and accordingly, this chapter adopts the term 'culture' to represent plural ideas. School culture displays unique institutional features, supported to differing degrees by governments and assigned specific tasks, missions and expectations (as distinct from other institutions like companies and hospitals). For example, modern schools take children of specific age groups and teach what is deemed to be necessary knowledge and skills in a systematic way. School culture is specific to the society's own history and institutional and social contexts. A distinction needs to be made between school culture as a normative benchmark and as something experienced and practised. We see the former in professional books and journals for princi-pals advising how to cultivate certain elements of school culture.[1] Insiders may also eagerly present normative views in response to the questions of an interested outsider. Even some academic literature assumes 'school culture' as a normative benchmark, for example, when examining non-mainstream institutions such as a non-regular institution for school dropouts.[2] My interest is in school culture that is experienced by participants and understood by observers in the anthropological and sociological literature.

The aim of this chapter is to illustrate the diverse school cultures of Japan, examining how they are formed, experienced and modified and with what consequences. I begin by discussing the continuing debates on Japanese school culture, and examine what have been deemed to be unique features of Japanese school culture vis-à-vis the Anglo-West, (Australia, Canada, the United Kingdom and the United States). Using the Anglo-West as a point of comparison is necessary due to its wide coverage in the literature and to my limited linguistic skills.[3] I then illuminate the diversity in school culture, reflecting local communities, social classes and minority compositions. Lastly, my focus turns to changes over time. This chapter draws on primary and secondary sources, in both English and Japanese languages. The primary sources include my fieldwork observations of schools, from a year of ethnographic fieldwork at high schools in 1989–90, and short-term observations at primary and secondary schools in 2006.

I suggest that school culture consists of students' culture, teachers' culture, and institutional culture, and that school culture is created and constantly modified through the process of interaction amongst: participants (students, teachers and parents); institutions both internal and external to schools (e.g. via national and local policies and requirements); and the community and other external factors. There are features of Japanese school culture – effort over ability, *ganbarism*, collaboration, the equality ethos, and 'whole person' development – that are distinctive, or more widely prevalent in Japan than in the Anglo-West, although the extent of these features varies. There are variations across regions, education levels, school types and individual schools in how these and other features manifest themselves in school culture and in how participants experience school culture. Variations result from interactions amongst participants, institutions and external conditions, and reflect the family backgrounds of students (social class and minority), composition of teachers, school missions and the nature of local communities. Diachronic changes in school culture often occur for individual schools facing changing local circumstances, while nationwide trends are also identifiable. In the last two decades, school culture has become more accommodating of diversities in students and their aspirations for the future.

Debates and controversies

Japan's present education system was established immediately after the end of the Second World War as a part of the postwar democratisation project under the Occupation force. It resembles the American system, consisting of six years of primary schooling and three years of lower secondary schooling (middle school) to complete nine years of compulsory education. Entry to a further three years of upper secondary schooling (i.e. senior high school) and then to tertiary education is determined by examination results. Almost all students proceed to senior high schools, and the great majority complete twelve years of schooling. The end product of the Japanese education system is a highly literate and numerate population.

There are two dominant understandings of distinctive Japanese school culture. One is the narrative of school culture which emphasises top-down control and passive learning under authoritarian teachers in an overtly competitive environment. According to this narrative, 'problems' that have emerged in the last two decades, such as students refusing to attend school, are attributable to the oppressive culture imposed by teachers and the central government.[4] The other narrative highlights positive aspects of Japanese school culture, such as nurturing, and lively and protective environments that encourage collaborative learning and teaching. Such a school culture is said to value 'whole person' development (cognitive, social and emotional) through lifestyle guidance.[5] These features are considered to be conducive to effective learning. While both narratives consider schools assuming the belief that students' effort is more important in determining achievement than innate ability, they interpret its consequences differently. The former view sees this belief as promoting excessive competition to the detriment of individual development, while the latter claims that it helps students maintain their motivation to achieve and prevents teachers and education authorities from 'labelling' students as academically weak and lowering expectations. While the scholarly literature is divided between the two narratives, the former, 'negative' narrative dominates in the media.[6]

I suspect that these differences are due to a combination of what researchers bring to their interpretations, such as outsider/insider status, Japan literacy and research interests, and their varying research methods. Foreign researchers may be privileged in being able to access information from participants who may be more willing to talk to foreigners than local academics. Conversely, these researchers may not obtain honest views since subjects may convey simplistic messages to outsiders who are seen to lack the insider knowledge required to appreciate complexities.[7] For example, participants may provide *tatemae* (normatively accepted, politically correct) answers that they think foreign researchers are pursuing. Outsider researchers may have a favourable perception of Japan even before they start their research, or may be looking for solutions to perceived problems in their own societies.[8] Alternatively, outsiders may be interested in what they judge to be malfunctioning aspects of society, and examine those who suffer as a result. In terms of research methods, I would suggest that studies based on long-term ethnographic fieldwork in schools, which allow researchers to observe more diverse, inconsistent and contradictory incidents and messages, are more effective in capturing the complexity of school culture[9] than those based on short-term observation and interviews with selected individuals. This is because schools are oppressive to students in some ways, and simultaneously nurturing in other ways. How children see, experience, and benefit from school culture is not uniform, but is instead determined by a combination of internal and external factors that are constantly changing.

I support a further, third narrative, in which Japanese school culture consists of elements that are both conducive and counter-productive to students' learning. For example, an element of school culture, like the effort-over-ability belief, can have differing impacts on school culture as a whole, contingent on other factors in a particular context. We can find such narratives in some of the English language studies that examine diversities across schools,[10] and more in the Japanese language literature.[11] This chapter develops this third narrative further, by examining diachronic and synchronic variations in school culture.

The third narrative emphasises the contingent nature of school culture. As mentioned above, school culture is conceived of as a product of interaction amongst institutional arrangements, participants, and other external factors. Institutions include the internal mechanisms of a school (e.g. the ways teachers are grouped, school events) and requirements imposed by national and local governments (e.g. the national curriculum, the teacher promotion and remuneration system, local education policies and directives, and teacher transfers). Participants include: students, who bring certain features specific to their families such as class and minority backgrounds; parents, with increasingly diverse expectations of schools and their children; and teachers with varying life histories, educational philosophies and commitment to the union cause. Because of interaction, school culture remains dynamic and displays great variations across regions and schools.

Changes both external and internal to schools affect the dynamism of school culture, which keeps school cultures constantly constructed and modified over years.

Japanese school cultures?

Japanese school culture shares basic global features with modern schools elsewhere. A modern school as an institution is expected to provide educational opportunities to everyone and to uphold principles of meritocracy and egalitarianism. They are globally considered to operate within dominant, so-called legitimate, middle-class, literate, 'rational' culture. Schools convey not only overt systematic knowledge and skills through classes, but also covert messages through school routines – these are termed the 'hidden curriculum'[12] and may include deferred gratification, self-discipline, and the promotion of an aspirational culture. Some argue that it provides everyone with a ladder to worldly success, while others contend that it only advantages the privileged and legitimates social inequality.[13] Institutions involved in the making of school culture include local governments, education boards and national government, all of which set out requirements and policies.

A further global feature is that students are ultimately the most important participants in the making of school culture. They bring their past experiences and ideas from home to school, and create student culture through interacting with their peers and teachers and negotiating the expectations imposed by institutions. Student culture varies across institutions and is influenced by catchment areas, school missions and the particular culture of the teachers. Within a school we can observe several distinctive subcultural groups such as the studious group, the sporty group and the somewhat rebellious group. Some of these groups emerge as more powerful than others in setting the dominant student culture of each school.[14] The interactions and negotiated hierarchies amongst these student subcultural groups are consistent with what we see in Anglo-Western schools.[15]

One of the most distinct basic assumptions underlying Japanese school culture is the belief that one's effort is more important than innate ability in determining school achievement, and that effort should be rewarded accordingly. It espouses that the process of learning is more valuable than the outcomes of learning, in terms of both cognitive and social development. This is often referred to as *ganbarism*, a word derived from a verb, *ganbaru*, which literally means 'to persist'. Anthropological studies of Japanese classrooms suggest several other features of Japanese school culture, after recording initial impressions of lively, carefree and often noisy classes.

Culture of learning

Collaborative learning process

A strong feature of Japanese school culture is the emphasis and value placed on collective and collaborative learning processes at earlier stages of Japanese schooling. Class size is relatively larger than in the Anglo-West, at thirty-five to forty students. In order to nurture collaborative processes of learning, a teacher often delegates his or her monitoring responsibility to students, rather than unilaterally directing activities and instructions to students, and tries to encourage interactions amongst groups of students. In order for mutual monitoring to take place effectively, the schools spend a considerable amount of time teaching children, and having them practise, a wide range of basic organisational and communal skills. These skills include: wearing appropriate shoes (outdoor, indoor, and gym), bringing what is required (textbooks, notebooks, physical education (PE) uniforms, stationery), following a weekly timetable, placing one's belongings in the designated place, maintaining school–home communication books, interacting peacefully with classmates, serving and eating school lunch properly, cleaning the classroom and performing various class monitor roles.

Another method employed to enhance collective learning is to create and work in small groups of four to six students, called 'han'.[16] These groups are established for a few months or a term, and form the basis for a wide range of learning activities such as dodge ball, cleaning duties, mathematics study and group discussions. Rather than being based on ability, group composition is deliberately heterogeneous – each group would have a slow learner, a fast learner, a sporty child, a compassionate child and perhaps an unfriendly student. Each student is expected to contribute what he or she can to the group. *Han* are most often used at the earlier stages of middle schooling.

'Whole person education'

An emphasis on 'whole person education'[17] is evident in the greater importance attached to non-academic activities such as PE, arts and music in comparison to most Anglo-Western schools, and in how various extra-curricular activities form an integral part of schooling processes. Furthermore, a central aspect of schooling is the process described as 'shidō',[18] which guides children to learn a series of traits and skills that are required to be a member of the adult world – such as being responsible, being considerate of others, setting one's own goals and making long-term plans. *Shidō* includes monitoring students' activities outside the school grounds such as smoking and part-time work. This could be interpreted as being excessively interventionist in what should be private family matters, but schools consider that such intervention is necessary in order for the school to ensure life chances for all children, regardless of their family backgrounds.

Culture of teaching

Teachers create the culture of teachers, an occupational culture, which assumes a set of shared values and norms and a sense of mission that guides the members' interpretation of the world and their activities. Some aspects of this culture are globally shared. One of the most frequently cited global features is the prevalence of collaboration amongst teachers[19] relative to other occupations, which in recent times has been encouraged more vigorously in the Anglo-West. [20]

Discussions of school culture in Japan attach relatively more importance to the culture of teachers in comparison to institutional and student culture. In one notable case, almost half of a book entitled *School Culture* is devoted to the culture of teachers,[21] and studies on the culture of teachers are more numerous than those on other aspects of school culture.[22] Shimizu's comparative study of comprehensive school cultures in the UK and Japan also focuses on what teachers collectively value as central to pedagogy.[23]

Collaborative work and development

Comparative studies have suggested that Japanese teachers are more collaborative in their work and professional development than their Anglo-Western counterparts.[24] It is most vividly observed in professional development patterns. Teachers constantly share experiences with each other. They work at desks in a large staff room next to colleagues in charge of the same year (rather than in their own classrooms). Teachers daily discuss marking, mistakes, teaching methods and curriculum content, as issues arise, and regularly invite colleagues to observe their own lessons in order to receive feedback. Japanese teachers see such daily interactions with immediate colleagues as the most valuable element in their own individual professional development compared with other forms of in-service training programs.[25]

American teachers, in contrast, consider that their professional development is helped more by those in formal positions of responsibility such as principals and head teachers, and in-service training programs provided by local authorities.[26] This process of professional development may have contributed to the strength of shared ideas amongst teachers about teaching and learning processes. Depending less on official guidance from the central and local education authorities, teachers in Japan are likely to be less familiar with government guidelines about specific issues and to therefore develop guidelines amongst themselves.[27]

Extensive responsibilities

Japanese teachers assume a greater extent of roles and responsibilities than their Western counterparts,[28] including fostering children's emotional, social and physical development. Further, teachers often refer to 'kizuna' (an intimate interpersonal relationship that fosters empathy and shared feelings of trust and inclusiveness between teachers and students), which they believe is central to teaching.[29] It is said that kizuna is distinct from the Anglo-Western conception of teacher-student relationships, in that Japanese teachers do not assert their authority as given, but instead authority emerges in the context of routine interactions with students.[30] Novice teachers are instructed to mix 'with students without disguise and pretence' in order to develop kizuna, which is believed to confer authority on the teachers. Conversely, in the US teachers are typically told not to make the mistake of befriending their students. Teachers' beliefs in their wider roles and in kizuna are said to be reflected in the fact that they pitch their lessons to slow and mediocre students. Japanese teachers tend to disagree with creating ability-based groups, since they are more concerned with the potentially negative effect of such strategies on slow learners.

Further, there is a strong ethos of equality amongst teachers where all teachers, regardless of experience and age, are equal in status once employed permanently. There is a tacit understanding that no teacher directly criticises a colleague unless invited to by that colleague.[31] This may have derived, at least partially, from the system of remuneration, whereby every teacher receives an almost automatic annual increment until retirement, which encourages long-term retention and in turn strengthens the occupation-based culture. Teachers in Japan perceive that principals exert less influence on school policies and practices than their Anglo-Western counterparts, and see their role as creating cooperative consensus amongst all teachers rather than exercising strong leadership.[32] The equality ethos amongst teachers was noticed by principals recruited from outside the education sector under a new policy, as I shall discuss later.

Variations in school culture

Regional variations

Specific features of the communities in which schools are located influence school culture in many ways. Local features include the history of the community, local industries, population composition (including unemployment levels, income levels, minorities and housing conditions), local government policies, the level and nature of civil movements and the degree of teacher unionisation in the area. Communities with many *buraku*[33] and ethnic Korean minorities often have a high degree of human rights activism – in particular, those in urban centres in the Kansai region. This activism extends to local schools, education authorities and teachers' unions. For example, a primary school serving a disadvantaged community with active grassroots movements, combined with unionised teachers, would be more likely to possess a teaching and school culture more actively interventionist in children's development than an elite secondary school. Another school with a similar student population but lacking community support would tend to offer less interventionist strategies to guide students' personal development. Studies of schools with minority students suggest that they continue to possess a weak aspirational culture[34] but that their interventionist strategies have some impact on raising aspirations.[35]

There are urban-rural differences in schooling culture. Urban areas allow high schools to conduct more finely grained differentiation at the entry point than those in rural areas. This is at least partially assisted by the relatively greater availability and use of private after-school cram schools, resulting in greater differentiation amongst students' academic achievement. Finer grained differentiation of urban high schools has led to higher internal homogeneity than in rural high schools. In rural areas there are more polarised forms of student culture within a school, such as the 'nerdy' students versus the outwardly delinquent students (called the 'Yankees'), without much differentiation in between.[36]

The two largest metropolitan centres display region-specific school culture, widely referred to amongst professionals as the 'Tokyo model' and the 'Osaka model', following the introduction of neo-liberal education reforms by the Tokyo metropolitan government since the late 1990s. The media refers to them as 'the Tokyo experiment'. The Tokyo metropolitan government, under a conservative governor, spearheaded initiatives to relax school zoning for primary and middle schools in 2002, and to abolish zones for senior high schools in 2003. The move, it was claimed, aimed to make government schools more competitive with private schools, and four schools were designated 'elite academic high schools with a focus on preparation for university'. The impact was an increase in the number of applicants (the first in eight years) and in the number of cross-zone applications. Schools became increasingly polarised.[37]

In contrast, the Osaka model opposes a greater degree of individual parental choice of schooling on the grounds that it neither brings advantages to the less privileged nor benefits the whole community's social cohesion. A central principal underpinning the Osaka model is that families are not equally equipped with resources to have their children attend schools outside their local communities, to access information, or to participate in the management of their children's schools, and that a more active interventionist role is required to compensate for this. Shimizu[38] describes the differences as follows: while both models advocate 'community-based schools', the Tokyo model sees such institutions as serving the communities of those who 'chose' such schools, while the Osaka model expects community-based schools to promote interaction amongst all residents of their school zones, including the least privileged, for the collective benefit of the entire community. I suspect that this emphasis derives significantly from the activism of *buraku* liberation movements and teachers' unions, which since the 1970s have forced local education boards and individual schools to focus on human rights and social justice.

The debates on the relative merits of greater parental choice have continued,[39] centring on social justice and effectiveness. On the continuum between the Tokyo model and the Osaka model, other cities and regions have offered parental choice only in relation to a few 'designated special schools' with distinctive features, which accept children from all zones (e.g. the Yokohama metropolitan area and some rural communities). Of the 15 metropolitan cities,[40] nine have refused to introduce parental choice in any form, and three cities have adopted only a 'designated special schools' system.[41] Thus Japan has not experienced neo-liberal education reforms to the same extent as we have seen in Anglo-Western nations over the last two decades.[42]

Variations at age-graded levels

Distinct differences are observed across the levels of schooling: preschool, primary school, middle school (aged 13 to 15), senior high school (aged 15 to 18), and tertiary institutions. Each level of schooling has missions that are age-specific, and accommodate students of specific age groups with age-appropriate needs and development. Primary schools are characterised by a nurturing and caring environment with an emphasis on collective learning and assessment, involving more extensive aspects of children's development within and outside school than higher educational levels.

Middle schools continue to engage in 'whole person' development, but now in the form of 'lifestyle guidance' (*shidō*) which aims to develop 'appropriate' lifestyles, life skills and attitudes such as time-management, manners, appropriate language use, self-discipline, and deferred gratification.[43] At the same time, students start receiving lessons from specialist teachers and preparing for entrance examinations to senior high schools. Compared to primary schools, instruction becomes more systematic and fact-filled and is based on textbooks rather than exploration. They also encounter, and learn to work in, an environment of age-based hierarchical relationships, typically seen in club activities and student committees.[44] The entry to senior high school at the age of fifteen marks the point of major differentiation amongst the young, and as such, senior high schools display a greater range of diversity in school culture.

Variations at different types of schools

It is useful to look at five categories of senior high schools to understand variations in school culture. The categories are elite academic, non-elite academic, vocational, evening and correspondence schools, and high school departments of schools for blind, deaf and otherwise disabled students.[45] The first three categories are examined here to illuminate variations. Non-elite academic high schools are 'mainstream' in terms of enrolment numbers. Differences in school culture across these categories of schools have been documented in anthropological studies.[46] The rankings of the first four types of schools are determined by their students' academic achievements at the end of compulsory education at age fifteen. This is measured by external examination and school reports. As is the case elsewhere, the rankings also reflect the general level of students' family resources. A diverse school culture has resulted from combinations of students' academic achievement levels, their family backgrounds, the schools' distinctive missions and their strategies to realise these missions. Peer group student culture and the culture of teaching also contribute to this diversity. The distinctive school culture in turn influences or reinforces further differences in academic achievement and aspirations.

At elite academic high schools, which constitute about 10 per cent of all academic high schools, preparation for entrance examinations to the nation's top universities is the foremost priority. Students are focused on this immediate goal and are equipped with self-discipline and other personal skills to make this possible. Such schools experience very few student behavioural problems. 'Non-elite academic high schools' see their mission as preparing their graduates to go on to the lower tier universities or junior colleges and private specialist schools (*senmon gakkō*) that teach vocational skills. As almost 65 per cent of high schools fall into this category, their school culture varies greatly, ranging from closely resembling elite academic high schools to a culture typical of vocational high schools.

Vocational high schools accommodate about 25 per cent of high school students in Japan. Offering courses in commerce, technical subjects, agriculture, home science, nursing and fishery, vocational schools aim to prepare their graduates for immediate employment after school. These schools generally rank lower and have less demanding entrance requirements relative to academic high schools. Evening high schools, originally created for workers who wanted to pursue post-compulsory education, now accommodate young people who missed out on places at day schools, and those who could not adjust to, or chose to opt out of, regular day school. Correspondence schools provide educational opportunities to a similar student profile as evening high schools, as well as those who cannot attend regular schools due to medical reasons.

School cultures at lower ranked non-elite academic schools are somewhat similar. Students do not aspire to build their post-high school lives on superior academic achievement, and are not at school to study so much as to socialise with their friends – a fact their schools are fully aware of and try to accommodate.[47] At these schools, many students are engaged in activities which violate school rules such as smoking, drinking and not conforming to school dress codes. The students are not overtly confrontational, in contrast to the British working class 'lads' in Willis' study.[48] While the 'lads' smoked at the school gate in order to be seen, boys at a Japanese technical high school smoked where they would not be readily observed, especially by teachers. To quote from my fieldwork at a technical high school:

... it was "cool" to be engaged in oppositional activities in a "tactful" (*yōryōgaii*) way without being caught. They enjoyed testing school authority to see how far they could "bend the rules", but always to the extent that they did not face confrontation with teachers. The capacity to estimate the "right" extent was important, and was the essence of "tactful" strategies.[49]

One of the few open confrontations that I witnessed was when a male student almost punched a teacher in an argument during a class – his close friends, sensing what was about to occur, quickly restrained him. The culprit not only received a one-week suspension from school, but also serious advice from his close friends that he was not 'playing the game' well. Student counter culture can be seen as young peoples' defiance against adults' control,[50] but I see it more as 'playful' activities that students create to entertain themselves and which, from their perspective, give meaning to their time at school.[51] One could see this counter culture as a process of learning useful skills for adulthood.

Finer variations within similarly labelled schools

Within similarly labelled schools, finer variations of school culture are noticeable to astute observers and experienced by students and parents. A case in point is the elite academic high schools – the top 10 per cent of all academic high schools. Within this category, there are widely acknowledged differences between long-established schools (*dentōkō*) and relatively newer schools. The term *dentōkō* refers to academic high schools established under the prewar education system, which maintain a legacy of cultivating well-balanced 'enlightened' all-rounders. In contrast, the relatively newer academic high schools, first established during the 1960s, have a narrow instrumental focus on success in entrance examinations to top universities. A case study of leadership change in the latter type of school[52] reveals that these differences were clearly understood by all the teachers. On his arrival the new principal stated his intention to transform this 'elite' school into a 'traditional elite' one (*dentōkō*), and set out to implement concrete measures to achieve this. A study of teachers' life histories[53] also documents this widely held perception. Indeed, the meaning of 'elite' school seems to have changed during the postwar period, in response to a rapid rise in the retention rate to post-compulsory schools and tertiary institutions.[54] The term 'elite' high school was used to denote a school of prewar origin for producing cultured elites, but has now come to mean any school which sends a large proportion of their graduates to the nation's top universities.

Amongst what are popularly called 'educationally difficult schools' (*kyōiku kon'nankō*) or 'bottom-line schools' (*teihenkō*) within the categories of non-elite academic high schools and vocational high schools, diverse pictures also emerge. These schools are often located in disadvantaged localities characterised by, for example, a high proportion of low-income families, high unemployment and people of minority backgrounds, or in the case of senior high schools, accommodate children with disadvantaged backgrounds. At one end of the continuum, some schools are seen as managing children with an authoritarian hand by enforcing rules about student behaviour in an oppressive manner.[55] At the other end of the continuum, some schools are seen as attempting to offer a very inclusive culture, precisely because of the family disadvantages which have caused students to suffer low self-esteem, low academic achievement and a sense of alienation from schooling. A teacher who was recently transferred to an 'educationally difficult high school' in Osaka commented:

> Shortly after being transferred to my present school (with a reputation of being the most difficult school in the region until a few years ago), a group of six students were caught smoking on the school grounds. Seeing their rough appearance and disrespectful manners, I had expected the head teacher would be angry and give them a pep talk. I was taken aback. He asked questions like "Is being at school tough for you?", and "When did you begin to feel lost in classes? At middle school, or primary school, in grade four or five? Or was it grade two or three?" When a student nodded, the teacher said, "Have you been sitting in class without understanding lessons for nine years? It must have been terrible experience for you. You have made a great effort and persisted a lot (*ganbaru*)." The students started shedding tears.[56]

Other studies of 'difficult schools' also depict school culture that is more complex and nuanced than that of autocratic authorities managing unmotivated and sometimes difficult students with oppressive measures.[57]

Changes over time

School culture changes over time, at the level of the individual school, the local area and the school system as a whole. Changes in school culture can result from individual schools taking initiatives to resolve emerging needs at the microscopic level. They can be induced by local-level institutions such as local governments and their education boards, and by local civil activism.

We can see overt changes in school culture when a prewar single-sex government academic high school renewed its 'traditions' and transformed itself into a postwar high school over the period 1941–55.[58] Amongst forces guiding this transformation were radical institutional changes imposed by the postwar education reforms, renewed expectations from students and parents for 'democratic education' and the community's growing stability and affluence.

Changes in school culture can also be triggered by mundane processes, such as the arrival of a new principal and regular changes in the composition of teaching staff (for example, the departure of union-involved teachers and the replacement of retiring teachers by younger teachers).[59] The system of recruiting principals from non-teaching backgrounds, introduced in 2001, is a case in point. By April 2006, 107 of these principals had been appointed, many from the corporate sector.[60] School reactions have been mixed. Some schools saw the benefits in having a principal with a fresh outlook, while others could not reconcile a different style of leadership. Some principals saw their assignment as being successful in bringing desirable changes to their schools, while others faced strong resistance and failed to bring about reforms, with one case resulting in suicide.[61] These consequences highlight significant differences between school and corporate culture, and emphasise that new principals possess the potential to implement significant change.

Accommodation of diversity

Two dominant changes in school culture are currently observable nation-wide. One is an increasing tolerance towards the diverse backgrounds that students bring to school. Some schools even go further in their efforts to build a more inclusive school culture. This trend began in the 1960s with Japanese families returning from lengthy postings overseas, which led to the creation of special transition classes catering for their Japanese language needs and 'cultural adaptation'.[62] More recent arrivals of new migrants with little Japanese language proficiency has also led schools to set up similar 'international classes' and forced schools to adopt a philosophy which celebrates diversity.[63] Teachers at schools with new migrants no longer adopt the long-held assumption that has underpinned Japanese schooling: that all students are 'Japanese', speak Japanese as their mother tongue, and have been socialised in mainstream Japanese lifestyles. The number of students in government schools who require Japanese as Second Language was 22 500 in 2006, an increase over the last two decades.[64]

Within this general trend towards tolerance and inclusion there are regional variations due to differences in the size and composition of migrant populations, and the activities of local governments, schools and activists. The constitutions of migrant populations vary: metropolitan centres where the long established minorities and newcomers co-exist such as Kawasaki, Tokyo, Osaka and its neighbouring cities; regional manufacturing cities with a large number of South Americans of Japanese descent; and other locations where newcomers reside in small numbers. How localities have responded to increasingly diverse students differs from place to place. Over 50 local governments have developed multicultural education policies[65] and provide concrete measures to accommodate, and benefit from, what these students bring to school, with varying degrees of success.[66] Localities with *buraku* and ethnic Korean minority activism[67] have built such measures on existing human rights-focused institutional infrastructures.[68] School culture is thus forced to adapt according to particular local conditions, such as population diversity.[69] Education is an area where globalisation impacts very much at a grass roots, bottom-up level.[70]

Waning aspirational culture

The other trend to note is that schools no longer offer the kind of strong aspirational culture that they did before the late 1980s. Even in its heyday, some no doubt questioned this aspirational culture on the grounds that not everyone benefited equally from schooling. The majority, however, felt that their improved life chances and lifestyles derived at least partially from their achievements in school.

Since the 1990s expectations of schools gradually became more diverse. Schools were pressed to provide opportunities for students to achieve 'self-realisation' and to be a place where young people feel comfortable.[71] Students increasingly seek more diverse post-school destinations in order to achieve self-fulfilment, and take diverse paths to reach them. Kariya[72] argues that this represents an 'incentive divide', that is, class-specific differences in the level of children's aspirations to gain worldly success. Takeuchi[73] suggests that increasingly diverse aspirations (in terms of destinations in the adult society and how one gets there) have resulted at least partially from the affluence and maturity of Japanese society as a whole.

In a study of senior high schools covering 1979–97, Hida and his colleagues[74] revealed that, regardless of the school's ranking, students became less committed to academic study and their school lives and less motivated by competitive examinations over time. At the same time, teachers became more tolerant of 'problematic' students and students expressed less overt dissatisfaction with, and less enthusiasm for, their schools.[75] These trends were confirmed by Ito,[76] who suggests that schools are now less interventionist in various aspects of students' education and more concerned with providing a 'comfortable' space for students in comparison to thirty years ago when schools tried to influence students to conform more closely to societal norms.

Recent national reforms have tried to address these new circumstances in several ways,[77] which I suspect will in turn affect the culture of schools. One such reform is the 'slimming of schooling' – a reduction in the school week from six days to five and in the coverage of the curriculum. This was expected to lessen the role that institutional schooling plays in children's overall education and provide children with more time to explore interests outside school. Another reform is an increased level of autonomy granted to individual schools and teachers to design curricula which build on and suit specific local conditions and their particular student populations. This has resulted in greater diversity across schools in terms of subjects offered and their content. The recent diversification of upper secondary schooling also addresses increasingly varied student interests and aspirations. Unit-based high school courses were introduced in 1988, allowing individual students to create their own curriculum by selecting from a wide range of subject units, rather than following a prescribed course with a few electives. Other new types of high school courses and high schools include integrated courses which combine academic and vocational courses, six-year secondary schools and specialist high schools (science/technology, English). The culture of these new high schools encourages exploration of students' own interests from a diverse range of options, rather than pursuit of a single track aspirational goal.[78]

Conclusion

This chapter has answered the following questions: What forms of school culture have been experienced and observed in Japan? How have they been formed, experienced and modified, and with what consequences?

There are features of Japanese school culture that are distinctive, or more widely prevalent in Japan than in the Anglo-West. School culture is diverse in terms of the extent and the ways these (and other) features are manifested, and in how they affect students. There are also patterns of variation identified across: (1) regions, in terms of the nature of the community, including socioeconomic context and local history, the urban-rural divide and Tokyo versus Osaka; (2) education levels such as primary, middle and senior high schools; (3) school types such as elite academic, non-elite academic and vocational high schools; and (4) between individual schools. School culture has undergone changes over time, and continues to be modified and renewed in response to changing circumstances at the levels of individual schools, localities and society as a whole. School culture has become more diverse due to increasing diversity in the student population, their aspirations and parental expectations. Recent institutional initiatives to make schools more accommodating of such diversities are, in turn, likely to influence school culture.

In order to understand both synchronic and diachronic variations, it is helpful to think of school cultures as being created and constantly modified through the process of interaction between participants, institutions – both internal and external to schools – and the community and other external factors. Seen in this framework, I suspect that in the coming decades school culture will continue to evolve into even more diverse forms, perhaps still maintaining 'Japanese' features to differing degrees. I remain unsure as to whether this evolution towards diversity will enhance the potential for all students, regardless of background, to benefit from schooling.

Notes

1. See, for example, Terada (2006); Aramaki (1990).
2. Endō (2002).
3. Since this book is published in English, I also assume that its readers are more familiar with schooling in the Anglo-West and their own societies, than elsewhere. When discussing education reforms, the distinction ('Anglo-West' rather than 'West', which would include the disparate continental European nations) is highly significant. Although I remain uneasy about making the Anglo-West a global reference point, I consider it is better than having this deliberate choice unstated and ambiguous.
4. See, for example, Cutts (1997); Horio (1988); Shoko Yoneyama (1999); Yoder (2004).
5. Duke (1986); Nancy Sato (2004); Lewis (1995); Stevenson and Stigler (1992); Tsuneyoshi (2001); Peak (1991).
6. See, for example, Sheffield (1990); Films for Humanities and Sciences (2003).
7. Hiroshi Usui (2001: 288–9).
8. See, for example, Vogel (1979); Duke (1986); Stevenson and Stigler (1992).

9. Ikeda (1985); Okano (1993); Rohlen (1983); Ii (2003); Shimizu and Tokuda (1991); LeTendre (2000).
10. See, for example, Rohlen (1983); Okano (1993).
11. See, for example, Ikeda (1985); Shimizu and Tokuda (1991).
12. Apple (1979).
13. See, for example, Apple (1979); Bourdieu (1984); Okano and Tsuchiya (1999); Urabe (1999).
14. Miyazaki (1993); Kiyoshi Takeuchi (1993); Hasegawa (1996); Price (1997).
15. See, for example, Willis (1977); Walker (1988).
16. See, for example, Tsuneyoshi (2001); Duke (1986); Nancy Sato (2004); Lewis (1995); Stevenson and Stigler (1992).
17. Nancy Sato (2004); Lewis (1995).
18. Shimizu and Tokuda (1991); LeTendre (2000).
19. See, for example, Hargreaves (1994); Lacy (1996); Imazu (2000).
20. See, for example, Lacy (1996).
21. Kihara, Mutō, Kumagai and Fujita (1993).
22. See, for example, Inagaki and Kudomi (1994); Kudomi (1988); Sawako Yū (1993); Arai (1993); Shinchika Yamazaki (1996); Imazu (2000).
23. Kōkichi Shimizu (2002: 6).
24. Stevenson and Stigler (1992); LeTendre (2000); Nancy Sato (2004); Imazu (2000).
25. Nancy Sato (2004); Manabu Sato (1992: 164–5); Imazu (2000).
26. Yasuhiro Itō (1994: 151–2).
27. LeTendre (2000).
28. Shimahara and Sakai (1995: 187); Nancy Sato (2004); Yasuhiro Itō (1994); Kōkichi Shimizu (2002); LeTendre (2000).
29. Shimahara and Sakai (1992: 156–7).
30. Shimahara and Sakai (1992: 157).
31. Shimahara and Sakai (1995: 154).
32. Yasuhiro Itō (1994: 150).
33. Descendants of a feudal outcaste population who still suffer from marginalisation.
34. Takayoshi Doi (1998).
35. Ikeda (1985); Okano (1993).
36. Naitō (2006).
37. Yoshio Murakami (2004: 30).
38. Kōkichi Shimizu (2005: 180–95).
39. See, for example, Fujita (2000).
40. Cities with populations over 1 million.
41. *Yomiuri Shimbun* (19 January 2007).
42. See Okano (in press).
43. Fukuzawa and LeTendre (2001); Shimizu and Tokuda (1991).
44. Le Tendre (1994: 47).
45. Okano and Tsuchiya (1999: 64).
46. Rohlen (1983); Okano (1993); Okano and Tsuchiya (1999: chapters 3 and 4).
47. Okano and Tsuchiya (1999: 104–7); Rohlen (1983); Okano (1993).
48. Willis (1977).
49. Okano (1993: 198).
50. Yoder (2004).
51. Okano (1993: 198).

52. Hiroki Ōno (1998).
53. Tsukada (1998).
54. Inoue and Yasuda (2002).
55. Yoder (2004); Shoko Yoneyama (1999); Cutts (1997); McVeigh (2000).
56. Ii (2003: 139–40).
57. Ikeda (1985); Shimizu and Tokuda (1991); Okano (1993).
58. Oh (1998: 200).
59. Tsukada (1998).
60. Endō (2004).
61. '*Shirīzu: Minkanjin shusshin kōchō ga yuku* (Series: Experiences of principals recruited from non-teaching sectors)', *Yomiuri Shimbun* (2–13 May 2006: 2 May).
62. Goodman (1990, 2003).
63. Tsuneyoshi (2004); Nukaga (2003).
64. Ministry of Education (2006).
65. Okano (2006a).
66. Tsuneyoshi (2004); Nukaga (2003); Kōkichi Shimizu (1998); Watabe (1998).
67. Minority activism in education has long existed in modern Japan. In the postwar period, the most notable and successful activism has been conducted by the Buraku Liberation League in pursuing a living standard comparable to the rest of society, human rights and the elimination of discrimination. It lobbied for legislation (The Special Measures for Regional Improvement Law, effective 1969–97) on one hand, and adopted the radical tactics of denouncing those deemed to have engaged in discriminatory activities on the other. So called 'Dōwa education' was introduced, initially focusing on *buraku* injustices and marginalisation, and later on human rights in general. Activism by long-established ethnic Koreans (descendants of formal Japanese colonial subjects) was influenced by the *buraku* activism both in terms of philosophy (e.g. human rights focus rather than celebration of cultural diversity) and concrete tactics; and was also built on infrastructures already existing for *buraku* education. For example, *buraku* education sections of local education board secretariats took on ethnic Korean issues, and then more recently, newcomer minority children's education. Positions of teachers initially in charge of *buraku* education at individual schools became inclusive of ethnic Koreans and then newcomers. Localities without a history of minority activism have not had the benefit of such infrastructure and experience in coping with influxes of newcomers (e.g. South American car industry workers in Aichi prefecture).
68. Okano (2006b).
69. Shimizu and Shimizu (2001); Tsuneyoshi (2004).
70. Okano (2006b).
71. Satoshi Suzuki (2002).
72. Kariya (2001).
73. Yō Takeuchi (1995).
74. Hida, Mimizuka, Iwai and Kariya (2000: 125–8).
75. Hida, Mimizuka, Iwai and Kariya (2000: 191).
76. Shigeki Itō (2002: 95).
77. See Okano (in press).
78. The details are reported in '*Shirīzu: Minkanjin shusshin kōchō ga yuku* (Series: Experiences of principals recruited from non-teaching sectors)', *Yomiuri Shimbun* (2–13 May 2006: 2 May).

Further reading

LeTendre, Gerald (2000), *Learning to be Adolescent: Growing up in US and Japanese Middle Schools*, New Haven: Yale University Press.
Okano, Kaori and Motonori Tsuchiya (1999), *Education in Contemporary Japan: Inequality and Diversity*, Cambridge UK: Cambridge University Press.
Rohlen, Thomas (1983), *Japan's High Schools*, Berkeley: University of California Press.

6

Work culture

Evolution of a tradition

The term 'culture' is a multifaceted concept, notoriously difficult to define. Without writing an extended preface defining the concept, it should be obvious that the culture surrounding the organisation of work in Japan has evolved in ways inseparable from the whole process of Japan's economic development. After the Meiji Restoration in the late 1860s, the challenge of industrialisation as a national issue focused attention on the relationship between social and economic development both as structural change and as cultural change. The nexus between culture and structure in development received concerted international attention as Japan re-emerged on the world stage, first in the 1960s in the Princeton series on the modernisation of Japan, then *circa* 1970 in the admonitions warning about Japan's threat to Western economies and ways of life, and finally in the 'learn-from-Japan' campaign from the late 1970s until the economic 'bubble' burst in the early 1990s.

This chapter pays attention to ways decisions made by Japanese regarding work are set in a larger socioeconomic context in line with the argument of Mouer and Kawanishi[1] that the long hours worked by many Japanese are more likely to reflect the way structural parameters delimit the choices in the labour market (e.g. by a work ethos or milieu) than by a value in work *per se*. It begins with an overview of the development problematic – the historic movement of labour to new industries in ways that generate economic surplus and set up a class-based dynamic. Discussion then moves to the period of rapid economic growth when the consumption and reproduction aspects of life interacted to reshape the consciousness and choices that were the ethos and milieu at the place of work between the late 1970s and the late 1980s. Before concluding with some comments on the changing notion of the household as the unit which binds the 'at-work' side with the 'at-home' side of each employee's consciousness, attention is paid to the extensive social changes occurring in the 1990s both in the labour market and the organisation of work in a narrow sense, and in the larger society in which employees found themselves as consumers and as individuals seeking new types of interpersonal relationships.

Economic development is, as noted many years ago by economists such as Nurkse[2] and Rostow[3], largely about generating a surplus that can be re-invested in physical capital, in human capital (through education, training and indoctrination), and in the upgrading and maintenance of management systems. In cultural terms it is about generating (or maintaining) an ideology and/or cultural outlook validating the sacrifices made in serving the nation, the family and the individual through the medium of corporations, other business establishments and entrepreneurial activity. The effort is justified partly by reifying or idealising such entities and by making claims about material outcomes in terms of rising standards of living through socially just mechanisms.

One world or many: the debates about convergence

The conditions for growth

Debates concerning work in Japan have revolved around the mobilisation of Japanese to generate surplus. Initially attention focused on the extent to which different cultures and different social arrangements could produce that surplus in ways that allowed it to be 'raked off the top' and channelled into growth. The process was conceived in terms of the fairly universal scientific principles behind a range of technologies that were introduced as individuals moved from rural agriculture to manufacturing in Japan's burgeoning urban concentrations. There was also a universal belief that schools would arm children for the labour force with minimal levels of literacy and numeracy and a certain discipline associated with all industrial societies. Finally, the vision rested on the efficiencies that came from having someone (i.e. a woman) at home who specialised in maintaining the physical and mental fitness of those going out each day to constitute Japan's new labour force for its factories, where startling advances in surplus-generating productivity were being realised.

A good deal has been written about the transition of Japan's labour force from life in rural agricultural villages to urban manufacturing contexts.

One view is that closely knit groups of workers brought to Japan's industrial and commercial enterprises 'feudal' outlooks, relationships and loyalties that fostered paternalistic approaches to work organisation At the same time, complex bureaucratic structures were being established in state enterprise by those more highly positioned from Japan's dismantled *samurai* class and then carried over into newly privatised offshoots early in the 20th century. This was particularly obvious in the large, interlocked *zaibatsu* firms which dominated the economy until Japan's Pacific War. To be sure, much of the work done in prewar Japan was carried out by small subcontracting firms and work gangs among which working practices and conditions varied considerably, and the state was also active in prioritising the use of 'voluntary labour' from young girls for Japan's Dickensian textile mills. Nevertheless, the large firms provided glimpses of what middle-class life buttressed by salaried income might look like.

Given that peasant rebellions to protest poor working and living conditions were not infrequent during the Tokugawa period (1615–1868),[4] it is not surprising that during the Taisho period (1912–26) labour unions formed and there was considerable voice for Japan's new urban poor. Many labour leaders found the vocabularies from various streams of socialism and anarchism overseas useful when articulating their views concerning social injustice. The Japan Communist Party was formed in 1921, and Japan's history of political repression at that time is fairly well documented. In the late 1930s a lively, drawn-out debate occurred among those concerned about the future of labour. One position suggested that Japanese capitalists would find it in their interest to look after the wellbeing of their labour force. The other position emphasised the exploitative tendencies and the need for pressure on 'the system' to improve conditions for Japan's labouring masses.[5]

Regarding the workers' daily livelihood, Nakayama[6] argued that workers also brought a rural living standard to their urban dwellings and were slow to demand wages equivalent to their higher productivity. The result was further surplus for Japan's corporate world and the wherewithal to invest for further development. The depression of household consumption was facilitated by the professionalism associated with the role of married women as household managers concerned with reproducing the labour force – a role which included bookkeeping and looking after household finances, sewing and monitoring nutrition and the next generation's education.

The ideological tension in postwar Japan's work culture

Looking at postwar Japan's growth mechanisms, Johnson[7] emphasised the role of government in developing market-conforming mechanisms such as administrative guidance and their prewar antecedents. However, a good deal of Japan's rapid development has occurred in an ad hoc manner. Following the end of the war, many of Japan's prewar social institutions were dismantled: the *zaibatsu*, the military, the nobility, the state system of education, etc. Freed from prison, militant labour leaders and left-wing intellectuals soon unionised 50 per cent of the labour force. Shortly afterwards a government-bureaucratic contract with big business became the major cornerstone of the 1955 system. Following on from the 10-year income doubling plan introduced in December 1958,[8] the economy grew annually between 1960 and 1975 by over 10 per cent in nominal terms.

As a result of that growth Japan came to be seen as a postmodern economy both with certain of the socialist features associated with many pre-industrial societies and with the vibrant markets associated with urban societies. Japan was regarded as an industrial economy that maintained a respect for traditional human relationships while pushing ahead to rationalise work practices. Many observers felt that balance facilitated the accumulation of savings to support sizeable investments in economic infrastructure and in the replacement of the capital equipment underpinning Japan's very competitive manufacturing industries. The 'Look East' policies of other Asian governments and the general interest shown by the advanced economies in Japan as a model tended to focus attention on a limited number of practices and institutions that were seen as generators of surplus at the micro-economic levels: enterprise bargaining, quality control circles, just-in-time production systems, and certain aspects of corporate culture and human resource management. This focus tended to emphasise the importance of worker involvement in decisions at the plant level. There was, however, another side to work culture during this period.

The 1955 system produced an uneasy truce – a kind of bi-polar balance of power between the forces for labour and those for management. The latter were linked to the LDP; the former to a fractionalised array of four to five parties laying claim to popular support. As the conservatives became more entrenched, the labour movement divided. One group supported both the growth policies of the government at the firm level and the efficiencies management sought to introduce with new technologies and planned redundancies. On the left, the other group attached importance to social justice and income equality over efficiencies. The former group's national centre was Dōmei; the latter's was Sōhyō.

During the 1960s many work sites were divided by competing enterprise unions – one pushing for efficiencies through cooperation with management and the other seeking more benefits for workers and a more equal distribution of income by pursuing a strategy of confrontation with management. The tug of war for union membership at many firms between a number one union on the left and a number two union on the right is amply described by Kawanishi[9]. It was a period of psychological tension, stressful for many workers but also producing a growth dynamic: the forces for productivity had to attend to the issue of equality, while those for equality had to recognise the importance of productivity-linked criteria. One outcome was an arrangement whereby an egalitarianism and a productivity-first ideology together yielded notions of an extensive middle class, efforts to develop a worker-oriented corporate culture and long hours worked by gung-ho employees under the guise of 'company loyalty'.

Toward a national culture of work and consumption: the 1960s to the 1990s

There was more to the milieu in which employees laboured than a dynamic, though delicate, balance of power. Inui,[10] for example, relates how a pattern of urban family life, education and the rhythm of work emerged out of the 1955 system during the 1960s. On the one hand, a common vocabulary emerged for describing the pulsations punctuated by the five-and-a-half-day work week, socialising after work, commuting considerable distances on crowded trains, stress from the enforced intensification of work, a relatively high expectation of promotion through internal labour markets in Japan's larger firms, a common recognition of the importance of further education for upward social mobility, and a fairly set transition from school/university to permanent full-time employment upon graduation. On the other was a culture built around the shared benefits of rapid economic growth, evident in the changing lifestyle of employees on the home front: the move from crowded living in cramped flats to individually owned houses in outer suburbs, the advance from the first three Ss (*suihanki* – rice cookers; *sōjiki* – vacuum cleaners; and *sempūki* – electric fans) circa 1960 through the three Cs (colour television, (room) cooler and car) in the 1970s to the more sophisticated three Ss (screen, sports and sex) in the 1980s. As the economy evolved to produce leisure-oriented services, individual employees came to replace the household as the main unit of consumption. Income differentials were increasing and society was re-stratifying itself, with access to education becoming an increasingly important avenue to the privileged lifestyle of the upper-middle class. The growth of popular culture and the mass media contributed to spreading an image of Japan as a highly sophisticated consumer society in which 90 per cent of the Japanese population could claim membership of a broadly-based middle class.

With the lifting of foreign exchange restrictions at the end of the 1960s, the *sarariman* began to be accompanied by his family when on overseas assignments. The number of Japanese tourists going abroad increased rapidly in the 1980s as the huge foreign exchange earnings from Japan's competitive exports in manufactured goods increased. With the 'bubble economy' at its zenith in the late 1980s, Japanese increasingly went abroad with renewed confidence as businessmen, tourists and residents.

From the mid-1960s workers increasingly came to focus on achieving a better material standard of living. By the mid-1980s shelves of bookshops through Japan carried an array of books bemoaning the move away from the earlier ascetic approach to consumption and the spread of a shallow infatuation with an individuated consumerist materialism. This shift was in part reflected in the growing number of unionists switching from the socialist-oriented number one unions on the left to the number two unions committed to individually linked measures of productivity. This occurred as management responded to the demands of productivity-oriented employees wanting to re-jig company wage systems to reduce the weight given to rather objective and ascriptive criteria such as age and years of employment with the same firm – criteria linked to basic livelihood needs – while increasing the importance of skill levels, job content and 'bottom-line' performance. In other words, the equation that set 'a fair day's work' against 'a fair day's pay' had shifted. With the dream of an upper-middle class lifestyle held high, a new materialism was beginning to drive more productive Japanese in their choices regarding work. Part of this shift was evidenced in the shifts in consumption; part in the refusal to lower oneself to work characterised by the three Ks (*Kitanai*, *Kiken*, and *Kitsui*), a formation known as the three Ds in English (for 'Dirty', 'Dangerous' and 'Demanding'). By the end of the 1980s, Japan was already coming to depend on foreign workers for the provision of lowly paid services and various types of unskilled or semi-skilled labour. The new consumerist outlook and the aversion to particular types of work were linked with Japan's rising levels of education across the board.

The lost decade and the fruits of rapid economic growth

The Heisei recessions in the 1990s could dampen these two trends, but not reverse them, as Japanese society and the economy had been integrating with the world for some time and the newly found patterns of consumption and living were becoming habits of the heart. Looking at the drop in economic growth rates, many came to talk about the 1990s as 'the lost decade'. However, many new habits were connected to far reaching social change and to altered ways of thinking about work. In terms of the evolution of Japanese society, the decade was certainly not 'lost'. Both Amanuma[11] and Hashimoto[12] have described how the younger generation, whose energy had built Japan, was starting to recede into retirement.

Steady at 35 per cent over the two decades to 1975, the unionisation rate began to fall, down to 25 per cent by 1990 and to 18.7 per cent by 2005,[13] the drop being most noticeable in the left-wing unions that had been central to the maintenance of a class-oriented view of interpersonal relations at work. It would be easy to conclude that this was consistent with the embourgeoisement hypotheses of Goldthorpe et al.[14] However, much more was in store as Japan headed for a decade of stagnant growth. Although a 'lost decade' for those who had celebrated the bubble years and believed that the new millennium would usher in the Japanese century, the 1990s was a period of immense change for those interested in the organisation of work.[15]

Globalisation and restructuring

In the 1990s moves were made to restructure the economy. Mergers and restructuring occurred across the banks, security brokerages and life insurance companies. Global restructuring in the automobile industry reverberated in Japan when the French Renault company stepped in to bolster the fortunes of Nissan in 1999, bringing to Nissan a non-Japanese chief executive. Restructuring occurred in retailing and telecommunications. Administrative reform was prioritised in government agendas, and Japan's national universities were privatised, some seeking a future by recruiting fee-paying overseas students. The Hei Consulting Group[16] commented that such events should be understood in the context of earlier mergers that had occurred among competing firms in North America and Europe responding to similar pressures.

An article on *nihonbyō* (the Japanese disease) in *Nihon Keizai Shimbun*, Japan's leading economic newspaper, in January 2003, highlighted four concerns related to the lives of working Japanese: (1) how corporate society is organised and run in Japan; (2) the attachment of Japan's innately conservative leaders to ways of fostering industrial growth *in the past*; (3) their imperviousness to the full impact of globalisation, multiculturalism and falling levels of literacy on Japanese society; and (4) the loss of the confidence needed to take risks.

During the 1990s Satō,[17] Tachibanaki[18] and Kariya[19] argued that the new inequalities in income, wealth and education were undermining the faith of many Japanese in the system. Satō,[20] Satō[21] and Miura[22] have argued that many Japanese were losing the drive to study and work hard, believing that chances for upward mobility had dried up. By the end of the 1990s the earlier sense of class conflict had given way to alienation from the system which had produced so much postwar wealth. Many began to question the wisdom of reforms based simply on notions of economic rationalism, unbridled free markets, and American-led capitalism/globalisation. As Japan nears the end of the first decade of the 21st century, many had become resigned to living with such globalisation in a 'gap society' characterised by disparities in income,[23] in education,[24] in managerial structures,[25] and even in the spread of English proficiency as the tool for participating in global affairs.[26] Some wrote about Japan's 'new poor'.[27] While authors of this ilk warned of the social consequences flowing from the gaps, others such as Suzuki[28] trumpeted the efficiencies of the ultra-gap society.

Deregulation

Restructuring also involved the deregulation of the labour market. Although education histories, gender and age continued to shape entry into Japan's labour markets, employees were increasingly casualised during the 1990s. Nikkeiren (the Japan Federation of Employers' Associations) pushed the Japanese Government to deregulate the labour market even though some employers warned that dismissing practices contributing to the maintenance of social stability and order at work would impact severely on worker morale. 'Reforms' enhanced management's ability to have employees work at its convenience, and altered the nexus between the economy and society in at least four ways. Nominal time standards were introduced as a kind of return to piecework. Provisions restricting the hours of overtime that management could require of its employees were loosened. Use of the variable working week was extended. The maximum time for a labour contract was lengthened from one year to three, allowing management to 'lock in' its casual labour force and to shift the boundary between regular and non-regular employees. Behind the last of these changes was Nikkeiren's[29] vision that regular employees in highly technical or professional jobs might be hired on such contracts in the future. Nikkeiren lobbied successfully to open the use of temporary labour from 13 to 16 occupational categories, then to 26, and finally to nearly all categories by the end of the 1990s. Further, a system of longer-term job placements through the use of temps was established in 2000. Organised labour resisted deregulation and lost on nearly every count.

Multiculturalisation

At the end of the 1990s, Morris-Suzuki[30] argued that many of Japan's narratives told of universal experiences that could be best understood within a comparative perspective. Yabuno[31] argued that the process of multiculturalisation was bolstered when peripheralised local communities responded to depopulation, rapid ageing, feminisation, and rising unemployment by establishing their own grass-roots diplomacy which allowed many Japanese to expand their horizons. A recent white paper[32] suggested that approximately 37 per cent of the adult population aged 15 to 79 are internet users, the majority logging on daily. This further enabled many Japanese citizens to expand their living space beyond the borders of their state and to imagine other life-cycle options within Japan.

Owing in part to labour shortages, the number of foreigners living in Japan began to increase markedly in the late 1980s. Komai[33] hints that Japan's newcomers are now reaching a critical mass that can fundamentally change Japanese society. Regarding Japanese identity, both Mouer and Sugimoto[34] and Fukuoka[35] observed in the mid-1990s that citizenship, blood, language and ethnicity no longer went together in defining Japaneseness. In 2002 a naturalised citizen from Finland was elected to the Diet (Japan's national parliament). Burgess[36] reported that about one out of every 20 Japanese entering matrimony today marries a non-Japanese, up from one in every 200 only 30 years earlier. He also noted that in about 80 per cent of those marriages the foreign partner is female, a reversal of the situation in the early 1970s. Rather than simply assimilating into Japanese society, he found, many foreign-born wives were actively participating in civil society and shaping the way Japanese social institutions were evolving.

This can be seen in the dissolution of barriers previously circumscribing the world of the foreigner in Japan. In the 1990s the National Sports Competition opened its senior high, junior high, university and open divisions to non-Japanese. Professional baseball lifted its three-person limit on foreign players in 1996, and foreign wrestlers have come to be a dominant force in the top sumo division. Restrictions on appointing foreigners to academic positions at national universities were relaxed. An oddity on Japanese television in the 1970s, foreigners now commonly appear.

There is room to speculate about the extent to which bi-cultural literacy is now required to reap the full benefits of living in Japanese society and to shape the directions it follows. English has been used to infuse the Japanese language with additional vocabulary – as Latin and Greek derivatives did for English elites some centuries ago – and its usage has tended to set Japan's more privileged citizens apart from many ordinary citizens. Foreign words often appear in the discourse used for public debate in Japan. A small number of Japanese firms have introduced English as a second language in running their business, and public debate was stirred in 2000 when a Prime Minister's advisory group suggested that consideration be given to having English as a second official national language.[37] While not receiving wide support at a time when English was being criticised for being the conveyor of cultural imperialism,[38] the debate underlined the importance of English for Japan's international interface. In July 2002 the Japanese Government introduced to schools a strategy to raise the English skills of Japanese children.

Civil society and voluntarism
After 1945, leftist intellectuals were outspoken in calling for the state to provide new civil minimums and to guarantee human rights associated with civil society. Although postwar conservatives dismissed such thinking as a foreign individualist ideology which had no place in a collectivistic Japan, the idea of 'civil society' existed in pre-Meiji Japan. In the early 1990s *shibiru sosaetī* came to be associated with an interest in the potential for voluntarism, an orientation acceptable to conservatives concerned about the costs of social welfare. The term 'NPO' became widely used in Japan to differentiate non-profit organisations as groups with an ongoing interest in 'serving society' from those with clear economic interests or long-term specialised political agendas.[39] Sugishita[40] argues that NPOs were stimulated by the passing of the NPO bill in March 1998 following the enactment of similar legislation in the US.

Two other developments worked to enhance involvement in NPOs. One was the increased number of aged Japanese with free time as life expectancy rose. The other was the across-the-board increase in leisure time as annual hours of work dropped from 2052 in 1990 to 1829 in 2005; and the percentage of employees with a two-day weekend increased from 39.2 to 60.4 per cent.[41]

The ageing population

The population aged over 65 increased remarkably in Japan over the past half century, reflecting a jump in life expectancy from 60 (males) and 63 (females) in 1950 to 69 and 75 in 1970, 76 and 82 in 1990, and 79 and 85 in 2005. In 2001 nearly a third of males and 13.8 per cent of females aged over 65 were still working, compared to only 4.5 per cent and 1.6 per cent in Germany or 16.9 per cent and 8.9 per cent in the US.[42]

Tamai[43] has argued that the pension system is quite inadequate for many Japanese. One set of problems rests in the very segmented pension system with its myriad of schemes that have had to be re-jigged several times since the mid-1980s. In 2001 the qualifying age for the pension was raised from 60 to 65. While those aged over 65 could previously keep their full pension without paying further premiums, after 2001 their pensions were reduced by some fraction of their earnings and they were required to continue paying into their funds.

The health insurance system is also complex and financially shaky,[44] although the benefits vary considerably from one fund to another. Outlays from the special old age fund now account for about a third of medical costs covered by all health insurance schemes. Though legislation has been passed that will allow employees family care leave similar to maternity leave, care of the aged involves a good deal of physical labour, and foreign labour is envisaged as the solution.

The *furiitaa*

Since the 1980s, Japan's graduates have become a much more diverse lot, and today fewer are seeking the secure but highly pressurised work life associated with regular employment in Japan's corporate sector. These kinds of changes reflect a new consciousness regarding work, and terms such as *furiitaa* (freelance worker),[45] *otaku* (devotees to a narrowly defined, mainstream passion), *niito* (NEET = not in employment, education or training),[46] and *parasaito shinguru* (parasite singles)[47] were created to describe sizeable numbers of young people bent on lifestyles different to that of the *sarariman*. They represent the first Japanese generation to have grown up in true affluence, one in which even Japan's poorly paid casuals can make ends meet without overly striving in the corporate world. While their refusal to accept the old work rigidities has been criticised as a new brand of selfish individualism, a different kind of social consciousness has emerged that is injecting a new dynamic into the labour force

Terms like '*furiitaa*' are seen as negative labels by many in the mainstream. For them the *furiitaa* are not buckling down to the realities of having a steady job with a steady income. They have not become respectable adults able to contribute adequately to society. As Yamada[48] and Kosugi[49] note, they often circulate through a series of under-paid positions lacking the job security, medical benefits and retirement prospects needed to support the ideal middle-class family. Many *furiitaa*, however, see it differently. Some have been victims of the restructuring which has resulted in a shortage of permanent full-time positions. Others have dreamed of a profession in a creative field where long apprenticeships without any guarantees are normal. Others see in casual work the flexibility to maintain friendships or even to build new ones with other youth having similar outlooks. Still others find in casual and volunteer work opportunities to learn critical skills and to mature emotionally before settling down to the rigors of regular employment. While Kosugi[50] recognises the great variety of motivations driving the *furiitaa* phenomenon, with some bordering on laziness and a stubborn refusal to 'grow up', she also notes that many want full-time regular employment but are more fussy than the traditional graduate who unquestioningly accepted the authoritarian framework and monotony of drawn-out in-house training rotations before being given challenging work. Deviating from the normal transition into full-time regular employment immediately following graduation, they symbolise not only an alienation from the older work culture found in many firms, but also a new independent creative force that challenges Japan's corporate sector to respond.

In the current competitive environment, firms are realising that they can no longer afford to discriminate against women or others with distinguishing features conceptualised in old prejudices. As Chan-Tiberghien[51] has argued, global standards are being adopted in Japan with regard to many gender-related practices. Equal Opportunity legislation has served to alter gender-related standards while also underlining the need for employers in the 'new globalised economy' to proactively embrace women in the labour force in order to have competitive staffing profiles. Although many foreign workers have for some time been hired to work in areas characterised by the three Ks, many Japanese companies have begun to open their doors to skilled foreigners in order to keep their workforce competitive. Conversely, once shunned by Japan's more able graduates, foreign firms have begun to attract a steady stream of young applicants wanting to be challenged in ways that would allow them to demonstrate a wide range of skills in IT, communication and the English language.

Work values and the Japanese household

When thinking about work in Japan, the word *'shūshoku'* provides a clue. The term is often rendered in English as 'getting a job', 'getting one's first job' or even 'obtaining employment upon graduation'. However, the term refers to obtaining regular or permanent full-time employment. Those who have found a 40-hour-per-week job as a casual employee have not completed *shūshoku*. One's first entry into full-time employment as a *seiki shain* (a credentialled company employee) signifies their coming of age as an adult member of society, qualifying them for a salaried income, membership in an enterprise union if one exists at the place of work, and the wherewithal to get married. It is also the first step to upward mobility in the corporate world. Marking an important rite of passage, it is a gender-neutral term, expected of women as of men (although until recently it was expected that women would voluntarily surrender their tenure as a *seiki shain* once they married and had children). Although the *seiki shain* was of central importance to an employment system that rewarded continuous employment with the firm, the system has also tended to more comprehensively reward better educated graduates and provided a gateway for them to elite status in the labour force as members of the 'aristocracy of labour'.

To understand the nexus between paid employment and being an adult member of society it is useful to consult Nakane's[52] delineation of the *ie* or household as an ongoing corporate economic entity. The continuity of the *ie* through time was symbolised by ancestor worship. As custodian of the *ie*, the household head would visit the family grave to report on the (financial) wellbeing of the unit. Patrilineal rules for succession were in place in most parts of Japan, but the rules also provided for adoption to bring in a more suitable candidate when required in order to ensure that adequate ongoing leadership was in place. As indicated above, wives were traditionally seen as professional members of the household with overall responsibility for its management, a system highlighting the husband's responsibility for the household's income.

In the households of artisans and shopkeepers, the practice was for the household head's nominee to follow in the footsteps of the household head. Other children established branch households when financially viable. In that context, household members assumed outside employment for instrumental reasons – either to support one's household of origin or to establish one's own household. The *dekasegi* were members of poor rural agricultural households who migrated to urban areas and remitted income back to their rural household. That employment model was important from the late 1950s through to the early 1970s. Although the acceptance of a young person as a permanent full-time employee represented a loose commitment by a firm to that person's household, firms were careful to limit that exposure. Having a fixed retirement age was one way to ensure this outcome. As life expectancy rose, however, so too did the retirement age. The extended use of subcontracting has been bolstered by the increased use of casual employees who include not only *furiitaa* but also large ranks of female part-timers.

As Japan's cities and industrial areas grew and established themselves, the ties to the rural household began to weaken, a process described in Nishimura's[53] prize-winning novel about a group who came from the Aomori region to work in Tokyo in the 1970s. During the 1960s and 1970s, many took annual leave each summer to return to their home town and visit the family grave. As they became more settled, however, such visits became less frequent and the sense of *ie* gave way to references to one's *kazoku* (a term which might roughly be rendered as 'nuclear family'). Over time the feeling that a family had to survive through generations as an economic unit faded. As many households came to enjoy unprecedented affluence, new burial sites were established nearer to home, the opportunities for relationships outside the home increased, and fewer children grew up with an urgent sense that the family finances need to be supplemented.

Many young Japanese identify with a wider range of collectivities, and continue to think about work in instrumental terms as did their parents. One difference is that many tie their end goals – their consummatory values – to a more diverse range of collectivities and are less tied to the needs of the standard *ie* or *kazoku*. This is reflected in the more diverse range of needs that employers have to consider when formulating a remuneration package that will attract the best and brightest recruits to their employ. The situation is complex; many young Japanese will continue to commit to a trade or profession outside the corporate world, and there will still be an army of graduates ready to fill administrative positions that lead to senior management. At the same time, opportunities will continue to open up to more individuated patterns of work for many Japanese in the labour force.

Conclusion: In the shadow of China

The world of work is one of the first places that the confluence of social and cultural change becomes visible. To a considerable extent the history of postwar Japan has been the history of economically driven social and cultural change. Greater affluence has resulted in an increased number of career pathways and lifestyle choices, more contact with the outside world, and more aged citizens. As Japanese struggled with casualisation and rising levels of unemployment and other aspects of the recession of the 1990s, such changes were reflected in the way Japanese prioritised work. Assumptions about automatic promotion and job security in the larger firms, the stalwarts of life in postwar Japan, came to be questioned.

The realignment of the global economy was connected to the recession as China took over the role of being the manufacturing hub of the world. Initially the cost of employing a seemingly endless supply of cheap, albeit less skilled, labour from China's rural areas and from bankrupt state owned enterprises (SOEs) was far less than that of acquiring automated equipment. Many Japanese firms found it hard to compete as China moved ahead with its market-oriented reforms in line with the promotion of socialism with Chinese characteristics. One could see in China and other Asian societies the frenetic energy that flowed from the sudden realisation that hitherto undreamt of affluence was within reach. The bar is now being lifted further as a new generation of more skilled and educated employees emerges in China's cities. Somehow the impulse that had fuelled Japan's leap forward in the 1960s and 1970s was being found in Japan's neighbouring economies.

China's challenge to Japan's economic pre-eminence raises a further question about the uniqueness of Japanese capitalism. For many years Japan's approach to work organisation raised questions about whether Japanese social structure and culture would come to replicate patterns found in the advanced nations of Europe and North America. Now, as China evolves along its own trajectory, questions are raised about how closely it will come to follow Japan's. In the first decade of the 21st century, Chinese workers are moving from rather regulated labour markets to freer markets, paternalistic systems of compensation found in the old SOEs (state owned enterprises) are giving way to productivity-linked payments, the rural-to-urban flow of labour continues toward its peak, an ageing population is increasingly pressuring an outdated pension system, management prerogatives are being devolved further down political hierarchies and censorship regimes are being relaxed, neo-nationalist outlooks heightened by the publicity surrounding the Beijing Olympics are colouring work choices, and China's interface with the global community is taking on new dimensions with Englishification and the extension of exports into the cultural domain.

Over the past three decades, Japan has confronted the transitions mentioned above. While some work practices are coming into alignment with global standards, Japan continues to experiment in many areas and its policy makers are well informed about successes and failures elsewhere. Many techniques associated with Japanese-style management have been widely accepted abroad, and Japanese firms are now having to respond to changes in the social, economic and political environments outside Japan, moving from a position of leading back into a learning role. In the past, Japan has learnt from developments in the West. It is now at a point where it will be informed by changes in many of the Asian nations as well. To respond to those challenges, the Japanese government has recently announced a new push to internationalise the production of science and technology in ways that will include steps to better encourage the active participation of its citizens in networks abroad. We can expect that the Japanese society and culture will be further internationalised, and that many of the social and cultural changes accompanying those moves will first become visible in how work is organised in Japan.

Notes

1. Mouer and Kawanishi (2005).
2. Nurkse (1953).
3. Rostow (1959).
4. See Sugimoto (1975).
5. Ōkōchi (1970) and Kazahaya (1973).
6. Nakayama (1975).
7. Chalmers Johnson (1982).
8. Actually the plan became four plans introduced in quick succession as the economy continued to grow beyond expectations.
9. Kawanishi (1992).
10. Inui (2002).
11. Amanuma (2007).
12. Katsuhiko Hashimoto (2007).
13. Japan Institute for Labour Policy and Training (2007: 71).
14. Goldthorpe, Lockwood, Bechhofer and Platt (1968 and 1969).
15. For more detail on the changes discussed in this section, see Mouer and Kawanishi (2005, especially chapters 5–10); Mouer and Sugimoto (2003) and Mouer (2008).
16. Hei Konsarutingu Gurūpu (2007).

17. Toshiaki Satō (2000).
18. Tachibanaki (1998).
19. Kariya (1995).
20. Takamitsu Satō (2003).
21. Toshiaki Satō (2000).
22. Miura (2007).
23. Tachibankai (2006).
24. Fukuchi (2006) and Toshiaki Satō (2000).
25. Fujii (2005) and Matsumoto (2007).
26. Ochi (2007).
27. Iwata (2007); Iwata and Nishizawa (2008); Hideo Aoki (2006).
28. Mamiya Suzuki (2007).
29. Nikkeiren (1995).
30. Morris-Suzuki (2000).
31. Yabuno (1995).
32. Ministry of Public Management, Home Affairs, Posts and Telecommunications (2001).
33. Komai (2001).
34. Mouer and Sugimoto (1995); Sugimoto and Mouer (1995).
35. Fukuoka (1993 and 2000).
36. Burgess (2003).
37. See, for example, Yōichi Funabashi (2000).
38. As described in Ōishi (1997).
39. Economic Planning Agency (2000: 8).
40. Sugishita (2001: 5–8).
41. Japan Institute for Labour Policy and Training (2007: 56–57).
42. Mouer and Kawanishi (2005: 102).
43. Tamai (2001).
44. Hamada and Ōkuma (2002: 459–63).
45. See Kosugi (2007).
46. See Honda (2004) or Kudō (2005).
47. See Masahiro Yamada (1999).
48. Masahiro Yamada (2000).
49. Kosugi (2007).
50. Kosugi (2007).
51. Chan-Tiberghien (2004).
52. Nakane (1967a).
53. Nishimura (1980).

Further reading

Rebick, Marcus (2005), *The Japanese Employment System: Adapting to a New Economic Environment*, New York: Oxford University Press.
Kosugi, Reiko (2007), *Escape from Work: Freelancing Youth and the Challenge to Corporate Japan*, Melbourne: Trans Pacific Press.
Mouer, Ross and Hirosuke Kawanishi (2005), *A Sociology of Work in Japan*, Cambridge: Cambridge University Press.

7

Technological culture

Introduction

There has long been a tension between tradition and modernity in Japan. We can see this tension at work in the relationship between technology and culture. Since the 19th century, this has been articulated in the slogan '*wakon yōsai*' ('Japanese spirit, Western technology'). This chapter argues that this dualism allows the Japanese to create a space for their own culture and to develop a sense of identity based on the relationship between Western technology and Japanese cultural traditions. The relationship between the two has fluctuated at times, especially during the Meiji period (1868–1912). In the late 1870s, the emphasis on Western technology gave way to a type of cultural nationalism. In the wake of defeat in the Second World War, *wakon* became discredited and was largely replaced from the late 1950s by rampant consumerism. With rising confidence in Japanese technology, people sought to account for Japanese success and interest in *wakon* could be seen in advertising and accounts of the Japanese economic 'miracle' from the 1960s.

Japanese technological culture is thus seen as an amalgam of Western technology and Japanese culture which combines the strengths of both. In a way, it can also be regarded as a compromise. This chapter examines the nature of Japanese technological culture, and the waxing and waning of *wakon* to provide a window to the Japanese embrace of modernity, and the concomitant confidence of the Japanese people in themselves and at times their traditions.

For example, some writers point to the importance of *wakon* and Japanese aesthetics in terms of the success of Japanese products not only in the Meiji period but also the post-Second World War period. Many

Japanese products are known for their compact and streamlined design. People draw connections with bonsai and suggest that the Japanese have a gift for miniaturisation. They link Japan's technological past and *karakuri ningyō* (automata or mechanised puppets) which date back to the 18th century to the widespread use of industrial robots in present-day Japan.[1]

Scholars have differed in terms of their view of the relationship between technology and the larger culture in which it is immersed. This has often been characterised not only in terms of how Japanese culture has contributed to technological change and innovation but also in examining how aspects of Japanese society and culture have been deficient or hampered Japan's embrace of technology.[2] For example, the Meiji era physician Erwin von Baelz suggested in 1901 that there was something wrong with the introduction of Western science in Japan: the Japanese treated it too much like a machine to crank out products 'instead of studying the spirit which made the acquisitions possible'.[3]

In this way, people have expressed the feeling that something is not quite right with Japanese science and technology. We can point to the gendered nature of technological culture as a constraining factor on female participation in innovation. It is also possible to show how other constraints in Japanese culture and society have served to limit Japan's ability to make the most of the technology that is being developed.

The *wakon yōsai* formulation has been used to argue that the Japanese are not sufficiently Western and hence Japanese technological culture and society are defective. We shall also see that the claims for the efficacy of the *wakon yōsai* dichotomy are time dependent. What is working against the usefulness of this concept is the increasingly transnational character of manufacturing, where it is difficult to trace the origin of a product to any one particular country.

Debate and controversy: *Wakon yōsai*

The idea of being able to separate Japanese culture from foreign influence can be traced back to the old idea of *wakon kansai* (Japanese spirit, Chinese skills). By 1854, however, when Sakuma Shōzan coined the phrase *Tōyō no dōtoku, seiyō no geijutsu* (Eastern morality, Western techniques), the Japanese were more interested in borrowing from the West. Sakuma tried to incorporate Western science and technology with a Confucian framework. It was through this hybridism that Japan would create a new order.[4] Both this slogan and the Meiji era slogan *wakon yōsai* are examples of how the

Japanese dealt with the threat posed by modernity to cultural traditions. They show a dilemma: while on the one hand these slogans indicate a desire to embrace a Western-inspired modernity, they also indicate concern regarding the effects of the introduction of foreign ideas and knowledge. This concern continues to this very day. While such slogans do rely on outmoded dichotomies between Japan and 'the West', they nevertheless articulate the idea that there is a 'Japanese' technological culture that is somehow different from elsewhere that enables the Japanese to Westernise (adopt Western technology) without becoming Western.

Watsuji Tetsurō embraced this idea in his 1935 essay 'Nihon seishin' ('The Japanese Spirit'), in which he attempted to separate the technologies from those who originally used them.[5] Although this doctrine was discredited after the war, Japan's postwar economic success suggested that there was something about Japan's technological culture that made it special.

This idea was famously evident in *Why Has Japan Succeeded: Western Technology and the Japanese Ethos*,[6] a book based on lectures given by the economist Michio Morishima at Cambridge University. He asks the question of how it was that the Japanese, who possess a 'remarkably idiosyncratic ethos', were able to 'gain such control over the industrial techniques produced by the West'.[7] He points to the importance of Confucianism in Japan and how it differed from Confucianism in China. The latter was humanistic whereas the former was nationalistic. Combined with Shintoism, Confucianism provided a powerful doctrine that helped propel Japan on a path of development that was very different from China's at the time. The result, he argues, was that the Japanese were able to

> retain their culture, their way of life, the specific relationship between superior and inferior, and their family structure, yet simultaneously to build a modern nation endowed with power that is comparable to that of Western countries.[8]

We must ask, however, whether these social attitudes and norms now hold Japan back. Are they necessarily conducive for technological innovation in the 21st century?

Success of *wakon*: Changes over time

What has been the focus of stories of Japanese success? Much has been written over the years about the role of government policies in Japan's rapid economic growth. The literature has been dominated by classics such

as Chalmers Johnson's *MITI and the Japanese Miracle*,[9] Daniel I Okimoto's *Between MITI and the Market*[10] and Scott Callon's *Divided Sun*.[11]
Takatoshi Ito,[12] in his well-known text *The Japanese Economy*, draws attention to how the Japanese were able to successfully adopt and adapt elements
of other cultures. In the pre-Meiji era, this propensity facilitated the transfer of technology from China. Ito attributes Japan's economic growth since
the Meiji period to a combination of heritage from the Tokugawa period
and wise policies implemented by the Meiji government. The Tokugawa
legacy included a high educational level, capital accumulation, a high level
of agricultural technology and advanced infrastructure (especially a major
road network thanks to the *sankin kōtai* system of alternate residence of
feudal lords in Edo, or present-day Tokyo).

This type of argument is extended into the post-Second World War
period to describe Japan's 'economic miracle'. It enables the Japanese to
praise American technological superiority and at the same time carve out a
sense of their own identity based on a propensity to assimilate others. Japan
can be said to have shown a strong technological orientation, epitomised by
the spectacular growth of the car and electronic industries in the postwar
years. It is possible to argue that a tendency towards a technological culture
in Japan has meant that not only have the Japanese quickly embraced new
technologies but they have been more open to borrowing from other cultures in general. Whether this is due to any 'inherent cultural peculiarities'
is, as James Bartholomew[13] suggests, open to debate.

Sheridan Tatsuno has compared Japanese creativity with its Western
counterpart. Westerners, according to Tatsuno, tend to be more 'linear,
rational, and individualistic' in their thinking whereas the Japanese are more
'adaptive, holistic, and cyclical'.[14] He argues that as the Japanese need to
make more technological breakthroughs of their own (rather than borrow
from the United States) they will draw on their cultural heritage, especially
aesthetic tendencies such as miniaturisation. The Japanese, according to
Tatsuno, like combining ideas to make hybrid technologies, fusing old ideas
with new to make new products. High Definition Television is cited as an
example of this phenomenon. More recently, the rise of *keitai shōsetsu*
(mobile phone novels) illustrates the Japanese liking for small things. In
the first half of 2007, half of the top 10 best-selling novels in Japan were
written as *keitai* novels (that is, for downloading on to phones) before being
republished in book form.[15]

The driving force behind technological innovation can change over time,
as can the definition of what constitutes Japanese 'spirit' and Japanese

technological culture. Rather than attributing Japanese economic success to some unchanging cultural essence, we need to acknowledge changes over time, often in response to external influences not of their making. The Japanese work ethic has been a contributing factor to Japanese economic success, but the image of a punctual Japanese worker may have been a relatively recent invention. In the mid-19th century, European visitors complained of the slowness and unreliability of Japanese workers. The Westernisation of Japan was accompanied by new ideas about time. Time became less rooted in nature and more closely aligned with machines and clocks. The introduction of railroads in 1872 and the building of Western-style factories required a level of precision and greater discipline in time-keeping. Life became busier and the Japanese were encouraged to work harder.

Today of course, foreigners marvel at the punctuality of bullet trains and how they manage to stop exactly at the right spot on the station platform. Japan's technological culture has definitely changed over time – the Japanese literally had to learn to live by the clock.[16]

Toyota's just-in-time system of technology management and lean production is considered to be one of the hallmarks of Japanese innovation. But such systems do place auto-workers under great pressure, almost transforming them into machines.[17]

In the 1960s, advertisements increasingly suggested that the Japanese should take pride in the products that were made in Japan by manufacturers such as Sony, Sanyo and Matsushita. Such technology was related to Japanese aesthetics, its history of craftsmanship and proximity to nature. Whereas technological products were originally heralded as symbols of Americanisation not long after the end of the Allied Occupation of Japan (1945–52), increased Japanese self-confidence (at least at home) changed the discourse to one which emphasised Japanese culture.[18]

Why are some Japanese products especially popular in Asia? We can point to the popularity of cute character culture such as 'Hello Kitty' in Japan and Asia. This phenomenon has been a feature of Japanese popular culture. Cute characters are attached as accessories to mobile phones and emoticons (face marks) help personalise messages.[19] Why has this tended to be more popular in Asia than elsewhere? It is possible to argue that 'cultural proximity' has facilitated the spread of Japanese popular culture in Asia,[20] and the same can be said of linguistic and cultural familiarity.

The Japanese do seem to have a penchant for electronic gadgets. By the year 2000, over 10 million Japanese accessed the internet via mobile phones.[21] The use of mobile phones now exceeds that of home phones. How do we account for this? Young Japanese enjoy the ease of communication afforded by mobile phones, and thereby avoid being overheard by parents or other family members. Cramped living space and limited privacy have, it has been argued, been factors in the popularity of text messaging by mobile phone.[22] In addition, the high cost of establishing a landline has encouraged many Japanese to purchase cell phones instead. NTT DoCoMo's i-mode system provides users with cheap and continuous wireless access to the internet, using cellular phones with a screen the size of a business card.[23] There are, thus, structural reasons as well as cultural justifications for the current levels of consumption.

We can point to a number of features of Japanese cyber-culture which differentiate it from elsewhere. Firstly, although 68 per cent of the Japanese population surf the internet,[24] it is mainly through mobile or cellular phones rather than personal computers. The WAP (Wireless Application Protocol) for mobile phones, which provides access to a basic version of the World Wide Web, became very popular in Japan, in contrast with the US. This has enabled those without computers to access the internet.

Also, it is clear that the traffic on the internet is primarily directed towards Japanese websites in the Japanese language. Although some web-sites have pages in the English language, the Japanese, not surprisingly, show a preference for their own language. Even the face marks that the Japanese use to personalise emailed messages show some differences when compared with those used in the US. American symbols tend to be read at 90 degrees to the line of words, whereas Japanese symbols often flow in the same direction as the sentence.[25]

As for the profile of users, the internet was initially particularly popular among males in Japan, but the percentage of female users has increased dramatically, rising from 16.5 per cent in 1997 to 44.5 per cent in 2001.[26] The popularity of internet shopping is one of the reasons for this increase. The fact that online shopping is popular in both the US and Japan is not surprising, but unlike in the US, purchased items are often collected and paid for at convenience stores rather than by credit cards and delivered to the home, reflecting the preference for cash over plastic.

We can account for some of the similarities in Japanese and Western technological culture by pointing to the fact that much technology in Japan originates elsewhere. This is one of the fundamental truths symbolised by the *wakon yōsai* slogan. Differences emerge, however, when the Japanese adopt and adapt foreign ideas and make them their own. For example, despite the early lead by the US in the introduction of robotics, by 1984 Japan was using four times as many industrial robots as the US.[27]

In 2007, General Motors attempted to show that it was getting serious about improving the quality of its vehicles by televising a commercial that suggested a new workplace culture where mistakes would no longer be tolerated. The commercial showed a robot in a GM factory getting fired after having made an error, and then committing suicide. Public outcry at the trivialisation of suicide portrayed in the advertisement resulted in the removal of the unhappy ending.[28] This poor attempt at humour was revealing, in that it showed discomfort with the idea of robots in the American workplace. Rather than a human being dismissed, it was a robot.

In contrast, the Japanese have taken their embrace of technology to extremes not countenanced elsewhere. Robots are seen as offering possible solutions for dealing with the increasing burden of caring for the aged in Japan. It is estimated that one quarter of the population will be over the age of 65 by 2020. While the prospect of having a human-like robot nurse the elderly might seem akin to science fiction, the concept of a robotics sick room with equipment to monitor bodily functions might not seem so far-fetched, given the already high-tech nature of hospitals today.[29]

How do we account for the popularity of robots in Japan? Robert Geraci[30] suggests that American researchers prefer to focus on artificial intelligence (AI) and virtual reality as Christian beliefs in salvation in purified unearthly bodies encourages a disembodied approach to information. In Japan, in contrast, he argues that Buddhism and Shinto beliefs of *kami* (deities) being manifested in nature allow even robots to have a spirit and be integrated into society.

Recently, there have been cases where real efforts have been made to put humanoid robots into the service of ordinary people. In January 2006, the People Staff Company announced that it would start making robots available to work in nursing homes and as receptionists. The robots include Ifbot, a 45-centimetre-high communication robot which retails at ¥495,000, the price of a used car in reasonable condition. Ifbot can talk, sing, and give quizzes to elderly residents. Hello Kitty Robo is marketed as a night receptionist. It has a sensor that recognises visitors, greets them, and relays images and sound back to computers at the staffing agency.[31]

A Kyoto nursing home was brave enough to install an Ifbot, but unfortunately it languished in a corner for two years after the initial novelty wore off. The director of the nursing home, Sawada Yasuko, concluded that stuffed animals are more popular.[32] The story of the Ifbot in Kyoto reflects Japan's fascination with and fear of robots. Given these problems, manufacturers are making an effort to meet the special needs of the elderly at a more basic level. Sony has produced an easy-to-operate radio cassette player[33] and the major mobile phone operator DoCoMo released a phone in 2001 with an easy-to-read screen and a bigger keypad.[34]

Western writers on Japan have criticised Japan's technological culture for only focusing on the instrumental aspects of Western know-how and not bothering to absorb the philosophical and religious aspects of what they were borrowing from the West. This was, as we have seen, the intention of the *wakon yōsai* concept. In an effort to understand the prevalence of social withdrawal (*hikikomori*) in Japan, Michael Zielenziger[35] has suggested that the Japanese ignored 'the individuation, inquiry, and risk-taking' that was associated with the technologies. He likens Japan to a bullet train that travelled at great speed from feudalism to industrialisation, without having experienced the Enlightenment.

There are clearly limits to which technology can be used to solve social problems. While the Japanese are keen to push the boundaries, some commentators suggest that there are aspects of Japanese society and culture that work against the Japanese realising their hopes for a hi-tech future.

Dealing with diversity and variation

In 2007, the Economist Intelligence Unit voted Japan as the world's most innovative nation, if innovation is defined as 'the application of knowledge in a novel way, primarily for economic benefit'.[36] This was measured by the number of patents generated per million people. At the same time, however, a majority of senior international executives voted the US as the best place for innovation. While these findings may appear contradictory, they suggest that some aspects of Japan's technological culture stand in the way of innovation.

Morishima[37] has argued that in contrast to Chinese Confucianism, its Japanese counterpart paid scant attention to benevolence and righteousness and focused on loyalty, filial piety and wisdom. It seems that the 'Japanese had no understanding of Western individualism and liking for liberalism'.[38] While we could debate the legitimacy of such claims, such ideas have been used to help explain the *hikikomori* phenomenon and why young men feel the need to withdraw from a highly competitive society which they feel has no place for them. The malaise is said to afflict up to 1.4 million Japanese, 80 per cent of whom are male. Of those affected, some 40 per cent are between

16 and 25 years of age.[39] These modern-day hermits shut themselves up in their small rooms for periods from six months to over 15 years.[40]

While the causes of this phenomenon are difficult to pinpoint, the affluence of Japanese families (despite the recession) coupled with technological advances have enabled these young men to lead the lives that they do, surfing the internet, playing video games, and eating food delivered to their homes or provided by their obliging parents. But something is not quite right. At a time of advanced communications, these young men turn away from social interaction and enter a virtual reality.

The sufferers of *hikikomori* are largely male, begging the question as to what extent technological culture varies according to class, region, gender, age and other socio-demographic variables. While technology might appear gender neutral, technological innovations often serve to empower some groups in society and to marginalise others. While there are class-specific factors related to affordability, sometimes differential access to new technologies may result from gendered socialisation.

Is there something about Japanese technological culture and the larger society that reinforces gender stereotypes? It does seem that young men are quick when it comes to adopting new technologies, but part of the problem may be that women and minorities are denied certain educational opportunities that more readily accrue to men. In 1960, only 0.5 per cent of university students enrolled in engineering degrees were female. By 1985, this rose to a slightly higher 3.9 per cent, and reached a plateau at 7.7 per cent by 1995.[41] This lack of participation by women will have an economic cost in the future when there are insufficient workers to support a largely elderly population. Technological culture varies from place to place within Japan, so those living outside of Tokyo have less access to the opportunities that characterise life in the nation's capital. Tokyo has long been the centre of technology-related activity, with some 59 per cent of Japanese major corporate headquarters based there.[42] What emerges today is a nation that can be divided into thriving urban centres like Tokyo and Nagoya, and rural areas that are economically depressed.[43]

While the Japanese like to think that they are all middle class, the reality is that the newest technological products are initially often very expensive and ownership is limited to the wealthy. Not all can enjoy the technological culture offered in the bright lights of the Tokyo shopping mecca of Akihabara. Only one small segment of the population can afford the most advanced products. In 1955, less than 1 per cent of Japanese owned television sets and refrigerators, but by the 1970s, this figure exceeded

90 per cent.[44] What is more, manufacturers deliberately target certain segments of the population. If we look at marketing in the 1970s, there is gender differentiation in advertising images associated with appliances, with
women often portrayed as consumers and men as the engineers responsible
for producing the products.

Women have tended to be absent from many narratives of Japan's technological success, not least because they are not in the 'driving seat' of
innovation and have tended to take more secondary roles. In 1996, women
made up only 3.8 per cent of the university faculty in engineering and 7.1
per cent of PhD students enrolled in that field.[45] It was only in August
2000 that for the first time in Japanese history two women received their
licenses to drive bullet trains.[46] In this way, access to technology in Japan
can depend on gender.

It was only in the 1990s that the internet became popular and use of
personal computers really took off in Japan. There are various reasons for
this delay, such as the popularity of Japanese language word-processors, an
interim technology. Furthermore, although Japan is the leading producer of
video games, the Japanese have tended to design game products (especially
catering for boys) which can be used as hand-held devices without the need
for other technologies such as computers or television sets. In contrast,
children in the US and Europe often play games on a computer using a
keyboard.

The audience for video and computer games in Japan still tends to be
male, but there are exceptions. The Japanese dance-simulation arcade game
'Dance Dance Revolution' (sometimes referred to as *karaoke* for the feet)
has proven to be very popular amongst young women, who are often better
dancers than young men.[47]

Women are still not seen as an integral part of Japan's technological
culture. Although women made up 37 per cent of Japan's online population in March 2000,[48] Japanese companies are slow to employ women
in IT-related positions. The bilingual internet forum DigitalEve Japan has
compared women working in IT in 20 countries, including Korea. Japan is
at the bottom of the list, with only 17 per cent of the IT workforce being
female.[49]

Japan's technological culture does not seem geared to recognise that
valuable contributions to innovation can be made by a range of diverse
players. At the end of the 20th century, Japan saw the emergence of what
has been described as 'the new *zaibatsu* (financial conglomerate)' or 'Net-
batsu', led by Masayoshi Son's Softbank Corporation, one of the world's

largest conglomerates of internet-related firms. Son's basic strategy was to import US World Wide Web companies such as Yahoo and to establish them in Japan. In the process, he aimed to transform Japan from an industrial to an information society.[50] But raising capital to realise his dream would not be easy. He experienced difficulties (partly relating to his Korean ethnicity) when he sought loans from a Japanese bank to establish Softbank.[51]

With an ageing population and a declining birthrate, Japan's technological culture needs to be more inclusive and encourage not only people of different ethnic backgrounds, but more women and older workers into the workforce. In the same way that Son, a Korean resident in Japan, experienced discrimination, women and those close to retirement age face bias. Many people have the potential to contribute to innovation. Kuwahara[52] suggests that with the rise of the digital revolution, the nature of work will change and that previous barriers to the participation of women will collapse, not only due to the reality of labour shortages, but due to the transformation of the Japanese economy away from heavy industry and a growing awareness of the need to have a productive female workforce.

Technology transfer from Japan to developing countries entails the export of some less savoury aspects of Japan's technological culture. For example, offshore manufacturing tends to reinforce Japanese domination over developing countries, reproducing the male dominance which somehow seems to be encoded in the machines themselves. The late Matsui Yayori[53] wrote of the case of Malay women in Japanese factories who suffered from mass hysteria, unused as they were to working on assembly lines and in a new environment of concrete buildings and complicated machinery.

The impact of technological change can be different for men and women due to gender relations in the workplace and the sexual division of labour. The assembly-line system which transformed the Malay women into 'robots' was designed for repetitious work, allowing the exploitation of 'unskilled' women workers for long hours at low wages, and placing men (who could 'understand' the system) in supervisory roles with higher remuneration.

Another more general concern has been the way in which technological culture, which placed economic growth before the environment, was exported to other parts of Asia. Japan now has to deal with environmental problems such as acid rain from China, where coal has been used to fuel economic growth.[54] Not all environmental problems have been shifted offshore. Some come back to haunt the Japanese.

Japanese confidence in the role of technology in their country's future has also been sorely tested in recent times by controversies surrounding incidents at nuclear power plants. The string of accidents raises questions about whether nuclear technology can be relied upon. Japan has 55 nuclear reactors which produce about one-third of its electricity. Japan is a resource-poor, earthquake-prone country that must depend on imported energy for much of its needs.[55]

Towards a transnational history of technology: The rise of hybrid products

In this global world, the simplistic dualisms suggested by *wakon yōsai* are increasingly problematic. Even if we look as far back as the end of the Second World War, we can see how crossing national borders, both physically and psychologically, was an integral part of technological development. Partner[56] argues that the US was pivotal to the development of the electrical goods industry in Japan. He points to the importance of the Allied Occupation of Japan (1945–52); the role of American-style anti-communism in promoting television in Japan; the role-model that the US provided as a consumer society; the transfer of US technology after the war; and the emergence of the US as a market for electrical components.

To better understand Japan's postwar trajectory, we need to acknowledge the importance of the American dream and American technological culture for the Japanese people. As Yoshimi Shunya[57] has found, advertisements from the late 1950s promoted the idea that through consumption, especially the purchase of electrical appliances, the Japanese could emulate the affluence and lifestyle of America. The housewife was portrayed as the catalyst for the Americanisation and 'democratisation' of Japan by introducing such goods into the home.[58] The postwar vision of a new Japan was placed against the backdrop of an affluent America. In this light, the concept of *wakon yōsai* seems less relevant.

We also need to acknowledge the increasingly hybrid character of products which have characterised the 'Made in Japan' brand. Indeed, the transnational nature of technology these days means that we can rarely isolate one country as the manufacturer of a product, let alone its sole inspiration. Japanese firms have often commercialised new products which have been partly or wholly invented elsewhere. Some examples are the transistor and integrated circuit, both of which originated in the US. Despite their American origin, the Japanese led the world in the commercialisation of transistors for radios and outstripped the US in the production of high-quality colour television sets.

With the 'hollowing out' of Japan in the 1990s and the shift of Japanese manufacturing to other parts of Asia, more and more 'Japanese' technology is being produced overseas. We can turn to the videocassette recorder (VCR), previously one of Japan's major exports, for further insight. As in the case of the transistor and IC (integrated circuit), much of the early work was done in the US. However, the Japanese solved many engineering, design and manufacturing problems which stood in the way of commercialisation. The VCR provides a good example of how the Japanese have gone from almost total dependence on foreign inventions (and a pattern of borrowing, modifying and commercialising) to a growing role as an inventor of products in fields such as fibre optics, new materials, biotechnology, semiconductors and computer-numerically controlled machine tools.[59] By 1996, it was estimated that over a third of Japanese car stereos and VCRs, more than two-thirds of colour televisions, and 80 per cent of hi-fi audio equipment made by Japanese companies will have actually been produced elsewhere. China and other Asian countries effectively provide the world with Japanese electrical appliances.[60]

The idea of a hybrid Japan rather than a homogenous Japan is becoming increasingly powerful. Commentators such as Douglas McGray have written of how 'Japan was postmodern before postmodernism was trendy, fusing elements of other national cultures into one almost-coherent whole'.[61] The ambiguity which arises from the hybridity of its products in terms of unclear nationality or country of origin has been skilfully used by the Japanese to appeal to multiple markets. Hello Kitty is said to be from London, helping to pander to Japanese tastes that often favour things Western. At the same time, Hello Kitty appears Japanese to those overseas who find Japanese things 'cool'. In this way, Japanese technological culture has become transnational.

Many Japanese 'products' are 'culturally odourless' and do not immediately conjure up associations with Japan. They are often localised by other countries and their origins made unclear. Iwabuchi[62] cites what he calls the three Cs as examples of this: consumer technology including VCRs (discussed earlier), the Walkman and karaoke; comics and cartoons; and computer and video games. Rather than viewing this lack of nationality as a problem, it can be seen as a positive: Japan is not only good at adopting and adapting, but its products are often exported and localised in turn.

The Walkman enabled consumers to take their music with them, but the rise of portable digital music devices such as the iPod have led to its decline, and Japan seems to have lost the lead. However, if we unpack the iPod, we see that this is not necessarily the case. Both iPods and the new iPhones help us to understand the transnational nature of the manufacture of technology which confounds attempts to attribute any one culture to the success of a single electronic product. How so?

Although the Apple iPhone is designed in California and assembled in mainland China, Taiwanese manufacturers play a major role in their production. The same may be said for iPods.[63] The manufacture of the Apple iPod is outsourced to a number of Asian companies. It is assembled in China but the most expensive part is the hard drive which is manufactured by the Japanese company Toshiba. Can we say then that it is actually made in Japan? Not necessarily, as most of the hard drives are made in the Philippines and China. Products such as the iPod are made in several countries but the bulk of the profit goes to Apple, as it is responsible for creating the original idea and design.[64]

The transnationality of products has made problematic any efforts to blame one country for the damage to the environment that they cause. The manufacture of one MP3 player releases 7.7 kilograms of carbon dioxide into the atmosphere. Should we blame the country where most MP3s are assembled, China, for the global warming that results or point the blame at countries that supply the components, such as Japan? Some policy makers suggest that carbon emissions are embedded in the products and that those who buy them in countries like the US should share some of the responsibility. In this way, the technological culture of a country can be inscribed into a product in ways that go beyond mere design and more broadly include even attitudes to the environment.[65]

Mia Consalvo[66] has argued that the console video game industry is, like the iPod business, a mixture of Japanese and American cultures. The hybrid nature of the industry can, she claims, be seen not only in the transnational corporations that have given rise to video games but also in terms of the global audience for the games and the style, format and content of them. Japanese products are a savvy blend of both Japanese and American culture, and are not too 'foreign' to suit American tastes. In August 2002, four Japanese games were amongst the top 10 video games sold in the US.[67]

In today's globalised world, it is impossible to confine skilled workers to national borders. The downsizing of Japan's electronics industry has been accompanied by the loss of thousands of Japanese engineers to Taiwan,

South Korea, China and Singapore where Japanese technological exper-
tise, especially in semiconductors, is highly prized.[68] This brain drain is
contributing to a greater awareness among Japanese that their futures are
tied to Asia. But the outflow of skilled workers is raising concerns about
whether Japan will be able to maintain its lead in areas like electronics.

Today, the technological sophistication that we had previously associated with the Japanese has become more widespread elsewhere, and firms in
many countries attempt to exploit opportunities as they arise. Rather than
use the words 'Made in Japan', it might be more appropriate to label many
products as having been 'Designed in Japan' or even 'Inspired by Japan'.
By adopting a more transnational approach to understanding technological
culture, we can paint a more accurate picture of how products are designed,
manufactured and consumed, and how Japan has contributed to the technological lifestyle that many of us now enjoy. *Wakon yōsai* has provided
a useful way of understanding how the Japanese have defined themselves
with respect to technology and to the West. When they are confident about
themselves, they point to the importance of cultural traditions; when they
are despondent, they point to inadequacies and deficiencies in Japanese
culture. But the world is an increasingly complicated place and our sense
of identity is more fluid. It is in this context of fluid identities that Japan
must situate itself, its people and its products for as we saw with the iPod,
products are often no longer identifiably their own.

Notes

1. Ken Nakamura (1989).
2. Inkster (2000).
3. von Baelz (1974: 150).
4. Van Sant (2004).
5. Tetsuro in Cox (2007); Koizumi (2002).
6. Morishima (1982).
7. Morishima (1982: viii).
8. Morishima (1982: 52).
9. Chalmers Johnson (1982).
10. Okimoto (1989).
11. Callon (1995).
12. Takatoshi Ito (1992).
13. Bartholomew (1978: 269).
14. Tatsuno (1990: 15–16).
15. Parry (2007); Hani (2007).
16. Takehiko Hashimoto (2002).
17. Kamata (1982); Sachiko Kaneko (2006: 236).

18. Yoshimi (2003: 474).
19. See Katsuno and Yano (2002); Hjorth (2005).
20. Iwabuchi (2002b: 122, 131).
21. Caruana (2000).
22. Castells, Fernández-Ardèvol, Qui and Sey (2007: 71).
23. Stevenson (2000).
24. Internet World Stats (2007).
25. Katsuno and Yano (2002: 206).
26. Onosaka (2003: 95).
27. Mowery and Rosenberg (1989: 219).
28. Elliott (2007).
29. Dethlefs and Martin (2006).
30. Geraci (2006).
31. 'Caregiver, receptionist robots to start working', *The Japan Times* (27 January 2006) online at: http://search.japantimes.co.jp/print/nn20060127b7.html.
32. Foulk (2007).
33. Dethlefs and Martin (2006).
34. Castells *et al.* (2007: 40–41).
35. Zielenziger (2006: 126).
36. 'Japan rated tops for innovation', *The Japan Times* (17 May 2007), online at: http://search.japantimes.co.jp/print/nb20070517a1.html.
37. Morishima (1982: 90).
38. Morishima (1982: 91).
39. Watts (2002); Hattori (2006).
40. Jones (2006).
41. Lenz (2001).
42. Cornell (2001).
43. Fackler (2007b).
44. Yoshimi (2003: 470).
45. Kuwahara (2001).
46. 'Women with a bullet', *The Weekend Australian* (19–20 August 2000: 15).
47. Jacob Smith (2004).
48. Howe (2007).
49. Pawasarat (2002); DigitalEve Japan (2007).
50. Kunii (2000).
51. Sender (2000); Gilley, Dawson and Biers (2000).
52. Kuwahara (2001).
53. Matsui (1987).
54. Batson (2004).
55. Fackler (2007c and 2007d).
56. Partner (1999).
57. Yoshimi (2003).
58. Yoshimi (1999).
59. Mowery and Rosenberg (1989: 220).
60. Skelton (1996).
61. McGray (2002: 48).
62. Iwabuchi (1998).
63. Belson (2007).

64. Varian (2007).
65. Spencer (2007).
66. Consalvo (2006).
67. Consalvo (2006: 125).
68. Fackler (2007a).

Further reading

Inkster, Ian and Fumihiko Satofuka (eds) (2000), *Culture and Technology in Modern Japan*, London: IB Tauris.

Iwabuchi, Koichi (2002), *Recentering Globalization: Popular Culture and Japanese Transnationalism*, Durham: Duke University Press.

Partner, Simon (1999), *Assembled in Japan: Electrical Goods and the Making of the Japanese Consumer*, Berkeley: University of California Press.

8

Religious culture

Perhaps it is only because we can witness life in contemporary Japan unfolding before our eyes or because the beginning of modern Japan is so recent, but the modern period has arguably been one of the most exciting and transformative in the long and rich history of Japanese religious culture. Modernity has not brought about the secularisation of Japan as was often predicted, but instead has seen the flowering of new religions, shifts in the practice of long-held traditions and extended debates among practitioners, government leaders and scholars as to what role religion has, can, does and should play in Japanese society. Moreover, the last few decades have seen the growth of a subfield within the study of Japanese religion that focuses on the modern period. Works by Shimazono, Inoue, Reader, Tanabe and others have all sought to explore the varied and fascinating religious life of modern Japan.[1] The aim of this chapter is not to neatly summarise a 'modern Japanese religious culture', rather it is to present the religious life of modern Japan from myriad viewpoints and to introduce the reader to approaches taken in the study of Japanese religious culture. This chapter attempts, thereby, to express the complexity of both the religious life of modern Japan and the study of Japanese religion.

Anyone who has been lucky enough to travel to Japan has surely been struck by the multifaceted religious life of the Japanese. There seems to be a shrine or temple wherever one looks, festivals pepper the calendar, the shelves of bookstores are filled with works on everything from Nostradamus to pilgrimage guides. Moreover, the visitor to Japan is often struck by the syncretic nature of religious practice. Attending a Buddhist temple in Tokyo around Christmas, for example, one can find people writing wishes on wooden tablets (*ema*, a practice that has its origins in Shinto) to Santa Claus. Studies on modern Japanese religions frequently note that in surveys of Japanese religion the number of believers of the various religions is generally twice the actual population of Japan. This statistic is used to show that Japanese do not hold exclusively to one religion but instead practice numerous religions depending upon their particular ritual need. This is where we get the famous phrase: 'Born Shinto, die Buddhist'. Most Japanese celebrate the birth of a child with a trip to their neighbourhood Shinto shrine to introduce the newborn to the local deity and seek blessings for the health of the child, just as most Japanese call on Buddhist priests to perform funeral rites and hold regular memorial services for the dead.

The study of modern Japanese religious culture is no less complicated and rich than the religious life of modern Japan. It entails the study of modern Japanese history, of ritual and doctrine, of ethnographic research and of law, to name but a few key areas. For example, there is a debate within Japanese Buddhism today led by Buddhist scholar-practitioners as to whether or not Japanese Buddhism is 'real' Buddhism. To understand this debate the student of Japanese religions needs to know the history of state-religion relations in Japan, the role modern Western studies of Buddhism have played in shaping Buddhist self-interpretation, and the history of east-west interactions in modern Japan. This chapter will introduce these and other issues as a way to better understand modern Japanese religious culture.

Background: The religions of Japan

It is impossible in the space of a paragraph or two to do justice to the complicated and rich history, teachings and practices of the many Japanese religions. This chapter provides a brief overview of some of the highlights of this fascinating set of traditions.

Shinto is the indigenous religion of Japan. That said, it was not until the introduction of Buddhism to Japan in the 6th century that Shinto took on its own identity and came to be known as Shinto. The Shinto we know today has been influenced over time by Buddhist teachings to such an extent that it is really very difficult to understand the history of Shinto without knowing the history of Buddhism in Japan. The core teachings of modern Shinto are sincerity and purity, and the practices of most Shinto shrines are for seeking the blessings of the *kami*. *Kami* can be roughly translated as 'deity', or more accurately, as anything that is awesome in nature. Practices include weddings, ground-breaking rituals, harvest and fertility rituals, and purification rituals.

Buddhism officially arrived in Japan in the 6th century. Its arrival tells us something about how Buddhism was viewed at the time and about how it continues to be viewed today: it was a gift from the kingdom of Paekche on the Korean peninsula, in other words, it was part of a diplomatic relationship between two kingdoms. Moreover, it was viewed as a wish-granting jewel, a powerful technology that could protect the nation and secure wealth. This is not to say that Buddhist teachings such as compassion and the conditioned nature of existence were unknown. But the interest in Buddhism stemmed from the perceived power inherent in its rituals to affect change, whether that be to heal the sick or defend the nation. A great number of forms of Buddhism were introduced to Japan or created within Japan. These schools focused on everything from understanding the teachings of emptiness to practising the moral code of conduct of the priesthood (the precepts), and from realising Buddhahood in this lifetime through esoteric rituals to achieving salvation through rebirth in a Pure Land.

Like Buddhism, Confucianism had a long history before penetrating Japanese society and going on to become the national ideology. In a nut-shell, Confucianism seeks to bring about a harmonious society. The basic teachings centre on how people relate to each other. For example, the five relationships – ruler and ruled, husband and wife, parent and child, elder brother and younger brother, friend and friend serve as the model for society. Of these, the parent-child relationship is the key; all relationships should be modelled on it. There is also an emphasis on self-perfection, which can be accomplished through self-cultivation. The legacy of this has been a strong value on education in Confucian societies.

Christianity first officially arrived in Japan in 1549 with Francis Xavier and met with initial success. There were stumbling blocks, though. Initially Christianity was seen as a new Buddhist teaching. Among other things, translation played a part in these early difficulties. For example, the word chosen to translate 'God' was Dainichi, the universal Buddha. By 1583 there were 200 churches and 150000 Christians reported. Christianity's success ended sharply when the leadership of Japan changed and Christianity was deemed dangerous, in large part because it was believed to represent the beginnings of Western encroachment. By the late 1600s Christianity was all but eliminated. A remnant church, however, survived underground, creating a type of Christianity unique to Japan. With the arrival of the West again in the mid-1800s, Christianity once again made inroads into Japan. In particular, many leading Japanese intellectuals and bureaucrats saw in Christianity the power of the modern Western states. Today,

Christianity remains in Japan with 1 to 3 per cent of Japanese claiming to be Christian.

In addition to Shinto, Buddhism and Confucianism, Daoism, Onmyō-dō, Shugendō, and a wide array of 'new religions' played roles in Japanese religious culture over time. Some of these will be touched on in more detail below.[2]

Debate and controversy

There are many debates concerning the study of modern Japanese religious life, including those over how to define religion, the methods used to analyse religion, and the related clashes over how we understand the relationship between such things as doctrine and ritual. Before addressing these debates one must begin by first questioning the term 'modern'. Stephen Vlastos and others argue that much of what we have come to know as 'traditional' Japanese culture is 'invented'.[3] Borrowing from Hobsbawm, Vlastos notes:

> tradition is not the sum of *actual* past practices that have perdured into the present; rather, tradition is a modern trope, a prescriptive representation of socially desirable (or sometimes undesirable) institutions and ideas thought to have been handed down from generation to generation.[4]

Japanese religious 'traditions' are no exception. State Shinto is perhaps the primary example of this, though modern Japanese Buddhism is no less an invented tradition.

It is also necessary here to question the term 'religion'. Within the broader field of religious studies there remains debate over the very term that defines the field. The word 'religion' has changed meaning over the centuries in the West. Regarding its use, Jonathan Z Smith writes, 'Religion is not a native category . . . It is a category imposed from the outside on some aspect of the native culture.'[5] Religion, Smith continues, 'is a term created by scholars for their intellectual purposes and is therefore theirs to define.'[6] As an imposed category, the very use of the term can be problematic. But it is widely agreed that the term, as a means of demarcating a field of study and drawing attention to facets of culture, politics and history that have otherwise often been ignored by scholars, can be useful. Smith further states that '[T]here is an implicit universality. Religion is thought to be a ubiquitous human phenomenon.'[7] This sense of universality often masks difference and has been used to imply hierarchies of sameness, ranking varieties of religious experience from primitive/local religion to world religions and within that category prioritising the dominant religion of the observer (generally Christianity in Western studies of religion).

Especially when considering as broad a subject as 'religious culture', it can be useful to turn to terms such as 'worldview', which can incorporate a variety of definitions of religion. Helen Hardacre's work on the Japanese new religious movement, Kurozumikyō, provides an excellent example of this. 'To delineate a worldview is to specify how a group of people understands itself to be related to the physical body, to the social order, and to the universe, and to show how its members think, feel, and act based on that understanding.' It is to understand 'how people appropriate' ideas and 'how they use them'.[8]

Even if one accepts the general category of religion, there remains controversy over how best to define the term as it applies to Japan.[9] Much of the debate centres on its translation into Japanese in the 19th century and the importation thereby of modern Western notions of what constitutes religion into Japanese cultural debates. Surveys of religion in Japan, for example, have been problematic because of their uncritical use of the term. Many surveys continue to ask questions about the respondent's 'religion' using the translation 'shūkyō'. However, this word has come to be associated in Japan with organised religion and survey results are often skewed because they do not take this into account.

Japanese religious culture is no less created by ideologues or the mass media within Japan than by scholars. The very methods chosen to observe religious culture inevitably colour how we come to view or construct that culture. Within the field of Japanese religious studies, work on religious traditions has often been divided between anthropologists and sociologists on the one hand, and Buddhist studies or religious studies scholars on the other. This rift is especially prominent in the study of modern Japanese Buddhism where, until very recently, scholars applying the methodologies of anthropology and sociology tended to focus on new religious movements or the rituals of Buddhism whereas scholars trained as Buddhologists generally ignored the modern period outright. As Rowe and Covell point out elsewhere, both the reasons for this split and the results of it are manifold.[10] On the one hand, anthropologists have not traditionally been trained in Buddhist discourse so when they approached Buddhism in modern Japan they tended to focus on ritual studies. Yet, in so doing, they 'contributed to the idea that Buddhist ritual and practice are better understood as examples of Japanese folk tradition'.[11] This further exacerbated the view that modern Buddhism was somehow moribund and therefore not a worthy object of study for Buddhologists. For their part, Buddhologists generally viewed modern Japanese Buddhism as degenerate or in decline. They tended to prefer the study of 'text and tradition' – focusing on philology and biographies of major figures – over socio-historical or ethnographic analysis. This was true for Japanese as well as Western scholars. In the case of Japanese scholars of Buddhism, most have been Buddhist priests. These scholar-priests inherited an earlier tradition of sectarian studies with its emphasis on founders and texts, and also expressed a certain uneasiness about analysing their own modern history, in part because they bought into the degeneration view (*daraku setsu*) and in part because of inter and intra-Buddhist political sensitivities. Put bluntly, as several scholar-priests have told me, they felt studies of their modern history would air dirty laundry far too soon.

The study of Shinto has been hampered by many of the same problems as the study of Buddhism. The concept of degeneration, for example, though rooted in a different field of study (folklore studies) has played a powerful role in the study of Shinto practices. Unlike Buddhism, which Buddhologists tended to approach as an ahistorical world religion, scholars often approached Shinto as a folk religion.

> Folklore studies in Japan tend toward what Marilyn Ivy has described as "discourses of the vanishing" in that they are characterized by a focus on the loss of tradition and thinning of ritual under the onslaught of urbanization and modernization. This degeneration model is premised on ideas of a pure Japanese essence that existed in communal practices (either in a mythic past or as recently as the turn of the century), but became gradually rationalized and simplified as local communities dissipated and traditional ritual knowledge was lost.[12]

Much as the degeneration view hampered the study of modern Japanese Buddhism, studies of Shinto have been hobbled by this idealised view of rural Japan and the 'essence' of Japanese culture.

Changes over time

The Meiji Restoration and the years that followed it brought about major changes within Japanese religious life. In 1984, Allan Grappard called the disassociation of Shinto and Buddhism that occurred in the mid-19th century 'Japan's ignored cultural revolution'.[13] In the intervening years this 'cultural revolution' became the topic of extensive study. James Ketelaar's[14] thorough examination of the impact of Meiji period developments on Buddhism, Helen Hardacre's[15] research on State Shinto, and Shimazono Susumu's[16] work on new religions will serve as our guides here.

The newly empowered Meiji government issued a series of 'separation edicts' beginning in 1868. These edicts furthered a process already begun in the Mito domain. The net result was the cataloguing and later removal of 'Buddhist' ritual implements from buildings designated Shinto and the removal of 'Shinto' implements from Buddhist temples. Priests of Temple Buddhism (also called 'established Buddhism', meaning the sects of Buddhism founded by the 17th century) were forced to choose to become Shinto or Buddhist priests; some were defrocked, lands were confiscated, and Shinto, for a brief time, enjoyed privileged status within the government. For decades, Temple Buddhism was faced with a reversal of fortune. Buddhist institutions, once closely allied with and generously supported by the state, fell out of favour with the new government. The disassociation of Shinto and Buddhism, once integral parts of a greater whole, created for the first time two clearly demarcated, separate religions. The effect this had on Buddhism and Shinto in the modern period on the institutional, doctrinal and ritual levels was incalculable.

Attacks on Temple Buddhism were launched from various quarters. The critiques were not new to the Meiji period. Critiques of Buddhist corruption and waste as well as those of Buddhism as a foreign religion had roots in pre-Meiji Japan. It was in the Meiji period though that they found resonance with the ruling powers and led to policy decisions detrimental to the Buddhist institutional status quo.

Buddhist leaders not only faced separation from Shinto, loss of land and funding, and attacks on the integrity of Japanese Buddhism, but were also forced to deal with a completely new place within Japanese law. Order number 133 by the Ministry of State, for instance, radically altered the relationship between the state and Buddhist institutions.[17] Under this so-called 'eat meat and marry' (*nikujiki saitai*) order, enforcement of Buddhist precepts was no longer a concern of the state. Centuries of teachings about the importance of Buddhism and the state working in close cooperation were suddenly and radically challenged. Buddhist leadership recognised the dramatic change in the state-Buddhism relationship and vigorously fought to bring the state back into enforcing precepts. Their efforts failed, yet they did serve to create new understandings of the precepts that have had a lasting impact on Buddhist practice in Japan today. Practices such as clerical marriage and the passing on of temples within priestly families expanded exponentially following Order 133. Today they are the norm. These practices in turn changed the face of local life at temples, where the wives of priests over time came to play a major, if unrecognised, role in the religious life of temples. The increased visibility of temple wives also served to call into question the position of women more generally within Temple Buddhism and the ideals of world-renunciation promoted by the male priesthood.[18]

The interaction between Buddhism and the state during Japan's modern period has not been one of two monolithic entities locked in struggle but has been marked by a variety of voices representing various causes and constituencies manoeuvring to maintain or create relevancy. In this process we see the creation of a number of new Buddhisms. Regarding Temple Buddhism, Ketelaar writes:

> Meiji Buddhists succeeded not merely in refiguring Buddhism from the heretical to the martyred; they also succeeded in producing a "new Buddhism" (*shin Bukkyō*) that in fact has come to be viewed as a bastion of Japanese culture. Our contemporary understanding of modern Buddhism (*kindaiteki Bukkyō*) as found in Japan (and to a large extent as found in the United States and Europe as well) can thus be traced to this crucible of persecution in the early Meiji era and the subsequent reconfiguration of its social institutional contours.[19]

In short, the enduring image of Buddhism as a rational philosophy in which ritual is downplayed or outright disparaged that is so dominant today came about at this time. For example, think for a moment of the image of Zen in the United States today. It is used in advertising to represent the serene, or moments experiencing a deep connection with oneself or the universe.[20] Buddhist monks are depicted bald-headed, robed and living a life of quiet contemplation and retreat. This is not to say rituals for everything from assuring safe childbirth to guaranteeing rebirth in a Pure Land did not continue in Japan following the redefinition of Buddhism in the modern period; far from it, they remain today the bread and butter of most temples. It is to say, however, that Temple Buddhism in Japan today suffers from a kind of schizophrenia – on the one hand it is envisioned as a modern, rational, philosophical system, while on the other hand it still serves the ritual needs of the Japanese for healing, protection and the afterlife.

The crucible of Buddhist persecution had an equally powerful effect on Shinto. Government efforts at unweaving strands from the cloth of

Japanese religion to create what we now know as Shinto and Japanese Buddhism had a lasting influence on the religious life of the Japanese. For example, government attempts to create a state religion, State Shinto, altered local and national religious practices. It was recognised early on in the Meiji period that religion could play a powerful role in creating a sense of national identity. State Shinto combined Imperial Shinto, which centred on the rites of the Imperial household, and Shrine Shinto, which consisted of the many shrines around the country. Its rites supported the emperor system, its priests were involved in national teaching campaigns and its shrines became a conduit between the centre and the periphery of the modern Japanese political landscape.

One example of the impact of the creation of State Shinto on the religious life of ordinary Japanese can be seen in the shrine merger policy implemented between 1906 and 1912.[21] Here state policy regarding shrines dovetailed with other state policies such as the Local Improvement Campaign. The state sought to integrate local shrines into a system of national shrines and, thereby, to turn local people into citizens of the nation. This necessitated the merger of many local shrines. The mergers coincided with new administrative districts. The shrine merger policy met with significant local resistance as shrine members fought to preserve local sacred identities, much as attacks against Buddhist temples had met with opposition at the local level from lay members who sought to save their temples, which had become caretakers of the ancestors.

From this rich soil of Temple Buddhist traditions, modernity, and the turmoil caused by State Shinto, not only did a 'new Buddhism' blossom but a monumental shift in religious culture occurred. The Meiji, Taisho and Showa eras saw the rise of new lay Buddhist movements and new religions. One early example of this is Reiyūkai, which was founded in 1925. Reiyūkai became the parent of many other Buddhist lay movements, including Risshō Kōseikai, which grew to become a much larger organisation than its parent. 'Reiyūkai's uniqueness lies in its combination of Lotus Sutra faith and ancestor veneration.'[22] Reiyūkai removed the priesthood of Temple Buddhism as mediator between families and their ancestors. Moreover, in recognising the changing structures of the modern Japanese family, Reiyūkai emphasised that the ancestors of both the husband and wife should be venerated at the home alter. These changes were maintained in its offshoots such as Risshō Kōseikai, which today claims six million adherents worldwide.

Buddhist lay movements were not the only new religions to arise in the modern period, indeed, religions claiming roots in Shinto and Christianity also appeared in great numbers with a similar emphasis on ancestor veneration and lay leadership. New religions and lay movements such as Reiyūkai flourished briefly during the Meiji and Taisho periods only to be suppressed during Japan's Pacific War. Following the end of hostilities and the Occupation of Japan in 1945, new religions once again grew in number. Today they claim tens of millions of followers worldwide and are a powerful force in Japanese society and politics.

Shimazono describes the relationship of the new religions and modernity as follows:

> The modernization process dissolved traditional communal social bonds. In the process, people began searching anew for a clear intellectual symbol of the ties between themselves and others, and between themselves and nature; these were ties that had been evident until that time. Such symbols became one type of support for people who were adapting to modern social relationships. This . . . can be identified as an intellectual question existing at the most fundamental level of human life. Japanese vitalistic thought, of which the populace was the principle bearer, attempted to answer this most fundamental intellectual problem of the people who were in direct confrontation with modernization.[23]

Vitalism stresses salvation in this life. Shimazono identifies 'vitalistic thought' as the core of much of modern Japanese religious culture.

Vitalistic thought is understood to be common to most religions in Japan today, both new and old, and to have its roots in what Yasumaru Yoshio identifies as 'the philosophy of heart' or common moral values developed during the 18th century. These values include sincerity, thankfulness and frugality and formed the core of the values later adopted by the Meiji government for use in mandatory ethics classes taught in the new compulsory education system, thus assuring that they became widespread and identified with a 'timeless' Japanese culture. The education system served to flatten out regional difference and had as one of its goals the creation of a Japanese identity based on these now shared 'common' values. Vitalistic thought underlies and overlaps these 'common' value sets, and understanding it is the key to understanding modern Japanese religion.

Shimazono outlines several characteristics that describe the vitalistic concept of salvation. Though Shimazono and Tsushima Michihito derive the concept of vitalistic salvation from the study of new religions, it can be seen within the teachings and practices of modern Temple Buddhism and

Shinto as well. Key characteristics include the following: (1) a view of the cosmos as a life-force possessed of everlasting fertility in which humans participate; (2) a primary religious being conceived of as the 'source of life'; (3) humans as born of the source of life and as 'tributaries of the Life-Source'; (4) 'salvation as the growth and efflorescence of life in this world'; (5) evil and suffering as stemming from the severing of the connection to the life-source; (6) salvation as reconnecting to that life-force; and (7) the saved state as being one of bliss and joy in this very life.[24] Robert Kisala (and elsewhere Helen Hardacre) describes a worldview that is helpful in understanding how Shimazono and Tsushima's vitalistic salvation might be enacted upon:

> The world is seen as an interconnected whole, and activity on one level will affect other levels. Therefore, a transformation on the most immediate level of the inner self will have repercussions within one's family, the surrounding society and eventually on the universe as a whole. Consequently, emphasis is placed on individual self-cultivation, centering on the virtues of thankfulness, sincerity and harmony.[25]

In this worldview, individuals are empowered to change their lives through self-cultivation. The details of cultivation vary from religion to religion. In some forms of Buddhism, for example, cultivation may occur through ritual practice (fire ceremonies, meditation retreats) or through the embodying of Buddhist moral codes through precept practice in daily life, whereas in some Shinto schools cultivation may take place through purification rites.

Ian Reader and George Tanabe's study of contemporary Japanese Buddhism, *Practically Religious*, echoes Shimazono's work.[26] Here Reader and Tanabe assert that the 'common religion' of Japan is that of worldly benefits integrally tied to the moral life of the practitioner. This 'common religion' has roots that extend centuries into the past but is particularly relevant today. Japanese religion, Reader and Tanabe conclude, is focused on this life and the palpable benefits – physical, emotional and spiritual – of practice. Common practices seen today include praying for success in school entrance exams and purchasing amulets to hang in cars to ward off traffic accidents.

In a similar vein, Reader elsewhere emphasises the 'primacy of action' as an explanation for the continued importance of religion in contemporary Japan. Situations demand actions that in turn express religiosity.[27] As Winston Davis notes, the criteria of believer versus non-believer is not easily applied to Japan, where praxis and feeling 'are the primary indicators of Japanese religious behaviour.'[28] Shimazono, Reader and Tanabe's work moves us far beyond simplistic explanations such as crisis theory for the rise of new religions and the continued relevance of Temple Buddhism and other so-called 'traditional' religions. The rise of new religions in Japan had long been tied to several moments of crisis in the modern period, such as Japan's defeat in the Pacific War, but as the work of these scholars demonstrates, the lasting influence and continued vitality of Japanese religion can best be understood through concepts such as vitalistic salvation and the primacy of action.

This model of religious practice remains relevant today, yet there have been significant changes since the 1970s. Whereas the new religious movements of the prewar and early postwar period, as well as Temple Buddhism and Shinto, tended to focus on the moral values made common during the Meiji period and the 'traditional' family and community structures that lay at the heart of those values, the movements that began in the 1970s, often called by the unwieldy term 'new new religions' (*shinshinshūkyō*), shifted the focus of practice. New new religions tend to be urban in focus, centred on a young membership, and concentrated on the individual rather than the group or family. Whereas new religions stress communal sharing of experiences and group counselling-like sessions, the new new religions emphasise personal transformation and individual practice. One marked difference between the new and the new new religions is the often pessimistic outlook of the new new religions. As can be seen within the vitalistic concept of salvation, the new religions have a very positive worldview in which salvation is possible through the efforts of the individual and where salvation can take place in this life. Moreover, such religions have taken the positive view that salvation is possible for all of humanity through the application of their practices. By contrast, new new religions tend to be shaped by a sense of impending doom. They do not all necessarily espouse an apocalyptic doctrine but the view that the world will meet its end in the not-too-distant future is not uncommon. This end is often envisioned as coming about at the hands of humans either through nuclear, biological or environmental disaster.

Diversity and variation

As we have seen, some of the most dramatic changes that took place in the modern period stem from efforts on the part of the state to control diversity, to create a notion of sameness and/or to control the powerful influence of religion in the lives of its citizens. But what is even clearer is that despite the great efforts of the state to control religion during the modern period, religion has remained as diversely practised as ever. It is often said that Japan is a homogeneous country, but even a cursory examination of Japan's religions proves this to be an overly simplistic view. We can observe regional diversity, diversity of gender roles, status and ethnic diversity, and generational diversity. And yet, to borrow from Byron Earhart,[29] there is unity within the diversity, even if that unity is often imagined.

The practice of Japanese religions has long been marked by gender-based role distinctions. As Confucianism, which entered Japan around the 4th century, came to play an increasingly dominant role in Japanese society, the prominent roles women once played in political and religious leadership were greatly diminished. In the modern period, women have often been relegated to behind-the-scenes or subservient roles, with the noticeable exception being in some new religions. In Shinto, women, who once played pivotal roles as active leaders and shamans, now mostly play less prominent performative roles as shrine maidens selling amulets, cleaning the grounds, and performing ritual dances for the deities. Within Buddhism, women are also bound by gendered roles. Nuns undergo similar training as monks, and yet are always in an inferior position within institutional hierarchies (though this is not unique to Japanese Buddhism). Some nuns today argue that their practices as renunciates are more in keeping with tradition than the monks. In particular, they point to clerical marriage and note that only the monks break precepts by marrying.[30] Yet these arguments fall on mostly deaf ears in the male-dominated sectarian hierarchies. Such arguments have also been the source of conflict among those nuns who enter the priesthood and maintain celibacy and those who enter the priesthood married and choose to remain married.

Gendered roles in which women are allocated domestic duties, nurturing and education of the next generation are still the norm. Leaders of the various denominations of Temple Buddhism call upon the wives of priests to support the priest, be a model housewife, produce a male successor and see to the education of the children.[31] Similar roles are espoused by many of the new religions. Hardacre observes a 'clear division of labor and moral responsibility by sex' within the new religion Reiyūkai. Women are encouraged to care for the domestic side of the family, be submissive and support their husband.[32] The new religions of Japan also provide examples of challenges to gendered role division, though these have met with limited success. The founders of Ōmotokyō, for example, practised inverting gender roles. The female leader took on aspects of male identity through her choice of clothing and behaviour just as the male leader did the same with stereotyped female attributes. While this may have had an effect on their ability to lead through projecting certain images, neither leader appears to have expected members to follow suit. Their experimentation with crossing gender boundaries stopped with them.

Religion has also been used to enforce status diversity. The best example of this is the treatment of Japan's once hidden minority, the *burakumin*, at the hands of the priesthood of Temple Buddhism. The Buddhist priesthood systematically discriminated against the *burakumin*. *Burakumin* were given discriminatory posthumous Buddhist names (*kaimyō*). These names singled them out in death as they had been in life and were used by businesses, potential marriage partners and others to determine whether or not a person came from a *burakumin* family. This practice, common across the sects of Temple Buddhism, only ceased in the 1980s.

Since the 1970s, Japanese religious culture has added new and diverse layers. We have already discussed the new and new new religions. To these we must add the new spirituality movements.

> From the point of view of these new spirituality movements, earlier religions with their hardened doctrines and institutional forms have restricted individuals and prevented them from realising their full spiritual potential.[33]

As noted at the outset of this chapter, the very definition of religion is contested in Japan. People involved in these movements tend to shy away from the term 'religion', which to them implies moribund institutions, in favour of 'spirituality'.[34] These movements share connections with the past just as the new religions do, but emphasise individual transformation of consciousness over institutionalised ritual and doctrine. The links to the larger religious/spiritual milieu, the unity within the diversity, can be seen in an emphasis on communication with divine beings, identification with leading religious practitioners of the past and active participation in the intellectual debates of their time.[35]

Another area in which we find the theme of unity and diversity played out in modern Japan is ancestor veneration. Ancestor veneration has been an important aspect of religious practice in Japan for centuries. Like so many other things, the content of ancestor veneration has changed over time even as the general concept has remained in place. In the modern period we see dramatic shifts in ancestor veneration playing out in response to changes in social structure. Moreover, religious practices such as ancestor veneration have themselves encouraged change in social structures. Modern ancestor veneration as conducted in many new religions and more often now in Temple Buddhism as well is marked by the veneration of the ancestors of both the husband and wife. This recognises the shift in household structures away from the extended family and towards the nuclear family. But it also finds its roots in the nationalism of prewar religious groups such as Reiyūkai, which believed that unsaved spirits could not serve to protect the nation.[36] By allowing more ancestors into the practice of each household the protection of the nation was assured.

More recently, as Mark Rowe's work shows, a handful of priests of Temple Buddhism have begun to change how ancestors are venerated.[37] Rowe's study of various associations for burial and memorial clearly demonstrates the changing nature of veneration and the manner it which it affects social structures. Rowe states:

> the two most common forms of relationship or bond (*en*) in Japan are those of blood and locale. What is fascinating to note about some of these burial groups is the way they are appropriating the *en* bond in new ways. The En no Kai offers no modifier for *en*, and becomes thus a "Society of Bonds." The use of the term *shienbyō* by the Society for a Women's Monument consciously modifies *en* by adding "will" or "intent" and thus enabling these women to form new types of bonds. In both cases as well as with other burial societies, the traditionally recognized forms of relations are being dramatically expanded, so that friends, acquaintances, even strangers, may now be buried together and memorialize each other.[38]

Religious culture does not simply reflect larger social trends, it participates in their construction. While the groups Rowe examines are still in the minority, they represent the beginning of a gradual shift in how people memorialise the dead.

It is important to observe and emphasise diversity in order to overcome misleading stereotypes of religious culture, however, it is equally important to understand that to look for the trees while ignoring the forest can create an unbalanced picture of religious life. State Shinto, the spiritual mobilisation campaigns of wartime Japan, compulsory education, the commercialisation of ritual, together with the mass media and increased literacy combine to have a flattening effect on many aspects of Japanese religious life.[39]

Morals education in prewar and wartime Japan, for example, served to propagate a common set of values derived from a variety of sources from Japan's religious heritage. Moreover, just as the Meiji, Taisho and Showa governments used moral education and the cooperation of religious organisations to create a common understanding of Japaneseness and a moral citizenry, successive postwar governments have sought to leverage moral education for these same purposes. All of these attempts appeal to a grounding in 'common' morals derived from religion. Postwar attempts have generally met with poor results, due to powerful opposition from the teachers' unions and the peace movement.

In 1966 the Chūo Kyōiku Shingikai (an advisory council established in 1953 that reports to the Minister of Education) declared that a desirable trait to be cultivated was that of a mind of reverence. The report then explicitly links this trait to religious sentiment (shūkyō jōsō).[40] 'True religious sentiment is [a mind of] reverence towards the source of life, in other words, the divine. Human dignity and love are based on this. A deep sense of gratitude wells forth from this. And, true happiness is based upon this.'[41] This clearly echoes the vitalistic thought discussed above.

In 2002, the Ministry of Education, Sports, Science and Technology (formerly the Ministry of Education) produced the *Kokoro no Nōto* (The Heart and Mind Notebook), a series of supplementary moral education texts for use in public schools across Japan. The focus of these books is fourfold: development of an awareness of self; development of an awareness of one's relationship to others; development of an awareness of one's relationship to the nation; and development of an understanding of one's relationship with nature and the sublime, which is described as 'furthering one's self-awareness through one's relationship with the beautiful and that which is beyond human power.'[42] In short, these books seek to instil a worldview rooted in religious values through the public school curriculum. This continued effort of government leaders has led, over the modern period, to the invention and perpetuation of 'traditional' Japanese values identified as the foundation of Japanese identity. The combined effect has led to a flattening of regional and other differences.

Commercialisation of practices has also had a flattening effect. For example, funerary rites were long the domain of Buddhist priests. Priests were responsible for guiding the grieving family through the ritual process and the customs related to funerals and memorials. As the funeral industry grew, and as national conglomerates bought out local companies, funeral companies came to play many of the roles priests once played. Moreover, economies of scale in production have led to changes in practices as implements required by local custom are phased out by companies that produce for a national market.

Conclusions

Modern Japanese religious culture is in flux. Great change has occurred in practices, institutions and worldviews over the last 100 years. This is not to say that religious culture was static before the modern period, as is often popularly portrayed. The Edo Period (1603–1868) was a time of great change, as political stability came to Japan. Temple Buddhist institutions underwent organisational change, local temples took part in government campaigns to control heterodox religious movements such as Christianity and certain Buddhist sects, and sectarian studies flourished. Confucianism also came to enjoy a place of honour within the Japanese government during the Edo Period. Though the modern period has been one of tremendous change, we would be remiss to assume it was somehow unique in this. To make such an assumption only serves to essentialise the past.

Change in the modern period has most often occurred at least in part through government action. Yet we must not understand this as the heavy hand of a government somehow disconnected from the rest of society. Government action, whether it was the disassociation of Buddhism and Shinto, the creation of State Shinto, the suppression of new religions, or the implementation of heart and mind education, did not take place in a vacuum. It could only occur through a process of negotiation between various factions within government, the input of competing religious groups, the voices of local leaders and the power of local traditions.

The modern period has also witnessed the creation of common value sets identified as the core of Japanese identity and the development of a shared vitalistic worldview. Both of these have come to be viewed as timeless traditions. Despite the pervasiveness of these, we already see within the new new religions and the new spirituality movements a shift away from these 'timeless traditions' and towards a new model based on individual practices. It remains to be seen what the 21st century will bring to Japanese religious culture, but change is inevitable.

Notes

1. See, for example, Shimazono (2004); Nobutaka Inoue (1991); Ishii (1997); Jaffe (2001); Hardacre (1997); Reader and Tanabe (1998); Davis (1992).
2. For a general introduction to the religions of Japan see Earhart (1982) and Ellwood (2007).
3. Vlastos (1998).
4. Vlastos (1998: 3).
5. Jonathan Z Smith (1998: 269).
6. Jonathan Z Smith (1998: 281).
7. Jonathan Z Smith (1998: 269).
8. Hardacre (1986: 7–9).
9. See, for example, Shimazono and Tsuroka (2004).
10. Covell and Rowe (2004). See also Sharf (1995: 417–58).
11. Covell and Rowe (2004: 246).
12. Covell and Rowe (2004: 247); Ivy (1995).
13. Grapard (1984: 240–65).
14. Ketelaar (1990).
15. Hardacre (1984).
16. Shimazono (2004).
17. See Jaffe (2001).
18. See Covell (2005).
19. Ketelaar (1990: x).
20. Many thanks to Sarah Horton for sharing her ideas on this at the American Academy of Religion annual conference in 2007.
21. Fridell (1973).
22. *The Lotus Sutra* is a Buddhist sacred text that is one of the most popular such texts in East Asia (Shimazono, 2004: 78).
23. Shimazono (2004: 51); Tsushima, Nishiyama, Shimazono and Shiramizu (1979: 139–61).
24. Shimazono (2004: 123–4).
25. Kisala (1999: 3).
26. Reader and Tanabe (1998).
27. Reader (1991: 15).
28. Davis (1992: 236).
29. Earhart (1982).
30. See Arai (1999). Nuns are permitted to marry but few choose to do so.
31. See Covell (2005).
32. Hardacre (1984: 196–7).
33. Shimazono (2004: 233).
34. Shimazono (2004: 275).
35. Shimazono (2004: 278).
36. Shimazono (2004: 78).
37. Rowe (2006).
38. Rowe (2003: 112–13).
39. See, for example, Shimazono (2004: 174).
40. Sugawara (1997: 9).
41. Sugawara (1997: 9).

42. Tetsuji Itō (2004: 8). The phrase *'Ningen no chikara wo koeta mono'* (that which is beyond human power) is used directly within the *'Kokoro no Nōto'* series, see for example, Ministry of Education (ed.) (2002).

Further reading

Reader, Ian (1991), *Religion in Contemporary Japan*, Honolulu: University of Hawai'i Press.

Reader, Ian, and George Tanabe (1998), *Practically Religious: Worldly Benefits and the Common Religion of Japan*, Honolulu: University of Hawai'i Press.

Shimazono, Susumu (2004), *From Salvation to Spirituality: Popular Religious Movements in Modern Japan*, Melbourne: Trans Pacific Press.

9

Political culture

The debate over Japanese political culture

Political culture is defined as a set of memories and identities, norms and values, beliefs and preferences, and practices and habits present in a certain community of people.[1] Thus defined, political culture is a patterned approach to thinking about politics. Politics, in turn, is defined as who gets what, when and how,[2] or as the authoritative allocation of values.[3] In this way political culture is shaped and shared by a certain group of people with common memories and experiences.

This chapter will first focus on Japanese political culture in terms of variations and diversity. Key themes include social capital, pacifism, authoritarianism, postmodernism and political ideologies. Sociological attributes by which variations are assessed include region, generation, class and uncertainty. The chapter will then outline a very long-term view of change in Japanese political culture since the late medieval period, focusing on a few noted artists in terms of individualist and collectivist orientations. Since collectivism is widely regarded as a key component of modern Japanese political culture, historically contextualising collectivism in Japanese society is a task of high importance. Further, comparisons will be made between Japan's political culture and that of other countries, most notably those of East and South-East Asia and Western Europe, using the survey data of the AsiaBarometer Survey[4] and the Asia-Europe Survey.[5] The study of modern Japanese political culture has often been conducted either holistically in reference to various features of Japanese nature, history, society, economy and politics or in implicit comparison to what Western authors regard as Western political culture. It is very important to situate modern Japanese political culture in systematic comparison to non-Japanese political cultures, near or far. The thematic foci of these comparative surveys are: citizens' identity, trust and satisfaction vis-à-vis the state and family values. Finally, two cautionary remarks about the study of political culture will be presented.

Variations and diversity of Japanese political culture

Japanese society is often said to be based on the relative homogeneity of culture. The immense variations that exist, but which are not easily detected in part because of methodological difficulties, are often forgotten. The regional variations of social capital or trust in interpersonal relations, for instance, from prefecture to prefecture or from city to city, are not well surveyed.[6] Yet the pattern of regional distribution of *oreore sagi* (money extraction through telephone scams) is rather revealing. *Oreore sagi* involves a telephone call from a deceiver informing his/her victim that, for example, their child hit someone with a car, that the deceiver represents the injured party's interests, and that the victim must immediately deposit a certain amount of money into the following bank account to resolve the case. Osaka, the centre of the Kansai region, is known as one of the regions where *oreore sagi* takes place least in Japan. People in Osaka apparently tend to be most cautious and suspicious, and tend to believe the adage that 'one cannot be too careful in dealing with people' rather than adopting the attitude that 'on the whole one can trust people'.[7] Robert Putnam's[8] intra-nation comparison between southern and northern-central Italy might well be made between the regions of Kansai and Kanto.

Variations among generations are also extensive. The major line of demarcation can be drawn between those schooled prior to 1945 and those thereafter. The former generation retains a strong preference for pacifism and anti-authoritarianism, while the latter tends to be politically more placid and compliant. Taking advantage of the increasing demographic dominance of generations who did not experience the Second World War, former Prime Minister Shinzo Abe strove to implement policies that would mark new departures from the postwar regime, an approach largely designed to overcome what he regards as excessive pacifism and anti-authoritarianism, two negative syndromes coming out of the experience and memory of the Second World War.[9] Within the postwar group, the schooling of the demographically densest groups born in the immediate post-1945 years and those thereafter is so different that they show contrasting orientations. The former group, the so-called *dankai* (a massive demographic cluster), exhibits strong energy and enthusiasm in their activities, whereas those born thereafter tend to be quiet and cool. For much of the 1945–65 period, primary schools accommodated on average 60 pupils per class, compared to the current average of 30 to 40 pupils per class. In the former situation, competition for food and friends was severe among pupils and extended, among other areas, into the examination process and athletic activities. The post-1965 groups that grew up in an affluent Japan do not show a similar level of 'hungry spirit'.

One of the areas where generational disparities are least pronounced is post-materialism, characterised by a lifestyle that stresses such values as individual freedom, gender equality, ecological harmony, a social safety net and social justice. Citizens have passed the stage of materialism where survival overrides all other considerations and have moved on to the stage of post-materialism where lifestyle is key to their satisfaction. The transition from materialism to post-materialism was slow and steady. Joji Watanuki[10] reports that compared to the preference for pacifism and anti-authoritarianism, generational differences regarding post-materialism were indistinct. In other words, the degree to which the post-materialist lifestyle permeated Japan does not exhibit large generational differences.

Variations among classes are no less noteworthy. In the 1945–75 period, class differences mattered.[11] In terms of political ideology, those highly educated, those belonging to unions, and those residing in metropolitan areas tended to be on the left, whereas those poorly educated, those possessing their own land and rice paddies, shops and factories, and those residing in non-metropolitan areas tended to be on the right. The ideological left signifies pacifism, union rights, anti-alliance and anti-patriotism, whereas the ideological right indicates self-defence, free enterprise, pro-alliance and patriotism. The Allied Powers' Occupation led to the expansion of the right-wing political parties, which later merged to become the Liberal Democratic Party with farmers and shop and factory owners as its support base. The Occupation reforms also helped to expand the left-wing parties supported by unionists, citizen groups, intellectuals and pacifists, mainly based in cities. At the parliamentary level, this dichotomy was conducive to the consolidation of the so-called 1955 system in which the LDP governed uninterruptedly until 1993 and the Japan Socialist Party had to put up with their semi-permanent major opposition party status.

From the mid-1970s onwards, the patterns changed somewhat. Union membership drastically decreased. Owners of land, rice paddies, shops and factories also dramatically reduced in number. In addition, the per capita income level increased significantly. This configuration created what is called the all-inclusionary middle class mass phenomenon[12] of the 1975–90 period. All these factors have made the left–right distinction less pronounced in politics and in terms of political support in voting and other types of political participation.[13] What was then called the new middle mass (*shin chūkan taishū*) became far more stratified. Although the class-based distinction between left-wing and right-wing ideologies have been moderated immensely, collectivist and authoritarian values on the one hand and social and economic networks on the other have remained two key factors that determine party support patterns during this period.

Between 1990 and the present, as part of the tide of globalisation generating the extremities of rich and poor, income gaps have increased significantly, elevating the Japanese GINI index to be among the highest in the Organization for Economic Cooperation and Development group.[14] A new class of 'working poor' has sprung up, and concerns about both their health and wealth have intensified.[15] Furthermore, there is a steady rise in the 'personalization of politics'[16] characterised by: (1) the increasing importance of politicians' personal appeal; (2) the growing emphasis on popular catch phrases and slogans, as disseminated by mass media and the internet; (3) the declining weight of political parties as mobilising forces and focal points of politics; and (4) the decreasing significance of national bureaucracies.[17] It seems that uncertainty is the key variable here. There are two types of voters: those facing uncertainty and risk with a modicum of optimism, on the one hand, and those hesitant to move forward, on the other. Old social and economic networks and collectivist authoritarian value preferences do remain important, but increasingly less so. This phenomenon is not confined to Japan, but is observable globally. Not only Tony Blair and Silvio Berlusconi, but also Shinawatra Thaksin and Junichirō Koizumi are the embodiment and therefore the vindication of the personalisation of politics. In tandem, political culture transforms.

Cultural change since the Meiji era

Given that the debate over Japanese political culture centres upon competing emphases on collectivism and individualism, it is useful to glimpse these shifting emphases in a brief analysis of the work of four Japanese representative artists. The artists to be discussed are Ikkyū Sojun, Chikamatsu Monzaemon, Natsume Sōseki and Murakami Haruki.

Ikkyū was a Buddhist monk and a poet in the 16th century. Many of his poems feature the theme of falling in love with nuns. His emotions and preferences were eloquently expressed in poems, none of which exhibit a hint of collectivism. He was writing at a time of individualism. During the medieval and warring periods, what mattered most was individualism. For warriors what was of importance was what Ikegami[18] calls 'honorific individualism'. For artists at Kyoto what mattered was art-tested civility.[19] Honorific individualism is a type of mental and cultural orientation that places self-esteem at the height of one's judgment and that stresses self-reliance or one's own capacity to defend this orientation. Art-tested civility is a form of mental and cultural orientation that singles out high-level artistic sophistication on the basis of one's own endeavours. During this era, divorce was common, and was often initiated by wives.

Chikamatsu, a novelist for the masses, had amassed his wealth and secured his position by the early 18th century. The early modern society of Japan was a mix of decentralisation akin to medieval societies and centralisation akin to modern societies. At the height of the Tokugawa family's reign, it permitted, except in the areas of defence, diplomacy, and external commerce, near autonomy to 300-odd domains. Yet the tide of centralisation in the form of tighter control over differences in social status steadily permeated Tokugawa society. From this point comes the key motif of Chikamatsu novels: Protagonists torn between social obligations and human sentiments. The former collectivist motive often overrode the latter individualist one. The only way to avoid the dilemma was *shinjū*, or double suicide by the lovers.

Sōseki, a novelist of the late 19th and early 20th centuries, was a professor of English. During his studies in London he was depressed by his new environment. Back in Japan, he was intermittently depressed for one reason or another. He wrote novels essentially about the inner private self. Only when he was writing about this inner private self, did he feel at ease. Novels prevailing during the increasingly centralist state penetration were called *shishōsetsu*, or I-novels. Sōseki can be called a state-suppressed individualist who immersed himself in the inner private self.

Murakami, a novelist of the late 20th and early 21st centuries, writes about his inner cosmos. Characters who appear in his novels enjoy encountering others in cosy settings. The active movements of memory of others and sentiments associated with them are key themes. The leitmotif of his novels preceded the neuroscientific discovery of the 'monkey-see, monkey-do' theory in which the monkey sees a human subject's movement and its memory is activated causing its muscles to move.[20] His characters are all individualist par excellence. They are interested in the inner self, but they are also open and associate with others. That is one of the reasons why Murakami's novels are bestsellers almost everywhere in the world.

As these artists – each of whom typifies their era – show, culture is not a fixed matter. In a sense, it is a complex and living collection of people's memories and habits. Over the centuries people change. Since collectivism is fairly firmly regarded as a key feature in the study of modern Japanese political culture, it is very important to understand collectivism (and individualism) over a long time span. Furthermore, as collectivism (along with authoritarianism) is a key component of modern Japanese political culture, its importance and the need to understand it across long-term political changes in Japanese society cannot be overemphasised.

To see more clearly how Japanese cultural change occurred in the last few centuries, a comparison between Tokugawa Japan (1603–1867) and Elizabethan England will be useful. The late medieval days of the warring period in Japan exhibited extreme individualism because hereditary status and class differences came to naught when competition was cut-throat. Strength was what mattered. The early modern period of Tokugawa brought some order and the tide of centralisation. But Tokugawa Japan, which was highly decentralised, was unlike Tudor England under Elizabeth, which exhibited absolutism, the highest degree of the will to centralise or concentrate power.[21] In Tokugawa Japan, the Tokugawa family allowed a large degree of autonomy to 300-odd domains. It was a bit like federalism, with the Tokugawa handling defence, diplomacy and external commerce. All the domains were autonomous as far as domestic politics were concerned.[22] In England, absolutism was maintained under the Tudors and the succeeding Stuart dynasty as well, although the monarchy faced increasing challenges from parliament and other social forces. These challenges forced absolutism to steadily transform itself in the direction of liberalism and democracy over subsequent centuries. In Japan, the Tokugawa Shogunate consolidated this quasi-federal system until the advent of the Western challenge.

Yet the Japanese response to this challenge did not result in an extreme concentration of power in the Emperor. When the Meiji Restoration occurred, the class distinction separating warriors, artisans, merchants and peasants was abolished. Most warriors were dismissed and channelled into state service jobs within the government. Those without jobs became politicians, businessmen or journalists. The way in which this bureaucratic recruitment took place was to reconstruct a quasi-federal system at the

height of the new central government in Japan in the mid and late 19th century. Ministries recruited bureaucrats, often on the basis of domains. Once
the government was set up and ministries had selected ministers, the ministers then recruited like-minded ex-warriors from their home domains. To
consolidate their power, each bureaucratic agency was quasi-autonomous.
Thus the Army was largely drawn from the Chōshū domain, and the Navy
from the Satsuma domain. Police were often from the Higo and Aizu-
Wakamatsu domains, while the Accounting Office was primarily drawn
from the Hizen domain. The Meiji Restoration repeated what the Pax Toku-
gawana had achieved, that is, the containment and retention of decentralised
power within the regime. Thus the Meiji Constitution gave an enormous
amount of power to each bureaucratic agency by the veto rights accorded to
each cabinet minister on all cabinet decisions. The prime minister remained
only slightly more than a *primus inter pares*. However, the state-society
relationship was extremely centralised. Each bureaucratic agency had its
local bureaus through which its policy action was implemented. Therefore
the picture of modern Japan was complex. At the height of the central government, power was fragmented and decentralised. Yet each bureaucratic
agency maintained its centralised power right down to the ground level.
Under this regime, collectivism progressed, with state power being visible
and tangible at the community level.

Two examples may be used to illustrate the absence of absolutist culture
in Japanese politics.[23] The first case refers to the situation which started in
September 2007, when Prime Minister Shinzō Abe was hospitalised immediately after he announced his resignation. He remained there for the ensuing two weeks without appointing an acting prime minister. This led the
Financial Times to comment that Japan might be governed without a prime
minister.[24] The second example can be taken from the way in which the
succeeding Prime Minister, Yasuo Fukuda, adopted a low-key posture vis-
à-vis the major opposition party, the Democratic Party of Japan, which held
a majority in the House of Councillors. To reactivate the Law of Supply-
ing Petroleum to fighter aircraft of the United States, the United Kingdom
and Pakistan in their war against terror in Afghanistan, set to expire on
31 October 2007, Fukuda could have legislated, as prescribed in the Constitution, a revised law that extended the deadline by passing it twice in
the House of Representatives, where the Liberal Democratic Party held a
comfortable majority. He did not. Instead, he waited about two months
during which he made an overture to Ichirō Ozawa, the Opposition leader,
to form a grand coalition between the Liberal Democratic Party and the

Democratic Party of Japan. After Ozawa was blocked from forming a grand coalition by seven lieutenants in his own party, Fukuda proceeded to pass a revised law by passing it twice in the House of Representatives, immediately after the House of Councillors said nay to it. Fukuda did not legislate a revised law immediately on ascension to power, although its legislation was urgently needed for the Japanese government to demonstrate its strong commitment to the US alliance. These two examples provide a glimpse of the lack of an absolutist legacy in Japan.

The Japanese pattern shows a stark contrast with England, where absolutism was consolidated. It was challenged, and yet state power – whether an absolutist monarch or a parliamentary umbrella – remained solid, as Michael Mann shows so vividly.[25] In Japan, the floundering of the first absolutist attempt seems to have determined the nature of the regime for a surprisingly long period of time. Following the Tokugawa regime's quasi-federal system, the Meiji regime concentrated its power vis-à-vis society, but at the height of the regime state power was fragmented and decentralised with each bureaucratic agency retaining its autonomy. The new Showa regime after 1945 did not change the overall picture of central control over society and of power fragmentation and power sharing at the top of the government. The centralisation of power to the state was reduced only gradually by the increased introduction of the market and the accommodation of its liberalising and globalising influences, especially in the Heisei period from 1988 to the present. The continuous existence of a quasi-federal system seems to make regime change less dramatic to political life in Japan.

Cultural change in politics took place in a particular fashion: from the barefoot individualism of the late 16th century to moderate collectivism during the gradual consolidation of central control in the early 18th century; to further modern collectivism under the Meiji and Showa governments, peaking in the mid-20th century; and to new collectivism under the new Constitution of the late Showa regime, peaking in 1991; then, finally, to the gradual individualism of Heisei Japan from 1988 onwards. In a sense Japanese culture is extraordinarily like a sponge: absorbing environmental and exogenous stimuli and transforming itself accordingly. The above shifts from individualism to collectivism of many kinds and currently back towards individualism exemplify this process. The transition from late medieval to early modern, from early modern to modern, and from modern to postmodern periods in Japan did not seem to be drastic or earth shaking. Thus, one can say that the absence of absolutism in Japan seems to give more continuity to Japanese cultural change.[26]

Portraying Japanese political culture as observed in the 1930s through the 1950s and branding it as the authoritative, eternal version of Japanese political culture is a little excessive.[27] Some noted political culture studies stem from the selective fixation on the observations made during this period, ranging from Kunio Yanagida, Ruth Benedict and Masao Maruyama to Chie Nakane.

International comparison of Japan's political culture

Organising the myriad threads of political culture in an international context is a daunting task. This section deals mostly with those propositions that have been systematically and empirically tested with a significant number of observations. Many theories on modern Japanese political culture have been presented without empirical foundations, and this tendency has contributed to the blossoming of unfounded *nihonjinron* (debates on the key features of Japanese and Japanese culture). The ensuing discussion endeavours to consciously conduct a 'reality-check' on a number of propositions about modern Japanese political culture and to restrict itself to those propositions that are related to the linkage between citizens and the state.[28] After all, this chapter deals with *political* culture.

Identity, trust and satisfaction

How one relates to the nation/state is one of the key questions underlying political culture. What is the individual citizen's primary identity? In other words, when people think about themselves, what do they think makes them truly themselves? Or what do they think resonates especially well with them? It is not surprising to see that some 20 per cent of respondents in the Asia-Europe Survey selected the 'don't know' category. Why? It may be because Japanese are hesitant to answer questions that do not contain some concrete and contextual information.[29] It may be because they really do not know what to say about their primary identity. It is a small surprise, however, to see that of all 18 countries surveyed, nine in Asia and nine in Europe, the Japanese respondents scored the lowest percentage in identifying themselves with their country, Japan. It seems that Japanese are intrinsically hesitant to identify themselves with the state/nation. Reasons vary from one person to another, an obvious one perhaps being their strong pacifism. The state that brought its citizens sacrifice and humiliation during the war cannot be easily pardoned. This is why the decision to have the Japan Maritime Self-Defense Forces fuel the military aircraft for the

Afghan war efforts of the United States, the United Kingdom and Pakistan on the Indian Ocean is not viewed very positively, even though it is the safest and most cost-effective cooperation Japan could undertake in the implementation of the Afghan war. Further, Japanese do not seem to want to place much confidence in the state for another reason. Whenever a prime minister has expressed the possibility of a consumption tax hike, he has faced close to 100 per cent chance of being forced to resign because citizens are vehemently adamant about this issue; at least they have been during the 1978–2007 period.[30] After all, the state had eliminated all government bonds by 1945. More recently the Social Insurance Agency pocketed some of the insurer's pension payments.[31] Popular distrust in this bureaucratic agency is registered as high, for obvious reasons. If distrust in a bureaucratic agency is so high, one cannot envisage citizens identifying strongly with the state/nation. They remain hesitant in this regard.

What about other identities? Asian identity is obviously an interesting question to pose. Like national identity, Asian identity is not very strong in Japan in comparison to other Asian states, such as the Philippines, Thailand and South Korea.[32] Japanese have ambiguous feelings about Asia. It is somewhat like English difficulties in placing England on the same level as the European continent. In an extreme sense, expressions such as, 'fogs over the channel isolated Europe', is broadly accepted in England.[33] Japanese acknowledge their civilizational debts to the Asian continent since time immemorial. Yet they feel that keeping the relationship at arm's length might be the best and safest approach to take.

In close relation to this ambivalence about Japan's Asian identity, two partially competing ideas exist on how Japan posits itself in the world. The maritime and commercial school of thought argues that it is best for Japan to be part of the maritime coalition in the Pacific and beyond, because Japan's survival depends on the defence of the free sea and free trade. In contrast, the continental and neighbourly school of thought argues that Japan is part and parcel of Asia and its survival cannot be separated from it for defence and commercial reasons. In surveys conducted on this issue over many years, 60 per cent of respondents supported the former view and 40 per cent supported the latter, if the 'don't know' and 'other' responses are omitted.[34] Islamic countries, like Indonesia and Malaysia, are torn in a way between Islamic and Asian identity. Normally, Islamic identity is chosen after national identity and Asian identity comes in third place. Culturally, Chinese societies, like Taiwan and Hong Kong, show ambivalence as to whether cultural Chineseness comes first or second in the hierarchy of identification. Singaporeans are largely untroubled by their predominantly cultural Chineseness. At any rate, of the Asian countries that do not have 'cultural Chinese' or Islamic identity, Japan has the lowest percentages in the Asian identity category.

Shifting away from identity with the state/nation, we move to issues of confidence/trust. Do the Japanese have confidence in the state and its institutions? The empirical findings show that their confidence in the state is not high. The two major reasons for their relatively low confidence have been touched on above: wars brought about humiliation and disaster; wars devastated livelihoods. The majority of Japanese do not want to be involved in wars again. That is why Japanese sent troops to Iraq only after President Bush declared victory in that country. It is also the reason that the main opposition party opposes the legislation on fuelling US and UK aircraft on the Indian Ocean. State taxation is visibly detested, whether it is personal income tax, consumption tax, local residence tax or legal entity tax. As noted above, a prime minister has a good chance of being forced to resign if he/she proposes a tax hike. Since Japanese citizens have continued to say 'no' to increased taxation, the government has accumulated an astronomical amount of deficit. Although Japanese are hesitant to place their money *in toto* for use by the state, they are not necessarily hesitant to keep their money in postal savings accounts, the world's largest savings account. Nor are they hesitant to purchase Japanese government bonds en masse.

What about the Japanese public's confidence in government institutions? Their pattern of confidence is not very different from other Asian citizens or, for that matter, from that of European citizens. First, publics in these countries exhibit a high level of confidence in the police and the military (in this order in Asia, and in the reverse order in Europe). In terms of confidence, public institutions come next, where recruitment is meritocratic and assigned tasks are technocratic. These institutions embody the legal and court system and government agencies. At the bottom, in terms of degree of confidence, the Japanese place democratic institutions: political parties and the parliament. This pattern of confidence is more or less universal.[35] Only the position of mass media, big business and international institutions varies from country to country. While Japan is no exception to this pattern, it may represent an extreme case of low confidence in democratically elected politicians and parliament. The six-month period of disarray of the Japanese government under Prime Minister Abe and his statement that he resigned from his office because of illness, led one, at least, to joke that in Japan the state might have withered away as Karl Marx predicted long, long ago. Akio

Kawato[36] argues that instead of coercion and legislation, communitarianism of a kind different from that envisioned by Marx might have prevailed in Japan. Irrespective of the vacuum of power at the highest level of the government, Japan seems to sail on serenely.

What about citizens' satisfaction with the state? Are they satisfied with its performance? The Japanese state boasts a great combination of achievements, such as the zero combat death of soldiers, the meticulous rise from a country devastated and lying in ashes to a country ranked number two for GNP in the world, and the miraculous transformation of the military-led authoritarianism of the war period to the mature democracy of the last 60 years. Yet, Japanese citizens are generally somewhat hesitant to praise the state and sceptical of its achievements.[37]

One seemingly strong answer to the question as to whether Japanese are satisfied is a post-materialist response.[38] Since lifestyle differs from one person to another, their degree of satisfaction depends on a myriad of factors and circumstances in which they find themselves. They may be most interested in their performance in their senior golf club's contest. Their happiness may come from seeing their grandchildren from afar. At any rate, they belong to the same club of not particularly satisfied peoples among the rich men's clubs of South Korea, Taiwan and Luxembourg.

Aside from the overall satisfaction with the state's performance, citizens are area-specific about their satisfaction. Not unexpectedly, many are attentive to domestic policies, especially social policy. They are not very satisfied with the state's policy on pensions, medical insurance, welfare, metropolitan-local income gap and gender equality. Nor are they satisfied with education, crime and corruption. Japanese are divided about foreign policy in that some are positive about sending troops abroad while others are not. The same can be said about the issue of Constitutional revision.[39]

Family values

Family values constitute one of the key components of modern Japanese political culture, as they are closely related to political authoritarianism. There are many threads that make up the composite picture of Japanese family values.[40] Still, these threads can be grouped into 'sets' of values. There is a 'traditional' set of values that includes such principles as filial piety, honesty, diligence, harmony, modesty, achievement, integrity and humbleness. Ruth Benedict added authoritarianism to this list. Thus, blind compliance to authoritarian-crafted consensus and excessive cults of guilt among groups are often said to be inculcated in families, the bastion of Japanese traditional values and virtues. However, the 'modern' set of Japanese family values and virtues seems to depart from tradition to a considerable extent. Most emphasised among the qualities that parents seek to nurture at home is mindfulness (*omoiyari* and *yasashisa*). This could be translated as tolerance, benevolence, thoughtfulness and care. *Omoiyari* stands above all other desirable qualities among Japanese respondents by 60 per cent.

This response makes Japanese unusual among East Asian respondents. Respondents from China, South Korea, Taiwan, Vietnam, Singapore and Hong Kong more or less uniformly depict the following three qualities as priorities at home: self-strength (self-standing, self-sustainability), diligence and honesty. All three qualities concern the self, not other social beings. Although honesty is also about relations with others, here it primarily means being honest to oneself. One must survive and stand alone. Conversely, Japanese respondents single out mindfulness or *omoiyari*. This quality concerns others in society. It may suggest that Japanese are more post-materialist, whereas other East Asians show the tenacious nature of materialism in which survival is the key virtue. Further, among the other East Asians there are many varieties of responses. In addition to the East Asian trinity of self-strength, diligence and honesty, South Korean respondents place more emphasis on deference to their elders than the rest; Vietnamese respondents give more weight to compliance than the rest; and Taiwanese, Singaporean and Hong Kong respondents exhibit more variety than the rest.

Related to family values is the authoritarian vision of pupils in the classroom. This view tends to portray Japanese pupils as obedient, compliant, consensual and deferential. A comparative study of school classrooms by Merry White[41] reveals quite vividly that Japanese children are characterised by a mix of cooperation and consensus on the one hand, and competition and intervention on the other. The latter is no less significant. Once guidance is given, pupils often take good initiatives. The style of running classrooms and the way in which teaching is conducted may also take into account this type of cultural difference.

A good example may be the American style of learning English (e.g. a subject is posed by a teacher and the debate is conducted, more or less freely). This method sometimes baffles some East Asian students; many of them do not necessarily ask questions, and many of them do not necessarily volunteer answers to teacher's questions. They expect the teacher to first provide careful and rich instructions on how to go about formulating an answer. If this level of instruction is provided, the pupils achieve quite a lot. One of the applications of this insight is that a number of parents in Asian countries send their children to Singapore to learn English rather than to the US, and that Singaporean-made English teaching kits are popular in China.[42] Using this method, children are able to learn much more each week in the same time-frame. Singaporean pupils are similar to Japanese pupils in that they combine obedience and competition.

Conclusion

Japanese political culture is rich. A single chapter cannot do justice to this rich and still largely unexplored subject. Instead of summarising what has been described, I would like to provide two short notes on two important subjects relevant to the study of political culture. First, Japanese political culture arguably has an enormous degree of malleability. Neither excessively stressing individualism or collectivism, nor single-mindedly highlighting competition or compliance, nor extremely underlining trust or distrust, Japanese political culture transforms itself according to endogenous and exogenous changes. Therefore, the study of culture in general and political culture in particular should not be conducted as if it were a DNA of people living over years in a given set of units often called the national cultural unit. Second, in studying political culture, language plays an important role. Language is part of culture. To better understand political culture, one had better know language as much as possible. Further, the inherently obtrusive and intrusive nature of interviewing in survey research when studying political culture needs to be kept in mind and, if possible remedied. Only armed with cultural sensitivity and linguistic thoroughness can one hope to grasp political culture.[43]

Notes

1. See Almond and Verba (1963); Pye (1982); Rich (2007).
2. Lasswell (1990).
3. Easton (1979).
4. See Inoguchi (2007d) and Inoguchi and Fujii (2008).
5. See Inoguchi and Marsh (2008: 280–310). Also available online at www.asiaeuropesurvey.org. See also Blondel and Inoguchi (2006); Inoguchi and Blondel (2008).
6. See, for instance, Subramanian and Kawachi (2006: 116–22); Lochner, Kawachi, Brennan and Buka (2003: 797–805); Subramanian, Kim and Kawachi (2002: S21–34).
7. The relationship between concerns about human rights and health in Asian people has been examined by Yasuharu Tokuda and his associates. See Tokuda, Fujii and

Inoguchi (unpublished 2007 manuscript). The relationship between social capital and public policy performance at local levels in Italy has been well examined by Robert Putnam (1994).

8. Putnam (1994)
9. These generational differences are well documented by the National Character Survey of the Ministry of Education's Institute of Statistical Mathematics from the early 1950s through 2000s (Tōkei Sūri Kenkyūjo Kokuminsei Chōsa Iinkai 1961; 1970; 1975; 1982a; 1982b). See also Chikio Hayashi (2001); Yoshino (2007).
10. Watanuki (1979).
11. Richardson (1974).
12. Yasusuke Murakami (1982: 29–72).
13. Kabashima and Takenaka (1988).
14. Tachibanaki (2006); Shingo Hayashi (2005). GINI index is one of the ways to measure the degree of income gaps among the population concerned.
15. Tokuda and Inoguchi (forthcoming).
16. Inoguchi (1997: 104–14; 2007b: 1–19; 2007e; 2008).
17. McAllister (2007: 571–88).
18. Ikegami (1995).
19. Ikegami (2005).
20. Rizzolatti and Arbib (1998: 188–94).
21. Inoguchi (2005a; 2005b; 1999: 19–28).
22. Inoguchi (2005a; 2005b; 1999: 19–28).
23. Inoguchi (2007e); Anderson (1975).
24. Pilling (2007).
25. Mann (1986).
26. Although absolutism was not generated outside Europe, it was transplanted onto the rest by colonialism. See Duland (2007).
27. Kunio Yanagita may have been unwittingly used for this purpose. Especially those social scientists like Masao Maruyama, Takeyoshi Kawashima, Jiro Kamishima, and Junichi Kyogoku might have presented such a picture of Japanese political culture.
28. Inoguchi and Blondel (2008).
29. Unfortunately, this linguistic-methodological inquiry has not been systematically and empirically tested.
30. Tax-hike related resignations include Masayoshi Ōhira, Yasuhiro Nakasone, Noboru Takeshita and Morifumi Hosokawa. Most prime ministers avoided policy choices which would lead them to increase taxes. Junichirō Koizumi was spectacularly successful in shirking from a tax hike for as long as five years of his tenure in power. One of the consequences was that it led many administrations to issue a huge amount of government bonds and without raising tax revenue – the government has accumulated a literally astronomical amount of government deficit over 30 years.
31. Inoguchi (2007a).
32. Inoguchi (2004).
33. Thakur and Inoguchi (2003).
34. The phrasing of questions makes a difference. These figures are my 'guesstimates', based on my reading of such questions over the years.
35. Inoguchi (2004).
36. Kawato (2008).
37. Inoguchi and Blondel (2008).

38. Inglehart (1993).
39. *Yomiuri Shimbun* (2002).
40. Inoguchi (2006).
41. Merry White (1993).
42. Minister Ong of the Singapore Embassy in Tokyo, September 21 (2007).
43. Inoguchi and Fujii (2008).

Further reading

Blondel, Jean and Takashi Inoguchi (2006), *Political Cultures in Asia and Europe: Citizens, States and Societal Values*, London: Routledge.

Ikegami, Eiko (1995), *The Taming of the Samurai: Honorific Individualism and the Making of Modern Japan*, Cambridge: Harvard University Press.

White, Merry (1993), *The Material Child: Coming of Age in Japan and America*, New York: Free Press.

10

Buraku culture

Burakumin as a genealogical minority

Japan is a mosaic society coloured by manifold layers of dominant and minority cultures. The representative ethnic minorities include the Ainu, Okinawans and Zainichi Koreans (Koreans living in Japan). This chapter deals with the so-called *burakumin*,[1] arguably the largest minority group in contemporary Japan.

While *burakumin* are Japanese both ethnically and in terms of nationality, they are discriminated against on the basis of belief about their descent: that they are real or purported 'descendants of outcastes' (*eta* or *hinin*)[2] of the status system which the feudal Tokugawa regime institutionalised about four centuries ago to implement its divide-and-rule policy.[3] The *burakumin* category was instituted in order to direct peasants' discontent over the heavy land tax they were required to pay away from the Shogunate and the local lords and towards the *burakumin*. Until today, many *burakumin* have lived in secluded communities and maintained a considerable degree of genealogical continuity. To be precise, *burakumin* constitute a modern social status group that forms a genealogical minority in contemporary Japan.

According to a 1993 survey, the most recent nationwide study available, there are 4442 areas in which *burakumin* live.[4] These areas have a total population of 2 158 789, of whom 892 751 are *burakumin*. However, the *burakumin* population far surpasses these figures. Some areas were not surveyed. There are *burakumin* who have left the designated areas to live elsewhere. There are some who do not know that they are *burakumin* because their parents did not disclose their descent to them. These people find out that they are *burakumin* when they experience discrimination.[5] Accordingly, it is a near impossibility to get an accurate count of the *burakumin* population.

To locate *burakumin* in the context of other minorities in Japan, it would be helpful to provide a brief description of the Ainu, Okinawans and Zainichi Koreans in contrast with the *burakumin*, the focus of the analysis of this chapter.

The Ainu is an indigenous ethnic group from the northern areas of East Asia. In the past, hunting and fishing were their primary means of subsistence, and they continue to possess their own unique culture (animistic faith, Ainu language, and oral tradition). In 1999, there were 23 767 Ainu[6] living in Hokkaidō and a few thousand Ainu in Kantō region, though the exact population number is unknown. The Ainu were attacked by what they call the *wajin* or *shamo* (dominant Japanese), and finally yielded to their colonial rule in the 15th century. With the establishment of the Meiji regime in Tokyo in the latter half of the 19th century, the Ainu were incorporated into the Japanese nation, had their land taken by force, were forbidden to pass on their traditions to the next generation, and were compelled to assimilate with the *wajin*. With the recent rise of multiculturalism, cultural revival movements were beginning to emerge towards the end of the 20th century, raising ethnic awareness among the Ainu. In 1997, a law was enacted to 'promote Ainu culture'. In 2008, the Japanese parliament passed the motion to recognise the Ainu as an indigenous group for the first time,[7] though such issues as land ownership, underground resources, autonomy, language and race, are still swept under the carpet.

The Okinawans (people from the Okinawan islands) also possess their own unique culture (Okinawan Shinto, language, and custom).[8] The Okinawans founded their own state (the Ryūkyū Kingdom) in the 15th century. However, it was attacked during the Edo era by the Satsuma [Kagoshima] domain in the south of Kyūshū, after which it became a dependent territory. In 1872, the Meiji government annexed it into Japan, after which the Okinawans suffered from discrimination and poverty under Japan's colonial policies. Towards the end of the Second World War, one third of Okinawans were killed during the Battle of Okinawa, which took place between the Japanese and United States armies. After the war, Okinawa was placed under US administration, and later 'returned' to Japan in 1972. However, US military bases remained concentrated in Okinawa, and the Okinawans suffer from higher levels of unemployment and poverty than Japan's mainland due to the dependency of the economy on the military bases and tourism. In 2007, the population of Okinawa prefecture stood at 138 000.[9]

Finally, Japan has a substantial number of Koreans, known as Zainichi Koreans, throughout the nation. Japan invaded the Korean peninsula and annexed it in 1910. The Japanese government then instituted colonial policies through which they exploited the land and resources of Korea. Koreans living under destitute circumstances migrated to Japan. During the Second World War many male Koreans were carted off for forced labour in Japan. Though many Koreans returned to their homeland when Japan lost the war in 1945, those who had lost their livelihood in Korea remained in Japan. 'Zainichi Koreans' refers to those who remained and their descendants. This group possesses special permanent residency status,[10] and their population numbered 443 000 in 2006.[11] Some Zainichi Koreans have been naturalised as Japanese, though the extent of this population is unknown. The Zainichi Koreans have been discriminated against in various ways, and many keep to their own networks of relatives and fellow Zainichi Koreans. The Zainichi Koreans possess their own ethnic culture (Korean Confucianism, language and custom); they have remained in Japan for over half a century and have formed their own identity, different from the national identity of Koreans in the motherland.

A few points of comparison will reveal the location of *burakumin* vis-à-vis these minority groups. Most important in this regard is the fact that the Ainu, Okinawans and Zainichi Koreans are ethnic minorities whereas *burakumin* are not. In terms of the official definition of nationality, *burakumin*, Ainu and Okinawans are Japanese, while Zainichi Koreans are not in the sense that they do not hold full Japanese citizenship.

All of these minorities emerged as products of modern Japan's external and internal colonialism. As Japan embraced modernity, discrimination against *burakumin* and Ainu intensified internally. At the same time, it brought about the creation of the Okinawan and Zainichi Korean minority groups externally. In other words, the dominant culture of Japan that gave rise to discrimination against *burakumin* contributed to the formation of the social structures that created ethnic minorities externally. In this sense, discrimination against *burakumin* is firmly connected with the matrix of structural ethnic discrimination and occupies a strategic domain in the context of contemporary minority issues in Japan, as Figure 10.1 shows.

There appears to be some status hierarchy among these minority groups. 'When I was growing up, people from the general public (non-*burakumin*) used to throw stones at me,' said a *burakumin* panellist at a symposium.[12]

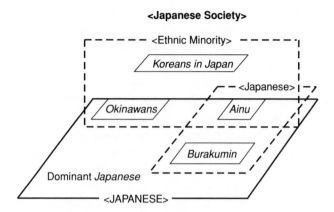

Figure 10.1 *Burakumin* and ethnic minorities in Japan.

Upon hearing this, a Zainichi Korean panellist said, 'When I was growing up, *burakumin* used to throw stones at me.' To which an Ainu panellist replied, 'When I was growing up, Zainichi Koreans used to throw stones at me'. This chain of internal discrimination within minority groups suggests the structural complexity of minority existence. Because *burakumin* are subject to discrimination by people who are no different in terms of nationality, race and ethnicity, they do not have a refuge in which they can completely escape from prejudice. In contrast, since other minorities are discriminated against by 'others' (ethnic Japanese), they have a refuge and a distinctive cultural tradition with which they can identify. Here lies the agony of the *burakumin*.[13]

Discrimination against *burakumin*

A number of fabricated allegations surround *burakumin* and form the basis for widespread prejudice. Some allege that *burakumin* are of a different race (racial origin theory), while others claim that they are of a different ethnic group (ethnic origin theory). There is also a popular belief that *burakumin* ancestors were placed at the bottom of feudal social hierarchy as outcastes because they engaged in cattle butchering, a practice regarded as unclean and profane (occupation origin theory). Though the Meiji government issued the Emancipation Edict in 1871 to abolish the designation as outcastes and the hereditary occupation system, discrimination against *burakumin* continues to this day. The reason behind this rests not only in the fact that non-*burakumin* have been very conscious of their feudal status, but also in the reality that discrimination against *burakumin* has functioned as a lever for social integration in the process of forming a modern Japan. Behind such integration is the Buddhist belief that slaughtering animals is an unclean act,[14] a construct that enables majority Japanese to see themselves as clean and to form the feeling of collective superiority, solidarity and togetherness. There is also Japan's *ie* system, discussed in chapter 4 of this volume, which has made it difficult for *burakumin* to conceal their lineage. Japan's strict and elaborate family registration system has enabled all Japanese to access information on anybody's genealogical background. Discrimination against *burakumin* extends to many areas of their lives, from being rejected as marriage partners to being discriminated against in job opportunities.

Prejudice, overt and covert, displayed in marriage situations presents the most serious aspect of *buraku* discrimination.[15] It is a product of pseudo-status endogamy, namely, the view that family continuity is highly important and therefore so is 'matched marriage' in terms of a family's social standing and lineage. At the core of such views lies the concept of uncleanness, which urges people to prevent the mixing in of base parentage. Some parents would investigate a potential son- or daughter-in-law's background and tear the young lovers away from each other if *burakumin* ancestry was revealed. Even those *burakumin* who managed to marry non-*burakumin* did so under difficult circumstances. Some were forced to keep their *buraku* parentage a secret, while others were allowed to marry on the condition that they leave the *buraku* communities and remain cut off from all contact with their relatives after marriage.[16] With the influx of foreign workers and migrants into Japan, international marriages are on the rise. When given the choice, some parents appear to prefer to see their children married to foreigners than to *burakumin*.[17] Similarly, there are some cases in which landlords have refused to rent their apartments to *burakumin*, preferring to lease them to foreigners.[18]

Asada Zennosuke, ex-chairperson of the Buraku Liberation League, who provided the ideological framework underpinning the *buraku* liberation movement, summarised the structure of *buraku* discrimination into three propositions: (1) its essence – *burakumin* do not have completely open job opportunities; (2) its social significance – the low wage levels of *burakumin* provides justification for those of workers at large; and (3) discrimination as social consciousness – prejudice forms in the unconscious levels of perception of the general masses.[19] *Burakumin* is a relational concept because one becomes a *burakumin* by experiencing discrimination as a *burakumin*; *burakumin* become conscious of their status after majority Japanese classify them (mainly on genealogical grounds). Majority hereditary categorisation comes before minority consciousness, a process that develops into interactive relationships. To this extent, the changing patterns of discrimination by majority Japanese alter the substance of *buraku* community culture.

The forms of discrimination enacted against *burakumin* have transformed over time. An awareness of equality, which rejects discrimination, has spread since human rights education was introduced to schools in postwar Japan. As a result, blatant discrimination based on language and gestures used by non-*burakumin* decreased. However, prejudiced views which lie hidden in the depths of consciousness cannot easily be swept away. Instead, the number of latent and indirect acts of discrimination against *burakumin* increased, with new forms of discrimination emerging. In a number of cases, anonymous individuals and private investigation agencies attempted to acquire *burakumin* family registers to identify them as undesirable persons. In one sensational case that became public in 1975, an underground publication entitled *A comprehensive list of buraku area names*, the compilers of which remain unidentified, was secretly sold to corporations and individuals. Many other new ways of conducting background checks on *burakumin* have been developed. Also still rampant are graffiti vilifying *burakumin*, blatantly discriminatory articles published on the web and prejudicial language used in the mass media, not to mention unfair treatment in terms of employment, wages, and personnel shuffling.[20] Secrecy, indirectness, anonymity and insidiousness constitute this trend, as more complex forms of discrimination and prejudice are faced by *burakumin*.[21]

Buraku culture

While *buraku* communities have diversified in many ways today, their most original form is found in those that have the characteristics Inoue Kiyoshi called trinity: lineage, space and occupation.[22] These communities have spatial boundaries in which *burakumin* with traceable genealogical background reside. In such communities, traditional *buraku* culture flourishes on the memories of a history of hardship that has been passed on since their days as outcastes.

Burakumin living in trinity communities generally engage in work in the industries they specialise in, such as butchery, meat processing and leatherwork. Most notable is craft such as leather bags, drums and footwear – *zōri* (Japanese sandals) and *setta* (Japanese sandals with leather soles) – and home appliances made from bamboo, straw and wood. In

performance art, traditional *buraku* culture includes *harukoma* (a congrat-
ulatory dance), *shishimai* (dance with lion doll), *manzai* (a comedic art) and
ōkagura (Shinto music and dance). One can also observe *burakumin* music,
dance, rituals, folklore, life-skills and even manners and customs that have
been handed down since the feudal period. Much of *buraku* traditional
culture is derived from a form of folk religion which focuses on worldly
benefits. While, on the one hand, *burakumin* were despised as outcastes,
they also acted as *hafuri* (person who controls rituals, such as festivals,
funerals and slaughtering, to purify the unclean things/situation) in charge
of purification rites for the 'ordinary people' (farmers who were members
of the general population). *Manzai, harukoma, shishimai* and the like were
all door-to-door forms of entertainment performed in order to drive away
impurity and taboos.

Contemporary *buraku* material culture is based on industry that
emerged in response to the new demands of the modern era. This type of
culture derives from work relating to shoemaking, gloves and mitts, bags,
slippers, sandals, processed meat, and the like. Everyday culture is also
created from work relating to small businesses and low wage-labour, such
as construction and public works, car and house wrecking, junk dealing,
garbage and human waste treatment, cleaning and peddling (green vegetables, sundries, bedding, etc.). Given that these jobs are unstable and poorly
paid, *burakumin* constantly endure the sense of anxiety involved in engaging
in these occupations. Such anxiety makes the culture of *burakumin* both
utilitarian and flexible. Since they have not possessed the means of production, and have lived the life of low-class labourers, they are inevitably
inclined to take up any opportunities useful for survival, as one *burakumin*
observed: 'Who in the world would want to go into the river in the middle
of winter to break off some ice if it wasn't because they had to?'[23] The arte-
factual culture of *buraku* communities is also flexible to the extent that their
cultural activities do not require licensing or accreditation, unlike the world
of tea ceremonies and flower arrangements of the middle class Japanese.
Anything that provides sustenance for life is seen as a cultural resource.
For instance, in forms of entertainment such as itinerant performance,
burakumin could engage in these activities without special skills and qualifications. In *buraku* craft and performing arts, too, the elaborate techniques involved have all been jointly owned and handed down through the
buraku communities, and anyone who is living in dire circumstances can
join without prior qualifications. *Burakumin* have developed orientations
to usefulness and flexibility, to deal with their plight in a pragmatic fashion.

Finally, *burakumin* have a culture of pride in their struggle for emancipation. The set of values derived from the pride of their resistance reverses the values resulting from the miseries of hardship and anxiety.[24] It is through this aspect of culture that *burakumin* history and hardships in life are reinterpreted, reversed, and carved into words, objects, and actions as symbols of *burakumin* 'pride'. *Burakumin* built their strength to fight against the difficulties they face by reminiscing about their struggles and achievements.

These feats include the Emancipation Edict of 1871, which abolished the status system institutionalised in feudal Japan. The Levellers' Association Movement from 1922 to 1942 marked the *burakumin*'s own political and collective action that put the issue of equality on the national agenda in prewar Japan. The All Romance Incident, which developed in Kyoto in 1951, is well known as the first postwar struggle to secure special budgets from local administrative bodies for the improvement of the conditions of *buraku* communities. For many years, *buraku* movements fought against discrimination through public denunciation of government officials and private citizens who exhibited their prejudice in one way or another. This saw the government execute a special policy called Measures for Dōwa Projects designed to provide aid to *burakumin*, though this policy ended in March 2002. The so-called Sayama campaign from 1963 to this day represents a long struggle to clear the name of an imprisoned *buraku* member who many *buraku* activists and their supporters believe was charged – and has been falsely imprisoned – only because he was a *burakumin*. The Dōwa Council Policy Report of 1965, a landmark achievement of the *buraku* liberation movements, enshrined the guidelines for special aid policies for *burakumin* and *buraku* communities.

Self-contradiction in *buraku* identity

Buraku culture is self-contradictory because of the structural position that *burakumin* occupy in Japanese society. On the one hand, *buraku* culture is hybrid to the extent that it is both continuous with and distinctive from Japan's dominant culture, leaving the borderline between the two cultures blurred. While *buraku* culture shares much with non-*buraku* culture, the pain of being discriminated against forms the core of *buraku* existence which the majority Japanese do not experience, and this shapes the line of demarcation between the two, making continuity and discontinuity the two ostensibly contradictory features of *buraku* culture.

On the other hand, *buraku* culture is double-faceted in the sense that it is both miserable and proud. It is a culture of misery embodying *burakumin*'s poverty, humiliation and alienation; it is a culture of lamentation. 'There is nothing good about being born a *buraku*. Nothing but bad things. In our case, we couldn't even get joint worship with the non-*burakumin* in Hakusan [a holy mountain]. We couldn't join the youth association either. The youth group for the festivals completely ignored us and wouldn't let us join in. It's the same even now.'[25] At the same time, it is also a culture of pride, in which many *burakumin* find themselves in their struggle against discrimination, their pursuit of human dignity and their commitment to liberation. 'Any foolish person who discriminates against shoemakers must not wear shoes!'[26] Through the struggle for liberation, many *burakumin* have found their pride as human beings: the culture of lamentation transformed into a culture of pride. 'I am happy that I was born a *buraku* because the fighting spirit has been ingrained in me since young. And because I have learnt that life is about plowing our own way forward.'[27]

Buraku culture, though a marginal one, overturns the values of the dominant culture. The 'elegant, fine, and sophisticated' dominant culture traditionally holds the 'vulgar, bold, and simple' *buraku* culture in contempt, but *burakumin* have carried out a kind of 'symbolic reversal'[28] of values by putting cultural superiority on the set of values belonging to the *buraku* group. Over the centuries they have discovered the beauty in their lives. Thus, misery and pride sit side by side in *buraku* culture.

'The most important aspect of a culture is the way people live – how people interrelate through their activities in order to survive.'[29] At the core of *buraku* culture lies *burakumin* identity, represented in Figure 10.2.

Burakumin identity is partly constructed by memories of history. These memories are made up of words, objects, and actions of 'discrimination and resistance' and 'poverty and endurance'. Their identity is also partly constructed by present everyday life experiences. These comprise the 'anxiety of discrimination and resistance' as well as the 'anxiety of poverty and endurance'. Finally, *burakumin* compare their everyday life experiences with their memories of history to gain a collective meaning of anxiety and resistance. *Burakumin* identity is formed in this way.

Diversity in *buraku* culture

Buraku culture adopts diverse forms depending on history, work, life, and place of residence. The industries of some *buraku* communities have

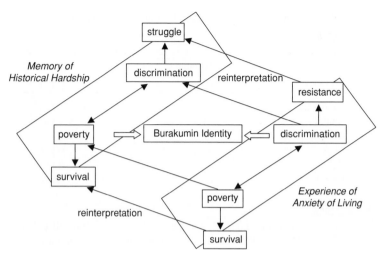

Figure 10.2 Formation of *burakumin* identity.

developed as a result of government aid while others have not. Some *buraku* communities are urban, while others are agrarian or fishing communities. Urban *buraku* communities are experiencing an influx of non-*burakumin*, while agrarian and fishing *buraku* communities have ageing populations and are becoming depopulated as they experience an outflow of young people. The regional distribution of the *buraku* communities and their populations is summarised in Table 10.1 on the next page.

The Kinki region contains many large urban *buraku* communities. The Chūgoku region is home to numerous small fishing and agrarian *buraku* communities. The Kyūshū region encompasses a lot of urban and agrarian *buraku* communities, its former coal mining areas containing *buraku* communities which formed in the modern era. The Shikoku region is home to many small fishing and agrarian *buraku* communities. The Kantō region has numerous small urban *buraku* communities. Meanwhile, the Chūbu region encompasses many small agrarian *buraku* communities. Many of the jobs in the urban *buraku* communities are in the manufacturing, construction and service industries, while the construction, agriculture and fishing industries dominate the fishing and agrarian *buraku* communities.

Moreover, the levels of activities of the liberation movements differ from one community to another. The emancipation movements have a long history in the Kinki region. Some leaders of the outcastes (*eta* leader Danzaemon and *hinin* leader Kuruma Zenhichi) were active in Edo (Tokyo)

Table 10.1 *Regional distribution of* buraku *communities and population*

Region	Number of communities	Population
Kantō	572	82 636
Chūbu	532	75 455
Kinki	781	372 918
Chūgoku	1052	115 565
Shikoku	670	105 612
Kyūshū	835	140 565
Total	4442	892 751

Source: Buraku Liberation and Human Rights Research Institute (BLHRRI) (2001: 736) Survey of Management and Coordination Agency in 1993.

before the Meiji era. Chūgoku, Shikoku, and Chūbu are coloured by a history of agrarian *buraku* community struggle, while Kyūshū has a history of joint struggle between the *buraku* emancipation movements and labour movements in the 1960s.

Transformation of *buraku* culture

Discrimination against *burakumin* has continued over four centuries. Consequently, *burakumin* and *buraku* culture have also continued to exist. However, the nature of discrimination against *burakumin* has transformed with time, and as a result, *burakumin* identity and *buraku* culture have transformed too.

In feudal Japan, outcastes were restricted in their choice of occupation and place of residence. After emancipation in the early Meiji years, *burakumin* gained freedom in this regard. At the same time, however, they lost their exclusive rights to the occupations they had had as outcastes. As most *burakumin* did not possess the funds or means to establish new businesses or change occupations, many of them were forced to take on odd jobs. They also had little choice but to live in areas that were located in the places whose habitation environment was inferior.

In more recent decades, *buraku* communities have undergone transformation, especially as a consequence of economic globalisation. *Buraku* communities located in city peripheries and agricultural areas became urban *buraku* communities as the cities expanded. Non-*burakumin* have come

Table 10.2 *Types of* buraku *communities by three factors*

Type	Community	Genealogy	Work	Comments
Trinity	•	•	•	Traditional *buraku* communities.
Genealogical and Territorial	•	•		Most *buraku* communities today, with no *buraku*-inherited industries.
Territorial only	•			*Buraku* residents are not *burakumin* in a genealogical sense.
Inherited industries operating outside		•	•	*Buraku*-inherited enterprise moved out of *buraku* communities, with their employees mostly *burakumin*.
Dispersal		•		Isolated *burakumin* who moved out of their communities, and their offspring.

Adapted from Noguchi (2000: 106–17). Two categories in his original table have been removed because they are analytical categories that are virtually non-existent in reality.

to live among *burakumin*. Independent *buraku* industries declined and *burakumin* became corporate employees. Finally, the boundaries defining *burakumin* became ambiguous as non-*burakumin* living in the *buraku* communities were discriminated against, or *burakumin* were no longer aware of their origins, and so on.[30] Consequently, the trinity principle consisting of community, occupation and descent collapsed, leading to the diversification of *buraku* communities in contemporary Japan. Using the typology of *buraku* communities that Noguchi Michihiko has developed, one can identify at least five categories as demonstrated in Table 10.2.

The first type, the trinity group discussed above, represents the orthodox *buraku* culture but now comprises only a small number of *buraku* communities, primarily because of the collapse of the conventional *buraku* industries. Yet, these communities are the bedrock of *buraku* liberation movements.

The second category, which may be called the residential/territorial type, forms the numerically largest group. While *burakumin* in this category live in identifiable *buraku* communities, they do not engage in traditional *buraku* work, and their occupational structure does not differ much from Japanese society at large, though the employment of middle-aged workers tends to be unstable and aged individuals tend to face difficulty in sustaining themselves. Sharing the historical memories of discrimination and conflict,

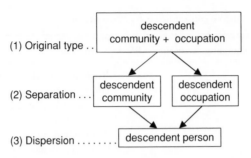

Figure 10.3 Transformation of *buraku*.

residents in this type of community have a sense of communal solidarity, though it tends to be diluted amongst the younger generation.

In the third type, there are a small number of areas which the majority population regarded as *buraku* communities, though their residents are neither the children of those who were genealogically classified as *burakumin* nor workers in the conventional *buraku* industries. These communities, which may be called simply the territorial type, drastically differ from the two types above because there is no blood relation between the current residents and the residents who identified themselves as *burakumin*.

The fourth category is made up of those communities whose members develop their *buraku*-inherited enterprises (such as abattoirs and meat processing companies) outside their own communities and use *buraku* communities only as their places of residence.

Finally, at the very end of the spectrum, there are *burakumin* who have moved out of their *buraku* communities and work in occupations that have nothing to do with the *buraku* tradition. These individuals, who may be classified as the dispersal type, are now scattered around Japan and their connection with *buraku* culture exists only through lineage. On the whole, this group used to be relatively well-off in their original communities and have had higher levels of education. Not surprisingly, the children and grandchildren of these individuals hardly relate to *buraku* identity. The dispersal type effectively ceases to be *burakumin*, in that they hardly experience discrimination and rarely participate in a distinctive culture.

In general, as shown in Figure 10.3 above, *buraku* communities appear to separate from their trinity prototype in two intermediate directions: (1) losing *buraku* occupational identities; and (2) losing residential and territorial identities. The final separation is the dispersal type, which has neither connection. These four types of groups coexist throughout Japan, an indication that *buraku* groups are in the process of reorganisation as well as dissipation, as a result of modernisation and globalisation.

Buraku communities are also stratified within themselves. Status hierarchies have sharpened in recent years with government aids and other forms of assistance provided to *buraku* communities. Those equipped with economic resources have taken advantage of these opportunities and acquired upward mobility, while the economic conditions of others at the subsistence levels have remained unchanged, with the result that intra-community social disparities have widened. Such increased social stratification within *buraku* communities cause *burakumin* to lose their sense of homogeneity and cohesiveness as a group.

Buraku culture at a crossroad

Buraku culture today is at a crossroad. Although, on the whole, *burakumin* live a life of poverty in the lower ranks of society, their sense of homogeneity and cohesion is declining. As a result, *burakumin* identity has become diffused along the lines of generation, occupation and region. Some continue to hold onto their identity as *burakumin*. Some feel that they are *burakumin* on occasion. Others strive to forget that they are *burakumin* at all. Still others, particularly the descendents of the above-mentioned dispersal type, are not aware that they are *burakumin*. This reality begs the question: where should one draw a line between *burakumin* and non-*burakumin*? The issue resembles the problem of defining who the Japanese are, a point discussed in the two opening chapters of this volume. The diffusion of *burakumin* identity reflects a diffusion of *buraku* culture.

First of all, the traditional cultural practices of the *buraku* are fast waning. The number of people who can hand down the production techniques of craftwork to the next generation has decreased dramatically. The few remaining craftsmen have become artists, solely producing works of fine art. Knowledge of *buraku* performance art has met the same fate. Both crafts and performance arts have been separated from the lives of *burakumin*. Furthermore, *buraku* culture has also become variegated, with the *buraku* industries derived from traditional industries being absorbed into large companies. *Burakumin* have become managers and employees of general occupations. As a consequence, *buraku* culture struggles to hold itself together as a distinctive entity.

Finally, the culture of emancipation is also facing a crisis, as *burakumin*'s memory of their history of hardship and resistance is beginning to slip into obscurity. Increased variations of *buraku* communities make it difficult for them to form a communal movement base, with the culture of mutual help waning.

In the past, *burakumin* sought the help of the *buraku* liberation movements when they faced discrimination or difficulties in life. The *buraku* liberation movements find their purpose in learning from the history of their struggle against hardships, reviving *burakumin* identity, fighting against discrimination and seeking to improve the standard of living for *burakumin*. To elevate the levels of education in *buraku* communities, they organise classes for illiterate people, mainly middle-aged and senior citizens who were unable to receive formal education because of poverty. In 1993, the illiteracy rate of *burakumin* was 3.8 per cent, 19 times greater than the national average.[31] *Buraku* liberation movements also organise 'liberation schools' where children, youth and women in *buraku* communities learn about their history and social issues to raise *burakumin* consciousness. These movements have also made attempts to revive special skills and arts accumulated in *buraku* communities and to create literary works as well as dramas to highlight the plight and struggle of *burakumin*. As such, *buraku* liberation movements are both cultural movements and creations based on the culture of emancipation, which pursue the creation of a new *buraku* narrative and tradition.

Regardless of the directions in which current *buraku* culture might shift, there is no indication that discrimination against the *buraku* will disappear from Japanese society. To combat this situation, the key agents of change would have to be *buraku* liberation movements. And *buraku* culture could be revived, created and disseminated only within these movements. They are the constant reminders that majority Japanese culture has harsh discriminatory ingredients, while the survival of minority culture depends much upon the political activism of its members as well as their supporters.

Notes

1. In Japanese the term *buraku* means a community and the term *min* means a person. *Burakumin* is a person who lives in a discriminated community.
2. The terms *eta* (unclean person) and *hinin* (non-human being) often appear in overseas literature. These were terms used to refer to outcastes during the Edo era; however, today they are considered obsolete and derogatory. Their descendants are referred to as *burakumin*.
3. The established view is that the formal status system of feudal Japan comprised four groups: samurai (warriors), peasants, craftsmen and traders. *Burakumin* were

placed beneath the four groups. While this is the established view, there are competing theories.

4. Buraku Liberation and Human Rights Research Institute (BLHRRI) (2001: 736).

5. Noguchi (2000: 16 and 18). However, this does not mean that being *burakumin* is a product of personal experience. *Burakumin* is a historically formed social group. One is *admitted into it* by being discriminated against.

6. Buraku Liberation and Human Rights Research Institute (BLHRRI) (2001: 37).

7. *Asahi Shimbun* (7 June 2008, morning edition: 2).

8. The Okinawans are considered to be Japanese nationals and residents of Okinawa prefecture in general. However, suffering from their oppressed political and economic status, they distinguish themselves from the Japanese (*Yamatonchū*) by calling themselves Okinawans (*Uchinanchū*).

9. Okinawaken Kikakubu Tōkeika (2007).

10. Special permanent residency status is granted to foreigners who have lived in Japan since the prewar era, as well as to their children and grandchildren. This category includes the ethnic Chinese in Japan or newcomers who have married Japanese. The majority of them are, however, Zainichi Koreans.

11. Ministry of Justice, Immigration Bureau (2007).

12. An episode at a symposium held by the Hiroshima Federation of the Buraku Liberation League, in Hiroshima on 10 March 1993.

13. George De Vos and Hiroshi Wagatsuma understand *burakumin* through concepts of race or caste (De Vos and Wagatsuma, 1972: xx). They apply racial and caste concepts to *burakumin*, as they believe that the mentality of the discriminators and *burakumin* response to discrimination is identical to that of American and Indian minorities. However, I believe that there are problems with both these approaches. Racial concepts tend to place an emphasis on physical characteristics (Cashmore, 1996: 297), yet *burakumin* do not have any different physical characteristics from dominant Japanese. Caste refers to people who have been classified based on 'endogamy', 'hereditary status', and 'class based hierarchy' (it is not easy to define the caste concept fully) (Cashmore, 1996: 66), however, *burakumin* in the modern age are not living within an ongoing system of social hierarchy as seen in the case of the Indian caste system. Religiosity does not play a big role in the contemporary situation of the *burakumin*, although the concept of uncleanness lies at the root of both discrimination against *burakumin* and caste discrimination. However, in the *buraku* discrimination the concept of uncleanness was connected with one of Metempsychosis of Japanese Buddhism. Finally, discrimination against *burakumin* is generally conceived as the 'remnants of the feudal status system'. This gives rise to the belief that discrimination against *burakumin* will disappear with the advent of modernisation.

14. Buraku Liberation and Human Rights Research Institute (BLHRRI) (2001: 281).

15. A *burakumin* girl committed suicide in Hiroshima on 28 October 1991. The reason was that her sweetheart, her former school teacher, cancelled their mutual matrimonial promise because his parents opposed their planned marriage.

16. According to the 2000 Osaka Prefecture Survey, 67.5% of married *burakumin* between the age of 15 and 39 had non-*burakumin* spouses, while the rate was 48.6% for those aged 40 to 59, and 30.9% for those aged 60 and above (Okuda, 2002: 11). It is clear that the number of *burakumin* marrying non-*burakumin* is increasing with time. In contrast, 24.7% of *burakumin* aged between 15 and 39 experienced discrimination in relation to marriage, while it was 19.7% for those aged 40 to 59, and 17.5% for

those aged 60 and above. The younger they are, the more likely they were to face discrimination (Okuda, 2002: 14). This gives us a glimpse of the reality that even young *burakumin* who marry non-*burakumin* cannot evade discrimination.

17. I sometimes have heard such comments in my fieldwork in Hiroshima and Osaka. A *burakumin* whose nephew married a Filipina told me that they were happy because nobody had investigated their family's descent (30 July 2005).

18. This point was brought to my attention by a friend of mine who has surveyed foreigners working in Shiga Prefecture (17 March 2008).

19. Buraku Liberation Research Institute (BLRI) (1986: 859–60).

20. Kiyoshi Inoue in *Buraku Kaihō to Jinken Seisaku Kakuritsu Yōkyū Chūō Jikkō Iinkai* (Central Executive Committee to Demand the Establishment of a Buraku Liberation and Human Rights Policy) (ed.) (2006: 21).

21. There is a town named Kamagasaki where many day workers live in Osaka. It is an underclass society where many workers from minorities including *burakumin* live. I have gone there to conduct surveys for more than 20 years. I met some workers who told me 'I am a Korean' and 'I am an Okinawan'. However, I met no worker who told me 'I am a *burakumin*'. I conclude that *burakumin* do not feel safe to reveal their descent even in such anonymous society.

22. Kiyoshi Inoue (1950: 4).

23. The words of a *burakumin* at a denunciation meeting, Hiroshima 1985, date and month unknown.

24. The emancipation culture is a kind of counterculture. 'Counterculture is all those *situationally* created designs for living formed in contexts of high anomie and intrasocietal conflict, the designs being inversion of, in sharp opposition to, the historically created designs' (Yinger 1982: 39–40).

25. Michiko Shibata (1972: 203–4).

26. The words of a *burakumin* (30 July 2005). Shoemaking is an industry predominant in *buraku* communities.

27. Michiko Shibata (1972: 256).

28. Babcock (1978: 14).

29. The words of a *burakumin* at a denunciation meeting, Hiroshima 1985, date and month unknown.

30. This does not mean that the group demarcation between *burakumin* and non-*burakumin* has become ambiguous. This demarcation, based on the notion of descendants of outcastes, in fact remains strong. It means that the scene of demarcation has become complicated.

31. Buraku Liberation and Human Rights Research Institute (BLHRRI) (2001: 414).

Further reading

Aoki, Hideo (2006), *Japan's Underclass: Day Laborers and the Homeless*, Melbourne: Trans Pacific Press.
Buraku Liberation and Human Rights Research Institute (BLHRRI) (ed.) (1998), *Buraku Problem in Japan*, Osaka: Buraku Liberation Publishing House.
Gordon, June A (2008), *Japan's Outcaste Youth: Education for Liberation*, Boulder CO: Paradigm Publishers.

11

Literary culture[1]

Text and context: literature in the age of transition

The relationship between literature and society/culture is complex. The act of writing is not a process of recording. Literary works interact with our sociocultural reality; they challenge, question, or sometimes reinforce our everyday values and assumptions. Reading modern Japanese literature means reading individual writers' experiences and their multifaceted interpretations of society and culture. In principle, therefore, any attempt at generalisation will fail. At the same time, however, literature is not created in a vacuum; writers' experiences are woven within a social and cultural fabric, and certain common literary features emerge during any given period in history. The individual writer's words are taken from, and the chain of words he or she creates is once again incorporated into, that very fabric. Sometimes these words may cause a tear or rip; or when they regurgitate the experiences of everyday life, they may be absorbed with little resistance, often becoming commercially successful in the process.

This metaphor may help explain the distinction between so-called pure and popular literature in modern Japanese literary history. The two genres have been commonly differentiated by the way they are received in the literary market: pure literature for those readers who 'seriously' enjoy reading literature and who have the ability to appreciate its 'literary' value; popular literature for the broader public who read for entertainment. Popular literature is 'light', and suited for pleasure reading – therefore, it circulates and sells well. Literary studies, however, at least in the Japanese academy, have largely concentrated on pure literature, often linking the themes expressed in literary works to questions about the state of Japanese culture and society, existing sociocultural values, the place of the individual, etc. Popular literature, by contrast, has been largely seen as complacent and unwilling to challenge the sociocultural fabric.

This distinction between pure and popular literature, however, has been called into question since the 1980s when a new generation of writers born after 1945 emerged. Murakami Haruki and Yoshimoto Banana – probably the best known of this generation, especially to readers of Japanese literature in translation – wrote works difficult to place into either the 'pure' or the 'popular' category. A new term, 'in-between' literature, was coined as a result. Since then, the Japanese literary scene has included a variety of such in-between writers, whose audience extends from literary specialists to casual readers.

This blurring of categories and the resultant breaking down of the hier-archical order that supported genre distinctions, can be found in various areas of Japanese culture. In fact, the assumption that there exists some-thing called 'high culture', which is balanced by 'low' or 'popular' culture, is no longer widely shared in Japan. We are entering an age when such familiar principles of modernity – which divide the nations of the world into the strong and the weak, the advanced and the backward, the central and the marginal, and set out clear categories within each national culture to distinguish the elite and the rest – are losing their legitimacy.

Needless to say, the role of the media has been pivotal in the populari-sation of literature. According to Matsuda Tetsuo, a publisher, essayist and commentator, the loosening of genre distinctions combined with the rapid spread of word-processors, personal computers, and more recently, mobile phones, has sent the overall number of people involved in the production and consumption of literature soaring.[2] The emergence of *keitai-shōsetsu* (mobile phone novels) is a symbolic case in point. These 'novels' first appear on websites accessed by mobile phone and are read on mobile terminals, then, if successful, they are eventually printed on paper.[3] So, at least demo-graphically, the literary population has been dramatically growing in Japan over the past decade. Matsuda concludes that the Japanese publishing world is witnessing an unprecedented market expansion, a 'gold rush' of sorts.[4]

The question, then, is: how far can literature evolve? We are witnessing a significant expansion of literature, moving further and further into, and often positively mingling with popular culture. Naturally, the extension of this is its interface with the realm of manga and animation. Even though the audience is still largely limited to the younger generation, literature in a broad sense has successfully found a means of survival in Japan's present-day consumer culture. One way to approach the question of modern Japanese literature, then, is to look at the writing culture in general and discuss literature in relation to the dynamics of popular culture. In the present discussion, however, I limit my analysis chiefly to the kind of writing that demonstrates a challenge to, or a critique of, existing sociocultural values. Accordingly, the focus will be on the production or the creative side – rather than the consumption of – literature, and references to works that have merged with the popular, consumer cultural scene will be limited. I also centre my discussion on contemporary trends and refer to early modern works only where a comparative or historical perspective is relevant.

Changes over time: out of the family

One theme that has continuously occupied an important place in modern Japanese literature centres on the notion of the family. Since the emergence of writers in Japan's early modern period, beginning with Mori Ōgai, Natsume Sōseki and Shimazaki Tōson, then Shiga Naoya and Dazai Osamu, to name only a few canonical authors, modern Japanese literary history abounds in works thematically related to the family, first identified by the term *ie*, later replaced by the term *kazoku*. In Yamazaki Masakazu's seminal work, *Ōgai: Tatakau Kachō* (*Ogai: The Combatant Head of the House*), he identifies that in Ōgai's historical fiction, as in his personal life, he struggled with the image of the righteous father.[5] Sōseki's stance was more cynical, and his later works depict a number of forlorn individuals who had left the *ie*. Shimazaki directly dealt with the theme in 1910 in his full-length novel, *Ie* (*Domestic Life*), setting the generational history of his family against the sociocultural context of Meiji Japan. Shiga, known as an 'I-novelist', wrote of his own family conflict, the plot often revolving around the protagonist's desire to free himself from the power of a father who embodied the ethics of the previous age. Dazai, too, struggled under the pressure of the *ie*, as we see in his fictional autobiography, *Ningen Shikkaku* (translated as *No Longer Human*), which depicts the protagonist's desperate attempt to escape and then denounce the haunting shadow of the *ie*. In the post-1945 period, the generation of writers that experienced Japan's defeat in their 20s attracted particular critical attention through their persistent attempts to explore the reality of the family after the breakdown of the *ie* order. Literary critic Etō Jun, in his influential work *Seijuku to Sōshitsu: Haha no Hōkai* (*Maturity and Loss: The Collapse of the Mother*), analysed how writers of this generation, such as Yasuoka Shōtarō and Kojima Nobuo, confronted the fall of the old family order signified by the loss of paternal dignity in postwar Japan.

The presence of a powerless father strengthens the tie between mother and son, according to Etō, but for the son to mature, the all-embracing mother image must disintegrate, allowing the son to make his departure.[6] Notably, Etō's analysis focuses on the son and his relationship with his mother, barely touching on the presence of any daughters in the family.

It is interesting to see that it is the 'daughters' of the previous generation who are actively pursuing 'family' themes in contemporary Japan. Some explore new ways of living as a family, while others take up the theme to demonstrate its emptiness and falseness, or simply negate the idea of 'family' altogether. One of the reasons for the sensational success of Yoshimoto Banana in the late 1980s was that she presented, in a remarkably relaxed and nonchalant manner, a new possibility for the forms a family can take. Freed from the older notion of the family as a blood-linked unit, whose domestic and social burdens and responsibilities are imposed upon its members, Yoshimoto presented, in her debut piece *Kicchin* (*Kitchen*, 1988) a portrait of a 'family' that consisted of a girl, her friend and his beautiful mother, who was, in biological terms, his father. In the 20 years since then, Yoshimoto has continuously written on themes that deal with human relationships, the nexus of which is the family. Many of the characters in Yoshimoto's works carry with them a grave sense of loss, often resulting from the death of someone close. The process of healing is depicted through developments in new relationships that are nurtured between those who care about one another, leading to the formation of something resembling a family. To say that Yoshimoto is projecting here a new vision of the family in the traditional sense is, however, misleading. Yoshimoto's success in gaining a broad and enthusiastic readership, including readers in translation in more than 30 languages, is at least partly due to her message that 'anything goes', that there is a way even for the deprived and the lost, in this age when the norms of the conventional family no longer possess absolute value. The absence of adult males in Yoshimoto's stories is symbolic – as Leith Morton notes, the father figure is almost always dead or divorced.[7] The works of Yoshimoto can thus be read to signify a further change in the conventional perceptions of the family, which in the olden days had centred around the dominating male of the extended *ie* family, and then shifted to the nuclear *kazoku* family, stereotypically a unit of three or four comprised of a hardworking father, a devoted mother and a child or two. The hardworking father did not, as Etō noted, necessarily possess power. Yet one can still argue that much of the literature of the past dealt with themes related to the difficulty of, or the sense of uneasiness in, playing the expected role within one's family. Such an assumption of expected roles no longer has significance in Yoshimoto's work. It is not that these assumptions no longer exist; rather, Yoshimoto's challenge, in her casual storytelling style, lies in her suggestion to her readers that not being able to play a role is no big fuss.

About 10 years after Yoshimoto's emergence on the literary scene, Yu Miri published *Kazoku Shinema* (*Family Cinema*, 1997), in which the very idea of 'playing the role' in one's family is ridiculed, knocked to pieces and put to an end. A portrait of a dysfunctional family that gets together for the shooting of a 'happy family' film is presented with a harshness that forces the reader in an almost threatening way to question whether or not the belief in so-called family values was ever anything but an illusion. A similar theme of a broken-up family is pursued in Yu's *Gōrudo Rasshu* (*Gold Rush*, 1998), in which the central character is a boy of fourteen who murders his father. Here again the theme is that of the falling father – in this case he is literally killed – and the estranged family is presented as a hotbed of cruelty and violence.

Looking over today's literary scene, we find the family theme unfolding further, so to speak. True, there are authors like Yoshimoto, who continues to weave this familiar theme into her new works. Also, Murakami Ryu, who has consistently produced socially challenging works since the 1970s, published a novel entitled *Saigo no Kazoku* (*The Last Family*, 2001), which depicts the process of recovery of a family inflicted with domestic violence, self-confinement and economic crisis. Yet, as its subtitle, 'Out of Home', written in English, implies, it is also about 'growing out' and becoming free of the family. It is suggestive that the father comes to realise amidst the confusion that he 'was never able to envision what an ideal family was like'.[8] In many other recent works, however, the family itself is negated from the beginning. The shadow of family looms everywhere; yet family life itself is scarcely visible. What have come to dominate instead are variations on the theme of being alone.

Symbolically, the recipient of the most prestigious Akutagawa Prize for 2007 was entitled *Hitori Biyori* (*A Perfect Day for Being Alone*) written by Aoyama Nanae. The novel revolves around the relationship between 20-year-old Chizu, who has no stable income or aspirations for the future, and 70-year-old Ginko-san, whose humble but vital life includes an interest in dance and occasional dates with a man around her age. Chizu's father is absent and her mother has gone off to China for work, so an arrangement has been made for Chizu to move in with Ginko-san. The two women form a relationship akin to that of grandmother and grand-daughter; yet something seems lacking, and even though there is affection and a sense of caring, the two are alone, each in their own way. A similar theme is developed in a highly acclaimed novel by Kawakami Hiromi, *Sensei no Kaban* (*My Teacher's Briefcase*, 2001). In this work the relationship is between Tsukiko, a woman in her late 30s, and Sensei, her 70-year old former high school teacher. It is a love story, perhaps, but the nature of the relationship is typically 'post-family': the two are alone and respect each other's aloneness. As the plot evolves, they become more and more fond of each other, and toward the end of the story Sensei tells Tsukiko of his special feelings for her. Yet, on reading the last pages of the work, where Tsukiko narrates the death of Sensei, one cannot deny the impression that despite their closeness the two lived their lives as two isolated humans; and perhaps because of that their love was genuine. What Kawakami seems to negate here is the illusion of the family as an ideal social unit, bonded by love, trust and responsibility. In another of Kawakami's novels, *Manazuru* (2005), the protagonist, Kei, yearns to be reunited with her husband, who disappeared one day and has apparently been dead for some years. She is drawn to the port town of Manazuru, a place name she found scribbled in his diary, and makes many visits there, often accompanied by a mysterious, ghost-like woman. Her husband's phantom seems to linger around the woman and the town of Manazuru, though the relationship between them is never revealed. Once again, this is a story of love, or rather, the impossibility of love in real life, and the vision of a happy family is evoked in its entire emptiness as something that never existed and will never exist.

Struggles in contemporary space: the invasion of the virtual

What is happening, then, to those individuals who have departed from, or abandoned the family? Many works deal with the individual's attempt to rebel against the values surrounding his/her personal or social environment. Though rebellion has always been a common theme in literature around the world, in Japan today it characteristically assumes the guise of artificial warfare, which may take place in the mind, in the imagination, or at a metaphorical level. Abe Kazushige's *Nipponia Nippon* (2001), is a case in point. Toya Haruo, a 17-year-old who has been living in self-imposed isolation for some years, mostly in front of his computer screen, plans to stage a revolution by killing a pair of crested ibis, or 'Nipponia Nippon', an endangered species kept in an enclosure on Sado Island. He is driven to embark on this project by what he sees as the hypocrisy behind the Japanese government's policy – an investigation on the internet has revealed to him that the only surviving bird of the species native to Japan is a male with no ability to reproduce, while the ones being so enthusiastically protected by the Japanese government are actually of 'Chinese blood'. Having nurtured a special sense of closeness to this bird (his surname is written with the character for ibis), he feels the urge to liberate them, which gradually evolves into a project to kill them, the project name being 'The Final Solution to the Nipponia Nippon Problem'. The attempt fails, and he is arrested.

What is being developed here is a record of a 'petit revolution', so to speak. Yet this 'revolution' has no sociohistorical dimension – rather, the protagonist claims that through his action he wishes to 'make everyone in the country regret that they left [him] alone'.[9] Here is the voice of an individual screaming out in frustration, tormented by loneliness and a sense of loss. It should not be assumed, though, that Abe is speaking for isolated youth in his highly metaphorical novel. For not only is the 'project' itself more performative than realistic; the central character too is 'unreal' in many ways. As we read through the work, which abounds in direct citations from the internet, the border between the real and the virtual blurs, as the virtual world of the internet invades reality, and reality begins to take on a virtual dimension. Katō Norihiro compares the unwavering 'brightness' of Abe's world with 'visibility' in computer graphics. The world of computer graphics has no depth, no hidden underbelly, everything is there on the monitor. Kato argues that the literary space created by Abe is similar in that the characters are devoid of internality, therefore, no matter how painful their experience may be, it lacks imminence.[10] Takahashi Gen'ichirō, himself an important contemporary writer, shares this view of Abe's work. In his commentary on Abe's *Gurando Finaare* (*The Grand Finale*, 2004), Takahashi points to the various 'strangenesses' in the work, and concludes that the biggest reason is that the central character himself is 'un-human'. He then adds, quoting one of his students, that, among the characters in the work this 'un-human' type has the most compelling reality.[11]

Abe's work is suggestive of the kind of situation that surrounds today's youth, and the prevailing loss of belief in revolution in the traditional sense of the word. Even though the youth in the above novel names his project a 'revolution', it is clear from the outset that it will have no social impact whatsoever. The idea of social solidarity is totally non-existent. The ultimate target is the state that has 'deceived' him, and he decides to take action to make the state know of his discontent. The motivation is painstakingly personal, as is the actual process of planning and carrying out the project.

From the beginning, it is clear that this 'revolution' is nothing but a rebellious gesture. We have also seen that this gesture takes us to the border between the real and the virtual, where the two can easily be reversed. Since the planning of the 'revolution' takes place in a confined room in front of the computer, the protagonist's actions acquire a virtual quality. Deprived of depth, they compel the reader to observe the scenes as if they were unfolding on a computer monitor.

A theme of tension between the individual and the state is also taken up in Misaki Aki's *Tonarimachi Sensō* (*War with the Town Next Door*, 2005). Unlike *Nipponia Nippon*, this is 'real' warfare involving the systematic killing of humans, even though that killing takes place behind the scenes. Two adjacent towns have agreed to embark on a 'war enterprise' for mutual administrative benefits, and the citizens have been systematically mobilised. Death tolls are announced in the local newspapers but the battles are invisible, and the towns' residents go on living their everyday lives as peacefully as ever. The story is narrated through the eyes of a young company worker, called up for service as a spy, who reconnoitres the enemy town together with a representative from the town's office, an attractive young woman whose determination to fulfil her mission is unshakable. He marries her on paper and performs his duty as she orders, without knowing the outcome of his actions. Suddenly, one day, she phones to tell him that a cease-fire agreement has been signed, and that he is released from his duties. He confirms later that the war was real, and, furthermore, that the killing was occurring virtually next door.

Whereas Abe's work illustrates how easily the real can slip into the virtual, Misaki's work, dealing with the theme of war, suggests that what looks virtual can actually be an impending reality. As Misaki himself suggests in his commentary on the work, his underlying theme is that anyone, and everyone, may be involved in war without being conscious of it.[12] How real was the Gulf War to the Japanese who watched the 'bombing lights' on television? The same can be said of the September 11 attack or the more recent war in Iraq. Misaki's work challenges the 'peace' discourse in a society permeated by virtual images of war that are deprived of all sense of reality.

Both Abe and Misaki deal with the question of social engagement in contemporary Japan. While Abe highlights the difficulty of taking meaningful action in a society whose solidarity has been shaken by the increasing fragmentation of experience caused by the spread of the electronic media, Misaki critiques the contemporary situation by illustrating the extent to which one's everyday life is controlled, not only by the media, but also by social and educational discipline, masterminded by a bureaucratic body that tactfully conceals where the power lies. Neither of their works takes the form of direct social criticism. In a style that resembles fantasy or science fiction, they create a 'noise' that shocks the nervous system of our common sense.

Machida Kō is another writer whose work characteristically creates 'noise'. His literary style is remarkably distinctive: a kind of punk monologue, outrageously casual yet pressing, hilariously fragmentary yet vividly real. In *Fukumi-warai* (*Pregnant Smile*, 2006), the protagonist, who is desperately running away from the spiteful, condescending 'pregnant smiles' turned his way by those around him, falls into a 'fissure' of reality and finds it filled with 'noise', which takes the form of wormy, sticky, eerie string. This poisonous stringy substance is flying about everywhere, sticking to human skin, melting it down until it eventually takes the last breath from its victim. The protagonist's fight with this 'noise' is futile, to say the least – there is no way out, even though reality is only 'fifteen meters away'.[13] This warp in reality is where Machida situates himself as a writer. Reality may be 'rotten', as the protagonist says, but to fight it in the hope of launching a revolution is not sensible; nor can you remove yourself from it to live the life of a recluse. Therefore you have to find a way of reconciling with it;[14] as a result you slip and get trapped in the warped space of its folds. Machida presents his literature as, symbolically, the 'noise' itself; yet, paradoxically perhaps, he believes this 'noise' will kill, not save, the world. In short, although Machida tears the fabric of the everyday in his writing, he sees these tears as being systematically reincorporated into that very fabric. In that moment they become superfluous – in other words, pure noise.

Machida's literary challenge is a kind of guerilla warfare, with no clearcut beginning or end. It does not attempt to overturn the system through classical strategies of rebellion, but rather, wiggles its way in, ripping and tearing, screaming and mumbling, abounding with malice and witty humour. Because it interacts with that which it attacks, it always stands on precarious grounds – is always on the verge of being incorporated.

The seeming incapacity of individual action in society has been a running theme in Murakami Haruki's work since the 1980s. Coloured by a sense of nostalgia for a past when the younger generation was able to cry out for freedom and for a 'real' revolution, Murakami's work presents individuals trying to get by in an age in which so many human actions are pre-empted by words and images. Compared to the works just described, however, the element of tension with society is minimal. Similar to Yoshimoto's pursuit of new styles of human interaction, Murakami provides his readers with a new picture of our times, not because he draws directly from our sociocultural reality but because he has created new models free from modernist values. He suggests that there are ways to live through this age, whether in Japan or elsewhere, as long as people gracefully abandon norms that governed them in the past: 'oh well' (*yare yare*), as the typical Murakami character would say, this is where we are.

Variations and diversity: crossing the borders

The blurring of borders between the real and the virtual can deprive the individual of the capacity to engage with society; sometimes creating, as we have seen, frustrated and angry individuals who are caught between the two realms. At the same time, however, the theme of crossing assumed boundaries has also opened up new areas of exploration, particularly for some women writers, Kawakami Hiromi, mentioned earlier, being one. Kawakami does not just transgress the border between the real and the virtual: she commits transgressions of all sorts. As we saw, in *Manazuru* it was the border between this world and the next that was broken down, allowing the protagonist to journey through time and space, accompanied by the shadow of the dead. This is a familiar theme in Japanese litera-ture, traceable to the ancient classics and later inherited by Ueda Akinari, Izumi Kyōka, and even Murakami Haruki in his *Wild Sheep Chase*. For Kawakami, the very act of crossing a border constitutes an important ele-ment in her writing. This can take place in myriad ways. In *Hebi wo Fumu* (*Stepping on a Snake*, 1996), the snake the protagonist accidentally steps on in the park becomes a woman who stays at her house, cooking meals for her, while her stories feature an octopus, a fox, a strange sea creature, giants, demons (from the short stories in *Ryugu*, 2002), and many other animals, monsters, and even plants, that mix and blend with humans. Even 'the night' is eligible, as we see in her story 'Atarayoki': 'I thought my back was a bit itchy, and found out that the night had grown into my body.'[15] All the categorisations and classifications that govern our lives lose relevance in Kawakami's world. The critic Kawamoto Saburo has described Kawakami's work as resembling a design on a thin, almost transparent sheet of paper that appears to be the tracing of something that lies underneath – yet, when you lift the sheet of paper, there is nothing there. The 'noises' that emerge from the frail yet compelling, dreamlike yet realistic array of images shake our senses. To use Kawamoto's words, they constitute a 'continuous series of little earthquakes.'[16]

Tawada Yōko is another woman writer who boldly crosses the assumed borders of our everyday reality. The 'body' takes many forms in Tawada's literary world: gender distinctions are blurred or erased; or sometimes the body itself is turned inside out, so that the internal organs flow out. Tawada has also crossed national and linguistic borders: she shares her time between Germany and Japan and writes in both languages. Abandoning the idea of literature as belonging to a certain national or linguistic tradition, she says she has instead strategically chosen to situate herself 'between' two languages: 'I am not that interested in learning many languages. My interest is not in the language itself but in the very gap between two different languages.'[17] The theme of travelling occupies an important place in her work, yet travel for her has no destination.[18] It is the constant process of moving and crossing borders, experiencing and feeling, that her words trace.

The transgression of borders takes on another dimension in Kanehara Hitomi, who sensationally emerged on the literary scene with *Snakes and Earrings* (2004), whose dark, gruesome portrait of today's youth encompasses sex, violence and death. Her 2005 novel, *Amebic*, deals directly with the theme of the body, its contours and transgressions. It focuses on the girl-writer as a 'writing machine', constantly typing her words in her room in a semi-delusional state. Ōtomo Rio has described how Kanehara's protagonist gradually loses the sense of her body's shape as the information-processing machine in front of her becomes an extension of her body, and she its 'terminus'. It is a record of suffering, to be sure, yet at the same time Ōtomo detects a sign of feminist defiance against the phallocentric order in the gradual breakdown of the unified self – flowing out, fluctuating, and blurring.[19]

Women writers have become more active, leaving the old 'women's literature' realm far behind.[20] In fact this very liberation from that gender-restricted genre has seemingly impelled them to write out of gender, out of nation, out of the Japanese language, and out of a number of other distinctions. Besides Yoshimoto Banana, Yū Miri, Kawakami Hiromi, Tawada Yōko and Kanehara Hitomi mentioned above, for example, there are many more, such as Ogawa Yōko and Matsuura Rieko who audaciously explore female sexuality, and Ekuni Kaori, Kirino Natsuo and others who started out writing children's fairytales, girls' comics and other non-mainstream literary genres, only to move on to create new streams of contemporary fiction.

Needless to say, it is not only the women who are boldly transgressing the boundaries of literary conventions; male writers are also attempting to challenge modernist assumptions of literature. Apart from those referred to earlier, writers such as Shimada Masahiko, Kobayashi Kyōji, Takahashi Gen'ichirō and Shimizu Yoshinori, to name only a few, are contesting the century-old myth of Japanese identity and the expectation that literature is supposed to question the meaning of Japanese modernity. Their works abound in satire and parody, which may be mischievous, obtusely metafictional, or manga-like and straightforwardly entertaining. Indeed, as we have noted, the distinction between 'pure' and 'popular' literature has become increasingly irrelevant in recent years. The literary market is drawing much of its energy from what would have been categorised as popular literature 20 years ago – mainstream literary journals, such as *Subaru*, *Bungakkai*, *Shinchō* and *Gunzō*, feature 'popular' writers, whose works are now often referred to as 'entertainment novels' and 'light novels'. Yet, are these voices from the periphery beginning to dominate the mainstream? Do their works create what Machida Kō terms 'noise'? Do they constitute an emancipatory discourse, or are they fundamentally incorporationist?

One other area of contemporary Japanese literature, essential to our discussion on difference and diversity, is the work of writers of non-Japanese origin who write in Japanese. Works written by Resident Koreans in Japan, generally referred to as the *zainichi bungaku*, have constituted an original stream in modern Japanese literature since the late 1930s, when Koreans were educated in Japanese (language education under colonial rule ended, of course, with the end of the war in 1945). Beginning with novelists like Kin Tatsuju, Kin Shiryō, Kin Sekihan and Tei Shōhaku, we see a succession of Korean writers producing works that deal with the predicament of the Korean people under Japan's colonial rule and its aftermath, and the harshness of their own experiences as Resident Koreans in Japan.[21] Ri Kaisei, born in Karafuto, who later settled in Japan after a failed attempt to go back to Korea, was the first Korean writer to receive the Akutagawa prize. Today, second, third and even fourth generation Resident Koreans are active in the Japanese literary world, although their works do not necessarily deal directly with the question of their Korean identity. Yū Miri, mentioned earlier, is one such writer. Kaneshiro Kazuki is a Japanese citizen of Korean origin, who calls himself 'Korean Japanese' (written in katakana), not *zainichi*. His works, *Revolution*, *SPEED*, and *Fly Daddy Fly* (original titles written in English), for example, enjoy an enthusiastic readership among the young generation and have been consecutively adapted into both manga and film.

Increasing the diversity of writers in contemporary Japan are others whose native language is not Japanese. American-born Levy Hideo can be seen as a pioneer of this kind. Arthur Binard, also born and brought up in the United States, writes poetry in Japanese. The 2008 Akutagawa prize was awarded to Yang Yi, a Chinese writer who began studying Japanese after moving to Japan at the age of 22. It is not only the fact that these writers have come on to the Japanese literary scene that deserves attention; it is that their works, including those of the *zainichi* writers, call into question the relationship between literature, language, ethnicity and nationality, compelling us to redefine and renew our understanding of what constitutes 'Japanese literature'.

A historical perspective: after the modern

Now, in the 21st century with nearly 150 years having passed since Japan's opening to the Western world, we are witnessing signs that many of the governing principles of the late 19th century, which pushed Japan through its modernisation process, are no longer at work. Japan has re-situated itself in the international context; or rather, the world's entire geo-political configuration has undergone a fundamental change, particularly since the end of the Cold War. This coincides with the spread of late-capitalist, consumerist societies and the subsequent information explosion, which has dramatically changed the nature of information flow around the world. Developments in Japanese literature can also be observed against this backdrop.

Many of the new 'novels' (*shōsetsu*) of the modern period revolved around themes related to the question of Japanese modernity: in particular, what it means to be 'Japanese' and 'modern' at the same time. With the overwhelming inflow of Western ideas, Japanese writers struggled to find a solution to the fundamental conflict between the nation's traditional values and newly imported Western values. This applied not only to the pioneering writers of the Meiji period but also to many writers of the Taisho and Showa periods. Of the Taisho writers, Akutagawa Ryūnosuke, for example, inherited much of the scepticism of his mentor, Sōseki, who had described Japan's modernisation as having been 'externally driven' (*gaihatsuteki*). Tanizaki Jun'ichirō began writing under the spell of the West but his vision changed significantly after he moved to Western Japan. Much of the work of Nagai Kafū, who was slightly older than Akutagawa and Tanizaki, is an elegy for the Edo culture he loved so well. Subsequent writers like Kawabata Yasunari and Mishima Yukio also dealt with the question of Japanese identity, respectively presenting their own visions of 'Japaneseness' in post-1945 Japan. Even writers such as Abe Kobo and Ōe Kenzaburo, who have upheld an 'international' perspective, possessed visions that were fundamentally and classically modern in the sense that they inherently asserted their Japanese identity in negating the culturally specific Japaneseness of their work.

One clear difference between these writers and those who emerged on the literary scene in the 1980s and after is that, among that younger generation, such a consciousness of Japaneseness no longer occupies a central place in their work. True, numerous references are made to issues that specifically concern Japan, but the question of conflict between tradition and modernity, and the quest for Japanese identity against the influx of Western values, do not constitute a dominant underlying theme. Take Murakami Haruki, for example, whose name is most frequently mentioned in discussions about this new generation of writers. The implicit message in his work is that he is writing in Japanese only by chance; that he only happened to be born Japanese. The author-nation relationship no longer marks the essential starting point of writing activity.

As was briefly touched on at the beginning of this chapter, the modernist worldview that had divided and categorised the world through the dualistic principles of power supported by a belief in the linear progression of history, has undergone radical changes in the last few decades. Accompanying this has been a profound change in the nature of a more than century-old power relationship in cultural exchange. As long as the West served as a frame of reference for Japan to measure the extent of its internal modernisation, information flowed predominantly in one direction. Japanese writers as recipients of this knowledge poured their energy into translation, but when they attempted to create their own version of modern literature, they were inevitably confronted with the question of originality. A successful case of importation and adaptation not only threatened Japan's cultural integrity but also left Japanese writers with products that were at best close to the original model. The constant references to the unique traditions of Japanese culture that dot the works of the writers mentioned above can be understood as a modernist response to Japan's cultural dilemma, 'modernist' because none of them meant to literally revive or restore traditional culture in its original state – they were already writing in the modern form. Given the recent change in the cultural scene, however, this dilemma has begun to lose relevance among the younger generation of Japanese writers, even though, of course, there is no indication that it has been resolved.

With the change in the global political and economic environment and developments in information technology, the power relationships between nations have shifted as the conception of knowledge and the means of its dissemination have undergone a major transformation. National boundaries no longer constitute the primary defining units of cultural activity. The global proliferation of the internet and other electronic media is accelerating the production of networks of all kinds. Literary activity, too, is much less domestically confined. The number of multilingual authors who choose their language of writing is increasing, and the flow of translation is much more diverse. A symbolic case in point is, once again, Murakami Haruki, whose works are actively translated into numerous languages as soon as they appear in Japanese. We have also seen how in the domestic realm, the hierarchical order of literature is steadily being invalidated, opening up space for an increasing diversity of forms, styles and writers.

All of these are suggestive of the liberating potential of our age. At the same time, however, we have seen in our examination of a few contemporary Japanese works the increasing presence of forces that inhibit people from becoming free and independent agents in society. The expansion of the media industry and the overflow of information make it more and more difficult for the individual to assert the originality of his/her experience. On the inter-cultural level as well, the largely shared recognition of the disintegration of the 19th-century global order does not necessarily lead to an equal interaction between different cultures around the world. In the case of Japan, the successful accumulation of capital and the emergence of a massive consumerist culture have dispersed the shadow of the West – indeed, the West has been 'consumed'. Yet, although the sense of backwardness may no longer be there, the question of identity has remained.

Looking at the 'literatures' of the world today, it is clear that works produced by writers in the world's metropoli share much in common, thematically and stylistically. But globalisation does not necessarily mean erasing local and regional differences. With the progression of what looks like a diasporic dispersal of values among the younger generation around the world, we are also witnessing a growth in awareness of locality and regionality. The complacency of similitude is inevitably accompanied by an urge for differentiation, since inherent differences are suppressed in the process of creating a common culture.

The acceleration in speed and the increase in quantity of intercultural exchange – and the resulting emergence of a global culture that allows people of different regions of the world to share common experiences – has given rise to a new consciousness of identity. This identity is based on the awareness of differences in one's historical and cultural experiences. It is a renewed sense of otherness that has come about as a reaction to today's predominating popular culture, so that, even in this age of globalisation, we are witnessing a renewed rise of nationalism. Confrontations between different ethnic groups and religious cultures are still stubbornly present. How Japanese culture will evolve within this world context remains to be seen.

One area in Japanese literature that has been left largely unexplored to date is its relationship with other Asian cultures. Perhaps, as Japanese writers move away from the Japan-West relationship, there will be room for them to look at their culture and history in relation to the cultures and histories of their neighbours. Since the beginning of the modern period, Japanese authors have held an ambivalent attitude towards Asia. In its pursuit of Westernisation, Japan's Asian identity was consciously left behind, as is reflected in the widely-quoted slogan proposed by Fukuzawa Yukichi, to 'leave Asia and enter the West'. When Japan advanced into its neighbouring regions in the name of Asianism, its imperial effort attempted to impose Japaneseness on the local people through the suppression of their cultures. During this period, few Japanese writers positively engaged with their Asian counterparts in their creative pursuits. By and large the situation has not changed to date; translation of foreign literature has been and is still dominated by works written by European and American writers. At the same time, we have seen how the voices of non-Japanese writers have been creatively challenging the traditional notion of 'Japanese literature'. As Japanese literature frees itself from the bonds of nationality, ethnicity and the discourse of cultural homogeneity, new space should open for it to expand and develop its encounters with the cultures and literatures of other Asian countries.

Notes

1. I express my special thanks to Ted Goossen of York University for his help in writing this article. I would not have been able to put this together without his assistance, though the entire responsibility with regard to the content is mine.
2. Matsuda (2007: 2–3).
3. The biggest hit to date, *Koizora* (Love Sky), a high school girl's love story, attracted approximately 1.2 million mobile phone readers and appeared on the bestseller charts soon after it appeared in book form. It was then made into a successful film. Mika (2007: back page).

4. Matsuda (2007: 2–3).
5. Masakazu Yamazaki (1972).
6. Etō (1967).
7. Morton (2003: 196).
8. Ryū Murakami (2001: 171). Page reference is to the 2003 reprint.
9. Kazushige Abe (2001: 70). Page reference is to the 2004 reprint.
10. Norihiro Katō (2004: 151–60).
11. Takahashi in Kazushige Abe (2005: 222–9).
12. Misaki (2005a).
13. Machida (2003: 187). Page reference is to the 2006 reprint.
14. Machida (2003: 139). Page reference is to the 2006 reprint.
15. Kawakami (1996: 105). Page reference is to the 1999 reprint.
16. Kawamoto in Kawakami (2002: 222). Page reference is to the 2005 paperback edition.
17. Tawada (2003: 31).
18. Tawada (2002).
19. Otomo (2007).
20. The Joryū Bungakusha-kai (Society of Women Writers) announced its dissolution in October 2007, putting an end to its 70-year history. The society was inaugurated by Yoshiya Nobuko, Uno Chiyo, Hayashi Fumiyo and other women writers who sought to create a ground for their activities through mutual recognition and criticism during the decades when writings by women constituted a distinct minority (*Asahi Shimbun*, 13 September 2007).
21. Korean names are written in accordance with the Japanese pronunciation.

Further reading

Goossen, Theodore (1997), *Oxford Book of Japanese Short Stories*, Oxford: Oxford University Press.
Karatani, Kojin (1993), *Origins of Japanese Literature*, Durham: Duke University Press.

12

Popular leisure

A revolutionary change

In 1991 the then prime minister of France, Edith Cresson, in the midst of an EU–Japanese trade conflict, caught much attention by comparing the Japanese to ants who stay up all night working. It might be that Cresson's impression of the Japanese was partly drawn from the debate on *karōshi*, death from overwork, which had begun in the second half of the 80s in Japan and was quickly adopted by those critical of Japan in the West. Such people, especially American intellectuals critical of the Japanese trade surplus with the US, the so-called revisionists or Japan-bashers, had accused Japan of 'social dumping' in the form of long working hours and short vacations. During the 90s, official Japanese economic policy changed, most probably in response to these critics: becoming prime minister in 1991 Miyazawa Kiichi (1919–2007), one of the LDP's most influential politicians for many decades, announced that the aim of his government was to make Japan a 'great country to live in' (*seikatsu taikoku*). Consequently, the Labour Standards Law (*Rōdō kijun hō*) was amended in 1993, providing workers with a 40-hour working week and 125 per cent overtime payment. Since management had been very reluctant to accept any further statutory reduction in working hours since the introduction of the 48-hour working week in 1947, this can be called a truly revolutionary change.

Furthermore, Japanese culture, which – apart from a considerable export of traditional culture such as *ikebana* flower arrangement or *haiku* poetry – never had had an important status in Japanese foreign policy, was suddenly seen in a more positive light by Japanese diplomats. Around 2005, Japan even came to be called 'cool Japan'; a catchphrase much used by the Foreign Ministry. Leisure and youth culture, which for a long time had almost been regarded as 'social evils', were re-evaluated and prioritised in cultural exports. Manga cartoons, anime films, playful Japanese design, J-pop music and Japanese-style cooking had first been eagerly absorbed in Japan's neighbour states and later all over the world. While for a long time Japan had been exporting the hardware for leisure to the world, now it is also exporting the software, and these exports seem to become ever more important year by year. The stereotypical view of Japan as a grey nation of working bees or ants, as expressed by Cresson, has given way to one of a colourful and youthful nation in which modern-style play is much more important than old-fashioned work ethics stressing diligence and devotion to one's employer. The German boys' pop group with the strange name Tokio Hotel, which formed in 2005 and has since become one of the most successful bands ever in middle Europe, is said to have taken its name because 'Tokyo is the most glittering city in the world'.

In this overview of contemporary leisure I use the framework of the convergence theory, meaning that economic development has a strong unifying impact on social institutions. Since Japan is one of the most advanced economies of the world, its society is likely to exhibit the features of a post-industrial society's leisure culture. This does not necessarily mean that Japan's leisure culture is completely adopting that of advanced Western societies, but that the importance of work ethics and related values is lessening, while privatisation and individualisation is increasing.[1] Another essential question is whether individual leisure behaviour has been emancipated from economic and political organisations, and to what extent Japanese citizens have achieved the freedom to use leisure not as other-directed but as inner-directed individuals, as defined by Riesman.[2]

Debates and controversies

One of the fundamental questions when dealing with leisure in Japan concerns the appropriateness of the Western concept of 'leisure' in the context of Japanese society.[3] Japanese critics of this concept like to point to the use of the loanword *rejā* for leisure as proof that this concept is alien to Japan. Even so, there also exists a Sino-Japanese compound word, *yoka*, as an equivalent for leisure, but critics tend to stress its negative meaning vis-à-vis the positive connotation leisure has in English or *Freizeit* has in German. *Yoka* means *amaru hima*, the free time (*hima*) left over (*amaru*), they argue, and *yoka* thus is nothing but a residual category in the time management of individuals. The genuine Japanese words *hima* and *itoma* signifying 'free' or 'available' time are not used for leisure, but in sentences like, *Ima o-hima desu ka?* (Are you free now to do this and that?) By contrast, one expression for 'to work', *itonamu*, has its origin in *ito nashi*, 'to have no free time', a hint at the high value placed on free time relative to work in years past.[4]

Rejā is a relatively new word, which, according to economic historian Ōtsuka Hisao, entered the Japanese language shortly after the high economic growth period began in 1955.[5] Around 1960, Japan experienced its first *rejā būmu* (leisure boom), heralded by the mass media. *Rejā* was a fashion word of the year 1961,[6] which points to its novelty at that time. Although it is a word of foreign origin, one can argue that it has now been in use for around fifty years and thus is thoroughly Japanised. This is clearly visible in words such as *rejā-sangyō* (leisure industries) or *rejā-zei* (leisure tax), *kamitsu rejā* (overcrowded leisure) or *kamikaze rejā* (leisure in a *kamikaze* fighter style, that is, until exhausted), which combine the foreign loanword with a (Sino-) Japanese word.

Of course the Japanese have always not only worked, but also liked to play. The verb *asobu* and the noun *asobi* denote this activity. Johan Huizinga in his 1938 fundamental study on human play, *Homo ludens*, already noted this Japanese expression and discussed its meaning, while at the same time pointing to the term *majime* (earnestness) as its contrary.[7]

In the 8th century, *asobi* was something connected with the sacred cult. Professional groups of 'players' (*asobibe*) performed dances and played music at religious occasions: these 'plays for the gods' were called *kami asobi*, later *kagura*. Typical occasions were 'field plays' (*ta asobi*, later called *dengaku*), festivals in the spring, which were held to pray for a rich harvest. It seems that *asobi* (Sino-Japanese reading: *yū*) was imbued with a negative connotation only when it came to be applied to purely sexual amusement, like in the words *yūkaku* and *yūri* (red light district) or *yūjo* (prostitute). *Asobi* in modern Japan retained this negative connotation. Further examples of this usage are words like *asobinin* (playboy) or *asobite* (rake), which have their positive counterpart in *hatarakimono* (hardworking person).

From the Meiji Restoration to the end of the Pacific War, the ruling elites tried to enforce a puritan samurai ethic on the whole of Japan. Every Japanese was expected to work for Japan's modernisation first and for the establishment of a huge Japanese empire second; time and infrastructure for play or leisure was lacking, with the exception of the larger cities during the 1920s and early 1930s. After the Pacific War, however, a change of values lead to a 'revolution of consciousness' (*ishiki kakumei*), as social psychologist Minami Hiroshi announced in 1960 in a book with the same title, in which he tried to give proof of these changes. From the late 1980s, to play and to enjoy one's free time finally became well-acknowledged goals in life, at least as long as they were not conflicting with one's professional or family life.

Turning to the academic study of leisure, it is notable that in several series of multi-volume sociology readers published in Japan from 1958 onwards, the 1995 edition was the first to contain a special volume on *Shigoto to asobi no shakaigaku (The Sociology of Work and Play)*. Prior to that, leisure or play had never had a place in these readers, an indication of their low evaluation in Japanese sociology up to the 1990s. This does not mean, of course, that the study of leisure had been completely ignored: already in the 1920s, Gonda Yasunosuke had initiated empirical research on the amusement and leisure behaviour of Japanese workers and urbanites.

One argument often put forward by those advocating Japanese uniqueness is the notion that the Japanese need no time for play or for leisure except as recreation from work fatigue. This idea was expressed as far back as 1919 by Mutō Sanji, the representative of the Japanese government at the convention of the newly founded International Labour Organization that planned to introduce a legally guaranteed 48-hour working week in all industrialised nations, including Japan. Mutō argued that the Japanese are used to working 10 or 12 hours per day and do not need more free time, because they are not accustomed to it. If Japanese workers were given more spare time, he argued, they would most probably only misuse it.[8] At the World Conference for Leisure and Recreation in Hamburg in 1936, Kitayama Junyu, the most active Japanese propagandist in Nazi Germany and professor for Japanology at Prague University in 1944–45, stressed firstly that Japanese workers in the family state[9] need no individual leisure for themselves, but only a creative break (*schöpferische Pause*). Secondly, in Japan, he contended, all holidays were related to the religious cult or the state. Moreover, to Japanese women, concepts such as leisure and recreation were totally unknown and meaningless, since they had to devote themselves entirely to the care of their children and husbands.[10]

After 1945, similar thoughts reappeared in a different form. The firm now replaced the family state as the institution to which workers had to devote everything. Adherents of this philosophy fought against the idea of leisure being an independent sphere in life and stressed that work and leisure must not be separated as in the West. MITI official Namiki Nobuyoshi, when reporting about MITI's 1971 industrial structure vision for Japan, stressed the necessity for a 'monistic acceptance of work and leisure', the 'meaning of life [lying] in the unification of work and leisure'.[11] It was imperative, he argued, to reject any dualistic view of work and leisure. Hence, after the introduction of the five-day working week, many big companies turned to appropriating Saturdays for the education of their workers.

In spite of such views, more and more Japanese over the last quarter of the 20th century have adopted an individual lifestyle not so different to that found in the West. With the exception of a small stratum of dogged 'company people' (*kaisha ningen*), they regard free time as their private time that they can use according to their individual liking and without any interference on the part of their employer.

Time for leisure

From 1992 onwards, Japanese workers have worked less than 2000 hours a year. If one compares this figure with international statistics, Japan is no longer among the top working nations regarding working hours. Scheduled working hours in establishments with 30 or more employees decreased between 1976 and 2003 from 162.9 hours to 141.7 hours per month, and total working hours, that is, scheduled working hours plus overtime, similarly decreased from 174.5 to 153.8 hours.[12]

The above statistics are based on the Ministry of Labour's *Maitsuki kinrō tōkei chōsa* (Monthly Investigation of Work Statistics) and only report paid hours of employment. Japan, however, is famous for employees working overtime without getting paid, either in the workplace or at home, which is known euphemistically as 'service overtime' (*sābisu zangyō*).

The Ministry of Public Management, Home Affairs, Posts and Telecommunications (Sōmu-chō) conducts its own Investigation on the Work Force (*Rōdōryoku chōsa*). In this survey, workers themselves fill out the questionnaires, and the resulting working hours are considerably longer than those reported by the Ministry of Labour. Even if we take into account the possibility that workers might exaggerate their work load, this alone does not explain the wide gap between results. In fact, workers often are expected to arrive at their workplace a quarter of an hour or so before work starts, and similarly feel compelled not to leave immediately after the end of their required hours.

What is also missing from the statistics is commuting. Workers in the Keihin area (Tokyo, Kawasaki, Yokohama) in particular, but also in the other big urban agglomerations, suffer from very long commuting times in overcrowded trains. In 1990 Rengō Sōken, the research institute of the biggest Japanese trade unions' association, conducted a comparative study of work-related time in five nations. Even though this report must be read with caution due to its authorship, the results are enlightening. Summing up commuting time, time at work and times of rest during work, while excluding eating time during work, Japanese workers, with approximately twelve hours per day, work 1.5 hours more than Americans and 2.5 hours more than Europeans (British, French and German). These working time patterns obviously have consequences for the time left for leisure purposes. While the Germans enjoyed 4:15 free hours on an average working day, the Japanese had to cope with only 2:28 hours, or nearly two hours less.[13]

Since many leisure activities take place on weekends, the forced introduction of the five-day 40-hour working week in all companies from 1997 onwards has brought about a great change in leisure behaviour and activities. IBM Japan had pioneered the establishment of the two-day weekend as far back as 1953. For the whole country, however, this revolutionary change took as long as 44 years to take place!

Japan today is the world's leading nation in number of public holidays. Over the years, the government has designated more and more public holidays to compensate working people for the postponement of the two-day weekend and for the small amount of paid vacations. The idea that the Japanese need more free time in order to be able to consume more, which again should stimulate the economy, might have been the ultimate motive behind these policies. The 'Happy Monday System', which instituted several Mondays as public holidays instead of holidays on fixed dates, guarantees that employees are able to celebrate national holidays. This makes it possible for people to enjoy three-day weekends on these occasions. Short vacations for two or three days to hot springs, 'leisure lands', theme parks or famous scenic spots correspond with traditional Japanese behaviour and are still very popular.

Three periods of the year are also by now customarily connected with longer absence from work: the time of the New Year festival, when most companies close for at least three days, although only New Year's Day is a national holiday; 'Golden Week' between 29 April and 5 May, with a cluster of national holidays; and the time of the Bon festival in the middle of August, at which time many Japanese return to their original homes to visit their ancestors' graves. Many companies take this traditional custom as an opportunity to close for a whole week or so. Needless to say, many Japanese nowadays also use these periods to travel abroad.

The most peculiar Japanese practice in regard to free time is Japanese employees' use of paid vacations. The amount of paid leave to which

Japanese workers are entitled is 10 days, but after six months with the same employer and a minimum attendance rate of 80 per cent, paid leave increases for two days per year until 20 days are reached after six and a half years. Of all industrialised countries, in terms of paid leave, Japan is second from lowest: only in the United States is there no legal guarantee for paid leave at all.[14] Taking into account the fact that Japanese companies have several regulations for additional days of paid leave, Japanese workers are not so badly off in comparison to workers in other highly developed countries.

What is truly astonishing is the low usage rate of paid holidays. Until 1995, the number of days of paid leave taken rose to 9.5 days per year, but since then it has started declining again and reached 8.4 days in 2005, which corresponds to a usage rate of only 46.6 per cent.[15] This rate is higher in large companies than in small ones. A study conducted in 2001 established that most workers avail themselves to the full of the regulation that unused days of paid leave can be saved for two years. In a sample of 3000 workers, men on average were allocated a total of 30.1 holidays, but consumed only 7.4 days, while women had 24.6 days and consumed 8.7 days. Even young women in their 20s and 30s who are often said to constitute a 'leisure aristocracy' did not deviate significantly from this pattern.[16]

The most often mentioned reason for saving a considerable part of the paid leave one is entitled to is a very rational one: employees want to have some days in reserve in order to use them when they get ill, despite the fact that sick leave is available to them. Thus they can boast of a perfect record of attendance, even in case of illness. Other reasons often mentioned relate to the working environment: to take too many holidays would affect one's colleagues; the working climate does not encourage one to take longer leave; etc. Some people even say that they do not know what to do with their days of paid leave. A Japanese government study in 2002 revealed that the full use of paid holidays and concomitant consumption would result in considerable economic growth and in the creation of 1.5 million jobs for people in the service industry.[17] From a purely economical point of view, Japanese frugality in holiday use is perceived to have considerable negative consequences.

Leisure activities

The relatively undeveloped state of leisure in Japan in the 1960s resulted in the creation of various institutions for the study of leisure which since then have resulted in a host of interesting research reports and data concerning leisure activities.

The Leisure Development Center (Yoka Kaihatsu Sentā) was created in the early 1970s by MITI, when the economic importance of leisure could no longer be overlooked, in order to obtain the necessary basic data on the leisure activities and wishes of the Japanese people. These were considered necessary in order to provide the leisure industries with data for their investment decisions. One of the activities of the Center consisted in the publication of a yearly *Whitebook on Leisure*, which reported the latest trends in the leisure activities of the Japanese. In 2000, the Center was renamed into a more fashionable, but short-lived Society for the Design of Free Time (Jiyū Jikan Dezain Kyōkai). It was dissolved in 2003 and became part of the Japan Productivity Center for Socio-Economic Development (Shakai Keizai Seisansei Honbu) as Yoka Sōken (General Research Institute for Leisure), which continues to publish the *Whitebook on Leisure* to this day.

Another important institution is the Japan Recreation Society (Nihon Rekuriēshon Kyōkai), which is financed by the Ministry of Education and Technology (Monbu Kagakushō) and has branches in every prefecture. Apart from research activities, it tries to provide the people with information on desirable forms of play. Furthermore, national broadcaster NHK has been investigating the time budget of the Japanese for many years for the planning of its TV programs, and these data are equally important for people professionally concerned with leisure.

A look into the *Japan Statistical Yearbook* reveals many interesting facts about the leisure habits of the Japanese. Leisure activities tend to differ on weekdays and on weekends, and according to gender. Table 12.1 shows that for most leisure activities more people engage in them on weekends than on weekdays and that they also spend more time on these activities on weekends, especially on Sundays. However, there are some exceptions: Fewer women exercise or play sports on weekends; and fewer men and women listen to the radio or read newspapers on Sundays, or take a rest on weekends. But the time engaged in conversations, exercise and sports, outings and walks, hobbies and television increases considerably on weekends. Fewer women than men participate in exercise and sports, have hobbies, or read newspapers, but more women seem to care for conversations, reading magazines and listening to CDs. What is also interesting is that there is no activity besides viewing television in which more than 50 per cent of all men and women engage. The other most common activities are reading newspapers and resting, at around 40 per cent, while hobbies, entertainment and

Table 12.1 *Daily action rates by kind of activity, average time spent, 2001*[a]

	Males			Females		
Activity	Weekday	Saturday	Sunday	Weekday	Saturday	Sunday
Conversation/Personal	12.8%	16.5%	17.3%	25.8%	26.8%	27.5%
associations	1:50	2:25	3:03	1:37	2:11	2:16
Exercise and sports	8.9%	12.2%	13.5%	6.8%	5.7%	5.7%
	1:58	3:13	3:47	1:37	1:33	2:39
Outings and walks	12.9%	18.0%	24.0%	14.8%	18.9%	23.5%
	2:11	2:53	3:20	1:51	2:54	3:17
Hobbies, entertainment,	17.3%	22.7%	25.4%	16.8%	20.2%	19.9%
cultural activities	2:40	3:34	3:58	2:19	2:50	3:00
TV	88.9%	90.5%	88.8%	91.4%	91.5%	90.4%
	3:34	4:29	5:03	4:02	4:24	4:25
Radio	15.0%	12.2%	12.1%	15.2%	13.1%	12.0%
	2:37	2:14	2:31	2:26	2:35	2:33
Newspapers	46.0%	48.1%	45.9%	42.1%	46.4%	40.9%
	0:51	1:00	0:52	0:43	0:45	0:46
Magazines, comic	17.4%	17.3%	19.0%	19.2%	21.1%	23.1%
books, books	1:16	1:32	1:32	1:03	1:16	1:15
CDs, MD, tapes	7.9%	9.2%	8.0%	10.8%	12.1%	11.9%
	1:36	2:05	2:01	1:32	1:50	2:05
Videos	7.1%	9.7%	10.4%	8.5%	10.5%	10.8%
	1:42	1:39	2:00	1:38	1:46	1:56
Rest	43.0%	41.8%	40.9%	43.0%	41.8%	39.3%
	1:09	1:17	1:24	1:07	1:10	1:13

[a] All data originally from the 2001 'Survey on Time Use and Leisure Activities' as contained in Ministry of Public Management, Home Affairs, Posts and Telecommunications, Statistics Bureau (2006: 750).

cultural activities, as well as outings, walks and reading magazines (this last carried out by women), transcend the 20 per cent level only on weekends. Since these statistics include all people – those who have a job, those who do not and housewives – we can assume that working people do not spend much time on leisure activities on weekdays.

Let us next examine the participation rate in a number of leisure-related activities that 10 per cent of all Japanese had engaged in at least once per year in 1995, 2000 and 2004 (Table 12.2). In the area of sports, the five sports with

Table 12.2 *Participation rate in leisure activities by type, 1995–2004 (%)[a]*

Sports Activity	Males			Females		
	1995	2000	2004	1995	2000	2004
Bowling	39.5	34.6	31.7	31.7	26.7	26.7
Jogging, marathon	25.9	28.0	28.1	21.4	21.7	19.8
Playing catch, baseball	27.3	25.5	24.2	5.1	6.3	7.1
Gymnastics	26.3	27.4	22.9	34.9	34.1	32.5
Fishing	27.4	24.3	22.4	8.0	6.8	5.1
Swimming (in pool)	21.2	19.6	18.7	22.9	24.4	21.3
Golf (courses)	23.6	21.0	17.6	3.6	3.0	1.8
Golf (practice ranges)	23.1	20.8	17.0	7.3	4.8	4.4
Training	14.8	18.3	17.0	8.9	11.0	11.4
Cycling	13.1	16.6	15.4	13.8	12.4	11.8
Table tennis	11.7	13.9	11.3	11.6	11.9	11.7
Soccer	12.0	10.9	11.0	1.9	2.0	3.1
Badminton	9.3	8.9	7.7	14.7	11.4	13.7

Amusement Activity	Males			Females		
	1995	2000	2004	1995	2000	2004
Eating out	64.4	67.8	63.1	70.1	71.4	68.4
Karaoke	58.5	49.4	48.4	56.0	48.0	41.2
Bar, snack bar, pub	54.6	50.0	45.6	31.8	25.9	23.0
Lotteries	43.3	39.0	44.0	35.0	32.3	39.6
Playing home-use video games	34.0	31.2	32.7	24.4	24.2	22.4
Playing cards, etc.	29.5	26.4	26.0	36.2	26.9	28.9
Pachinko	38.7	28.3	24.8	16.5	9.1	8.3
Playing video games at game centres	25.6	22.5	22.6	21.5	18.5	22.1
Shōgi	18.9	17.1	13.9	3.7	1.7	1.7
Betting at horse race	21.8	15.9	13.1	7.5	3.8	3.1
Mahjong	21.3	17.2	11.6	5.3	3.6	2.6
Sauna	11.5	10.4	10.2	8.2	7.0	7.0

Hobbies and creative works Activity	Males			Females		
	1995	2000	2004	1995	2000	2004
Enjoying videotapes	47.1	44.6	46.7	39.8	40.7	42.0
Personal computers	–	38.0	46.6	–	24.7	34.5
Enjoying music (CD etc.)	38.1	40.4	37.6	43.2	40.0	39.3
Watching movies (excluding on TV)	26.4	28.2	36.6	35.9	35.5	43.0
Gardening	29.1	31.2	27.8	37.8	42.3	40.0

(*cont.*)

Table 12.2 (cont.)

Hobbies and creative works Activity	Males			Females		
	1995	2000	2004	1995	2000	2004
Watching sport games (excluding on TV)	25.7	22.5	25.0	16.7	13.1	14.4
Do-it-yourself carpentry	24.1	22.1	19.1	3.2	2.7	4.2
Studies, research	11.7	16.9	17.3	11.8	14.3	16.7
Photographing	12.6	11.3	15.4	7.7	6.9	9.8
Music concerts, etc.	14.0	16.4	15.4	30.8	30.7	30.7
Knitting, weaving, embroidering	0.7	0.7	0.3	27.4	26.8	22.6
Watching plays (excluding on TV)	6.7	6.5	7.7	19.4	18.7	16.6
Enjoying fine art (excluding on TV)	13.0	10.4	9.9	22.9	17.8	15.1
Sewing, dressmaking	0.5	0.7	0.8	22.6	18.4	13.7
Cooking (excluding ordinary duties)	7.0	6.1	6.3	19.3	10.7	13.5

Travel and excursion Activity	Males			Females		
	1995	2000	2004	1995	2000	2004
Domestic sightseeing tours	55.3	51.3	53.4	61.9	59.1	57.1
Driving a car	58.4	58.1	52.8	54.2	53.6	47.6
Zoological and botanical gardens, aquariums and museums	36.9	35.3	33.3	44.8	41.9	40.2
Visiting amusement parks	31.9	30.6	26.2	38.7	34.8	31.5
Picnic, hiking, field walking	30.2	29.2	26.0	37.8	34.5	29.6
Sea bathing	30.5	23.4	20.0	26.4	21.6	16.6
Visiting one's home town	21.7	20.5	19.8	22.6	23.1	22.5
Entertainment, exhibitions	22.8	18.4	17.0	28.0	24.9	22.3
Overseas sightseeing tours	10.9	12.8	11.0	14.9	13.4	10.9

[a] All data newly arranged from the 2001 'Survey on Time Use and Leisure Activities' as contained in Ministry of Public Management, Home Affairs, Posts and Telecommunications, Statistics Bureau (2006: 752–3).

the highest participation rate for men were bowling, jogging, baseball, gymnastics and fishing, while the five top sports for women were gymnastics, bowling, swimming, jogging and badminton. In general, women engaged in sports, and especially in baseball, fishing, golf, training and soccer, to a lesser degree than men, but in other areas the female participation rate was higher than the male, namely in gymnastics, swimming and badminton. Sports not shown in Table 12.2 are only practiced by very small segments of society.

In activities classified as 'amusements', eating out and playing cards are the only activities in which the female participation rate is slightly higher than that of men. On the other side of the equation there are many favourite male amusements, in which very few women participate, such as visiting bars, playing *pachinko*, playing *shōgi*, betting at horse races and playing mahjong. All these can be called typical male leisure activities. In the category 'hobbies and creative works', watching movies and plays, going to concerts and enjoying fine arts have a much higher female participation rate. It seems as if Japanese women are much more 'cultured people' than men, but it is probably the case that fewer men are able to engage in such activities because they often occur during working hours. All the other activities in which many more women than men participate are those that can be classified as 'half work-related': gardening, knitting, weaving, embroidering, sewing and dressmaking, as well as cooking. The only comparable male-dominated activity is do-it-yourself carpentry.

In the final category, 'travel and excursion', the gender differences are not as pronounced. That visiting zoological and botanical gardens, aquariums and museums, going to amusement parks, and enjoying entertainments and exhibitions have a higher female participation rate might be due to many mothers visiting such institutions with their children and without the children's fathers.

Age is another important variable influencing leisure activities. This can be best observed in sports, which show rapidly declining participation rates for both sexes after a certain age. The most conspicuous example is baseball, the favourite sport of most Japanese. In the 10–14 years age group, 55.9 per cent of boys and 10.1 per cent of girls play this sport, but this rate decreases to the around 20 per cent for males aged 20 to 44, and to less than 10 per cent after age 50.[18] Most sports follow this pattern of lineal decrease. Some, however, show an increase with age before starting to decrease again, while others peak in youth and again in terms of adults.

Sports with a lineal decrease in participation rates for men include baseball, volleyball, table tennis, badminton and jogging, but some of these sports show a small peak for men between ages 35 and 44, probably due to the time of life when they practice these sports with their children. Golf has its peak (over 25 per cent participation rate) with men aged 35 to 59. It can thus be said to constitute the most popular sport for adult males, in age grades called *sōnen* (prime age – approximately 35 to 45) and *chūnen* (middle age – approximately 45 to 60). Another adult male sport is fishing, but here the peak occurs between ages 25 and 49. The only sport that has its highest participation rate at a higher age is 'taking a walk as sports or light gymnastics', which from 45 until old age shows a higher than average participation rate. Females display a return to badminton, table tennis and volleyball between ages 35 and 44, after a considerable decline between 25 and 34. From 45 onwards very few women participate in any sports, with the exception of 'taking a walk as sports or light gymnastics', bowling and swimming.

One sport catering to the needs of the elderly is gate ball (gētobōru). This is a kind of cricket played by men and women in many public parks during the early morning hours when the parks are not used by anyone else and before it gets too hot. Played by two teams with at least five members each, gate ball is a very sociable sport. It gained ground among Japan's elderly about 30 years ago, and in a very short time became tremendously popular. In contrast to other sports, gate ball is a sport practiced only by the elderly, complete with their own gate ball association and national championship.[19] Another sport/game that has more recently gained popularity among Japan's elderly is boccia, a national game in Italy. Both sports seem to be popular because they are so sociable, and thus help participants to avoid loneliness.

A leisure activity thought to be engaged in by women to a much greater degree than men is sightseeing travels, be it in Japan or overseas. According to the 2001 Survey on Time Use and Leisure Activities, however, there are no great differences in this regard in the behaviour of men and women with one exception: many more young females than males in the age group 20 to 29 embarked upon a sightseeing tour either in Japan or abroad. In this age group, the participation rate of women in foreign sightseeing was almost twice as high as that of men. This corresponds to what many women say: that they have to go abroad for sightseeing before marriage because they do not know whether it will ever be possible afterwards. It is also an indication of the high purchasing power of women in their 20s.

Travel agencies have also paid a lot of attention to those women whom they classify as 'nice midi' (naisu midi): women relieved of the upbringing of children, who have time on their hands to spend sightseeing with their friends. The survey data show that, indeed, women in the age bracket between 50 and 64 years engage in domestic and international sightseeing more often than their male peers. Among those 65 years and older, however, men again dominate.

What is difficult to extract from these survey data are visits to hot spring spas, a national passion in Japan. Recent media reports tell us that several

Table 12.3 *Participation rate in domestic and foreign sightseeing travel by sex and age (%)*[a]

Age group	Domestic		Foreign	
	Male	Female	Male	Female
10–14	61.4	59.0	4.6	5.6
15–19	43.6	49.5	5.3	7.0
20–24	49.8	63.9	9.8	19.0
25–29	54.5	63.9	12.3	21.4
30–34	56.5	60.8	11.2	13.8
35–39	61.6	62.0	8.9	8.9
40–44	59.9	55.9	8.9	7.7
45–49	52.9	51.9	8.8	8.8
50–54	51.4	56.0	9.1	11.4
55–59	55.6	59.7	10.7	14.0
60–64	57.2	59.4	12.7	12.6
65–69	55.2	55.6	10.6	9.2
70+	44.2	38.0	6.9	4.2
Total	53.7	55.3	9.2	10.8

[a] All data from the 2001 'Survey on Time Use and Leisure Activities' as contained in the Ministry of Public Management, Home Affairs, Posts and Telecommunications, Statistics Bureau (2006: 755). Respondents were asked whether they had undertaken domestic or foreign sightseeing travel during the year preceding the interview.

spas nowadays have discovered a new function befitting 'grey Japan'. Some of these establishments have come to be used as custody places for the elderly during the week, when none of the young folks at home have time to care for them. The spas profit from this arrangement by attracting more customers during the week, and the elderly benefit by having a place to stay with company, and being able to use the hot baths as often as they want to.

Variations in leisure usage: Gender, class, age, urban-rural differences

Gender and age, as I have already indicated above, are important determinants for the choice of leisure activities. As befits a society with a very high proportion of people of an advanced age – presently more than 21 per cent of the Japanese are aged 65 or more and over 7 per cent are 80 years and older – the elderly have been actively trying to establish their own leisure patterns. This has led to the creation of old people's clubs, in many of which

Japanese dancing is the favoured activity, old people's universities, in which the elderly pursue life-long learning, and gate ball, walking and *boccia* as typical sports engaged in by the elderly. Other contemporary hobbies have had a longer history, such as the cultivation of dwarf trees (*bonsai*) or reciting Chinese poems (*shigin*), which have been leisure activities of elderly men since the Edo period.

Salarymen are often criticised for having no hobbies, because as real 'company men' (*kaisha ningen*) their thoughts supposedly centre only on the firm. But it is sometimes overlooked that these men have their own sport – golf – with the whole culture surrounding it, and that many of them are very good at *karaoke* singing, which constitutes for them a kind of musical escape from the strict rules of the company society they live in. Furthermore, many use the long commute to and from work for avid book reading.

Women who have passed child-rearing age and therefore no longer devote themselves to their children's education often start to redevelop their friendships from schools or universities. With their former and new friends, they practise sports like tennis or go to exhibitions, theatres and concerts, and undertake domestic and foreign travel. Many attend courses at one of the numerous 'culture centres', run either by NHK or one of the national newspapers. As long as the children are not yet going to university, mothers are supposed to help them in every respect, and are thus often rather busy. Such mothers, like workers, do not have much spare time for leisure.

The four years or so spent at university for many Japanese are the best time in their life, which many of them devote to club activities rather than to earnest study. Every university is proud of its many club activities, and these attract students – often to a greater extent than the academic programs. Many students do not want to change their lifestyle immediately after graduation and therefore try to postpone entering a company. Rather, they choose to work as 'freeters' (a word contracted from 'free arbeiters') and for hourly pay, and thus remain free from the pressures big organisations usually place on their members. They hope that to work in this way for several years will allow them to continue a more leisure-oriented life.

Children are supposed to study hard from the age of 10 or so, and especially before they enter high school or university there is not much time for leisure activities. Due to the shrinking birthrate, there are fewer and fewer students competing for entrance into the well-known universities, which makes the once feared entrance examinations marginally easier.

Because the ideology of Japan as a classless society is still strong, in spite of many publications arguing the contrary since the economic crisis swept Japan in the 1990s, Japanese scholars investigating leisure generally avoid researching differences in leisure behaviour by class. To cite just two simple examples: it is clear that, even though there are examples of famous people being *pachinko* addicts, playing *pachinko* is rather a lower stratum leisure activity, while playing golf, even if there are some blue collar workers practising it, is an upper middle class and upper class sport. An empirical study like Bourdieu's *La Distinction*[20] would most certainly reveal that in Japan, too, aesthetic judgments visible in one's free-time behaviour are related to social space.

Urban-rural differences in leisure are also important insofar as many rural areas are depopulated, with mostly elderly people living there. However, some of these old people are very creative, as is the case in a rural region in Fukui prefecture where the elderly organised a rather successful theatre group, the Rōjo Gekidan Babāzu, which tours the region performing for other elderly people. For young rural people, though, the manifold leisure possibilities the cities offer are a main reason for their migration to urban areas.

Changes over time

In the villages during the pre-modern period *asobu*, to play, and *tanoshimu*, to amuse oneself, were mostly limited to days of *hare* (bright days), which were special holy occasions, as opposed to days of *ke* (dark days), meaning plain everyday life. On *hare* days, people wore special cloth, used special spaces (rooms), ate special food and drank sake. The amusement was collective, not individual.[21] In the cities, and this clearly was the most attractive aspect of city life, people could play individually, and did not have to wait for *hare* occasions. The marvellous development of the theatres and the red-light-districts in all larger cities of the Edo period, as well as the existence of numerous people who made their living from teaching others literary and martial arts, are proof of the great demand for individual amusement at that time.

After industrialisation, many companies tried to gain control over their workers' free time. Young female factory workers were taught *ikebana* flower arrangement and other *o-keikogoto*[22] in the factories during their little free time with the promise that this would make them more attractive as brides. Especially after the Second World War, big companies set up their own sports and leisure facilities in order to make their employees spend not only their work time but also their leisure time under the control of the company. Company sports in Japan thus became famous worldwide. Companies especially encouraged team competitions, like basketball, volleyball or soccer, because they believed that sports such as these would make employees develop a strong team spirit, which could be easily transferred onto the firm. With the deterioration of Japanese management principles during the past 20 years, due itself to the success of Reaganomics and neoliberal economic thought, and with companies no longer so eager to secure workers for their whole working life, company sports and leisure are no longer as common as they once were.

In contemporary society, individual control over one's free time has become the norm and not the exception, as it once was. Neither patriarchal small firms nor the big companies retain the power to force their employees into what they think is 'healthy leisure usage'. Of course, socialising and drinking together after work with the company group is still very common, but the implementation of the two-day weekend helped most individuals to attain independence from their organisation during leisure time. In addition, many survey data show an increasing tendency to stress leisure-related values rather than work-related ones as guidelines for one's behaviour. Although most people are satisfied with the amount of leisure time at their disposal and do not wish to have more free time, a majority of people say that leisure or the family are more important for them than work or the company. Japan is not only exporting leisure culture, be it either hardware like electronic goods or software like *manga* and *anime*, its people by now have also come under the strong influence of leisure culture itself,[23] as was the case with the inhabitants of Edo two hundred years ago.

Cross-cultural comparisons

Most leisure activities carried out in Japan are not typically Japanese, but can be found in many countries and cultures of the world. Some of them are, however, performed in a typically Japanese way, and there are some activities that are rare outside Japan. Some activities which were once thought to be 'typically Japanese' have been exported to other countries, and leisure activities of other countries were adopted in Japan and afterwards 'Japanised'. Of course there are great differences in participation rates according to cultures, as well as in the frequency of engaging in a certain activity.

Golf is a good example of a foreign sport having become Japanised. First played in the early Taishō period (1912–26) by foreigners on Kobe's Rokkō mountain range, it was practised by about 140 000 of Japan's elites in 1940, or about 0.2 per cent of the population. While remaining the sport of the elites, after the war golf also became a sport of the middle and upper middle classes, being practised especially by people aspiring for a career in a large organisation. In order to impress people from the company, these middle class members had to practise, and since normal golf ranges were much too expensive, they went to golf practice grounds, which nowadays can be found in every large city in Japan. Furthermore, department stores set up mini golf practice sets on their roof tops, and some people even practise at home with a mini golf set. The salaryman swinging his umbrella like a golf club on the platform while waiting for the train is a common sight. Thus golf has many connotations in Japanese society, not only that of an elite sport, but also that of the miserable efforts of a non-elite member aspiring to climb the social ladder.

Typically Japanese leisure pursuits include flower arrangement (*ikebana*), calligraphy (*shodō*), tea ceremony (*sadō*), miniature landscaping (*bonseki*), martial arts like *jūdō*, *kendō* and others. While some of them, especially *ikebana*, found enthusiastic reception in Western countries, their popularity in Japan is gradually declining, probably because they were not taught primarily as a means of self-expression during one's free time, but rather as aesthetic skills which men sought in their future brides.

But 'typically' Japanese leisure behaviour can also originate from present-day society and culture and does not necessarily have to be 'traditional'. The great number of fans of comic books and journals (manga) as well as of animated motion pictures (anime) developed their own culture, which is now imitated all over the world as 'Japanese' culture. The over-concentration on these hobbies led to one of the strangest social phenomena in modern Japan – the appearance of people living solely for their hobbies, perhaps as a kind of antitheses to their fathers living only for their work. These '*o-taku*' people hardly leave their homes, and communicate with other fans mainly via the internet. Said to number between one and two million, they are the object not only of social criticism, as one might expect, but also of admiration by other anime and manga fans, who feel unable to similarly devote their lives wholeheartedly and radically to this one and only specialisation, which in the case of the *o-taku* can no longer be called a leisure activity, but rather becomes hard work.

Final note

One important aspect of Japanese leisure is the high cost involved. Many Japanese excuse their somewhat passive leisure behaviour by saying that they cannot afford to be more active in this regard. Similarly, the tendency of Japanese tourists to prefer short trips in Japan to long journeys is related to the fact that such trips are two to three times more expensive than, for example, similar trips in Europe. Quite a number of leisure facilities built in the 1980s, during the so-called bubble economy years after the Resort Law had been issued in 1987, had to be shut down again. One representative leisure project from the bubble period is Miyazaki Seagaia, the largest indoor pool in the world, with a fake volcano and an artificial 300 × 100 metre beach, near the beautiful Miyazaki coast. Opened in 1993 and operated by 3000 employees, it had to be closed in 2007 due to low visitor numbers. Many theme parks and leisure lands are experiencing similar financial troubles. Huge modern shopping complexes are in no better situation. Often located far away from the traditional urban centres, they tend to become rather depressed places with few customers after an initial upsurge.

Although this development might be sad for Japan's big business, it can also be interpreted positively as an indication that many Japanese have become self-conscious citizens who devote their free time to activities of their own liking, often with a low budget, rather than allowing large organisations to direct their desires towards consuming leisure facilities and goods that create the best short-term profits.

Notes

1. Beck and Beck-Gernsheim (2002).
2. Riesman, with Glazer and Denney (1950).
3. Linhart (1989).
4. Linhart (1984: 210).
5. *Nihon Kokugo Daijiten* (1976, 20: 491).
6. Okuyama (1974: xx).
7. Van Bremen (1996: 88).
8. In Fujimoto (1963: 44).
9. The 'family state' is a technical term for the ideal Japanese state created by nationalistic state ideologists in the late 19th and early 20th century. The basic idea is that the whole Japanese nation is one family, the emperor being the father and the citizens his children.
10. Linhart (1989: 210–11).
11. Namiki (1975: 228).
12. SM Fuess (2006: 14).
13. *Japan Labor Bulletin* (1991); Linhart (2000: 140).

14. Ray and Schmitt (2007: 3).
15. Noda (2006: 57).
16. Ogura (2006: 15–16).
17. 'Full use of paid holidays would buoy economy by 2.3%: study', *Japan Weekly Monitor* (7 June 2002); Kyūka Seido no Arikata (2002).
18. All data from the 2001 'Survey on Time Use and Leisure Activities' as contained in Ministry of Public Management, Home Affairs, Posts and Telecommunications, Statistics Bureau (2006: 754).
19. See Iwamoto (1984).
20. Bourdieu (1984).
21. See Linhart (1984).
22. Leisure activities that require a lot of training like the tea ceremony, calligraphy or playing a Japanese musical instrument like the *koto*, a kind of zither.
23. Manzenreiter and Ben-Ari (2004: 496–519) contains a good overview of the changes in Japanese leisure behaviour from 1945 to the present.

Further reading

Hendry, Joy and Massimo Raveri (eds) (2002), *Japan at Play: The Ludic and the Logic of Power*, London: Routledge.

Leheny, David (2003), *The Rules of Play: National Identity and the Shaping of Japanese Leisure*, Ithaca: Cornell University Press.

Linhart, Sepp and Sabine Frühstück (eds) (1998), *The Culture of Japan as seen through its Leisure*, Albany: State University of New York Press.

13

Manga, anime and visual art culture

Introduction

Manga and anime are at the centre of significant innovations and cultural debates in Japan. While manga and anime are not identical fields – manga can be loosely defined as Japanese comic books, while anime encompasses the breadth of Japanese animation – they have become synonymous with a distinct Japanese contemporary visual culture and aesthetic in the eyes of many media and culture scholars and commentators around the world. While this chapter will refer to both mediums interchangeably to reflect their mutual contribution to Japan's contemporary visual culture, it is important to distinguish between them and acknowledge their differences as well as their similarities. Many consider manga to be the origin: the creative vitality that spawned anime, and later video games and merchandising spin-offs. In many cases manga defined the template for the key genres – *shōjo*, *shōnen*, *gekiga*, and so on (see Table 13.1) – which have come to dominate the wider popular culture of Japan today. However, while manga established the roots of this style during the postwar period, it was through anime that a broader global audience became aware of a distinctive Japanese visual culture. Japan's anime industry is large and continues to grow overseas. The scale of the industry varies according to how one defines anime's breadth; for instance revenue earned from film, game and merchandise agreements alone has been estimated at more than ¥20 billion per year.[1] However, at its core anime consists of three major forms: (1) feature-length films; (2) TV shows; and (3) video and DVD versions of anime shown on film and TV, and produced only for video and DVD formats.

In 2003, the broadcast of TV anime programs in Japan increased to 2850,[2] making TV the main platform for anime consumption. There has also been some growth in anime and manga consumption through handheld mobile devices such as mobile phones, laptops and personal digital assistants (PDAs). This trend in new media is sure to continue as wireless media develops.

The significance of manga and anime to Japanese visual culture is more than economic: it has increasingly been related to Japan's culture and national image. Academics and critics have connected manga and anime to various aspects of Japan, including architecture,[3] motherhood,[4] social life and customs,[5] homosexuality,[6] gender,[7] history,[8] popular culture[9] and religion.[10] As Douglas McGray observed:

> Japan is reinventing superpower – again. Instead of collapsing beneath its widely reported political and economic misfortunes, Japan's global cultural influence has quietly grown. From pop music to consumer electronics, architecture to fashion, and animation to cuisine, Japan looks more like a cultural superpower today than it did back in the 1980s, when it was an economic one.[11]

Advocates for Japan's recent cultural resurgence, such as the Prime Minister (as of late 2008, Tarō Asō), and the Japanese Commissioner for Cultural Affairs, Tamotsu Aoki, point to the concept of 'soft power' in relation to the popularity of Japan's visual culture.[12] This refers to the possibility of a new cultural renaissance of increased artistic freedom for Japan and a level of respect, admiration, and interest in the culture and history of Japan's visual art both domestically and internationally. Joseph Nye, Jr, who coined the term 'soft power', sees manga and anime as ideal soft power products – claiming they are 'immediately recognised and widely admired' everywhere.[13] He notes the global success of anime such as *Pokemon*, which 'projects a soft and friendly image' that appeals to children all over the world.[14] Japan's Ministry of Economy, Trade and Industry (METI) itself has identified anime as having an important impact on Japan's image overseas, as well as being at the centre of technological innovations and global media trends through increased overseas investment and collaboration.[15]

Critics of this boom, however, express concerns about the narrow image of Japan these texts convey: the violence and sexism of some titles – particularly violence towards women[16] – and the alienation and obsession of some readers/viewers.[17] While these themes are important I raise them only to indicate the broader social context that manga and anime are often placed within. I will sidestep a more detailed discussion of manga and anime's effects on society, as these debates are mired in the unsolvable problem of how to prove claims of 'media effects' (i.e. a convincing causal link between consuming or circulating a media text and changes in audience behaviour). In addition to concerns around 'media effects' Japanese critics have expressed worries over new stereotypes of Japan appearing today. In particular, this group accuses Western advocates of manga, animation and visual art of Orientalism, or of promulgating the reduction of Japanese culture to a series of binary opposites vis-à-vis the West. They argue that reducing manga, animation and visual art to cultural stereotypes is a convenient way to claim some authority and dominance over these forms, and avoids more complex questions of the diversity and variation within Japan. These scholars[18] have criticised this 'essentialist' approach by highlighting manga and anime's transnational virtues and arguing that anime's popularity overseas is caused by its softened Japanese presence, making it an easy art form to domesticate. Further, authors such as Kinsella[19] and the Japanese Economy Division[20] have pointed to various areas of concern within the industry, such as the working conditions and stress levels among manga and anime creative talent, and the challenge of funding anime productions and expanding into overseas markets.

In this chapter I examine the history of the manga and anime industries, with particular reference to the transformations it has experienced over time. I begin by focusing on manga, as this art form established the basic styles and genres from which anime developed, and it is through manga that various scholars[21] have articulated a distinct Japanese aesthetic. I discuss the cultural associations between Japan and manga/anime pointed to by key scholars, and observe how certain images and information dominate the translation of manga and anime into national (Japan) and hybrid (Western appropriation and collaboration) environments. I conclude with some consideration of future changes in the industry and culture of manga, the new issues being raised by global or OEL (Original English Language) manga, and the Western communities based around manga culture, as well as looking at the work that maintains the evolution of the global manga market.

Manga demographics

While manga is popular throughout all segments of Japanese society, there have been significant demographic trends and developments identifiable its recent history. As shown in Table 13.1, even a small cross-section of some of

Table 13.1 *Typology of six key manga forms*

Types of manga	Description	Major examples	Major consumption groups	Initial publication form	Prevalent period
Yonkoma (four cell) manga	Four cells, typically of equal size. Usually gag or nonsense stories	*Sazae-san* (1946–74), *Nono-chan* (1991–97)	All readers, originally adult and young adult	Newspapers and magazines	1920s to today
Story manga	Longer, novelistic format using 'cinematic techniques', e.g. close-ups, various angles, etc.	Popularised by Osamu Tezuka's work, e.g. *Buddha* (1974–84), *Adolf* (1983–85)	All readers, originally children	Cheap *akabon* (red books) in the postwar period	Postwar to today
Kodomomuke manga	A 'cuter' graphic style, initially influenced by US Disney comics and cartoons distributed during Allied Occupation (1945–51)	Popularised by Tezuka's work, e.g. *Shin Takarajima* (*New Treasure Island*) (1947), *Tetsuwan Atomu* (*Astro Boy*) (1952–68)	Children	Cheap *akabon* (red books) in the early postwar period	Postwar to today
Gekiga manga	More mature, serious drama, depicted in a more realistic and graphic style. The principal graphic contrast to the cuteness of children's manga	*Ninja bugeichō* (*Secret Martial Arts of the Ninja* (1959–62), *Kamuiden* (1964–71)	Working class youth, and later high school and university students	Book rental shops (*kashihonya*)	Emerged during the 1950s, peaked in significance during the late 1960s and early 1970s
Shōnen manga	Broad variety of genres, commonly associated with action-based plots with male protagonists	*Dragon Ball* (1984–95), *Slam Dunk* (1990–96), *Rokudenashi Blues* (1988–97)	Boys (under 18)	Serialised in manga magazines (*Shōnen Jump*), reprinted in *tankōbon* from 1970s	Became dominant from the 1960s on
Shōjo manga	Covers all genres, but commonly associated with slender elegant male characters and romantic, fantasy-based plots	*Sailor Moon* (1992–97), *Ataku Nambaa Wan* (*Attack Number One*) (1968–70), *Nana* (2000–continuing)	Girls (under 18)	Serialised in manga magazines (*Ribon*), reprinted in *tankōbon* from 1970s	Boomed in the 1970s

the more popular and influential manga genres shows niche areas within the broader manga reading public. This typology of manga is significant because it reveals the diversity of manga content and readership, extending across layout and composition (*yonkoma* compared to story manga), graphic style (the cuter style of *kodomomuke* compared to *gekiga*'s graphic realism), and gender (the segmentation of the manga market into *shōnen* (boys) and *shōjo* (girls)). As will be discussed below, each manga type has distinct cultural and historical roots. While an overall trend of manga's content 'growing up' with its readers from the 1960s onwards has been discussed elsewhere[22] this table helps show that the different origins of manga, such as *gekiga* in the rental market appealing to a working-class and counter-cultural youth demographic of the 1950s and 60s, reveal that there has always been a more mature, adult content linked to an older demographic sitting parallel to the more mainstream success of children's manga.

Manga history

The term 'manga' can be traced back as far as the 1770s[23], and has been used to describe the wood block prints of Katsushika Hokusai, such as his caricatures (*Hyakumensō*) in 1819. However, while the term 'manga' may have been coined in the past it did not attain widespread, popular usage until the 1930s for two reasons. First, the popularity and national circulation of newspapers modelled on Western layouts brought serialised *yonkoma* manga into homes and workplaces throughout Japan. Second, the growing job market for *manga-ka* (manga authors) – another term which attained widespread use from the 1930s – fostered a sustainable manga industry.

One of the difficulties that arises in both academic and journalistic writing about the history of manga is the dominance of dualistic thinking. Much of the literature on manga is framed by the question of its origins – is it located within Japan's past and therefore a distinctive Japanese aesthetic, or is it a contemporary phenomenon influenced by the West? Those arguing for manga as a continuation of earlier forms of Japanese graphic art point to stylistic similarities between past and present graphic art, citing the similar 'dynamic effect'[24] that manga and anime share with narrative picture scrolls (*emaki-mono*) from the 9th century. Critics of this continuity express two concerns with this focus on the past. Firstly, they claim that it sidelines or ignores the very contemporary nature of this form[25] and the important influence of Western artistic styles. Secondly, they argue that it has less to do with art history and more to do with responding to current political and popular concerns of manga's negative effects on youth and culture – that is, linking manga to the past is a defensive argument that hopes to prove manga is part of traditional Japanese culture and thus circumvent attempts to censor or ban it as trash culture.

This tension created by asserting a resiliently particular image of *Japanese* manga and anime at the expense of acknowledging the significance of foreign influence is a key problem when surveying manga history.

Prewar

Paving the way for the widespread acceptance of manga in the 1930s was the establishment of two types of comic strips in the 1920s:

1. Comic strips for children published in newspapers and journals bought by parents. These publications were heavily influenced by United States newspapers and contained United States comic strips translated into Japanese, such as George McManus's *Bringing up Father* and Pat Sullivan's *Felix the Cat*, as well as Japanese original comic strips based on the US/European template, such as Bunshirō Suzuki's *The Adventures of Little Shō*.
2. Short political cartoon strips for adult readers. These included cartoons influenced by ideologies such as Marxism appearing in publications like *Workers' News* and *War Banner*.

This division between mainstream children's manga and alternative/political adult manga would remain a lasting feature of the manga industry. The industry experienced a downturn in the 1930s, partly triggered by the changing political environment as increased media regulation and censorship narrowed content to conform to national political objectives.

Postwar

In the early postwar period, manga succeeded as a form of cheap entertainment for an impoverished, war-weary Japan. The development of manga during this time felt the impact of US comics, as Japanese translations of well-known titles such as *Blondie, Popeye, Mickey Mouse, Donald Duck* and *Superman* appeared.[26] These comics, along with Disney animation, came to have a significant impact on the style of manga created for children. Writing on the translation of these United States comics into Japanese, Ito suggests that an important reason for their success was that 'the [Japanese] people longed for the rich American lifestyle that was blessed with material goods and electronic appliances'.[27]

In the early postwar period, manga appeared in three main forms: picture card shows (*kamishibai*); rental manga (*kashihonya*); and manga booklets (*yokabon*). 1946–48 saw a boom in storytelling (*rakugo*) and picture card shows performed in theatres and outdoors throughout Japan. The picture card shows would use cheaply produced picture cards that the storyteller would speak to, performing a miniature theatre play. The popularity of these shows endured until the early 1950s, with eager crowds of up to five million people entertained by these lively performances.

The second factor that supported the growth of the manga industry was the emergence of the book-rental shop. Artists would write manga for books and magazines that could be rented out at as cheaply as ¥10 for two days. This trend peaked during the mid-1950s as book-rental outlets appeared at train stations and street corners, totalling around 30 000 outlets. The *gekiga* (dramatic pictures) style was developed primarily in rental manga. As opposed to the cuter, anthropomorphic characters that filled many children's manga, the *gekiga* style contained more mature, serious drama, depicted in a more realistic and graphic style that reflected the tastes of its older readers during the 1950s. However, *gekiga*'s major impact lay not in its graphic style, but in its popularity amongst poorly educated young urban workers and, during the 1960s, university student activists, where it became part of the anti-establishment politics of the time. Sanpei Shirato's *Ninja Bugeichō* (*Secret Martial Arts of the Ninja*, 1959–62) was influential in this regard. Many critics saw this story of peasant uprisings as reflective of student and worker anger over current issues such as the Japan-America Security Treaty.

The third form of manga that flourished in postwar Japan was published in small books (*yokabon*) sold directly to the public. These manga books were priced between ¥15 and ¥20 and sold in discount book shops (*zokki*) and children's toy shops, with deluxe higher-quality manga albums priced between ¥70 and ¥90. The initial high cost of these manga is a partial explanation for the growth in the rental manga market, a preference which lasted until prices decreased in 1959 when two of the largest publishers of manga, Kōdanasha and Shōgakukan, produced cheap weekly manga anthologies for retail sale. In the Osaka market, small manga books known as *akabon* (red books), due to the red ink they were printed in, attained wide popularity through the phenomenally successful *New Treasure Island* (*Shin Takarajima*), which sold 400 000 copies from its launch in 1947. Osamu Tezuka, author of *New Treasure Island*, quickly became one of the most significant figures in manga. Through the enormous popularity of his work, serialised in children's manga magazines such as *Kimba the White Lion (Janguru Taitei)* and *Astro Boy (Tetsuwan Atomu)*, a dominant 'cute' manga style was established. As opposed to the gritty realism and overt politics of *gekiga*, Tezuka's manga founded an archetypical manga style featuring cute characters with large saucer eyes. This style was influenced by Disney animation and US comics, which had flooded Japan during the Allied Occupation between 1945 and 1951.[28] Tezuka also incorporated cinematic techniques inspired by French and German movies: 'I experimented with close-ups and different angles, and instead of using only one frame for an action scene or the climax (as was customary), I made a point of depicting a movement or facial expression with many frames, even many pages'.[29] Tezuka's manga became epics – often spanning thousands of pages – and popularised a longer, serialised form of manga known as 'story manga' which would become a standard format evident in today's manga industry.[30] Primarily read by children and regarded as cute, wholesome entertainment by their parents, these 'story manga' were an innovative break from the rigid layout and brevity of the 'gag manga' genre and four-panel (*yonkoma*) comics popular in newspapers and magazines of the time. The development of the manga industry from picture card shows to rental manga and finally to the manga magazine industry is reflected in the employment history of significant manga artists such as Shigeru Mizuki (who created the popular *Ge Ge Ge no Kitarō* manga series) and Sanpei Shirato (creator of *Ninja Bungeichō*). These artists both worked their way up through picture cards, rental manga, and then the manga magazine industry during the 1950s and 1960s.

The 1950s established manga as a lucrative and popular element of Japanese entertainment through the success of children's titles such as Tezuka's *Astro Boy* (1951) and the first weekly comic magazine for boys, Kodansha's *Shōnen Mangajin* (1959). One of the dominant divisions in the manga market is the split between male and female demographics. Critics have suggested that this division may have become entrenched through the segregated school system in Meiji Japan and the launch of early children's magazines such as *Shōjo kai* (Girls' World) in 1902 to raise literacy rates.[31]

Manga such as *Astro Boy* became typical of the trend for original manga to lead to various spin-offs in other media, becoming one of the first children's TV cartoons in 1963, with various remakes since (1980 and 2003). *Astro Boy*, broadcast in the United States from 1963, also launched the trend for the global export of popular TV anime.

During the 1960s manga broadened its content to include popular genres such as sport. Two important early sports stories that helped establish the genre in weekly comic magazines for boys and young adults were the boxing story *Ashita no Joe* (1968) and the baseball story *Kyojin no Hoshi* (1966). The 1960s also saw the steady maturing of the manga market and titles which reflected this expansion beyond the children's audience. Young adults, who had read manga as children, began demanding more sophisticated and adult material. This included not only stories set in the adult workplace and the world of leisure but also avant-garde manga such as the alternative manga magazine *Garo* (1964–2002). *Garo* serialised the popular peasant revolt story *The Legend of Kamui* (*Kamuiden*) and became an important platform for alternative 'art' manga in Japan.

The 1970s were marked by a group of female manga artists who pioneered a new approach to *shōjo* manga. *Shōjo* can be narrowly defined as manga aimed at girls less than 18 years of age, but is often more broadly applied to manga aimed at a female readership. While *shōjo* includes a range of genres such as sport, horror, science-fiction and historical drama, it is commonly associated with slender elegant male characters and romantic, fantasy-based plots. Matt Thorn estimates that today 'more than half of all Japanese women under the age of 40 and more than three-quarters of teenaged girls read manga with some regularity'.[32] The *shōjo* artists are mainly female and the market is a lucrative one, with *Ribon*, a popular manga magazine for girls, reaching a peak of one million sales per month during the late 1990s.[33] Successful *shōjo* artists such as Naoko Takeuchi (creator of *Sailor Moon*) have also become millionaires through the popularity of their manga. While initially dominated by male authors,[34] by the 1970s a group of female artists known as *Nijūyonen Gumi* (Year Twenty-Four Group) pioneered a new approach to *shōjo* manga introducing new themes and approaches such as homosexual love.[35] These artists, all born in the 24th year of Showa (1949), depicted themes such as romantic love between beautiful young boys, for example, Keiko Takemiya's *Kaze to Ki no Uta* (*The Sound of the Wind and Trees*, 1976) and Moto Hagio's *Tōma no shinzō* (*The Heart of Thomas*, 1974); while Yumiko Ōshima's short manga *Tanjō* (*Birth*, 1970) depicted teen pregnancy and abortion. These titles helped broadened the audience and content of *shōjo* manga.

As shown previously in Table 13.1, developments in manga's layout and composition, graphic style, and gender-specific formats had become firmly established by the 1970s. The following six illustrations represent key aspects of these developments.

Risu Akitsuki's *OL Shinkaron* (Office Lady Theory of Evolution) (Figure 13.1), published in Kodansha's comic magazine *Morning* from 1989,

Figure 13.1 *OL Shinkaron*'s simple four-panel layout and gag structure is typical of the *yonkoma* manga form.
Source: Risu Akitsuki 'OL Shinkaron' ('Office Lady Theory of Evolution')
Shūkan Mōningu, (18 April 1996) p. 62 © 秋月りす/講談社 © Risu Akizuki/Kodansha Ltd.

demonstrates the *yonkoma* convention of a short, self-contained gag delivered in four panels. Most content is drawn from everyday observations, as in this example, where a new female employee misunderstands the special consideration she receives from her male colleagues, as emphasised by the title of this manga *Byōdō ni Tokubetsu* (*Equally Special*). The humour draws upon the stereotype of the male-dominated workplace where the female employee has received kindness from the male workers (the first two panels), however her senior female colleague dismisses this kindness as being only a temporary male prerogative for patronising new female employees. This simple four-panel layout worked perfectly for the newspapers and magazines that often carried *yonkoma* manga, as they had limited space and fixed measurement requirements. However, the story manga form reacted against these limitations, offering epic narratives with an equally epic diversity of panel sizes and dynamic graphics. Tezuka's *Buddha* (Figure 13.2) is representative of this approach. In this example we see the main character, Siddhartha, disarming Bandaka – a scene that is comprised of many frames, in contrast with *yonkoma*'s format where one scene equals one frame. The tension and drama is carefully developed and prolonged through the use of close-ups and variations in panel size. Tezuka's *Buddha* also offered a novelistic approach to manga, telling the story of the historical founder of Buddhism spread over fourteen volumes.

Tezuka was also significant in popularising the cute graphic style often associated with *kodomomuke* manga. *Jungeru Taitei* (*Jungle Emperor* – or as it became known in the West, *Kimba the White Lion*) portrayed cute, humanised animals while also offering humanitarian principals to its audience. This style is evident in Figure 13.3, where the recently orphaned Leo assumes his role of Jungle Emperor after contemplating the fate of his father. While Tazuka is also notable for responding to changing political and cultural sentiments of the 1960s and 70s through his *gekiga* manga such as *Bomba!* and *Song of Apollo*, one of the best examples of this form is Shirato's *Ninja Bugeichō* (Figure 13.4). As this example shows, *gekiga*'s graphic violence offered a grittier 'realism' than the cuter style of *kodomomuke* manga. *Ninja Bugeichō*'s portrayal of the harsh conditions faced by peasants in feudal Japan also offered a more dramatic theme for an older audience that resonated with post-Occupation issues such as criticisms of the Japan-America Security Treaty.

While *gekiga* reflected political and cultural concerns of the time, as already noted, it was in *shōnen* and *shōjo* manga that the biggest market for manga was to be found. These two examples (Figures 13.5 and 13.6)

Figure 13.2 Siddhartha's disarming of Bandaka in Tezuka's *Buddha* shows the greater layout complexity of the story manga form.
Source: Osamu Tezuka *Buddha* (US reprint) Vertical: 1st American edition (11 July 2006) *Buddha* vol. 2, p. 339 © Tezuka Productions.

Figure 13.3 Cuteness and melodrama combine in Tezuka's *Jungeru Taitei.*
Source: Osamu Tezuka *Jungeru Taitei.* © Tezuka Productions.

exemplify the different approaches associated with *shōnen* and *shōjo* manga. Son Goku's battle in *Dragon Ball* (Akira Toriyama, BIRD STU-DIO/Shueisha) (Figure 13.5) conveys *shōnen* manga's greater emphasis on action centred on male protagonists. Figure 13.6, a page from Tachikake's *Hana Buranko Yurete* demonstrates *shōjo* manga's more creative page layout, reflecting the internal emotional intensity of the main character. While these examples illustrate manga's key changes since the postwar period, manga's development did not end in the 1970s.

A further significant innovation was to occur in the 1970s with the popularisation of the *tankōbon* (paperback) format for manga. Popular manga previously serialised in weekly and monthly magazines were compiled in a

Figure 13.4 Shirato's *Ninja Bugeichō* conveys the darker adult themes of *gekiga* manga.
Source: Sanpei Shirato *Ninja Bugeichō* (*Secret Martial Arts of the Ninja*) 1959–62 (1997 reprint) vol. 3, p. 388. © Sanpei Shirato/Akame Production.

higher-quality paperback more portable for commuters and more attractive for collectors. The *tankōbon* soon replaced manga magazines as the main revenue stream for manga publishers.

By the 1980s sales of manga had peaked, but continued to do well into the 1990s. Even after the collapse of Japan's bubble economy in the 1980s

Figure 13.5 Toriyama's *Dragon Ball* is an excellent example of *shōnen* manga's ability to do action and adventure perfectly.
Source: Akira Toriyama *Dragon Ball* (1985) vol. 1, p. 124 © Akira Toriyama, BIRD STUDIO/Shueisha.

Figure 13.6 The story of a young girl coping with the divorce of her Japanese and French parents forms the emotional nexus typical of *shōjo* manga in Tachikake's *Hana Buranko Yurete*.
Source: Hideko Tachikake *Hana Buranko Yurete* (1978–80) © Hideko Tachikake/Shueisha.

manga sales still totalled ¥586 billion in 1995.[36] By the 1980s and 90s manga had become mainstream and were read by nearly everyone of all ages. *Kyoyo Manga* (academic or educational manga) is an example of the mainstream appeal of new forms of manga as they were used to inform and educate readers on a range of topics from history and annual festivals to cooking and other DIY areas.

Manga changed again in the 1990s as editors asserted a stronger role in the creative processes of manga production. Kinsella[37] argues that because most editors were more wealthy and educated than artists, adult manga in particular was reformed around their more privileged tastes and interests. This move away from the working class, artist-created, counter-culture stories of the 1960s and 1970s such as *Ninja Bugeichō* (*Secret Martial Arts of the Ninja*, 1959–62) and *Garo* can be seen in the more factual and niche-interest manga such as the political and economic series *Osaka Way of Finance* (*Niniwa Kin'yūdō*) and the extensively researched nuclear-submarine story *Silent Service* (*Chinmoku no Kantai*). This period also saw the expansion of the global market for manga. Manga began to gain a stronger foothold in the US, long a niche market for Japanese popular culture. With the release of *Akira* (1988 Japan release, 1989 US release) and *Ghost in the Shell* (1995 world-wide release), both based on original manga, Japanese manga and anime began to attract greater international attention than ever before. These titles were much more 'adult' that the standard animation of the time, and their dystopian, cyberpunk themes came at a time of great interest in the approaching millennium. In 1998, *Ghost in the Shell* reached number one on Billboard's video chart in the US.

By the early 2000s, the manga industry had broadened beyond the familiar Japanese publishers (Kōdansha, Shūeisha, Shōgakukan) to include a smaller number of transnational manga distributors and publishers (Tokyopop, Viz Media and Seven Seas Entertainment) and achieved a globally dispersed audience, a trend discussed in more detail in chapter 19. For companies such as Kōdansha, manga was still an important generative source for other media platforms – TV animation, video games, merchandise and so on. While there are current concerns that the Japanese manga market is becoming stagnant and its fortunes are declining – the circulation of weekly manga magazines has been in steady decline for the last decade – many of the most successful anime, video games and merchandising lines began as manga. *Naruto* began in the comic magazine *Akamaru Jump* (1997) and has gone on to become a world-wide hit through anime, card-game, video game and merchandise spin-offs. The enormously successful *Dragon Ball* franchise likewise began as a manga series in 1984. In addition to these manga-inspired titles, the 2000s have been dominated by the growth of large, globally successful brands that exist across various media platforms. *Power Rangers*, adapted from the live-action Japanese TV show, was broadcast in the US in 1993, and by 2007 it had expanded to 15 television seasons, 14 series and two films. Its success was overshadowed by the greater popularity of *Pokemon*, produced by the video game company Nintendo and created by Satoshi Tajiri, which became a successful video game, anime, and character-related business franchise.

Shogakkan's *Pokemon*, the animated version of Nintendo's portable game software, was the first huge success by a Japanese anime overseas. Released in 45 countries and regions around the world, as of the third instalment of the series it had generated overseas box office revenue of ¥38 billion, double its earnings in Japan. *Pokemon's* gross global earnings, including related products, are estimated at ¥3 trillion.[38] *Pokemon's* global success has helped establish the enormity of Japan's character-related industry, and has maintained Japan's contribution to the global children's entertainment sphere.

Manga has also moved into online environments, with both Kōdansha and Shōgakukan offering online manga content and various downloads that extend the audience's access to manga in a more interactive online environment. Mobile phone manga is also available through companies such as Toppan Printing, allowing readers to enjoy manga without worrying about weight or bulk. This move away from print media to digital formats is extended even further by hand-held video devices such as Sony's PlayStation Portable (PSP) and Nintendo DS which offer a number of titles based upon popular manga (*Dragon Ball, Naruto*) or drawing upon the manga style (*Cooking Mama* and *Phoenix Wright: Ace Attorney*).

Manga industry

Manga's development and distribution over varied media platforms reveals shifting relationships between the industry and audience. In recent times, manga's development has been impacted by the rise of OEL (original English-language) manga, which straddles the Japanese/Western divide. OEL manga involves taking the 'design engine' of Japanese manga and using it to tell stories created by non-Japanese artists for a non-Japanese audience. An essentialised 'manga style' of big-eyes, cute girls, beautiful boys and dynamic action that was used as the engine to create the OEL manga stories and art represents a move to standardise the manga product.

Central to the sustainability of the manga industry are the artists and writers involved in the creative work and the larger production team employed in the creation of related media spin-offs such as anime, video games, and merchandising. Criticism of the pressures and stress impacting on manga artists and those in related industries such as anime is growing,[39] and low wages have resulted in an exodus of talented young artists to other creative industries such as the video game industry.[40]

A recent report into the Japanese animation industry[41] identified the following significant trends in the globalisation of anime:

1. Japan is the largest provider of animation worldwide, with approximately 60 per cent of animation shown around the world made in Japan.
2. Japan is struggling to monitor and enforce intellectual property rights (IPR) with a shortage of skilled personnel familiar with international legal affairs related to IPR. Bandai Visual has measured its lost royalties in overseas markets in the tens of millions of yen annually.
3. Japan is actively targeting the foreign market with new anime, as opposed to the past where only titles which had first become popular in Japan were exported. Examples of the trend include the *Ghost in the Shell* movies.
4. The co-production and co-financing of anime by foreign businesses has increased.

The last of these factors is particularly interesting, as it suggests that anime and manga are representative of the shift occurring within Japan's visual culture from a national to a global market. The implications of this global manga trend are discussed further in chapter 19, however it is worth briefly noting that manga's influence and 'brand recognition' has helped open up a global market for manga-style work including South Korea's *manhwa*, China's *manhua*, France's *la nouvelle manga*, and manga-like comics in the US going under various labels such as Amerimanga, world manga or OEL manga.

One key trend not mentioned in the industry report is the growing impact of the *dōjinshi* (fan or amateur manga) community. The *dōjinshi* community has matured in Japan to become strongly integrated within the overall industry, with an 'unspoken, implicit agreement' (*anmoku no ryōkai*) between *dōjinshi* and publishers allowing fans to produce parody-manga based on copyrighted content and characters as this maintains and revives interest and sales in existing titles and sustains a talent pool of manga artists.[42]

Manga cultures and manga studies

As manga and anime have become more popular, involving more people in the various industries that produce and distribute them, Japanese visual culture has become an increasingly important area of scholarly analysis. Early manga studies debates revolved around explaining the mechanics of manga through reference to Japanese culture, society and aesthetics.[43] These articles and books written during the 1980s define a Japanese visual culture that was different and confronting for the West, particularly in its depiction of sex and violence towards women.[44] In this body of work, written well before the current interest in anime, manga is described as being violent and aggressive. However, the focus on manga in the 1980s and on anime in the 1990s shared a number of similar discoveries and problems: both defined manga or anime as having a distinctive Japanese aesthetic, and both engaged with the debate over the sensationalist reporting of manga or anime as being shocking sites of violence and titillation.

Later developments in this field have included a growing analysis of the political economy of manga and anime production. Kinsella[45] pays close attention to the economic dynamics of manga production in Japan, while Allison[46] discusses the global merchandising and anime industry as it has changed and developed since the postwar period. Further, Napier[47] provides an analysis of some of the key anime motifs which have become popular in Japan and around the world.

In Japan, there has been a significant expansion in manga studies through Japanese University programs such as Kyoto Seika University's Faculty of Manga, which opened in April 2006. In addition to the extensive analysis of manga and anime within Japan, these media have become a fast-growing field of study in the West through specialist journals such as *Mechademia*[48] and texts such as *Dreamland Japan: Writings on Modern Manga*,[49] *Adult Manga: Culture and Power in Contemporary Japanese Society*,[50] *Anime from Akira to Princess Mononoke: Experiencing Contemporary Japanese Animation*,[51] and *Millennial Monsters: Japanese Toys and the Global Imagination*.[52]

To conclude this analysis, two recurring issues illustrate the significant innovations and cultural debates manga has been part of in Japan: the effect of manga on society and intellectual property rights management. Both address the conflicted status of the manga consumer as someone either to be embraced by industry as passionate proponents of the manga form or to be policed as potential deviants and criminals.

Manga's effect on Japanese society

Critics of manga include a range of groups such as parents, women's associations and PTAs concerned over school children reading vulgar and sexually explicit manga[53] and scholars concerned over the sexism and violence directed towards women in manga[54]. At the most extreme, critics of manga claim that it can have a negative effect on society, making people less informed and more violent.

There are three broad areas of concern identified. Firstly, that too much information, from driving manuals to business information, is being conveyed through manga – a form of caricature that inevitably distorts, simplifies and exaggerates. These critics suggest that the complexity or depth of an issue cannot be conveyed through manga in the same way as prose or film documentary can facilitate. Secondly, critics claim that the increasing popularity of manga as an information tool reflects a broader trend in politics, religion and education where the entertainment value of information is highlighted in order to create appeal. Additionally, further concerns exist that information that is too complex to be compressed into manga will be ignored.

A final concern is that violent and sexually explicit manga may cause more violent behaviour, particularly amongst younger readers. This issue came to public attention after several sensational 'moral panic' controversies from the late 1980s where manga readers were portrayed by the media as either threats to social stability and order, or at risk of becoming corrupted through their manga consumption. The case with the highest profile in this regard was the trial of Tsutomu Miyazaki in 1989 for the murder of four young girls. He became know as 'The Otaku Murderer' due to the large collection of porn videos, including anime, which police found in his apartment. While incidents of moral panic generated by concerns over manga's effect on society have achieved great notoriety in Japan, it is usually simplistic and unrealistic to isolate one factor – such as manga – as the sole cause of behavioural problems in an individual. Other factors may include mental illness, family dysfunction, poverty, or drug addiction while an increasing body of research such as Hugh McKay's work[55] attempts to broaden the debate beyond an exclusively media-effects framework.

Fan-generated content and intellectual property rights management

Manga and anime should be understood as exemplar products within Japanese visual culture. One thing that makes manga culture important in Japan is its penetration into nearly every facet of Japanese life and culture today. Manga are read in many different private and public settings and consumed by a broad segment of the community. Further, manga and anime have become increasingly popular around the world. Networks of Japanese and overseas fans are translating and distributing manga, both original and commercial works. The manga style provides an engine for various fans to depict their own stories and relate to each other through this world. There are online communities such as *Wirepop.com* that assist fans in developing their art style, allow them to socialise with others who share similar interests and provide a platform for amateur artists to be noticed by industry. The manga 'text' is added to and changed by the audience through these fan-art productions, and existing characters are parodied or re-written into *yaoi* stories where previously heterosexual characters are, for example, re-imagined as gay lovers. As noted earlier, within these communities manga is no longer finished by the publisher or original artist, and publishers increasingly rely on fans to continue the awareness of and interest in existing titles. One implication of this is that these fan-producers have become an important part of manga's development cycle, some becoming 'scanlators' – people who scan and distribute their translations of Japanese manga online – such as the Australian-based *LostInScanlation* community, who scan underground Japanese *dōjinshi* bringing it to a broader audience, or the anime music video (AMV) artists who 'mash-up' anime sequences with alternative music. These fans have become an important part of the process of adoption of new manga styles and narratives, leading to further innovation and investment in this area.

Today, industry members are faced with choices about the extent to which they embrace the fan creators as part of their structure. Some within the industry openly encourage such communities, allowing them to produce fan comics and anime based on characters and settings from copyrighted work, thus using fan creativity to further research and development and recruit new talent. Others employ heavily enforced and policed copyright laws which criminalise the creation of derivative works by fans, continuing an older approach to intellectual property rights (IPR) regimes and production. These choices are not restricted to manga and anime, but are part of general shifts occurring in the management and regulation of media such as video games. The more global and interactive the manga culture becomes the more issues of ownership and regulation will arise and require new approaches based on the interconnected nature of today's visual culture and media texts.

The choices facing the manga and anime industry today reveal innovative new industry opportunities. The online, networked community of fans raises questions such as how to embrace the passion and creativity of *dōjinshi* communities while maintaining IPR. Further, the rise of non-Japanese manga such as OEL manga or *manhwa* raises questions as to how Japan can maintain cultural ownership or develop a 'soft-power' advantage through the popularity of these increasingly hybrid goods – is this model of ownership and control even the most appropriate to use?

The global market and *dōjinshi* communities face the challenge not only of resolving issues of manga and anime's continued success and popularity, but of Japanese approaches to community management and globalisation. To return to an earlier point, while the anime industry may turn a blind eye to its local *dōjinshi* community, Bandai Visual's determination to secure lost overseas revenue 'aiming to expand its overseas sales from ¥7000 million to ¥2 billion in a three-year plan'[56] suggests their main goal is the generation of profit rather than social equity or community collaboration. This apparent contradiction between a flourishing local fan-market re-imagining copyrighted content, and the threat of an increased enforcement of IPR in global markets suggests that the major debate ahead will be over an appropriate model for IPR management that balances the demands of industry and fans. These issues of IPR management and fan-production will rise in importance as more and more people actively engage with copyrighted goods and contribute to existing media narratives and franchises.

Manga and anime are successful entertainment products within contemporary Japanese visual culture. They have shown the way forward – during the 1920s manga comic strips were part of the political and cultural ferment of the time as alternative political organisations were established and overthrown. During the early postwar period manga provided cheap and exciting reading for poor workers and children. In the 1960s it was at the forefront of counter-culture thought. While its working class origins and radical counter-culture politics of the 1960s may have diminished from the 1980s, it remains an innovative element of Japanese visual culture today. Through manga's influence on anime and appearance in the digital world it continues to identify where change, negotiation and controversy arise in

Japan today. The issues pertinent to manga and anime today are well worth consideration: the cultural and social changes that underpin its use and popularity; the globalisation of media content and the impact on industry; the change in the role of consumer as active fan; and the impact on intellectual property are just some areas that have wide significance for Japan and justify further attention.

Notes

1. Japan External Trade Organization (2007: 4).
2. Japan External Trade Organization (2005: 8).
3. Nitschke (1994).
4. Allison (1996).
5. Gill (1998); Poitras (1999); Kinsella (2000a).
6. McLelland (2000).
7. Allison (2000b); Buckley (1991); Imamura (1996).
8. Schodt (1983); McCarter and Kime (1996).
9. Standish (1998).
10. Levi (1997).
11. McGray (2002: 44).
12. Tamotsu Aoki (2004: 8–16).
13. Nye (2004: 3).
14. Nye (2004: 4).
15. Japan External Trade Organization (2005).
16. Darling (1987); Ledden and Fejes (1987); Hadfield (1988).
17. For a critical analysis see Kinsella (1996; 1998; 2002b).
18. Kenji Sato (1997); Ueno (1999); Iwabuchi (2002a).
19. Kinsella (2000a).
20. Japan External Trade Organization (2005).
21. Schodt (1983); Loveday and Chiba (1986); Lent (1989); Schodt (1996); Yaguchi and Ouga (1999).
22. Thorn (2005).
23. Isao Shimizu (1991).
24. Loveday and Chiba (1986: 162).
25. Kenji Sato (1997); Ueno (1999); Iwabuchi (2002a).
26. Kinko Ito (2005).
27. Kinko Ito (2005: 466).
28. Kosei Ono (1983).
29. See Schodt's discussion (1983: 63) on Tezuka.
30. Schodt (1996: 234); Thorn (2001).
31. Thorn (2001).
32. Thorn (2001).
33. Thorn (2001).
34. Tezuka's *Ribon no Kishi*, ('Princess Knight', 1953–56) is an early example of this.
35. Thorn (2001).

36. Schodt (1996: 20).
37. Kinsella (2000a).
38. Japan External Trade Organization (2005: 13).
39. Kinsella (2000a); Japan External Trade Organization (2005).
40. Japan External Trade Organization (2005: 9).
41. Japan External Trade Organization (2005).
42. Pink (2007).
43. Schodt (1983); Buruma (1985); Loveday and Chiba (1986); Kato, Powers and Stronach (1989).
44. Darling (1987); Ledden and Fejes (1987); Hadfield (1988).
45. Kinsella (2000a).
46. Allison (2006).
47. Napier (2001).
48. See http://www.mechademia.org.
49. Schodt (1996).
50. Kinsella (2000a).
51. Napier (2001).
52. Allison (2006).
53. Kinko Ito (2005: 469); Kinsella (2000b: 139–61).
54. Buckley (1991: 163–95); Kuniko Funabashi (1995); Kinko Ito (1995); Newitz (1995: 2–15).
55. McKay (2002).
56. Japan External Trade Organization (2005: 14).

Further reading

Allison, Anne (2006), *Millennial Monsters: Japanese Toys and the Global Imagination*, Berkeley: University of California Press.
Kinsella, Sharon (2000), *Adult Manga: Culture and Power in Contemporary Japanese Society*, Richmond: Curzon.
Napier, Susan Jolliffe (2001), *Anime from Akira to Princess Mononoke: Experiencing Contemporary Japanese Animation*, New York: Palgrave.

14

Music culture

Perspectives regarding 'Japanese music'

The expressions *hōgaku* and *yōgaku* are among the terms regularly used when people discuss music in present-day Japan. These words stem from the idea that music (*-gaku*) as a whole is divisible into that of Japan (*hō*) and that of the West (*yō*).

While *hōgaku* stands for 'Japanese music', and *yōgaku* for 'Western music', the actual concepts are a little more complex than this simple division suggests. Let us thus attempt to compare the *hōgaku* and *yōgaku* distinction based on a native Japanese perspective, with the three domains of 'art music', 'folk music' and 'popular music'. These domains, frequently employed in the classification of music, constitute so-called 'ideal types' and do not necessarily illustrate the substance of the music. 'Art music' signifies music which has as its audience the upper echelons of society and the elite; its composers can be identified; it is written down in advance in musical notation; it is accepted over a long period of time; and it aspires to artistic values. 'Folk music' has the members of a regional community as its audience; its composers are unidentifiable; it circulates by oral transmission; it is accepted over a long period of time; and it aspires to a unification of sentiment among the community. 'Popular music', assumes a large-scale audience; its composers can be specified; it circulates through a medium which records its sounds; its period of acceptance is relatively short; and it aspires to financial gain.

First, let us examine how art music has been regarded in Japan. The *koto* music (termed *sōkyoku*) composed by Yatsuhashi *Kengyō* (1614–85), for example, is *hōgaku*. By contrast, the orchestral works written by Japanese composers trained in Western music, such as Takemitsu Tōru (1930–96), are seen as 'Japanese *yōgaku*'. As these examples illustrate, the basis for division into *hōgaku* and *yōgaku* is not their place of origin, but their musical style.

Conversely, in the case of 'popular music', different criteria are used. Works written by a Western composer and performed by Western musicians fall into the *yōgaku* category, but if Japanese lyrics are attached to the same tunes and sung by Japanese singers, they are regarded as *hōgaku*. The 1978 song *YMCA*, sung by the United States group, the Village People, is *yōgaku*, but its Japanese-language cover version, entitled *Young Man*, which was performed by the Japanese singer Saijō Hideki is deemed to be *hōgaku*. Moreover, *yōgaku* within the category of popular music also includes songs sung, for example, by artists from Turkey or Singapore. In other words, in the case of popular music, the *hōgaku* and *yōgaku* distinction is based on the language of the lyrics and the performer's place of origin, and *yō* means 'apart from Japan'.

In Japan, the notion of dividing various phenomena into the two categories of *hō* (or *wa*, also signifying Japan) and *yō* is also evident in areas other than music, but the classification into *hō* and *yō* according to different criteria in different domains is peculiar to matters relating to music.

In addition another factor further complicates the issue: the connotations of the expression '*Nihon ongaku*'. In semantic terms, *Nihon ongaku* means 'Japanese music'. Fundamentally, however, *Nihon ongaku* refers to *hōgaku* within the art music domain, as well as Japanese folk music, but does not extend to popular music. Simplistically interpreted, it would appear that temporal antiquity, as signified by 'acceptance over a long period of time', is covertly included in the judgment criteria. Still, though any *sōkyoku* (*koto* music) composed in the latter half of the 20th century would be regarded as 'Japanese music', a popular song created way back at the beginning of that same century would not be seen as such. While giving the impression upon first glance of making 'temporal antiquity' a criterion, this term exercises the ability to make a specific part of 'Japan' represent 'Japan' as a whole.

In Table 14.1, each cell illustrates the relationship between the various attributes and the notion of 'Japanese music', with the three domains of art, folk and popular music on the horizontal axis and the two divisions of *hōgaku* and *yōgaku* on the vertical axis. The contribution of each attribute leads to a summary classification of each type of music as being 'Non-Japanese music' or 'Japanese music'.

The fact that the expressions '*hōgaku*', '*yōgaku*' and 'Japanese music' are employed on a regular basis, despite having such fluid definitions, shows

Table 14.1 *Concepts of* hōgaku, yōgaku *and 'Japanese music' in Japan*

3 domains 2 divisions		Art music	Folk music	Popular music
Hōgaku	Composers	● (○)	●	● ○
	Musical styles	●	●	○ (●)
	Performers	● (○)	● (○)	● (○)
	Language	●	●	● (○)
	Instruments	●	●	○ (●)
	Classification	Japanese music	Japanese music	Non-Japanese music
Yōgaku	Composers	○ ●	○	○
	Musical styles	○ (●)	○	○
	Performers	○ ●	○ (●)	○
	Language	○ (●)	○	○
	Instruments	○ (●)	○	○
	Classification	Non-Japanese music	Non-Japanese music	Non-Japanese music

Note: ● = Japanese ○ = Non-Japanese (●) = Japanese in limited cases (○) = Non-Japanese in limited cases

that negotiation as to 'what is 'Japan(ese)' and what is not 'Japan(ese)' is constantly occurring in the background of people's consciousness, a point discussed by Befu in chapter 1 in a broader context.

Diversity and types in music culture: five areas

This section establishes five areas as a way of classifying the music of Japan and its people's musicking[1] since the Meiji era, and records their respective transitions. These five areas are: School; Interest; Performance opportunities; Corporeality; and Venues incorporating consumption of food and drink.

School

In Japan, the Education System Order (*gakusei*) was promulgated in 1872, and a subject called 'shōka (school songs)' was established. Three published volumes of music textbooks, *Shōgaku shōka shū* (Primary school song collection) (1882–84), contained a total of 91 songs with staff notation, having first demonstrated staff notation, its precursor, figure notation, and the diatonic scale of Western music. Most of the published songs were those in which Japanese lyrics had been attached to a Western tune, and 12 hymns, the Scottish *Auld Lang Syne*, and Heinrich Werner's *Haidenröslein* were included. Among the music which had continued since before the Meiji era, the melodies of *gagaku* (court music) were mainly used in these textbooks, whereas neither *warabe-uta*, which are children's traditional play songs, nor *min'yō* (folksongs) were accommodated.

The lyrics of the songs in S*hōgaku shōka shū* were written in adult literary language, the content describing the beauty of nature or providing moral lessons. Then, around 1900, criticism of the content of such lyrics triggered the creation of school songs in colloquial language (*genbun itchi shōka*) whose lyrics matched children's actual speech. The majority of such school songs, with melodies also penned by composers in Japan, were rendered in the pentatonic major scale (*yonanuki chō-onkai*: do-re-mi-sol-la-do), a tonal scale which was a blend of the Western diatonic major scale and the pentatonic mode that had been used in Japan since before the Meiji era. Together with the repertoire of teaching materials, a style of instruction in which students in a class would all sing the school songs in chorus became established as the foundation of music education in schools in Japan.

It was after the end of the Second World War that instrumental music was introduced into school music education, which hitherto had consisted solely of singing. A program comprising learning rhythmic instruments in lower primary years, then adding melodic instruments from the middle primary years onwards was consolidated in the 1950s. Western instruments such as the harmonica and recorder were placed in an important position as melodic instruments. As for the songs themselves, both those created for children under the influence of the prewar trend for colloquial-language school songs and Western musical compositions continued to be adopted, while popular music from Japan and elsewhere began to be introduced from around 1990.

From the end of the 20th century, the reappraisal of Japan's traditional music came to be raised as a policy issue. This led to the active incorporation of material from Japanese folksongs, and a new general rule that students would learn Japanese instruments (*wagakki*) at junior high school.

As music at school has directionality – first, from the state to ordinary people, and second, from adults to children – it can be said to be a perspective 'from above' in a dual sense. In Japan, this top-down perspective vis-à-vis music has developed as follows. From the 1880s, while Western music was positioned as the basis of school music education, Japan's folk music was excluded, and chorus-singing style was consistently emphasised. Around 1900, a melding of the West and Japan occurred in relation to the tonal scale. From the 1950s, education in instrumental music using Western instruments began. From around 1990 popular music was incorporated. By the end of the 20th century, a reappraisal of Japanese 'traditions' has been carried out.

Interest

Japanese instruments such as the *shamisen* (three-stringed plucked lute) and the Chinese flute and *gekkin* (the Japanese name for a round-shaped lute) had been played as a hobby amongst the middle social stratum since before the Meiji era. By the 1920s, Western instruments like the mandolin and harmonica and various kinds of newly-developed instruments had made inroads into the area of interests. The playing of Chinese instruments gradually declined. The instrument most widespread in Japanese households around 1940 was the harmonica, with a diffusion rate of just under 50 per cent.

Collections of music published for hobby purposes contained Japanese *koto* pieces and *min'yō*, Chinese popular tunes, and so on. From around the turn of the 20th century, the repertoire was augmented by colloquial-language school songs and *gunka* (martial songs); *hayari-uta* (popular songs which were mainly orally transmitted); and, from around 1910, Western melodies from opera and the like. Most *gunka* and *hayari-uta* melodies were in the pentatonic scale. Chinese tunes, which made up part of the repertoire, vanished at the juncture of the Sino-Japanese war of 1894–95. In the 1930s, songbooks began to be dominated by Japanese popular songs which, in association with the recording industry, came to be dubbed *kayōkyoku*. Western opera, whose melodies had been familiar to the middle social stratum during the first quarter of the 20th century, became 'art' accepted by the upper social stratum after the Second World War.

Kayōkyoku were predominantly written in the pentatonic scale until the 1950s, but tunes in the diatonic scale proliferated rapidly in the 1960s under the influence of European and American popular music. In opposition to this trend, a style of dramatic ballad called *enka* emerged in the late 1960s as a kind of Japanese popular music which imitated an older style based on the pentatonic scale, sharing the same nomenclature as a genre of political *hayari-uta* of the Meiji era, and winning support among middle to older age groups. Conversely, in mainstream *kayōkyoku*, a succession of 'idols (*aidoru*)' targeting young people of the opposite sex started to make their debuts from the 1970s. *Aidoru* refers to a singer who is 'life-sized, cute and above average'.[2] Moreover, from around 1990, 'J-pop' began to be employed as a term to broadly encompass Japanese popular music, including musical numbers influenced by rock, hip-hop, and the like.

Another example worthy of special mention in the 'interest' area is the playing of instruments by girls as '*keiko-goto* (exercises for cultural enrichment)'. Before the Meiji Restoration, the *koto* was the instrument which unmarried daughters of the elite were supposed to learn, while the *shamisen* was for middle-class girls. After the beginning of the Meiji era, the *shamisen* came to be looked down upon as low class by the intelligentsia, but it continued to survive as an interest for the middle social stratum. It was after the mid-20th century that the *koto* and *shamisen* declined markedly as a cultural enrichment practice for women and girls. From the mid-1950s, music lesson venues operated by musical instrument retailers such as Yamaha and Kawai were widely established, and the piano became the dominant instrument for *keiko-goto*. To have an upright piano in the living room became the target of middle-class aspirations. These dreams became reality as the diffusion ratio of pianos, about 3 per cent in 1964, grew to about 19 per cent in 1985 and to 24 per cent in 2003.[3] There is, however, a disparity in the number of pianos according to income, with families earning an annual income of ¥12 million or above boasting a diffusion ratio of about 50 per cent. From the end of the 20th century, furthermore, learners of the piano have begun to emerge from among the middle-aged and elderly, including men.

In the late 1960s, the guitar, which came to dictate the direction of subsequent popular music, also showed signs of firm establishment. The permeation of the guitar prompted young amateurs to form bands. The beginning of the 21st century has seen moves by middle-aged and older male amateur musicians with previous experience in bands to form bands once more.

Musical activities as hobbies include not only performing but also listening. Music listening has been supported by the media of each era. Radio and records in the 1920s, television in the 1950s and CDs in the 1980s promoted listening to music in the home environment. Listening to music in an individual, portable mode, as inaugurated by the 'Walkman' in 1979, has been accelerated since the beginning of the 21st century by means of portable digital music players such as the iPod, and the downloading of ringtones (*chaku-uta*) to mobile telephones.

In addition, the way individuals behave in relation to music as an interest has been transformed through the spread of the internet. One example of this is the interactions among fans of the same musician via online message boards. In the 21st century, there have even emerged trends such as amateur orchestras which specialise in performing music from computer games, provoked by intercommunication on fan site message boards.

As the above discussion shows, in regard to the area of 'interest', many things have functioned as new stimuli to the emergence of hobby activities. From the end of the 19th century, in addition to Japanese and Chinese musical instruments, Western instruments came to be played in the middle social stratum. In the mid-20th century, the focus of female *keiko-goto* shifted to Western instruments. From the end of the 20th century, the playing of musical instruments as a hobby showed an expansion to a broader age range. Hardware for listening to music stimulated music-listening first at a household level, then at an individual level. Finally, the internet has come to function as a new impetus for the generation of hobby activities.

Performance opportunities

From the early years of Meiji until the end of the Second World War (1871–1945), military bands were the driving force behind the diffusion of Western music. Military bands included in their repertoire not only martial tunes, but also Western classical music. In the 1880s, civilian brass bands also began to be active in various parts of Japan, and provided music to people at balls, horse-races and sports carnivals. In the period in the early 20th century when silent films were shown as touring attractions, small-scale bands equipped with Western wind instruments accompanied them on their rounds. When silent films started to be screened in permanent cinemas, Japanese-instrument players belonged exclusively to picture-theatres showing Japanese films, while small groups of musicians playing Western instruments, including the piano, were attached to cinemas screening Western films. The latter performers would play marches and excerpts from operas before the film and during intermission.

While, on the one hand, the streets and cinemas became 'sites' for the delivery of music to people in this way, 'concerts' began to be held from the end of the 19th century purely for music appreciation. At the open-air concert hall (*yagai ongaku-dō*) completed in Tokyo in 1905, military bands held public performances with programs including *koto* tunes, band music by Philip Souza and Richard Wagner's orchestral works. Music using

Japanese instruments such as the *koto*, hitherto restricted to parties and pupils' recitals, also gradually came to be performed at concert venues.

Concerts fulfilled the role of nurturing professional performers and composers, as well as audiences. In 1915, at the inaugural concert of the Tokyo Philharmonic Orchestra Club (*Tōkyō firuhāmonīkai kangen-gakubu*), Japan's first professional orchestra, music by Yamada Kōsaku (1886–1965), the first orchestral work ever to be written by a Japanese composer, was performed alongside waltzes by Johann Strauss. From then on, pieces by Japanese composers of the same generation had equal billing with Western works at concerts by Japanese orchestras. National policy during the Second World War, which encouraged the performance of orchestral works by Japanese composers, as well as the practice evidently established from the late 1950s of orchestras commissioning Japanese composers, stimulated the creation of 'Japanese *yōgaku*'.

From the second half of the 1960s, one increasingly conspicuous trend in orchestral music by Japanese composers was their inclusion of Japanese instruments. One example of this is Takemitsu Tōru's *November Steps* (1967), which employs the *biwa* (plucked lute) and *shakuhachi* (vertical bamboo flute).

During the period from the 1950s to the 1960s the number of professional orchestras in Japan increased. In tandem with this, from the 1960s onwards, the number of concerts given by orchestras also grew. At present, there are more than 20 professional orchestras in Japan. The listeners at concerts which feature 'Japanese *yōgaku*' are from the intelligentsia, while concerts featuring works by Western composers from the 18th to 19th centuries, such as Mozart, attract a wider audience. One trend seen in 21st century orchestras is the quest to expand their support-base beyond the confines of a fixed socioeconomic group. Outreach activities which endeavour to forge a link with the local community, such as guest performances at schools, have become vigorous.

Concerts have also been instrumental in widening the scope of amateur performance activities. From prewar days to the present, brass band music and choral singing have robustly developed with the support of amateurs. Both these forms have permeated deeply into school club activities, citizens' groups and workplaces. Currently some 70 per cent of junior and senior high schools throughout Japan have a brass band club. In terms of the composition of their membership, the proportion of females participating surpassed that of males around 1970, and now females account for the vast majority of school brass band club members.

One aspect of amateur activities can also be observed in concerts featuring Beethoven's Symphony Number Nine. In Japan, it was in the 1950s that year-end concerts of Beethoven's Ninth became a regular event, but examples of ordinary citizens' participation in the chorus have become conspicuous since the 1970s. Participants range from teenagers to the elderly, and the majority are people who come into contact with the German language for the first time through the lyrics of this work, nicknamed *Dai-ku* (Number Nine).

Another point in connection with amateur performance opportunities is that the 'street' re-emerges in the domain of popular music from the end of the 20th century. Amateur performance activity in the street and in plazas, meant for the ears of passers-by, has become a fixture not only in metropolitan areas but also in regional cities.

As detailed above, performance opportunities have come full circle. The shift from street to concert led to the cultivation of professional musicians and audiences and widened the scope of amateur activity. For popular music, the 'street' has come into its own again since the 1990s.

Corporeality

One example related to corporeality in outdoor music venues is the sports carnival introduced to Japan during the Meiji era. Initially, brass band music was performed live, but now it is usual for recorded music to be used. Every recording company annually releases new CDs for use at school sports carnivals, and in recent years it has become common for arrangements of J-pop numbers to be used. Conversely, long-time favourites used during foot-races are Jacques Offenbach's *Orpheus in the Underworld* and Hermann Necke's *Csikos Post*. These are examples of how Western classical music, which is deemed uncongenial to corporeality, has forged a connection with corporeality in response to opportunities for use.

One example which has continued since pre-Meiji times of an outdoor venue which involves dancing is that of the *bon-odori* (Bon dance) at summer festivals. This involves people dancing in a circle around a platform (*yagura*) in the centre of the plaza according to the rhythm of dancing songs (*ondo*) sung atop the platform. Bon dances were banned on numerous occasions during Meiji, by reason of being 'vulgar folkways', but they have lived on in all parts of Japan to the present day. *Ondo* can be roughly divided into those which have been handed down since the Edo period in limited areas such as rural communities; those which were popularised after the Second World War on a slightly wider regional level; and those which spread nationwide through recordings, without being restricted to particular areas. One example of the second category is the Kawachi Ondo of Osaka, and examples of the third category include Tōkyō Ondo (1933) and *ondo* from the late 20th century which are sung by protagonists from television and anime films.

Indoor venues accommodating dancing also have had a deep connection with music. At the Rokumeikan, which was built as a place to entertain foreign guests in the 1880s, balls were held and foreign dignitaries and members of the upper echelons of Japanese society danced waltzes and so on to the accompaniment of music played by Japanese performers playing Western wind and string instruments. At dance halls (*dansu hōru*) from the end of the 1920s, jazz and tango numbers were played by live bands, and, in most cases, professional female dancers were partnered by ordinary adult men. At the 'go-go cafés (*gō-gō kissa*)' of the end of the 1960s, bands wielding electric guitars played live rock music, and young people in their teens and 20s danced along. At the discotheques (*disuko*) of the 1980s, urban youth danced to Eurobeat records being played at high volumes. At clubs (*kurabu*) since the mid-1990s, urban youth can be seen dancing, urged on by the playing of the DJ.

A new site that has appeared since the turn of the 21st century, which relates corporeality to music, is the computer game. Within the tide of games called 'music games (*ongaku gēmu*)', some have emerged which synchronise the body with music through an input device in the shape of a Japanese musical instrument, such as *Taiko no tatsujin* (Taiko Virtuoso) (2001–) and *Shamisen burazāzu* (Shamisen Brothers) (2003–). The former uses a Japanese drum (*wadaiko*) and drumsticks to manipulate visual data on the display screen, while the latter uses a *shamisen* and plectrum. The music playing during the games covers a wide range, including old school songs and J-pop. Such games have won acceptance among young people in urban areas.

Venues incorporating the consumption of food and drink
Some venues that incorporate eating and drinking have had a connection with music that transcends its use as mere background noise. In Japan from the 1950s through the 1960s, numerous varieties of such venues prospered. Establishments that played classical music records in response to customers' requests were called 'famous-melody cafés (*meikyoku kissa*)', reflecting the fact that high-quality audio systems had not yet spread to households in Japan. The diffusion rate of home stereos was no more than

9 per cent in 1964.[4] At so-called 'jazz cafés (*jazu kissa*)', which played imported jazz records, live performances were sometimes held at night. Another type of establishment which differed markedly from the above two in terms of the presence of music was the 'singing-voice café (*utagoe kissa*)'. This was associated also with the *utagoe undō* (singing-voice movement) which had developed from the end of the 1940s as a music movement in workplaces and local communities. At these 'singing-voice cafés', customers sang Russian folksongs and the like, in chorus. The popularity of *utagoe kissa* dwindled with changing social conditions and the infiltration of *karaoke*.

Karaoke (from 'empty orchestra') emerged at the beginning of the 1970s, and became established as a replacement for the *nagashi* (itinerant musicians) who used to make the rounds of down-market drinking-places. These *nagashi*, continued the pre-Meiji lineage of street musicians who carry their instruments with them. In the 1960s, guitars and accordions joined the conventional *shamisen* as established instruments for *nagashi*. The greater part of their repertoire consisted of popular songs (*kayōkyoku*): the *nagashi* doing the singing themselves in some cases, while in other cases accompanying clients' singing, the latter becoming the direct impetus for the birth of *karaoke*. Ogawa[5] cites the existence since at least the 1960s of drinking-places that would play tunes to their customers' liking through music boxes and cable radio (*yūsen hōsō*), and the custom established even earlier of singing songs in front of other people at various gatherings, as other background elements in the lead-up to the emergence of *karaoke*.

Initially, *karaoke* functioned as auxiliary entertainment for middle-aged and older men at night-time drinking places, but in the mid-1980s, its customer base widened through the birth of establishments called 'karaoke boxes', the primary purpose of which was karaoke-singing. Since the 1990s, *karaoke* has developed into a pastime appealing to a wide age-range, including children and the elderly. Its repertoire has come to be occupied in part by theme songs from television anime programs, and recent years have also seen its enrichment through popular songs from China and Korea. Moreover, from the 1990s a custom emerged of individuals borrowing single-track CDs from CD-rental places – businesses unique to Japan – and practising their songs, but since 2006, the habit of using online video clips with music to practise singing has been gaining popularity.

The above discussion relating to venues incorporating eating and drinking can be summarised as follows. While opportunities for listening to

Western music have been provided by multiple venues from the mid-20th century onwards, sites where amateurs sing songs in front of other people have been secured through the developmental trend from 'singing-voice cafés' to *karaoke*.

Social strata

Piecing together the previous sections, it can be seen that the music culture of Japan from the Meiji era to the present day has developed in two directions: the importation and absorption of Western music, and the flourishing of popular music.

If we overview a cross-section of music surveys conducted in the past,[6] we can see that the developmental process has passed through two stages. The 1930s saw the emergence of the first stage: *kayōkyoku*, a new genre of popular vocal music which had incorporated Western music, began to be consumed in large quantities, causing the decline of several genres of vocal music that had continued since before the Meiji era, such as *gidayū* (narrative *shamisen* music). From the 1960s into the 1970s the second stage emerged. In this period, the preference ratio for Western instrumental music, such as jazz and orchestral music, began to overtake that of Japanese traditional instrumental music, including *biwa* and *koto*, which had endured from pre-Meiji times. At that point, the basis of the musical perspective and music literacy of Japan's people can be thought to have shifted to Western music, in both name and substance.

The next question is whether each musical genre whose degree of consumption has variously fluctuated over history is connected to any particular social stratum. Here, also with reference to the results of past surveys, I have sorted the representative musical genres and their consumption ratios into high or low consumption strata by three time periods: prewar; 1960s to 1970s; and the 21st century. In Table 14.2, I subsequently extracted the dimensions thought to relate to the degree of consumption (far right column) and grouped the genres common to each dimension in the same category (indicated by alphabetical letters in the far left column). The entries in italics within cells show that the population itself which consumes the genre in question is numerically small, and the cell relating to the 'low-consumption stratum' has therefore been left blank. For the 21st century, I have only set up a column for the 'high-consumption stratum'.

From here on, I will describe each category in the left-hand side of the table.

Table 14.2 *Musical genre and social stratum*

Era/stratum Genre	Pre-war High-consumption stratum	Pre-war Low-consumption stratum	1960s–70s High-consumption stratum	1960s–70s Low-consumption stratum	21st century High-consumption stratum	Dimension of disparity
Min'yō	Middle-aged/elderly Regional	Teens	Middle-aged/elderly Regional	Teens	Middle-aged/elderly Regional	Age; location
A *Naniwa-bushi*	Wide range	Young females	*Middle-aged/elderly Rural*		*Middle-aged/elderly Regional*	
Enka			Middle-aged/elderly Regional	Young people	Middle-aged/elderly	
Jazz	Young people	Middle-aged/elderly	Young people Urban	Elderly	Middle-aged/elderly	Generation
Rock			Young people	Elderly	Young to middle-aged	
B *Kayōkyoku*	Wide range	Non-specific	Wide range	Non-specific	Middle-aged/elderly	
J-pop					Young people	
Anime songs			Children	Elderly	Children to middle-aged	
C *Gidayū*	Middle-aged/elderly	Young people	*Middle-aged/elderly*		*Middle-aged/elderly*	Age
Sōkyoku	Wide range	Young males	*Middle-aged/elderly*		*Middle-aged/elderly*	
Orchestral music	Young people	Elderly	Highly-educated White-collar, major firm	Agriculture Blue-collar	Highly-educated White-collar	Level of education; occupation (income)
D Opera	Young people	Elderly	*Highly-educated White-collar, major firm*		*Highly-educated Middle-aged/elderly*	
E Male idol singers			Young females	Males	Females	Sex

A. The genres in which 'age' and 'location' are considered to be the dimensions determining consumption are: *min'yō*; *naniwabushi* or *rōkyoku* (narrative singing with *shamisen* accompaniment); and *enka*. In addition to these genres having high rates of consumption by middle-aged to elderly people, they also have the following characteristics: *min'yō* have a repertoire peculiar to each part of Japan, with support for *min'yō* in the Tōhoku region in north-eastern Honshū, in particular, having remained stable over a long period. *Naniwabushi*, which emerged in Osaka at the end of the 19th century, received strong support from older age-groups and regional strata, but its consumption declined in the final 25 years of the 20th century. In recent years, however, though its consumption could not be called great, some expansion has been seen on the social-stratum dimension, stimulated by the emergence of players who have introduced new elements, such as the incorporation of rock phrasing into their *shamisen* performance. The relatively new genre of *enka* has developed by incorporating musical elements of the other two genres, including vocalisation and titles. The stylistic similarity arising from this can be considered a factor in these genres sharing the support of common strata.

B. In relation to the five genres from jazz to anime songs, as can be appreciated from the fact that the high-consumption stratum for jazz has shifted from young people in its early days to middle-aged or elderly people at present, the relatively young strata which supported 'new' music have sustained their consumption as they have grown older. From this, the primary dimension relating to consumption is 'age', based on the period in which the genre was first experienced, that is, each consumer's 'generation'. Moreover, the fact that opera and orchestral music in category D were popular among young people in prewar days implies that even though all kinds of Western music initially were consumed by the young as 'new' across the board, each genre has specialised its strata of consumption over time. With *kayōkyoku* and J-pop, one can see situations in which the compartmentalisation of consumers into young people and middle-aged/elderly strata has begun upon the emergence of new genres within Japan's popular music, which has continuously incorporated elements from Western music.

C. In the case of *Gidayū* and *sōkyoku*, 'age' is considered to be the determining dimension of consumption. Within *hōgaku*, these two genres, whose artistic aspirations are strong in comparison to the *min'yō* and *naniwabushi* of category A, are characterised by their near lack of connection with any dimension, such as region, except that of age.

D. The dimensions dictating consumption for both orchestral music and opera are thought to be 'level of education' and 'occupation', with 'income' predicated on the other two. Opera especially, as I have already stated, which was a familiar genre until the first quarter of the 20th century, underwent a transformation in its social positioning in postwar years to become 'art'. This changed its dimension of consumption dramatically.

E. Consumption relating to 'idols' is basically supported by consumers of the opposite sex from the singer. That basis stands firm, though a transformation has been evident in recent years in the consumption of male idols, whose young female fans have been joined by a surge in fans from their mothers' generation, thus expanding the age-range of the high-consumption group.

In summary, the consumption of musical genres and their rise and fall includes: category A in cases where the foundation is the same social stratum, but different new genres are consumed over time; categories B and C, where a certain musical genre is consumed continuously by a fixed social stratum; and categories D and E where the consuming stratum shifts or expands.

International comparison

Let me reiterate that Japan came face-to-face with Western music in the Meiji era and has undertaken its importation and absorption. This, on a greater or lesser scale, can be said to be an issue which all non-Western countries have confronted in the process of modernisation. Now let us locate the music culture of Japan from the perspective of Japan in East Asia.

School education

In Japan in the 1880s, *shōka* (school songs) were developed under a policy designed to form a compromise between Western and native music. In China at the start of the 20th century, music education shaped around *xuetang yuege* (school songs), inspired by their Japanese counterparts, was initiated by Shen Xingong and others who had studied in Japan. The spread of *xuetang yuege* functioned to diffuse the Westernised melodies of Japanese *shōka* and to popularise both Western staff notation and numbered musical notation in China. In Korea, in the period from the start of the 20th century until 1945, education pivoting on Japanese *shōka* was conducted. The pentatonic scale which permeated Korea through the *shōka* also influenced Korean popular songs. In this manner, when viewed from the perspective of the importation of Western music into East Asia, Japan played the role of a mediator at the beginning of the 20th century, through school education.

Importation and absorption of brass band music

Western style military bands emerged in China in the 1890s. As for civilian bands, there had been a privately established brass band formed prior to that, in 1885, by a Briton, Sir Robert Hart. This group was augmented by string instruments in 1890. In both cases, their repertoire is said to have been limited to Western music. In Korea, Franz Eckert, who had led military bands in Japan during his sojourn from 1879 to 1899, later led the Korean Lee Dynasty imperial band. The band's activities and influence endured for only a short period, however, due to the dismantling of the military in 1907. In Japan, the following can be said to be the characteristics of bands: firstly, until the establishment of professional orchestras, military bands functioned as their substitutes; secondly, the repertoire of brass band music by composers from Japan started to take shape from the end of the 19th century; and, thirdly, the influence of military bands extended to the civil population, and brass band music has continued to be a nucleus of amateur musicking to the present day. •

Absorption of orchestral music

Composers from China, Korea and Japan all produced orchestral works incorporating traditional elements from their own countries. In China, folk-songs, ethnic music scales and so on have been used since the first half of the 20th century. In Korea, there was rising momentum for the handing-down and development of traditional music from the mid-20th century onwards, and in orchestral works the introduction of elements from traditional music has also been attempted. In the case of Japan, there have been two distinct time-periods in which composers have created works with an unequivocal awareness of 'Japan': during wartime and from the late 1960s. Such attempts were made under state policy in the war years, but were based on the consciousness of individual composers from the end of the 1960s. Unlike the other two areas, Japan has the distinctive feature of having experienced both state-led and spontaneous music movements.

The music industry

As I have discussed above, the establishment of 'concerts' in Japan has contributed to developing both *yōgaku* and *hōgaku*, as well as music by professionals and amateurs. Among Asian countries, one salient feature of Japan is the growth of its concert business. In addition, Sekine[7] cites the uniformity of music recording prices, the expansion of outlets dealing with record rentals (from 1980), and the world's highest ratio of singles to albums in the CD market as being characteristic of Japan when viewed from the perspective of the music industry in Asia as a whole.[8]

As we have observed above, though the issue of 'the traditional music of their own country' versus 'Western music' is common to all of East Asia, each area is unique and individual as to how it balances the two, and also in relation to the process in which music culture has been developed with the additional support of industry and education.

Points at issue

Given the discussion thus far, I now raise three points in relation to contemporary music culture in Japan.

Changes in the meaning of 'yōgaku'

Western music imported during Meiji was something 'new' and 'lofty' to the people of Japan. With the passage of time, however, these meanings have changed.

Until the verge of the Second World War, Western music which had once been consumed as 'new' became increasingly difficult to associate with 'newness' in the process of being imported and absorbed over a long period of time. Instead, among the increasingly segmentalised genres of music, it is those which boast only minor levels of consumption that have won the position of 'newness'.

As for 'lofty', as indicated by the diffusion rate for pianos, Western music has already ceased to be something so lofty that it is out of reach. That being said, evident by the motivation which spurred the popularisation of pianos and the consumer strata for orchestral music and opera, Western music still retains its significance as an 'upper-middle-class' status symbol. The construction in metropolitan areas of dedicated music auditoria equipped with bars and chandeliers from the 1980s makes their meaning as status symbols both obvious and more easily understood.

Changes in the meaning of 'hōgaku'

The status of Japanese traditional music, which in Meiji times was imbued with such sentiments as 'backward' and 'vulgar' vis-à-vis Western music, has also undergone changes.

In the case of Japanese traditional musical instruments, until about 1950 a practice persisted in which different notation was used for different instruments, and even with the same instrument, there was almost no mutual exchange between rival schools. From the mid-1950s, attempts were made under the auspices of broadcasters to cultivate young players of Japanese instruments, leading to changes in this situation. Through the teaching of staff notation, the way was opened for combined performances by disparate schools and with different instruments. In the same period, moves by Japanese-instrument players to commission new works from composers of 'Japanese *yōgaku*' began to occur. In this way, from the late 1950s onwards, Japanese traditional instruments started to take on a tinge of 'newness'.

Changes also emerged in folk music. Music rooted in 'regional areas' began to be transmitted to and accepted by a wider audience. One example is the Tsugaru-*jamisen* (Tsugaru *shamisen*).[9] In the 1960s, the Tsugaru-*jamisen* enjoyed a boom, thanks to Takahashi Chikuzan (1910–98), and its influence even extended to Europe and America through Takahashi's overseas performance tours in the 1980s. In the 21st century, the genre-crossing activities of young performers such as the Yoshida Brothers (Yoshida Kyōdai) have reignited the boom, and Tsugaru-*jamisen* tunes have also joined the ranks of mobile telephone ringtones.

The policy of reappraising Japanese traditional musical instruments, which was hammered out in school education at the end of the 20th century, has given rise to several concrete moves. The instrument industry responded swiftly, developing such products as a compact *koto* which is easy to use in the classroom, and a *shakuhachi* made of plastic. Moreover, it was decided that *enka* songs would be included in senior high school music textbooks from the 2008 academic year.

A reappraisal of 'Japan' can be seen also in the realm of popular music. A 21st-century male idol group, Kanjani 8, has made hits with songs which combine *Kawachi-ondo* and Japanese-language rap.

Numerous examples above show that for the people of Japan, who have achieved such proficiency in Western music, a paradoxical situation has arisen where Japanese traditional music, rather than Western music, is considered 'new'. Further, while forging close connections with both education and industry, 'traditions are being invented' in the present tense in Japan.

Transformations in consumption

Changes have also occurred in patterns of consumption. Since the 1990s, it has become difficult to consider age, location, level of education and the like as dimensions determining consumption. Against a background of the compartmentalisation of popular music into ever smaller subgenres, for the youth of today music has become a means by which to identify others who share the same taste, using musical preference as a clue.

Additionally, when, for example, young people sing *karaoke*, they vary their choice of song according to the people accompanying them. In other words, music has come to function as an antenna for testing the 'air' around individuals and finding a place where one can feel at ease with one's presence, or, in a more negative sense, as a tool for ameliorating an uncomfortable atmosphere. Music is consumed while being used in different ways according to the venue.

Conclusion

If we synthesise the three issues discussed above, contemporary music culture in Japan has taken a vastly different trajectory from the ideas of the Meiji era, when only 'Western music' was valued. We can now see the emergence of a kind of grassroots cultural relativism which evaluates and consumes a diversity of music on an equal basis. However, the fact that such cultural relativism has provoked a 'reappraisal of Japan's own culture' in a country that has taken Western music as its benchmark, represents both its greatest distinctive feature, and a kind of perversity.

From here forward, the cultural relativism which is emerging in current Japanese music culture has the potential to move in two different directions according to whether or not it again undergoes a process of relativising its 'own culture'. If it does undergo another process of relativising, it will slip out of the robust framework used in connection with music of 'Japan' versus 'other than Japan' and head towards cosmopolitanism; if not, it will follow a path leading to absorption into the framework and on to soft nationalism.

Notes

1. This is a neologism coined by music scholar Christopher Small (1987), based on the desire to think of music not as a noun, but as a verb of action that 'people do'.
2. Aoyagi (2000).
3. Cabinet Office, Economic and Social Research Institute (2003).
4. Masui (1980: 49).
5. Hiroshi Ogawa (1998: 45).
6. Masui (1980), NHK Hōsō Yoron Chōsa Kenkyūjo (1982), '*Sedai koete uta wa tanoshi* (Songs enjoyed across generations)', *Yomiuri Shimbun* (4 December 2003).

7. Sekine (2007).
8. In 2006, however, the gross sales revenue for user-pays music distribution in the form of songs downloaded via the internet to personal computers and mobile telephones surpassed that of single CDs. *Nihon Record Kyōkai* (Recording Industry Association of Japan) (2007).
9. Tsugaru is one area in Aomori Prefecture, at the northern tip of Honshu. The Tsugaru-jamisen is distinctive in the way it is played by striking the strings with a plectrum.

Further reading

Galliano, Luciana (2002), *Yōgaku: Japanese Music in the Twentieth Century*, Lanham: The Scarecrow Press.

Stevens, Carolyn S (2008), *Japanese Popular Music: Culture, Authenticity, and Power*, London: Routledge.

Wade, Bonnie C (2005), *Music in Japan*, New York: Oxford University Press.

15

Housing culture

Housing codes

On encountering the term 'housing codes', most people are likely to think of building regulations: what kind of dwellings can be built where, what provisions need to be made for gas, electricity and sewerage, etc. Such regulations certainly do exist – and constitute one of the major ways in which public policy impinges on the 'private' realm of the home – but I use 'housing codes' in another sense here, to mean the prevailing assumptions we have about houses and the standards we have internalised for evaluating the exteriors and interiors of the houses we encounter. Just as we are influenced by 'dress codes' and 'dietary codes', so too are we influenced by 'housing codes', and these codes are both socially constructed and variable over time.[1] A remotely controlled iron gate leading to a garden and off-street parking or a front door just a few paces from the street; a spacious entry hall or immediate access to the living room; a separate dining room or an eat-in kitchen: these and other design features convey messages not only about the type of house we are visiting, but also about the lifestyle of its occupants. The 'novel' layout of rooms – bedrooms on the ground floor and social space on the floor above, for example – may suit the site or the occupants, but it will strike most visitors as a reversal of the prevailing code for the location of 'private' and 'public' spaces.

Japan's housing codes, and domestic dwellings themselves, have changed dramatically since the late 19th century, reflecting not only the economic and demographic transformation of the country but also its ideological transformation, especially after the Second World War. The cumulative result of these changes has been the emergence of a new housing culture, which is similar in most respects to the housing cultures of other fully developed countries elsewhere in the world.

Around the time of the Meiji Restoration of 1868 and for some decades thereafter, Japan was still a predominantly agrarian society, with 80 per cent of the population living in the countryside and some 70 per cent of the labour force engaging primarily in farming activities. In rural villages home and workplace overlapped, and the typical dwelling included space for farm tools and a few chickens or trays of silkworms as well as for the farm family itself. Even in Japanese cities, the separation of these two basic loci of human existence – one of the significant developments wrought by modernisation throughout the world – had only just begun. A relatively few government officials, factory owners and factory workers commuted from home to work – on foot or by rickshaw or horse-drawn tram – but most urban residents were either shopkeepers or artisans, who ate, slept and raised their children in or just behind the same premises in which they earned their livelihoods.

Of course, dwellings varied in size and quality, reflecting the socioeconomic status of their occupants. The poor occupied small dwellings, sometimes little more than crudely built shelters against the elements. Affluent Japanese, whether rural or urban, had larger, better-built dwellings, which included space for servants and for the celebration of familial and communal events – there being hardly any restaurants and certainly no funeral parlours, wedding chapels or community centres (other than local shrines and temples) in those days. Such differences in housing standards were accepted as normal, a reflection of the natural order of things in a society where social stratification was taken for granted and, as in much of the West at roughly the same time, where poverty was regarded as the result of lax behaviour and moral depravity on the part of the individuals concerned.[2]

A 'proper' house at this time was considered to be one that provided accommodation for members of an *ie*, the multi-generational stem family discussed by Imamura earlier in this volume, and like the *ie* itself, space within the house was arranged hierarchically. The prime space – usually opening onto a garden – was reserved for the male head of the household, or patriarch; rooms in the dark recesses of the dwelling were occupied by servants and/or employees of the patriarch's business; and at least one 'good' room in between was used by family members other than the patriarch for sleeping, meals and diverse daytime activities. The kitchen tended to be in a remote corner of the house, usually in a lower, dirt-floored area, reflecting both the need to protect the rest of the dwelling from the fires that were lit there on a daily basis and the lowly status of women and women's work within the household.

In the countryside and in the less densely populated districts of cities, the house itself would be set apart from other houses by a gated wall or hedge; in the more congested 'downtown' districts of cities, where row houses predominated, a rather stern facade with few, if any, windows would face the street. In all cases, and essential to the 'proper' house, the outer sliding entry door would lead to a *genkan* (vestibule) at ground level, marking a significant boundary between outside (*soto*) and inside (*uchi*) the residence. Here, casual visitors would be dealt with, and here too occupants of the house or the invited guests of the head of the household would remove their footwear before stepping up into the raised interior. Also essential were a *tokonoma*, an alcove in the 'best' room in the house – that is, the patriarch's room or a larger reception room nearby – where a seasonally suitable hanging picture scroll and flower arrangement would be displayed, and a *butsudan*, or Buddhist altar, for commemoration of the *ie*'s ancestors.

The architectural design of these 'proper' houses in the early Meiji era incorporated key elements of the *sukiya-zukuri* style of architecture developed during preceding centuries for the dwellings of Japan's elites. The houses were one- or at most two-storied, with a superstructure of thick wooden posts and beams bearing the weight of a heavy tiled or thatched overhanging roof. Rooms other than the *genkan* and kitchen were raised at least 30 centimetres above ground level and their floors were covered with one of a set number of woven *tatami* mats. There were thin, full-width sliding doors between most interior rooms and sliding doors with rice-paper insets to let in light along the veranda under the overhanging roof, and these made it possible to open up larger interior spaces as and when needed and to provide ventilation during the humid summer months. In most rooms there were floor-to-ceiling cupboards for the storage of futon, floor cushions, individual lacquered dining trays and other items that would be needed as the use of rooms changed during the course of a day. Rooms were not only of modular size (4.5 mats, 6 mats, 8 mats, etc.) but also multipurpose: sleeping, eating, playing games, sewing, etc. Co-sleeping, that is the bedding down of family members other than the patriarch in one room – with young children or a mother and her youngest children often sharing one set of bedding – was the norm.

Such houses were, of course, well beyond the reach of poor Japanese, or even those with ordinary incomes. Yet it is likely that they visited such dwellings on a fairly regular basis – to deliver goods, to take part in some annual events and to provide kitchen or serving labour at others – and so they were exposed to what constituted the 'good life' in a 'proper' house at the time. As in the early modern West, the lifestyles and living environments of the aristocracy and wealthy farmers or merchants were visible to their 'lesser' neighbours and some of the features of the houses of the former – in the Japanese case, *tatami* mats, a *genkan* and a *tokonoma* in particular – became aspirations of the latter, to be realised as and when their resources permitted.

Conspicuously absent from this aspirational wish-list in the late 19th century was furniture, for the simple reason that furniture – chairs, tables, beds and the like – was conspicuously absent from the houses of Japanese elites. For reasons that remain unclear, Japan retained what is described in the literature as a 'floor-sitting' or 'squatting' culture[3] far longer than was the case in nearby China or in the West, where chairs and a 'chair-sitting' culture appeared during the Tang Dynasty (618–907 AD) and the late Middle Ages (c. 1400 AD), respectively and slowly diffused to much of the population thereafter.[4]

Today, and since the 1970s, the vast majority of Japanese people are urban residents, with adults employed in the industrial or service sectors of the economy. Commuting from home to work is the norm. And the homes from which these employees set off in the morning and to which they return at night are radically different from those of a century or so ago. Whether detached houses or apartments in low- to high-rise buildings – or indeed, on the non-commuting side of urban life, the living space behind one of the numerous small, family-run shops still to be found in Japanese cities – the typical dwelling is occupied by a nuclear family consisting of a married couple and their children (although as we shall see later the number of 'non-standard' occupants of dwellings – young single people, single-parent households, the elderly living on their own – has been increasing). Interior rooms are now functionally specific as in the West, with solid walls and doors demarcating such private spaces as bedrooms, and almost all the rooms are filled with furniture. Hardwood floors have replaced *tatami* mats, although one such 'traditional' matted and multipurpose room remains in many urban dwellings for use as a dining room on special occasions, as temporary accommodation for visiting relatives or as the parental bedroom at night. At the centre of the dwelling, metaphorically if not literally, is a well-lit kitchen, fitted out with a wide range of labour-saving appliances, and a dining area where the occupants can gather for meals around a table.

Nearby or often as part of the same open-plan family area is a living room with sofa, chairs and all the electronic equipment now deemed essential to modern living.

In short, there have been two major transitions in the housing culture of modern Japan, both of them taking place over a relatively short span of time. One is from housing that was a fairly rigid expression of patriarchy to a more egalitarian culture in which both the status of women in the family and the privacy afforded to individual family members, especially children, has risen. The second is from a floor- to a chair-sitting culture, a transition which required more housing area per household than had previously been the case for the simple reason that furniture takes up space. Before examining these cultural shifts in greater detail, however, it will be useful to locate contemporary Japanese housing in a comparative perspective. I will also deal with a few problematic stereotypes in the process.

International perspectives

Chief among the problematic stereotypes that merit attention are those which portray contemporary Japanese dwellings as exceedingly small – as 'little more than rabbit hutches' in the vivid phrase used in 1979 by a high-ranking British official in the European Community, as it was then known[5] – and those which cite the 'scrap and build' trend in Japanese housing as a profligate use of resources, especially of timber imported from developing countries in South-East Asia rather than from Japan's own extensive forests.[6]

The first of these stereotypes stems from undue attention in the West (and in the Japanese media) paid to housing conditions in Tokyo Metropolitan Prefecture. As I have documented in greater detail elsewhere,[7] Tokyo ranks as the very lowest among the 47 prefectures of Japan in terms of the average size of dwellings, while ranking at the very top in terms of the cost of both owner-occupied and rental housing. Granted, Tokyo has a large population, the prefecture itself being home to some 9 per cent of Japan's total population and the Capital Region (which includes four adjacent prefectures) home to over 28 per cent. But when housing conditions in the rest of the country – where the majority of Japanese live – are taken into consideration, it is clear that Japan has been on a par with most Western European countries since the early 1990s. Indeed, in terms of the average size of dwellings, Japan ranked ahead of France and West Germany and

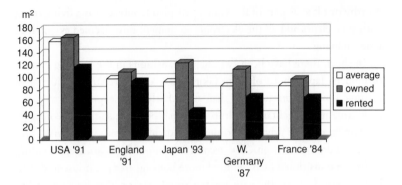

Figure 15.1 An international comparison of housing space, in square metres.
Source: Ministry of Construction, Japan (1994), table 9.1, p. 138.

almost level with England in 1993 (Figure 15.1).[8] Typical Japanese homes are small in comparison with homes in such land-rich countries as the US, but so too are typical homes in most of Western Europe.

The second stereotype fails to give adequate attention to the seismic challenges facing Japan and the impact of those challenges on housing, past and present. As noted previously, the traditional Japanese house was built of wood, and it was generally assumed that a well-built house would last at least 40 years, barring a natural disaster of one sort or another. This was not an unusual projected lifespan for such a house, although of course some wooden houses in Japan as well as elsewhere have lasted considerably longer. But natural disasters in Japan were and remain relatively common, with earthquakes ranking along with typhoons at the top of the list in terms of destructive power. In sparsely populated areas, wooden houses are still considered relatively safe, owing to the inherent flexibility of wood and hence the ability of support posts to absorb seismic waves. In densely populated areas, however, residents are at great risk from the fires that often follow in the wake of a major earthquake, as demonstrated in the aftermath of the Great Kanto Earthquake of 1923 when fires caused by overturned charcoal or wood cooking stoves raged throughout Tokyo, and the Great Hanshin Earthquake of 1995 when broken gas mains ignited and fires consumed hundreds of wooden houses in the centre of Kobe.

In response to the former disaster, in which over 140 000 people lost their lives, the authorities took steps to fireproof Tokyo by widening roads and promoting buildings of concrete or stone, but the impact of these measures was limited to the central business districts of the city. Those residents of Tokyo who could afford to do so, mostly members of Japan's new middle class (about whom more will be said later), relocated to the suburbs of the city in the aftermath of the earthquake, where lower population density provided a margin of safety. This sort of suburban migration, in search not only of lower cost housing or housing land but also of greater safety, continued in the early postwar decades. With the massive influxes of new migrants to the capital and other major cities during the so-called 'economic miracle' years (1955–72), however, suburban districts became increasingly congested and, with most dwellings still constructed of wood, the risk from fire increased.

It was to accommodate the workers deemed essential to Japan's postwar economic recovery and growth and at the same time to fireproof major cities that the authorities now turned to the construction of large, mid-rise apartment blocks built of reinforced concrete. This building technology was also adopted by private construction firms to provide housing for rent or sale to swelling urban populations. More affordable than a detached house in the now distant lightly-populated suburbs and promoted as both 'modern' and safe, these apartments became home to many urban Japanese. In the meantime, even more sophisticated building technologies were developed for high-rise office buildings in expensive city-centre locations, where the substantial rental rates would offset higher construction costs – first, structures like the 36-storey Kasumigaseki Building in downtown Tokyo whose upper floors would sway safely if a bit disconcertingly in a powerful typhoon and later, much taller buildings with computerised sensors in the basement which would activate weights on the roof or elsewhere in the structure within one-hundredth of a second to counteract seismic waves. When the Great Hanshin Earthquake made a direct hit on Kobe in 1995, analysts were surprised by the large number of 20-year-old apartment blocks built of reinforced concrete that collapsed, or pancaked, at the fifth floor,[9] with obviously dire consequences for those living at that level. The building regulations for such structures nationwide, which had been revised in the early 1980s, were now revised again to incorporate many of the recent technological innovations in office buildings previously considered too expensive for the would-be renters or purchasers of units in residential buildings.

Nor were the lessons of the Hanshin earthquake lost on ordinary Japanese households. Already for some years, increasing numbers of those owning fire-prone wooden houses built decades earlier in densely populated urban areas had been rebuilding their homes in more fire-resistant materials, taking advantage of the progressively greater building heights now permitted for such structures. Now those about to acquire an urban apartment were impelled to give serious consideration to paying the extra cost – in rent or purchase price – of a unit in the newest development on offer, because 'newest' meant safer for themselves and their families. Construction companies responded to these new market conditions, and new official standards for earthquake-resistant structures, not only by building anew, but also – after their initial construction costs had been amortised to an extent – by demolishing and re-developing existing housing sites. The pace of what had been a relatively slow but steady process of adapting home construction to new technology now quickened.

Wood is used in all Japanese dwellings, as both a structural and design element in traditionally built houses and as an important design element in the interiors of high-rise apartment units, and there is no denying that more of this wood comes from the forests of South-East Asia (as well as from the US, Canada and Russia) than from Japan's own forests. Some high-quality wood is also ground up and made into disposable plywood frames for the poured-concrete panels used as building trim. Japanese timber importers and construction companies have no doubt contributed to problems of deforestation elsewhere, and certainly could do better in this regard. But it is important to recognise that there has been an underlying life-saving rationale to 'scrap and build' construction practices in Japan over recent decades, as new construction technologies have been invented and diffused to create more durable, disaster-resistant structures. Far from being the expression of some inherently wasteful Japanese preference for the 'new', the interest of Japanese consumers in new-build homes – and government policies which facilitate urban re-development – make a great deal of sense.

One consequence of this consumer interest, which differentiates Japan from many other developed countries, is that there is a comparatively limited market for 'used' or second-hand dwellings, which is reflected in generally lower prices for older housing stock, whether detached houses or apartments, than for new-build properties.[10] That the Government Housing Loan Corporation (GHLC), until recently the major source of loans for the purchase of domestic dwellings in Japan, provided longer repayment periods for mortgages on new-build properties and refused to mortgage any property over 25 years old,[11] no doubt contributed to this outcome, but the contrast with markets for older homes in Britain and the US, for example, is still striking. In those two countries, not only do the sales of such homes far outnumber new-build sales,[12] but also many would-be purchasers consider older properties to be more desirable than brand new homes, and may even be willing to pay somewhat higher prices for them – exactly the opposite of the Japanese case. It seems increasingly likely that more durable (that is, more disaster-resistant) construction technologies will eventually create a comparably mature housing market in Japan, in which older stock plays a crucial role in housing transactions.

Like Britain, the US and many other countries, however, home owner-ship has become the norm in postwar Japan, and slightly over 61 per cent of all dwellings are now owner-occupied. Although it is often portrayed in such countries as the realisation of a 'natural human instinct' as and when personal resources allow, home ownership on this scale is in fact much more than the product of increasing middle- and working-class affluence since the mid-20th century. Government housing and tax policies, the availability and cost of mortgages, the construction and marketing of relatively low-cost dwellings by property developers and an assessment of the alternatives to and advantages of house purchase by consumers have also played an important role.

In early 20th-century Japan, as in many Western countries at the same time, most urban residents rented their dwellings from private landlords,[13] and housing systems based on the mass provision of rental housing – whether private, social (that is, built and managed by public bodies) or a mixture of the two – continue to exist in a number of European countries today.[14] There had been advocates of social housing provision in early post-war Japan, but they failed to have much impact on the Japanese government. The government instead opted to give priority to the country's economic recovery, to provide a limited amount of strategically located housing for workers who could contribute to that goal and, when shortages of vital construction materials ended, to leave housing construction largely to the private sector.[15] The state's role thereafter was increasingly confined to the provision of low-interest loans to qualified (exclusively middle-income) home buyers and, importantly, to issuing guidelines every five years for the structure, basic fittings and steadily increasing minimal size of dwelling units that would qualify for such loans.

Private rental housing did not disappear from Japan. On the contrary, it has long ranked second after owner-occupied dwellings in available housing stock, accounting for roughly 27 per cent of stock in 2003, far ahead of public rental housing at slightly less than 7 per cent. A subcategory within private rental housing, company or 'issued' housing – which partly compensated for the limited supply of public rental housing for those Japanese employees

Table 15.1 *An international comparison of housing by form of tenure (% of total stock, year of observation in parentheses)*

	Owned	Rented		
		Total	Private	Social
Sweden (2002)	46	39	21	18
Denmark (2002)	51	45	26	19
Netherlands (2002)	54	46	11	35
France (2002)	56	38	21	17
Japan (2003)	**61**	37	30	7
United States (2005)	69	31	27	4
England (2003)	71	29	10	19

Note: 'Other' forms of housing – free housing, vacant housing – are not included.
Source: Ministry of Land, Infrastructure and Transport, Japan (2006), Table 9.3, p. 170 for Japan, the US and England; National Agency for Enterprise and Housing, Denmark (2004), Tables 3.4 and 3.5, pp. 39, 41 for Sweden, Denmark, the Netherlands and France.

not yet earning middle-income salaries in earlier decades – is now down to slightly over 3 per cent of stock. It appears to be destined for even less significance as Japanese corporations continue to rationalise their operations in the aftermath of prolonged recession during the 1990s.[16] As shown in Table 15.1 above, private rental housing is considerably more prevalent in Japan than in all other countries listed, except the US.

The salient fact about this private rental housing is that it has always provided comparatively small dwelling units, almost exclusively apartments in densely populated urban areas, that are suitable for a single person or a couple with one infant at best, and those units have been and remain of generally poor quality. Granted, there are some spacious, high-quality (and high-cost) rental apartments now available in Tokyo and a few other major cities, but these are the exceptions that prove the rule.[17] Various factors have been at work here, chief among them the exemption from officially mandated construction standards enjoyed by small-scale housing developments, the small size of building plots owned by the individuals interested in profiting from the construction of rental units and, last but by no means least, the legal protection provided to sitting tenants, which has made periodic rent increases, the eviction of tenants for non-payment of rent and the recovery of the premises for personal use exceedingly difficult.[18] The latter factor, in particular, made designing rental units for a high-turnover market – singles who soon will marry and move on, young couples who eventually will have a second baby and move on, employees on temporary assignment away from their home bases – an attractive option.[19]

This left ordinary Japanese urban residents who had outgrown the rental accommodation of their early adult working lives with very little choice. As affordable family-sized rental accommodation was exceedingly scarce, they could either make do in increasingly cramped quarters or they could buy a larger apartment or detached house within as manageable a commuting distance to their workplace as they could afford. It is hardly surprising that many of those with the necessary middle incomes to qualify for loans – and, before that, to save up the substantial down payments required (about 30 per cent) – wanted to purchase their own homes.

At some stage during this decision-making process, if not earlier on, two other considerations were likely to intervene, both of which were important elements in establishing and normalising aspirations of home-ownership not only in postwar Japan but in many other countries as well. The first was that real estate was an asset that steadily appreciated in value and hence a good investment. The second, was that being able to purchase one's own home conferred enhanced social status, its degree varying with the perceived quality of the home that was purchased perhaps, but distinguishing the home owner from the 'mere' renter nonetheless.

Changes over time

China, like Japan, had been a floor-sitting culture in ancient times, but by the early Tang Dynasty chairs – introduced from Central Asia – were in increasingly widespread use, and high tables for eating, writing and painting soon followed. Why Japan, which borrowed so much of its technology and culture from China at this time and later, did not also adopt Chinese-style chairs and other furniture remains an intriguing question.[20]

Whatever the reasons, Japan's leaders were set for a rude awakening when the country was constrained to re-open to the West in the 1850s after two centuries of national seclusion. Considerable numbers of Western diplomats, traders and missionaries soon arrived in Japanese treaty ports, bringing their chair-sitting housing culture and ethnocentric confidence with them. Most of these Westerners were appalled by the housing conditions they encountered in Japan, and they were not reticent in expressing their views on the subject. To the leaders of the new Meiji government, keen on protecting Japan from further Western incursions and on revising the 'unequal' treaties the preceding Tokugawa Shogunate had been constrained to sign, it must have been a shock to discover that the housing they occupied was considered 'uncivilised' and that 'squatting' – sitting, eating and sleeping on the floor, no matter how carefully swept the *tatami* mats and how elegant the immediate surroundings – was associated in the Western mind with, for example, the 'backward' tribes of Africa. Some high-ranking officials of the new Meiji government swiftly had Western-style houses built for the entertainment of foreign dignitaries, although they and their families continued to spend most of their days and nights in the traditional Japanese dwellings still nestled within the gardens of their Tokyo estates.[21] This obviously was not a solution that many could afford, nor were most Japanese – in Tokyo or elsewhere – much aware of these Western criticisms. What began to attract attention, and lead eventually to some modest but significant changes in housing design in the early 20th century, was the discovery by a small number of Japanese of the then-prevailing emphasis on 'warm family life' based on the strong bonds of affection between husband and wife and between parents and their children in Britain and the US. They became Japan's first housing reformers, soon to be aided and abetted by some of the country's first professionally trained architects, and their main aims were to provide a degree of privacy within domestic dwellings – not for individual family members, but between family members on the one hand and household servants and visitors on the other – and to promote such wholesome and purely family gatherings as meals taken at set times around a common table in a suitably central and attractive room.[22] The main audience for the articles they wrote, and eventually for the relatively small number of 'modern houses' (*bunka jūtaku*) that were built in the 1920s and 30s, were members of Japan's new middle class.

Despite the 1898 canonisation of the multi-generational and patriarchal *ie* in the Meiji Civil Code, there had always been nuclear families in Japan, each one consisting of a married couple and their children and usually still dependent on the husband's natal *ie* for support if and when hard times struck. After the Meiji Restoration, the number of such families increased along with greater employment opportunities in the non-agricultural sector, as the younger sons and daughters of farming families moved to the towns and cities where those opportunities were concentrated. Some, especially daughters, would eventually return home to marry and settle down, but others married and established permanent residences near their places of employment, returning home only if forced to do so by economic necessity.

At the upper socioeconomic level within this category were some fairly self-sufficient nuclear families, economically independent of the husbands' natal *ie* by virtue of the mens' higher educational qualifications and relatively stable, well-paid employment in government, industry, universities or the military. Such men tended to marry young women who had benefited from the more limited higher education then available to girls, which prepared them for their future roles as 'good wives and wise mothers'. These couples came to be seen – and to see themselves – as members of a 'new' middle class, distinguished from members of the 'old' middle class in cities who remained tied to inherited occupations – and to inherited dwellings – as successful merchants and artisans. Although relatively few in number, probably constituting no more than 4 or 5 per cent of the economically active population as late as the 1930s,[23] it was these new middle class households that rented the fairly small 'modern houses' that first became available in new suburban developments in the 1920s. These houses featured an interior corridor to separate family space from the kitchen and other space used by servants. They also included one or more reception rooms just off the entrance to serve as the husband's domain, where he might entertain his visitors or pursue his personal interests without interfering with normal family life within. One of these reception rooms might well be furnished in Western style with chairs and a desk or table,[24] although *tatami* mats and floor-sitting prevailed elsewhere in the dwelling.

The justification commonly given by architects at the time for the Western style of this masculine space within the home was that 'no one sat on the floor in government and company offices',[25] the places of work to which many men of the new middle class commuted on a daily basis. That was indeed the case, and a marked contrast with Japan's pre-Restoration past. It was part of a larger trend that had been introducing many Japanese – whether rich or poor, living in countryside or city – to a chair-sitting culture for decades. Classrooms in the schools built early in the Meiji period to provide every child in the nation with an elementary education were furnished with desks and chairs. The barracks built for army conscripts were fitted out with beds, and for meals conscripts sat on benches at long tables. There were tables and chairs in the canteens for workers in large factories, too, and not a *tatami* mat in sight in the railway carriages and trams in which increasing numbers of people travelled. But this was the outside world of work in the new nation of Japan. The inside world of home remained relatively unchanged for the vast majority of the population. Although there would be some modest improvements to kitchens in the 1920s and 1930s in both urban and rural dwellings to render them more sanitary and efficient,[26] a floor-sitting culture persisted.

With Japan's defeat in the Second World War in 1945, the widespread destruction of dwellings in Japanese cities as a result of aerial fire-bombing in the year or so preceding Japan's surrender and a postwar Occupation set on democratising not only the polity and economy but also the society of a defeated enemy, the scene was set for unprecedented change in both housing and housing codes.

As Imamura has documented earlier in this volume, the patriarchal *ie* system was abolished in law early in the Occupation years and gender equality proclaimed in both a new constitution and a new civil code. Rural land reform laid the basis for improved incomes and living standards in the countryside, where roughly half the Japanese population still resided. Although the Occupation did not directly concern itself with housing, it did not prevent official Japanese efforts to deal with the severe housing crisis then facing the nation: an estimated crude housing shortage of some 4.2 million dwellings, with the shortages most acute in large cities.[27] As noted earlier, the Japanese government prioritised economic recovery and growth, but that meant providing housing of some sort for workers in critical industries. That in turn provided an opportunity for housing reformers, many of them active since the late 1920s, to realise the now significantly amended goal of 'democratising' the typical Japanese dwelling. Baldly put, what that meant was getting the Japanese 'off the floor' at home at long last and into chairs around 'proper' tables for family meals in a designated space within the home that could not also be used for sleeping. It also meant the elimination of all the 'feudal' elements of the past within the home – no patriarchal or masculine preserves, either for the male head of the household himself or for the exclusive entertainment of his guests, and no wasted spaces for 'ostentatious' display such as elaborate *genkan* or *tokonoma*. Finally, it meant the provision of separate sleeping rooms for parents and children and of functional, labour-saving cooking and bathing facilities to enable the wife, now the equal partner of the husband in Japan's new democratic families, to discharge her duties without the aid of a single servant.[28]

Given severe housing shortages in early postwar urban Japan, which did not abate until the late 1960s, these reformers enjoyed a seller's market for their design initiatives. The most fundamental of these was the 'nDK' model for urban apartments in the housing estates (*danchi*) built by the

Japan Housing Corporation, a government agency, after 1955. 'DK' stands for a wooden- or vinyl-floored combined dining and kitchen area featuring a Western-style table and chairs and a small but efficiently organised cooking space, and 'n' stands for the number of other rooms, *tatami*-matted and envisioned as sleeping rooms, which were originally two in number: one for the parents and the other for their children. With some modifications, most notably the addition of an 'L' (living room) to the DK, and an increase in both the number and size of other rooms, this model won general public approval and became the template for virtually all house construction in Japan subsequently, not only of apartments but also of single-family dwellings.

The spread of Western-style furniture from the original DK to virtually all the other rooms in these dwellings stemmed in part from the lack of built-in storage space in both publicly and privately built housing. This impelled residents to purchase chests of drawers and wardrobes for their clothing and other personal possessions. But there were other factors at work as well, not least among them the growth of a domestic Western-style furniture industry. Kick-started by the sudden demand for tables and chairs for all those DKs, the new industry was soon offering easy terms for purchase of such expensive items as sofas and beds. The spread was further stimulated by the considerable publicity in magazines targeted at housewives and at local PTA meetings given to the need to provide children with private, well-fitted study and sleeping spaces.[29]

Another innovation within the separate units of early *danchi* apartments, was a family bathroom with a deep tub for soaking Japanese-style whose water was heated by a specially designed gas-fired boiler. This eventually brought about the demise of public bath-houses in most of urban Japan. A separate Western-style 'sit-down' flush toilet also became well-nigh universal in Japanese dwellings, leading eventually to the invention of high-tech toilets with heated seats and variable flushing controls that make most Western toilets seem backward indeed.

Although bathrooms and toilets, even if improved in diverse ways, took up roughly the same space as originally provided, the (L)DK and other n-rooms seemed increasingly crowded to their occupants as they became filled with space-consuming furniture. The progressively larger per capita and overall dwelling sizes stipulated by the GHLC for middle-class housing loans, and by other government agencies as new five-year targets for home construction took this dynamic – and increasing urban middle-class incomes – on board, inching or more accurately metering up the mandated space standards each quinquennium, until basically adequate standards for a Western-style, chair-sitting housing culture were achieved.

Variations and stratification

There always have been, and continue to be, variations in the style, size and quality of housing within Japan, as in other countries. Some of these are basically geographical or climatic in origin – houses in regions with harsh winters have more steeply pitched roofs and better provision for winter heating than houses in more temperate regions. Others have more complex demographic and socioeconomic origins, leading to contrasts between, for example, rates of home ownership, average housing size and the internal layout of rooms within houses among rural, urban and metropolitan areas of the country. Considerably lower land prices in many parts of rural and small-town Japan than in Tokyo and other large cities have contributed to higher rates of owner-occupancy in these areas. Residents of rural areas, small towns and the numerous medium-sized regional cities of Japan also tend to live in larger homes than the vast majority of their metropolitan counterparts. Moreover, many of these homes – including some built fairly recently – feature not only modern DK and private bedrooms, but also traditionally designed 'public' spaces in the form of sizable *genkan* and linked *tatami*-matted rooms that exist only in attenuated form, if at all, in dwellings in the nation's largest cities.[30]

Finally, it is essential to mention what have recently become the two key issues in studies of Japanese housing and housing policy, both related to increasing stratification within Japanese society: (1) the growth in the number of 'non-standard' households in need of appropriate and affordable accommodation; and (2) the growing divide within the nation's largest metropolitan areas between those middle-income households who can realistically contemplate eventual home-ownership and those who cannot.

As noted earlier, the nuclear family of a married couple and their (two) children became the norm in early postwar Japan, and it was for such families – or more accurately, the skilled blue- and white-collar workers within them who were deemed essential to Japan's postwar economic recovery and growth – that a limited amount of state-subsidised social housing was built and on which much subsequent private housing provision focused. But the percentage of such nuclear families reached a peak in Japan in the late 1970s and the number of 'other' households began to increase.

These included: single-parent nuclear families; one-person households of either working-age adults or elderly widows or widowers; childless couples; and 'new' three-generational households in which either an elderly parent or parental couple took up residence in the home of one of their adult children or an adult child (often a son) and his nuclear family took up residence in his parental home.[31] For reasons also noted earlier, small units of accommodation – essentially studio apartments with kitchen, bath and one other room – were built for rent or sometimes for sale to working-age singles or young couples in large cities. Construction firms also began to market designs for 'two-household homes' which promised to provide a friction-free, non-'feudal' balance of shared and private facilities for those with the land and financial resources to take the 'new' multi-generational housing route.[32] But absent from this list was suitable and affordable housing not only for low-income 'standard' households, who were left as previously to find whatever social or private rental housing they could, but also for single-parent households, especially those headed by relatively low-paid working mothers, and for the elderly, whether home owners seeking to downsize into rental accommodation to be closer to their children or long-term renters seeking suitably sheltered accommodation as they encountered the infirmities of old age.[33]

Attracting at least as much attention in recent studies have been the difficulties faced by increasing numbers of middle-income Japanese households in climbing the established postwar housing ladder from renting to owner-occupation in the major metropolitan regions of the country, particularly in greater Tokyo and greater Osaka. For years many households in these regions had been constrained to purchase apartments or detached houses at ever greater distances from the main breadwinner's workplace in order to secure the living space they needed at a cost they could afford.[34] Dramatically rising prices for land and housing during the 'bubble' years of the 1980s did not merely intensify these problems, they put home-ownership of any reasonable sort beyond the reach of such households unless they had parental or other familial wealth on which to draw. The collapse of the bubble economy in the early 1990s led to a significant decline in land and housing prices in these same metropolitan areas, leaving anyone who had purchased an apartment or a house during the bubble years with an asset worth considerably less than the housing loans they remained liable for.[35] In addition, the ensuing long recession – the so-called 'lost decade' – and the unprecedented economic and employment uncertainties it generated trapped many younger Japanese households possessing what had previously been regarded as very good career prospects in rental accommodation, unless they inherited land or housing from their parents or otherwise received familial assistance. Put another way, inherited advantage which privileged the children of middle- or higher-income families, especially those who already owned their own homes, over the children of families of lesser means, especially those who rented their homes, began to play a noticeable role in movement up the metropolitan housing ladder. This posed a considerable challenge to one of the basic tenets of postwar Japanese meritocracy, that of upward social mobility by dint of the individual's own efforts and achievements regardless of family background.

The implications of this latter development in the housing sphere, which impinges directly on those Japanese who have achieved notable success in educational selection, has contributed to greater academic and public attention to social inequalities within Japan than has been the case for decades.

Notes

1. See Ravetz (1995: 149–65) for a discussion of changing codes of room use in 20th-century England.
2. Garon (1997: 25–40).
3. Rybczynski (1986: 78–81).
4. Perkins (1999: 172–3); Rybczynski (1986: 26, 81–5).
5. 'Obituary: Sir Roy Denham', *The Times* (19 April 2006), online at: http://www.timesonline.co.uk/tol/comment/obituaries/article706856.ece.
6. Bob Johnstone (1997: 18).
7. Waswo (2002: 110–13).
8. Varying definitions of habitable space in national surveys, not to mention the differing categories of the housing included in those surveys, render such international comparisons imperfect. Whether or not kitchens are included, or only kitchens of at least a certain size, is a major variable. US and, until recently, English surveys exclude apartments, which tend to be smaller than single-family dwellings. Japanese housing surveys have always tended to maximise the area of housing units, but they have also included apartments as well as single-family dwellings. When apartments were eventually included in English surveys in 2001, the average area of all housing fell below recorded Japanese levels. See Ministry of Land, Infrastructure and Transport (2006: 169).
9. See Louie (1996) for illustrations of this 'anomaly' and other explanations of the heavy casualties incurred in Kobe.
10. Hirayama (2007: 26).
11. This is the limit cited by Hirayama (2007: 26), but a limit of 10 years is cited by Kanemoto (1997: 534). It could well be that the GHLC amended its policy toward providing loans on used houses sometime in the late 1990s or early 2000s.

12. Eiji Ōizumi (2007: 69–70); Kanemoto (1997: 634).

13. Waswo (2002: 39–43).

14. Harloe (1995).

15. Waswo (2002: 45–60).

16. Iwao Sato (2007: 79–85); Waswo (2002: 92–4).

17. As shown in Figure 15.1, the difference in living space between owned and rental housing in Japan was greater than in the other countries listed in the early 1990s, and the space available in rental housing – predominantly apartments – was considerably lower than in the other countries. This remained the case in 2003. See Ministry of Land, Infrastructure and Transport (2006: 169, table 9.1).

18. Kanemoto (1997: 632–4).

19. Waswo (2002: 87–8).

20. Chairs had been introduced to Japan from China late in the Nara period, it appears, but they never came into widespread use among the court aristocracy (Morris 1964: 31) and disappeared from elite dwellings thereafter.

21. Nishiyama (1989: 100).

22. Sand (2003: 21–54).

23. This is a very crude estimate, using data from the 1930 Japanese census and the occupational categories devised by British sociologists for the analysis of class in post-war Britain. See Halsey (1995: 40–1) for the application of these categories to prewar Britain.

24. Sand (2003: 43–4).

25. Sand (2003: 44).

26. Sand (2003: 62–94); Partner (2001).

27. Nishiyama (1989: 290–1).

28. Waswo (2002: 69–75), Nishikawa (1999: 485–93).

29. Waswo (2002: 82–4).

30. Sumita (1983).

31. Hinokidani (2007: 118, 127).

32. Coaldrake (1989: 64–6).

33. Hinokidani (2007: 122–3, 128–9); Izuhara (2007: 107–8).

34. Waswo (2002: 110–15, 121–2).

35. Hirayama (2007: 25–6).

Further reading

Hirayama, Yosuke and Richard Ronald (eds) (2007), *Housing and Social Transition in Japan*, London: Routledge.

Sand, Jordan (2003), *House and Home in Modern Japan: Architecture, Domestic Space and Bourgeois Culture, 1880–1930*, Cambridge: Harvard University Asia Center.

Waswo, Ann (2002), *Housing in Postwar Japan: A Social History*, London: Routledge-Curzon.

16

Food culture

The conventional meal of Japan comprises four types of food: rice, the staple diet; *okazu*, secondary components like fish or vegetables; soup called *shiru*; and *tsukemono*, vegetables pickled in salt or rice bran. The traditional practice in Japan is for all food to be served on individual plates and bowls at individual, low tables. Unlike typical meals in the West today, where dishes are served chronologically, in Japan it has been common for all dishes to be placed together on a serving tray at the beginning of the meal.

This chapter first deals with rice as a significant part of Japanese cultural life and fish as the most important *okazu*, the two key components of Japan's food culture for both pre-modern and modern Japan. Changing patterns of food culture in and after the Meiji period are then examined,[1] with the concomitant transformation of the dining table. Finally, the chapter presents a model that shows the way in which the Japanese today mix different styles of food, and concludes by discussing issues faced by contemporary Japanese food culture.

Rice as symbolic food

Rice constitutes the staple diet for the Japanese, both as essential food and as an important symbol of cultural life. Japan's rice is the so-called *Japonica* type short grain which is normally eaten on its own without seasoning or flavouring. The Japanese have long regarded rice as central to their meal culture and all other food as a secondary component of their diet. In the Japanese language, to eat rice (*meshi o kuu*) means to have a meal (*shokuji o suru*).

Before the establishment of the modern nation state, feudal lords collected tax in rice, not in money. Japan's feudal economy was thus built upon the production of rice. Japanese village life follows the calendar of rice cultivation, with village festivals organised according to this cycle. Villagers pray for a rich harvest at spring festivals at the time of planting seedlings into paddy fields. At summer festivals, farming communities pray for the protection of rice against harmful insects and typhoons that hit Japan late in the season, while autumn festivals are harvest celebrations.

In Japan, as well as in countries in South-East Asia, rice has been regarded as a sacred grain in which the divine spirit dwells. During festival periods, people in the lower classes, who had to 'extend' their everyday rice by mixing it with barley, foxtail millet and Japanese millet, ate pure white rice with no additives, festive meals made from glutinous rice and also drank *sake* made from rice. The belief underlying this practice was that these rice products would empower their consumers with the sacred energy of rice.

Mochi, made from glutinous rice steamed and pounded in a mortar, has special significance for many Japanese, who believe that it gives much physical power to the eater. While dietics and physiology can scientifically corroborate this belief, it is based upon the folk notion that *mochi* as condensed rice imbues the eater with supernatural energy provided by the sacred spirit that dwells in rice. This is why the Japanese celebrate New Year's Day, the most important holiday on the nation's calendar, by eating *zōni* soup that contains *mochi*.

Sake is also made from rice. The method of brewing *sake* was initially brought to Japan from the Chinese continent and the Korean peninsula. Japan has developed its own technology, producing *sake* of 20 per cent alcoholic content, the highest level among brewed liquors without distillation. *Sake* is an indispensable part of Shinto festivals in which all gods are supposed to enjoy drinking the beverage. Festival participants offer *sake* to Shinto shrines, which they later drink together in an act that cements community solidarity.

Conventionally, people enjoy *sake* in *tokkuri* (a small ceramic flank-shaped bottle) after it is warmed in hot water and served in *choku*, a small ceramic cup. However, since the 1980s, *ginjōshu*, high-quality fruity *sake* brewed at low temperatures, has been marketed successfully in a chilled form to be enjoyed like white wine.

Fish – sashimi, sushi and whale meat

Although the typical Buddhist believer did not eat animal products on specific Buddhist events, funerals, or anniversaries of the death of a family member, they were able to eat fish and shellfish on other days without any feelings of guilt. As a result, fish came to be perceived as the greatest delicacy in traditional Japanese cooking, resulting in a large range of fish-based dishes. Although various techniques were developed in Japan for the preparation of fish dishes, in comparison to China and Korea where meat was eaten, cooking methods featuring a range of spices and using oils and fats did not develop in Japan.

The philosophy behind Japanese food culture appears to be a paradoxical belief that no cooking is the best kind of cooking. This manifests itself in the treatment of fish in Japanese gastronomy. If fish are fresh enough, they ought to be sliced raw and served as sashimi. If they are not sufficiently fresh, the second best preparation is to grill them and sprinkle them with salt. Only when fish lose freshness would they be cooked with such flavourings as shōyu or miso as a last resort. The thinking here is that the extensive use of cookery and processing methods is vulgar; the natural initial flavours of ingredients should be retained and eaten in the form as close as possible to nature.

Sashimi, carefully sliced raw fish meat to be eaten with wasabi and soy sauce, reflects this value orientation most sharply. Most Japanese consider sashimi the simplest and therefore the most refined food. High-quality Japanese cuisine almost invariably includes sashimi.

Sushi[2] is often wrongly thought to be an extension of this idea, because it is served as a small amount of rice shaped by hand and topped with sashimi. In fact, sushi originated from the culture of fermenting fish meat in pre-modern Japan and differed markedly from what we recognise as sushi today. The idea started with the knowledge that fish preserved with salt and mixed with cooked rice can be stored for a long period of time because rice undergoes lactic acid fermentation which raises its acidity level and thereby prevents bacteria from propagating. Rice grains used this way break down and become pasty and are normally inedible. Removed from rice, the preserved fish tastes sour and smells like strong cheese. This was the type of sushi available before the Edo period. Similar food exists in paddy regions in South-East Asia, an observation that gives some credence to the theory that sushi had initially developed in the upper and middle reaches of the Mekong Delta area in ancient times as a method of preserving freshwater fish meat and was brought to Japan with the paddy field method of rice cultivation. While this type of sushi was eaten in China for some time, unprocessed food gradually disappeared from the Chinese table, with only some ethnic minority groups in south-western China still retaining the practice today.

From around the 15th century, the Japanese began to develop their own style of sushi, based on a new technique that enabled them to begin eating it three or four days after preparation and to consume it within one or two months. The short fermentation method made it possible for both fish and rice to be eaten at the same time and therefore for sushi to serve as a snack.

Towards the end of the 17th century during the Edo period, *haya zushi* (quick sushi) became available, with both rice and fish being flavoured with vinegar. This method opened the way for the diversification of sushi, which now included mixing vinegared rice with flavoured and cooked vegetables. Around the same time, *nori maki*, which used paper-like dried seaweed to wrap rice, became popular.

The so-called *nigiri zushi*, which is served at sushi restaurants today, acquired popularity in the 1820s in Edo (present-day Tokyo) and became the standard version, comprising a small ball of vinegared rice shaped by hand by a professional sushi chef with a slice of fish and a bit of *wasabi* to be eaten with a few drops of soy sauce. From around this time, *nigiri zushi* ceased to be made in the home altogether and began to be served at sushi restaurants where chefs were supposed to make various kinds of sushi on the spot at the request of customers. Thus, the sushi that originated as long-term preserved food transformed itself into a kind of 'fast food' in Japan, which has recently been popularised around the world.

While the *nigiri zushi* type is in national and international vogue, it should be emphasised that there is much regional variation of sushi within Japan. *Funa zushi*, for example, the noted product in Shiga Prefecture, is made from carp caught in Lake Biwa and subjected to lactic acid fermentation based upon the ancient method of sushi production. At community festivals and functions, various types of sushi are served in different localities.

The consumption of mammals such as whale and dolphin was not prohibited in Japan by the Buddhist establishment as these were viewed as *large fish*. Whale was not only consumed; oil was extracted from the whale's blubber and sprayed onto the surface of rice paddies to prevent pests. After the whale oil was extracted, the remaining fatty layer was dried and used as a preserved food. Whale meat, in particular, has been ranked as one of the top ingredients for fish dishes and is often served on festive occasions. As early as 1832, a specialist book that detailed various methods of preparing whale meat was published. The book, titled *Kujiraniku ryōrikata* (Ways of preparing whale meat), classified the body of a whale into 70 parts, including its internal organs, and provided ideal preparation details for each part.

While recognising the importance of preserving animal resources, a majority of the Japanese find it difficult to comprehend the argument,[3] frequently advanced in Western countries, that whales should be given *special* protection because their intelligence level is close to that of human beings. The animistic perspective long embedded into the Japanese psyche regards *every* being, including plants and minerals, as having a life of its own. This worldview has been combined with the Buddhist thinking that human and animal lives are on equal footing: human beings live depending upon the lives of other beings. In the endless cycle of some animal beings eating others, some lives are maintained at the expense of others. Based on this belief system, whaling communities in various areas of Japan erected towers for the repose of whales' souls and held ceremonies to honour their memories.

Transformation of food culture: some guideposts

Lifting of the ban on meat consumption and the rise of *sukiyaki* – early Meiji years

Though there are many common features in food and cooking techniques among the three countries, the decisive difference between traditional Japanese cooking and that of China and Korea is that meat was absent from the Japanese diet until relatively recently. One exception to this rule are the islands at the southernmost tip of Japan that formed the Ryūkyū Kingdom, which had claimed its independence from 'mainland' Japan before it was annexed during the Meiji period. The Ryūkyū Kingdom was not influenced by Buddhism and therefore eating meat was not prohibited. As a result of exchange with China, the people of Ryūkyū farmed pigs and goat for meat and developed a unique style of cooking distinct from traditional Japanese techniques. Similarly, the Ainu, indigenous to Hokkaidō in the north, were also not converted to Buddhism and hunted game such as deer and bear.

By the 10th century, both Buddhism and Shintoism began to view meat-eating as contaminating. In feudal Japan, those involved in slaughtering mammals or the production of leather goods began to be socially isolated and classified as an outcaste group that suffered discrimination (see chapter 10). It was not until the latter half of the 18th century that shops selling wild mammals and poultry made their appearance in cities, creating opportunities for members of the urban population to eat meat,[4] though this did not affect the majority of the Japanese, who lived in rural areas.

In order to realise the national goal of modernisation immediately after the Meiji Restoration of 1868, there was a need to cultivate healthy workers and soldiers. Many intellectuals at the time claimed that the reason behind the small and weak physical build of the Japanese people was the lack of meat and milk in their diet. In 1872 it was reported in newspapers that the Emperor Meiji consumed beef, and in turn, Japanese people were encouraged to do the same. In the same year, the government permitted priests – who previously had to shave their heads – to grow their hair, marry and consume meat. Under these new conditions, the consumption of meat was increasingly perceived as something that 'civilised', modern people did, and those who rejected this notion were viewed as conservative nationalists.

The general populace first tried meat at restaurants called *gyūnabeya* where *gyūnabe*, a prototype of *sukiyaki*, was served. *Gyūnabe* was a dish in which beef, spring onions and tofu were simmered in familiar seasonings such as miso, soy sauce, and *mirin* (sweet *sake*), and was eaten with chopsticks. During the Meiji years, this dish was considerably cheaper than the beef meals served at Western style restaurants in Japan.[5]

As *gyūnabe* is based on traditional cooking methods, it eventually made its appearance in private homes. In more conservative households the beef would be prepared outside, or the *kamidana* (household shrine) or *butsudan* (Buddhist altar) would be covered in paper to prevent the smell of the beef from contaminating the gods and Buddha enshrined inside. By the beginning of the 20th century, *gyūnabe* was consumed throughout Japan, while being perceived as a family meal to be served on special occasions.

In the cities of Osaka, Kobe and Kyoto in the Kansai region, *gyūnabe* began to be referred to as *sukiyaki*. The dish still featured sliced beef cooked with spring onions and tofu, but now also included ingredients such as vegetables or *ito konnyaku* (thin devil's tongue noodles), simmered in soy sauce and sugar and served with beaten raw egg. The term *sukiyaki* also became established in Tokyo during the 1920s and the dish became extremely popular around the nation at this time. In Japanese butcher shops, beef and pork is normally sold sliced, rather than in large pieces, because *sukiyaki* is still regarded as the most commonly prepared meat dish.

Spread of Japanised Western-style dishes – the turn of the 19th century

Other meat dishes featuring traditional Japanese food preparation methods included *nikujaga*, a *shōyu*-flavoured, stew-like dish of simmered sliced beef and potatoes, and *yamatoni*, or beef and ginger simmered in soy sauce. The origins of *nikujaga* lie in a dish that was served in the navy, later becoming popularised as a family dish. Enormous quantities of tinned *yamatoni* were used as a portable military meal during the Sino-Japanese War (1894–95) and the Russo-Japanese War (1904–05), and the dish was popularised by soldiers throughout Japan after their discharge. *Yamatoni* remained the most popular tinned food in Japan until around 1950.

As there were few varieties of meat dishes that could be prepared using traditional Japanese cooking techniques, many Western preparation techniques were adopted in order to prepare the new ingredients. The meat dishes of China and Korea which featured seasonings similar to miso and soy sauce, and which were also eaten with chopsticks, would have been more familiar to Japanese at the time. However, in the late 19th century, a time when society was being modernised based on the Western model, Western-style dishes were perceived as 'civilised' cooking. The colonisation of Korea and the Japanese victory that ended the Sino-Japanese War generated a growing tendency to view China and Korea with disdain. As a result, instead of attempting to learn from Chinese and Korean cooking, Japanese people adopted Western-style cooking methods to create meat-based dishes.

Although French-style cooking was served in the dining rooms of hotels and early Western-style restaurants that were patronised by the elite, the Western-style cooking adopted by the general populace was largely influenced by Anglo-Saxon cooking. English was primarily used to convey Western civilisation to the Japanese people, and many of the missionaries, university lecturers, engineers, and merchants who went to Japan were English and American. Most of the books on Western-style cooking were translated into Japanese at missionary schools, while the Western-style cookbooks published during the Meiji period were predominantly translations from English.

By the late 1880s, chefs who had learned Western-style cooking at hotels and restaurants began establishing Western-style restaurants called *yōshokuya* that were targeted at the general populace.[6] *Yōshoku* means 'the food of the West': it did not refer to a specific style of Western cooking, such as French or German, but something more nebulous. Main dishes often used meat products, and many Japanese at the time viewed this style of cooking as something that used a lot of oil and fats, such as butter. The ingredients of these dishes were replaced with those that were easily sourced in Japan, and Japanese food preparation techniques and taste preferences were partially applied, resulting in a Japanised style of Western cooking. The alcohol served with the meal was either Japanese *sake* or beer. Wine was not yet available. Beer, which had recently begun to be produced in Japan, was more expensive than *sake* in those days, and was the most popular choice. Few customers ate bread with their meal, instead it was common for rice to be ordered as an accompaniment. Nonetheless, the meals served at *yōshokuya* were eaten with knives, forks and spoons.

The main items on the menu of a typical *yōshokuya* were: rice curry, *hayashi* rice (hashed beef served with rice), omelet, beef steak (called *bifteki*), pork cutlet (now called *tonkatsu*), croquettes featuring mashed potato (called *korokke*), and *ebi* fry (deep fried prawns). In lieu of accompanying sauces, bottled Worcestershire sauce was poured over each dish. Japanese have a habit of using soy sauce on all dishes, and so when they encountered Worcestershire sauce they quickly embraced it as a Western-style soy sauce. The unique Japanese-style Worcestershire sauce that is based on soy sauce to suit the Japanese palate made its appearance at the beginning of the 20th century, and soon became an essential item to accompany dishes originating in the West.

Urban middle class and *chabudai* culture – early 20th century

Although Japanese living in large cities occasionally visited *yōshokuya* and Chinese restaurants, foreign meals were not prepared in the home. Cooking schools aimed at daughters of the upper and middle classes began to make their appearance from the end of the 19th century, and from around 1910 large numbers of these schools emerged in the cities, with cooking classes held throughout Japan. By the 1920s, large numbers of articles in women's magazines featured Western and Chinese-style dishes that could be prepared at home, and by the 1930s cooking was a topic that featured frequently in radio programs and newspapers. The media thus played an important role in popularising the concept of nutrition based on modern science and foreign cooking.

By 1919 Japan's industrial production exceeded its agricultural production and Japan was transformed from an agricultural to an industrial nation. It was around this time that the middle classes began to grow, and this sector became the driving force behind the modernisation of food in the home. This was prior to the mechanisation of agriculture, and agricultural households required labour from many family members in order to be largely self-sufficient in terms of food. The middle class families in the cities, in contrast, were nuclear families comprising husband, wife and children, who obtained all their consumer goods through the monetary economy. These families purchased beef, pork, chicken, Worcestershire sauce and tomato ketchup, and prepared 'Japanised' Western meals or Chinese meals in the home. These people also, by incorporating dishes that originated overseas, developed the prototype of Japanese home cooking today.

In these middle class families the use of traditional, individual low dining tables called *zen* was eliminated, and instead the family would sit around a communal table called a *chabudai* on *tatami* mats and eat as a family. In the conventional kitchen the housewife would crouch on an earthen floor or sit on a wooden floor to cook, but in the cities the middle class families, with the growing introduction of running water and gas, began to use sinks and cooking benches designed to allow people to prepare meals standing up.

However, it is important not to over-emphasise the prevalence of this new lifestyle. Half of the population of Japan in the 1930s were farmers, and for many farming families rice was only eaten during festivals and at events. At all other times barley and millet were used to 'extend' rice, and this was served with soup made with home-made miso accompanied by home-made vegetable pickles and a simmered vegetable dish. The diet of many Japanese at the time remained unchanged from the Edo Period. There was very little consumption of meat, and according to the statistics of 1934–38, only 6.1 grams of meat was consumed per person per day. If this was converted to *sukiyaki* meat, the most frequently eaten meat dish, it would equate to eating the dish only once per month. Incidentally, according to the 'demand and supply tables of food' compiled for 2007 by the Ministry of Agriculture, Forestry and Fishery, 76.1 grams of meat is now consumed per person per day in Japan.

Wartime and postwar devastation and food shortage – 1930s to 1960s

The Great Depression that began with the collapse of Wall Street in 1929 spilled over to Japan in the following year, and Japan experienced the greatest economic slump since its modernisation. This had an enormous effect on the middle classes in the cities and the new style of eating that had been cultivated had to be abandoned.

War raged between China and Japan for 15 years, triggered by the Manchurian Incident of 1931. The Pacific War began in 1941. The living standard of the Japanese fell under the economic policies that prioritised the military until Japan's defeat in 1945. The outbreak of the Pacific War resulted in the conscription of farm workers, leading to a fall in agricultural productivity, while food importation ceased. A serious food shortage followed, with rice and grains being rationed from 1941, after which all food, seasonings, vegetables, and even fuel could not be purchased without a ration card. As the war situation deteriorated, the food that could be rationed became increasingly scarce and people could no longer rely wholly on rations to survive. People living in cities began to grow vegetables in every available vacant block of land, turning these plots into fields of sweet potatoes, consumed instead of rice to avoid starvation.

As a result of the slogan 'luxury is the enemy' under the war-time state-controlled economy, hedonistic eating behaviour was perceived as immoral. *Bentō* boxes containing only cooked rice mixed with barley, in the middle of which was a single bright red, extremely sour pickled plum called *hinomaru bentō* (the circle of red in the middle of the white barley inside an oblong bento box symbolised the national flag, or *hinomaru*), were recommended for school students and workers. Although this was a nutritionally inadequate meal, the government's promotion of it is testament to the fact that they prioritised nationalism and the war effort over the health of the Japanese people.

The food shortage that followed Japan's defeat meant that the focus was more on restoring food quantity rather than quality, the catch-phrase at the time being 'increase food production'. It was only around 1950, when the Japanese economy began to grow as a result of the effects of the Korean War, that people no longer faced the fear of starvation, and it was not until 1955 that rice production levels recovered to prewar yields.

Return to a richer diet – post-1960s

During the 1960s Japan entered a period of high economic growth. Increase in income resulted in a richer diet both in quantity and quality, and a greater choice of food types was available to consumers. When this happened, people did not return to eating traditional Japanese meals and instead, there was a shift to a new style of eating.

In 1962 the annual consumption of rice per person reached a record 117 kilograms, but rice consumption gradually fell to 61.5 kg in 2004. It is often argued that this was because people began to eat bread on a regular basis, but this is not strictly accurate. In order to maintain the health of school children during the food shortage following Japan's defeat in the War, lunch consisting of bread and milk began to be provided at school in many regions of Japan. Although this resulted in the popularisation of bread in Japan, it does not necessarily mean that Japanese preferred bread to rice. Because of the increase in the number of dishes served for lunch and dinner the focus of the meal shifted to the side dishes, and so people began to fill their stomachs with other food and thus ate less rice at each meal.

Changes in the dining table

Not only did food culture undergo changes over the last century, but the table that was used by the family at mealtimes, and the atmosphere in which the meal was eaten, also transformed. Instead of the traditional individual *zen* (low dining table), a type of table known as *chabudai*, mentioned earlier, made its appearance. *Chabudai* is a small table seating five to six people, with four short legs that can be folded inwards.[7] With the use of *zen* tables, once the meal was finished, each would be stored in a cupboard in the kitchen. In the case of the *chabudai*, the legs would be folded and the table placed on its side in a corner of the room, so that after the meal the same room could be used for another purpose.

From 1925, more families began eating from *chabudai* rather than from trays, after which the *chabudai* was adopted by the majority of Japanese families and became part of the national culture. In 1971, however, eating at the dining table rather than the *chabudai* emerged as the preferred style and has been adopted by the majority of Japanese families since.[8]

Concrete apartment buildings began to be constructed in Japanese cities from the end of the 1950s. As discussed in chapter 15, it was in this type of residence that a room dedicated to eating meals made its appearance, and as a result, Japanese people began sitting in chairs around a communal table to eat.

During the years that the *chabudai* was popular in Japan, intellectuals who opposed the patriarchal system and who advocated the democratisation of the family welcomed this new style of eating. It was widely claimed that the family sitting around the same table and eating the same food meant that the family could express themselves equally, regardless of gender or age, and enjoy each other's company as they ate. According to the results of our survey,[9] however, this ideal was not realised during the years that people ate from *chabudai*. The patriarch controlled the meal, it was considered bad manners to eat while conversing and it was believed that silence should be maintained at mealtimes. The atmosphere that surrounded mealtimes in the *chabudai* era was therefore little different from when *zen* tables were used.

The introduction of the dining table into Japanese family life, however, was accompanied by democratisation of the family and a change in the atmosphere at mealtimes. After the Second World War, there was a rejection of the male domination that had been established during the feudal system of the Edo Period, as well as of the traditional family system with its emphasis on patriarchal authority. Within this social context the era of the dining table was ushered in.

Few families today prohibit conversation during meals, and it is the wife and children who determine the topic of conversation at the meal table – there are few examples in which the father plays the main role at mealtimes. Much of the conversation centres on the news or entertainment media, testament to the fact that many families watch television while eating, and that television programs are a key source of conversation at the meal table.[10]

When Japanese ate using *chabudai*, the entire family generally ate breakfast and dinner together. Few families today eat breakfast together on weekdays, as family members eat separately depending on when they are commuting to school or work. Although dinner time is an opportunity for the entire family to get together, the father often goes out for dinner and drinks after work with his colleagues, while members of the younger generation who enjoy the benefits of more spending-money increasingly eat out with friends. It is therefore quite normal for at least one member of the family to be absent during a meal, and there are concerns that this trend is weakening family ties.

In contrast to the meals served on *chabudai*, which consisted primarily of rice, soup and one or two side dishes, it has become normal for modern meals to feature at least three side dishes, with Japanese *sake* or beer also being served for those who like to drink. In family meals in the past, multiple dishes and alcohol only appeared during special events such as festivals. Modern Japanese are now enjoying, on a daily basis, festive food in the absence of the gods.

The way in which meals were served has also undergone a change. When meals were served on trays or *chabudai*, all food was served on individual plates for each person. Today, however, only rice and soup are served in individual bowls and the side dishes are served in communal plates or bowls and placed in the centre of the table.

Food compatibility model

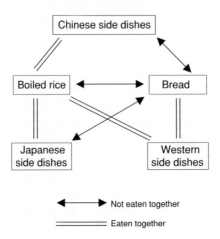

Figure 16.1 Compatibility between main and side dishes.

One of the questions related to eating habits asked of respondents in a national survey[11] of 3600 people held in 2005 was, 'What kind of cooking do you like?' The top 20 responses included curry rice, grilled meat (Korean barbecue), hamburger, salad, spaghetti and pasta, ramen noodles, fried chicken, dumplings such as *gyōza* and *shūmai*, *tonkatsu* and sweet and sour pork. Along with Japanese dishes such as sushi, sashimi, *sukiyaki* and tempura, 10 types of dishes that originated overseas were mentioned.

To what extent do Japanese today mix 'Japanese style', 'Western style' and 'Chinese style' meals'? Figure 16.1, which attempts to answer this question based on a survey,[12] shows the way in which most Japanese find some types of food compatible and others incompatible in the same meal.

As Figure 16.1 shows, the Japanese can be divided into those for whom rice represents the staple food in a meal and those for whom bread fills this role. Rice and bread are thus 'in opposition'. Like Chinese and South-East Asians, Japanese believe that a normal meal should include two categories of food – the staple food and side dishes – as well as the strong perception that there should be only one type of staple food in each meal. Eating two types of staple foods in the one meal is perceived as 'strange'. Noodles are also thought to be a staple food and therefore traditionally noodles and rice were never eaten together. Although imported noodles like spaghetti are becoming increasingly popular, they are never served with rice.

Bread is only served as a staple food with the accompaniments of a Western-style meal and is never served with Japanese- or Chinese-style side dishes. Although bread is frequently eaten at breakfast, it is accompanied by salad, ham and eggs, cheese, butter, and jam, while the drink served at breakfast is either coffee, tea, or fruit juice – recognised by Japanese as Western-style drinks – and milk. Japanese tea, however, is never served with such a meal.

Even the side dishes accompanying bread at lunch and dinner are restricted to those originating in the West such as beef steak or salad. Only Western-style meals feature bread. This is therefore a 'closed system' that does not allow the inclusion of Japanese- or Chinese-style side dishes.

The only exception to this rule is curried rice. Japanese curry was not imported directly from India but was introduced as a Western-style meal. However, Japanese curry rice underwent a transformation from Western-style curry to a uniquely Japanese dish that became a national dish. It is not so much a Western-style dish but should be seen more as a new type of Japanese dish, with Japanese people eating curry today on average once per week.

It is normal for Japanese tea to be served at the end of the meal when rice is the staple food. The accompaniments can be a combination of Japanese-, Western-, and Chinese-style dishes. Beef steak and salad are served as accompaniments to rice, while stir-fried Chinese-style dishes and sweet and sour pork are also served in this way. It is not unusual for three dishes, each with different origins – Japanese, Western and Chinese – such as miso soup, omelette, and *shūmai* to be served as accompaniments in a meal featuring rice.

A meal featuring only Chinese-style cooking would rarely appear at the family table. According to the results of our survey, there was only one example of a family which ate out at a Chinese restaurant. Although two or three Chinese dishes may be served at a family meal, this would be accompanied by Japanese pickles or miso soup, with Japanese tea being served at the end of the meal. There is therefore no consistency in terms of place of origin in the style of dishes served. Dishes originating in China eaten with chopsticks, and which are similarly eaten with rice as the staple, are served together with Japanese dishes. Even Korean-style barbecued meat and the Korean pickles (*kimchi*), which have been 'Japanised', are now eaten frequently in Japanese homes and have achieved the same position as the Chinese-style accompaniments shown in Figure 16.1.

Thus we can see that dishes served in Japanese homes today do not represent a haphazard combination of internationalised, or Westernised, or Sinosised dishes, but a clear structure of 'eligible' combinations based on the choice of staple food. Bread is always accompanied by Western-style dishes. In other meals, it is essential that the dishes are linked in some way with rice in order for an imported dish to be accepted into the everyday diet of Japanese families. Therefore imported dishes that go well with rice have been adopted, with the cooking technique and seasoning altered over time. In this way, foreign dishes have been Japanised to become established as part of the family meal.

Decline in meal preparation at home

Restaurants serving Japanese food first became fashionable in the US towards the end of the 1970s and there is now a Japanese restaurant boom in cities around the world. There were 800 Japanese restaurants in New York and 300 Japanese restaurants in Moscow in 2006. Japanese food has also come to be perceived as healthy. Sushi, made with rice and raw fish, is the most popular dish served in Japanese restaurants overseas, and the general perception is that Japanese enjoy the longest life expectancy in the world because they eat large quantities of rice and fish.

However, traditional Japanese food cannot be described as healthy, lacking animal protein as well as oils and fats. Until the 1960s, the government conducted promotional campaigns encouraging Japanese to eat more meat and dishes cooked with oils and fats. As Japanese society became wealthier as a result of the rapidly-growing economy, meat dishes, which at the time were more expensive than fish, came to be eaten everyday, so that the Japanese diet came to be supplemented with animal proteins that had been lacking from the diet until that time, resulting in improved nutrition for Japanese people. Other than excessive salt intake and a slight shortage of calcium in the Japanese diet, the Japanese nutritional balance was close to ideal by the end of the 70s. As a result, Japan achieved the status of having the world's highest life expectancy. Today, however, many Japanese have grown accustomed to American-style fast foods that contain excessive meat and fats. Like other developed nations, Japan is also facing the growing problem of adult-onset diseases resulting from over-eating, and as a result, there is a high possibility that it will lose its status as the nation with the world's highest life expectancy.

Despite the increase in the amount of meat consumed, there has also been an increase in fish consumption. Japan has the sixth largest ocean mass in the world, with its territorial waters amounting to twelve times that of its land mass. However, only half of the seafood consumed by Japanese is fished in Japan's domestic waters and Japan's fish self-sufficiency rate is only 56 per cent, according to the Ministry of Agriculture, Forestry and Fishery's 2007 'demand and supply tables of food'. Although only 50 per cent of tuna, popular as sashimi or in sushi, is imported, Japan is being increasingly attacked by international environmental protection groups which claim that the world's tuna resources are in danger of being depleted as the fish is supplied to the tables of Japanese families.

The food and restaurant industries have grown with the Japanese economy. Japan's food industry ranks fourth, in monetary terms, of all the Japanese industries, after the electrical appliances, motor vehicle, and oil industries, while the restaurant industry ranks sixth, after the steel industry.

A groundbreaking moment in the Japanese food industry was the invention of 'chicken ramen' in 1958. Simply adding hot water and waiting three minutes produced Chinese-style noodles in chicken soup. This product was followed by many different variations, and instant noodles soon achieved the status of an international product. The Japanese food industry continues to direct its efforts into developing foods that require little preparation in the kitchen, such as miso soup and other soups that only require the addition of hot water, as well as curry and Chinese food that only needs heating while contained in a metallic envelope. The popularity of these products throughout Japan means uniformity in taste, flavour, and preference, and the tastes and flavours unique to home cooking or the distinctive features of regional cooking are in danger of being lost.

The popularity of eating out is also significant. Today one can find, as well as restaurants serving Japanised foreign dishes, Western-style, Chinese-style, Korean-style, and American fast food restaurants where one can eat Japanised foreign dishes even in small regional towns. And in cities, one can also find restaurants serving genuine Chinese, French, and Italian meals prepared by foreign chefs or chefs who studied cooking overseas, as well as restaurants specialising in ethnic foods such as South Asian, and Central and South American food.

The first fast food outlet capitalised with American funds opened in Japan in 1970, followed by the rapid development of chain restaurants. By the late 1970s, restaurant chains known as 'family restaurants' where families could eat out at affordable prices began to appear, and people began eating out frequently, which resulted in a decline in home cooking.

The food industry represents society's kitchen, while the restaurant industry can be described as society's meal table, and Japanese today are enjoying quality meals as a result of the development of the social kitchen and dining table. Meanwhile, there is a growing sense of anxiety that the social kitchen and the social dining table are eroding the Japanese family's kitchen and its meal table. One of the major issues facing food culture in the future is how to best achieve a favourable balance between meals in the home on one hand and meals in 'society', or meals outside the home, on the other. This is perhaps an issue that not only applies to Japan but to all developed nations in the world today.

Notes

1. For a full analysis of the relationship between Japanese modernisation and food, see Ishige (2001a; 2001b) and Cwiertka (2005).
2. The term 'sushi' derives from the Japanese word *sui*, which means sour.
3. See note 11 of the Overview of this volume.
4. Ishige (2007: 80–92).
5. In 1877, there were 558 *gyūnabeya* restaurants and shops selling beef in Tokyo. See Okada (2000).
6. By around 1900 there were around 1500 to 1600 *yōshokuya* in Tokyo. See Itō Kinen Zaidan (1990: 249–50).
7. Ishige (2005: 92–108).
8. Ishige (2005: 183–9).
9. Ishige (1991: 69).
10. Ishige (2001a: 178–219).
11. NHK Hōsō Bunka Kenkyūsho Yoron Chōsa-bu (NHK Broadcasting Culture Research Institute, Public Opinion Department) (2008).
12. A team of investigators based at the National Museum of Ethnology, led by the present author, conducted this survey in 1975, with a sample of 50 households. Despite the limited sample size and the fact that the survey was held 35 years ago, the pattern that it showed should still apply to people today because no new conditions have emerged to alter it since then.

Further reading

Bestor, Theodore C (2004), *Tsukiji: The Fish Market at the Center of the World*, Berkeley: University of California Press.

Cwiertka, Katazyna J (2006), *Modern Japanese Cuisine: Food, Power and National Identity*, London: Reaktion Books.

Ishige, Naomichi (2001), *The History and Culture of Japanese Food*, London: Kegan Paul International.

17

Sports culture

Sport, as an idea, has come to mean a fusion of modern forms and traditional exercise in Japanese culture. Modern forms of sport represent the inclusion of foreign culture in Japanese thought. Since the Meiji Restoration, traditional physical exercise has represented traditional culture and has been practiced in close relation to Shinto rituals or the samurai code. These activities include sumo wrestling, *kyūsha* (ceremonial Japanese archery), *kenjutsu* (traditional Japanese fencing and the predecessor of kendo) and *jūjutsu* (judo's predecessor). During the Meiji Restoration, physical training was systematised into *taiiku* (physical education) through the introduction of modern school education systems and Western-style military training. When attempting to understand Japanese sports culture, we must bear in mind that it is a complex amalgamation of physical exercise, including foreign sports, traditional culture that follows uniquely traditional codes, and physical education carried out in the school system.

This fusion of foreign and traditional physical exercise cultures takes a particular shape. The paradoxes contained in this fusion have often caused disagreement over Japan's comprehension of its own sports culture. In particular, the fact that foreign sports were initially established for students to emphasise the significance of training mind and body through activity, prioritised seriousness over enjoyment in practising sports. This remains a key feature of contemporary Japanese sports culture.

This chapter will provide an overview of Japanese sports culture, incorporating an outline of historical changes leading up to the present and a discussion of current forms of Japanese culture that are recognisable in sport.

Japan's unique sports

The foundation of Japanese teenagers' exercise/sports practice rests in extracurricular club activities (commonly known as *bukatsu*), for which schools secure time, space and instructors to support student participation. *Bukatsu* plays an important role in the formation of Japanese sports practice. For many junior and senior high school students, it occupies a very important place in school life. These activities are held at school after hours and are roughly divided into cultural/artistic and sports activities. School teachers are assigned to specific clubs as advisors and lead club activities in liaison with students' initiative. Most students choose to pursue one of these activities and work hard to achieve in this regard. In 2005, a survey found that 77 per cent of male and 57 per cent of female junior high school students, and 35 per cent of all high school students, participated in school sports clubs. The three types of sports with the largest numbers of registrants were: baseball, soccer and soft tennis among junior high school boys; soft tennis, volleyball and basketball among junior high school girls; baseball, soccer and basketball among high school boys; and volleyball, basketball and badminton among high school girls.[1] The popularity of team ball games seems to be a phenomenon unique to Japanese teenagers' sports activities within the *bukatsu* tradition. However, many students also work on other sports, including non-team sports, such as track and field, swimming, and martial arts such as judo, kendo and *kyūdō* (Japanese archery).

Well-known representatives of uniquely Japanese sports culture include *ōzumō* (grand sumo tournaments), *Kōkōyakyū* (National High School Baseball Championship or High School Baseball), *radio taisō* (radio gymnastic exercises), soft tennis and *ekiden kyōsō* (long-distance relay road race). With the exception of sumo, all of these sports have developed after the arrival of foreign sports during the Meiji period. All continue to occupy important positions in contemporary Japanese sports culture.

Sumo

Sumo is a Japanese martial art with deep traditions. Its first appearance in literature dates back to the 8th century, in the oldest work of Japanese history: *Kojiki* (Records of ancient matters). Sumo takes place in a round earthen ring of about five metres diameter, called *dohyō*. In the most common pattern, two wrestlers stand face-to-face in the ring, grapple with each other, and one gives the other a hard pull and throws him to the ground. Sumo developed and matured as a unique culture of physical exercise by blending Shinto ceremonial elements and agricultural rituals with an entertaining contest of strength, fought by wrestlers gathered from all over the country. In 1927 the Dainippon Sumō Kyōkai (Great Japan Sumo Association) was established, in which four official tournaments were fought each year by professional wrestlers. This was the beginning of modern sumo. Live radio broadcasts of grand sumo tournaments began the following year. Once television became widespread, grand sumo tournaments were broadcast live on NHK (Nippon Hōsō Kyōkai or Japan Broadcasting Corporation), and this further promoted sumo's popularity as a spectator sport. The present six-tournament-per-year system was established in 1957. High-ranking wrestlers in divisions called *makuuchi* (senior grade) and *jūryō* (intermediate grade) each have 15 bouts per tournament in 15 days, while those in the *makushita* (junior grade) or lower divisions each have seven bouts. The winner is determined for each division by the number of bouts won. In this modern competition, sumo wrestlers wear topknots and wrestle naked save for their loincloths. Before each bout, the wrestlers throw salt to purify the ring and rinse their mouth with water called *chikara mizu* (literally, power water) to 'purify' themselves. The sumo referee, or *gyōji*, gives the command to start the match and decides and declares the winner. The *gyōji* wears traditional costume and supervises the bout by giving oral instructions with unique intonation. The distinctive atmosphere of the grand sumo tournaments containing these Shinto ceremonial elements has attracted many tourists from all parts of Japan and from abroad.

High school baseball

Of all foreign sports to be introduced to Japan since the Meiji period, baseball is the most popular. Beginning in 1915 as a sport for middle school students under the old system of education (today's high school students), inter-school matches have developed into the Yūshō Yakyū Taikai (Baseball Championship Tournament) national competition. This was the beginning of today's Kōkōyakyū, or High School Baseball, which symbolises high school baseball as a uniquely Japanese sports culture with a popular and proud tradition emphasising strict discipline and order. In this championship, preliminary tournaments take place nationwide, with about 4000 schools participating today. Every summer season, after winning local preliminary tournaments, school teams represent local districts at the Kōshien Stadium in Hyōgo Prefecture. The Kōshien Stadium is not only a holy place for high school baseball players; for spectators, it is a symbol that evokes recollection of attachment to hometown school teams.

Radio taisō

Radio taisō (radio gymnastic exercises) is free exercise conducted to the music and instructions broadcast on an NHK radio program for 10 minutes from 6.30 am every morning. These exercises were originally modelled after a program employed by the United States post office insurance business. The Seimei Hoken Kaisha Kyōkai (Life Insurance Companies Association of Japan) and NHK started *radio taisō* in 1928 and spread it throughout Japan for the purpose of promoting health. *Radio taisō* are now also broadcast daily on television. After several revisions, the exercises took on their current form after the Second World War and have been established as a form of physical exercise known to every person in Japan. A particularly significant contributing factor for this is summer holiday programs for primary school children employed in all parts of Japan, which encourage children to participate in *radio taisō* exercises every morning so they can keep early, regular hours during their summer holidays. Most Japanese people share the same memory of summer holiday mornings during their primary school years, of gathering in a park or an open space in the neighbourhood, doing the *radio taisō* and having their attendance card stamped. However, a significant number of people – mainly those of middle or advanced age – habitually do these exercises alone at home. For these people, the *radio taisō* is their essential daily routine and familiar habitual exercise. The exercises are so well known that they are often employed as warming-up exercises at school or community field days. In this regard, although low in intensity, *radio taisō* is representative of life-long participation in Japanese sport.

Soft tennis

Lawn tennis was introduced to Japan during the Meiji period. A shortage in supplies resulted in the use of rubber balls as an alternative to conventional tennis balls. Tennis played using these rubber balls was named 'soft tennis' and became widespread in Japan. Soft tennis is characterised by its lightweight rackets and balls vis-à-vis those used for lawn tennis and is easier to play, a fact that enables soft tennis players to continue to enjoy playing the game later in life. Soft tennis matches are played in either singles or doubles, with procedures and rules basically similar to those of lawn tennis. It remains a relatively minor amateur sport unique to Japan, due to the lack of recognition by international sport competitions and the absence of professional players. Soft tennis, like lawn tennis, is competitive in nature, has high exercise intensity and has great excitement associated with games.

These features make it particularly popular as a junior high school *bukatsu* activity. Teenagers, housewives and retired people are the most common soft tennis players. In this regard, it seems to be another representative lifetime sport of the Japanese, loved by people of all ages from children to the elderly.

Ekiden kyōsō

Ekiden kyōsō is a track and field sport in which several athletes run respective legs of a long distance relay race. It is a sort of traditional Japanese sport, in that it was invented in Japan in 1917. In the *ekiden kyōsō*, the runners wear a sash of cloth called *tasuki* across the chest from one shoulder, instead of carrying a baton, and pass the sash to the next runner. This long-distance team race, which demonstrates the runners' loyalty to their team, their patience and determination to carry on, and strong ties among team mates, has touched the hearts of spectators and has aroused strong sympathy among Japanese people who value moral integrity. The Hakone Ekiden race, which takes place on the 2–3 January each year, is particularly popular as a spectator sport. In this race, 10 runners who are college or university students run 217.9 kilometres (approximately 134 miles) in a round-trip between the centre of Tokyo and Hakone in two days. In addition, late autumn and winter seasons see a number of *ekiden* races, including the national high school championship, inter-prefectural competitions, competitions between corporate teams and international competitions. Many of these competitions are broadcast on television. *Ekiden kyōsō* has now become a spectator track and field sport as popular as marathon among the Japanese people.

Current sports practice

These above-noted culturally unique sports are complemented by international forms of exercise and sporting practice. The sports which are widely practised by or are popular among Japanese people clearly reflect the position occupied by sport both in Japan's history and in its contemporary culture. This chapter now draws upon various data on the trends in sports participation by Japanese people published in *Sports hakusho: Sports no kachi no aratana hakken* (Sports white paper: Rediscovery of the value of sports) issued by the Sasagawa Sports Foundation.[2] The practice rates by age are shown in Table 17.1, with a total percentage calculated across all age groups in the far right-hand column.

Table 17.1 *Changes in sports practice by age (%)*

Year	Practice level	20–29 yrs	30–39 yrs	40–49 yrs	50–59 yrs	60–69 6yrs	70–79 yrs	Total
1994	Level 0	40.3	38.5	44.0	57.3	63.5	71.8	50.1
	Level 1	36.4	42.9	34.1	22.8	10.6	9.4	28.3
	Level 2	6.7	5.1	8.6	6.2	7.1	3.4	6.6
	Level 3	7.4	4.0	5.5	9.8	9.4	11.1	7.5
	Level 4	9.2	9.5	7.8	3.9	9.4	4.3	7.6
2004	Level 0	17.2	20.2	20.5	26.2	32.5	44.8	26.6
	Level 1	43.7	44.2	29.9	22.2	15.8	13.2	28.1
	Level 2	9.0	7.9	14.0	10.9	6.6	6.5	9.2
	Level 3	14.5	12.8	19.2	24.3	26.2	21.9	20.0
	Level 4	15.7	14.8	16.4	16.4	18.9	13.5	16.1

Level 0: Practised no exercises or sports during the previous year.
Level 1: Practised exercises/sports at least once per year but less than twice per week (1–103 times/year).
Level 2: Practised exercises/sports at least twice per week (≥ 104 times/year).
Level 3: Practised exercises/sports at least twice per week, at least 30 min per time.
Level 4: Practised exercises/sports at least twice per week, at least 30 min per time, at exercise intensity of 'fairly hard' or harder.
Source: Sasagawa Sports Foundation (2006), p. 27.

The results found in Table 17.1 demonstrate that age disparities in sporting participation at levels 2 through 4 (those who exercise regularly at least twice per week) are comparatively minimal, while those at level 0 (who practise no exercises or sports) increase with age and those at level 1 (who exercise on an irregular basis) decrease with age. This implies a general tendency for people to exercise less with increasing age. This trend has not changed for 10 years. Conversely, people at levels 3 and 4, who exercise regularly and relatively actively, have increased in proportion during the decade. In this regard, the white paper points out that with increasing age people tend to divide into two groups – those who do and those who do not practise exercises/sports.[3] The past decade has also seen, in all age groups, a significant reduction in the proportion of people at level 0 and an increase in the proportion of people at levels 1 through 4. These results show that the Japanese people's participation in exercises and sports has steadily increased during the past decade.

An analysis by sex reveals that more men than women participate in exercises/sports on a regular basis, but this difference is small.[4] Similarly, an analysis by region seems to indicate that there are no significant differences in sports practice rates among different regions in Japan. However, differences are observed in types of sports preferred in different regions in Japan, due to the geographical characteristics of the Japanese Archipelago which extends north and south and has seasonal changes. In particular, in cold regions such as the northern parts of Japan and mountainous regions, skiing, skating and other winter sports have traditionally been practised actively.[5]

From these survey results analysed by age, sex and region, the level of participation in exercises/sports practised by adults (aged 20 years and older) in contemporary Japan is generally on the increase.

A similar survey on exercises/sports practice has been conducted among people aged 10 to 19, and the distribution of people of this age group across different practice levels (by frequency, time and intensity of exercise) has been calculated. The results of this survey, conducted in 2005, are shown in Figure 17.1.

The particularly high proportions of those who practise sports at level 4 during the junior and senior high school stages (46.4% and 36.9%, respectively) are likely to be due to sports *bukatsu* activities at schools. As mentioned above, junior and senior high school students seem to be pouring significant portions of their youthful power and energy into sports through *bukatsu*. Among adults, high-ranking exercises/sports practised by those who exercise at least twice per week (the total of levels 2 through 4) include: 'strolling', 'walking', 'gymnastics (light physical exercises, *radio taisō*, etc.)', 'swimming', 'strength training' and 'jogging/running'. These are types of exercises/sports that people can enjoy individually to develop their physical strength. This suggests that the characteristics of sports that Japanese people can (easily) continue to practise on a regular basis are that the sport does not require particular equipment, place or partners and can be practised easily at any time.

The survey determined that high-ranking exercise/sports practised regularly by people aged 10 to 19 years included soccer, basketball, baseball, volleyball and badminton.[6] These sports roughly correspond with those noted as popular *bukatsu* sports above.

Another survey conducted in 2005 by the Sasagawa Sports Foundation has revealed the numbers of people practising selected competitive sports. The largest sport population in terms of the number of registered individual players is kendo, which is practised by 1 386 404 fighters. This is followed by soccer (862 045 players), basketball (597 597 players) and soft tennis (540 271 players). In terms of the number of registered teams, baseball is the

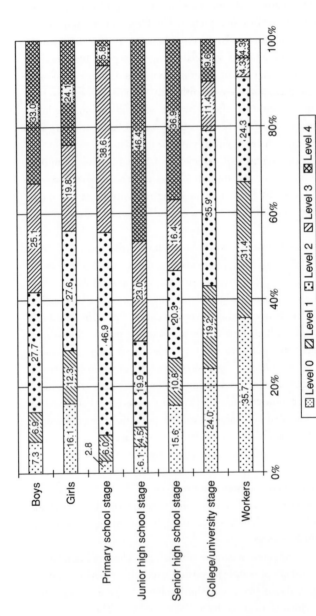

Figure 17.1 Exercises/sports practice by sex and school stage.
Level 0: Practised no exercises or sports during the previous year.
Level 1: Practised exercises/sports at least once per year but less than once per week (1–51 times/year).
Level 2: Practised exercises/sports at least once but less than 5 times per week (52–259 times/year).
Level 3: Practised exercises/sports at least 5 times per week (260 times and more/year).
Level 4: Practised exercises/sports at least 5 times per week, at least 120 min/time, at exercise intensity of fairly hard or harder.
Source: Sasagawa Sports Foundation (2006), p. 30.

clear winner. The number of baseball players, estimated from the number of teams, is 1 180 000, representing the second largest sport population next only to kendo.[7] Based on the above data, as a general trend the types of sports practised in Japan primarily for competitive purposes are kendo, baseball, soccer, basketball and soft tennis.

In terms of the estimated number of people practising sport or exercising, not necessarily for competitive purposes, walking attracts the largest number of participants (23 786 000), followed by bowling (19 705 000), swimming (12 546 000) and golf (11 639 000). Most of these sports do not involve teams and are leisure-oriented.[8] In terms of sport population size, the non-competitive sports population is overwhelmingly larger than the competitive sports population, supporting the fact that a European-style civic sports and exercise culture, in which people enjoy sports as part of their daily activities, has begun to take root in contemporary Japanese society.

Historical changes and disputes in Japanese sport

The changes in Japanese sports culture since the Meiji Restoration can be summarised as follows: the acceptance of modern sports introduced from Western countries; the establishment of these sports in Japan with local adaptation; and the development of these sports as a uniquely Japanese culture of physical exercises. Sports that were perceived as reflecting and projecting Western culture were accepted and rapidly spread to Japanese society in the name of 'civilisation and enlightenment'.[9] They also served to arouse the public's desire for Western civilisation and awareness of the nation's intended development into a modern state. At the same time, *jūjutsu*, *kenjutsu* and *kyūjutsu* represented the traditional culture of physical exercise. These developed into judo, kendo and *kyūdō*, respectively, based on the respect for traditional norms and on the concept of mental and physical training, while seeking ways to become more competition-oriented under the influence of imported sports. This cultural transformation arose over three successive stages: the acceptance of foreign sport during the period from the Meiji Restoration to the Russo-Japanese War; the establishment of a sports culture against the backdrop of the Russo-Japanese War through the First World War to the Taishō Democracy; and the transformation which started from around the beginning of the Shōwa period and the Manchurian Incident (1931) and continued during the so-called Fifteen-Year War, during which Japanese sports culture declined temporarily.

The movement of people promotes the spread of culture and, after a process of acceptance involving consent, refusal and transformation, activates contact between different cultures. Likewise, most of the first Japanese contacts with foreign sports as forms of foreign cultures have occurred as a result of the movement of people. In 1878, George A Leland, an American thinker on physical education, was invited to Japan as a teacher at the newly-founded Taisō-Denshūjo (National Gymnastics Institute). It was Japan's first government-funded training school for school physical education instructors. This school introduced modern physical education theories and instruction methodologies, adopting both free exercises and exercises involving the use of hand apparatus and equipment as 'normal gymnastics'. Later, 'military gymnastics' were introduced to school physical education as a required subject. The military physical exercises were part of a Western-style military training program adopted by the Japanese army in line with the national prosperity and defence policy. To provide the space to practise these exercises, schools began to construct flat playgrounds about 6600 to 10 000 square metres in size. This ground was also used as a space to practise baseball, track and field and other imported sports activities and to hold sports competitions. Practising traditional Western gymnastic exercises and sports changed the traditional Japanese walking style into a Western one. This change was also linked to the change in Japanese people's clothing from traditional Japanese attire to Western clothing, which is more suited for practising physical exercises.[10] Despite strong resistance, mainly by people from the former samurai class, against the active introduction of foreign sports with gaming and entertaining elements, these sports continued to be taken up, resulting in significant visible changes to Japanese-style physical movements.

While Japanese people learned a new style of physical exercise from these imported sports and physical education in accordance with the Western-style modernisation described above, in 1882 Kanō Jigorō standardised the rules and skills in *jūjutsu* and compiled them into 'Kōdōkan Jūdō' with some physical educational components. The 'Japanese spirit and Western learning' policy played a major role in the formation of sports culture: while foreign cultures, skills and knowledge were actively absorbed, at the root of these activities was a determination to protect the uniquely Japanese spiritual support that has its sources in Confucianism, Buddhism, Japanese classics and Shintoism.

When the turbulent age in which Japan was exposed to Western civilisation in all respects, including its political, economic and social systems, was over for the time being and the Sino-Japanese and Russo-Japanese Wars that followed were settled, Japan started to seek its proper position as a modern state in the international society. By that time, imported sports had taken root in Japan and the national slogan 'Overtake the West and pass it' began to assume significance in sports culture. National sports organisations were founded and they soon began to hold regular nationwide competitions. The year 1911 saw the foundation of the Dainippon Taiiku Kyōkai (Japan Amateur Athletic Association), the predecessor of today's Nihon Taiiku Kyōkai (Japan Amateur Sports Association), which was authorised to send athletes to the Olympics as one of its functions. In 1912, Japan sent its first two athletes, the track and field athletes Shisō Kanakuri and Yahiko Mishima, to the Fifth Olympic Games, in Stockholm. Over the years, increasing numbers of Japanese athletes were sent to compete in an increasing range of events at the Olympics. Japanese people became progressively more interested in each Olympic Games as sports events that increased national prestige and symbolised modernism. Amid the expansion of sports to the international arena and the domestic organisation of sports groups, Japanese society was experiencing the steady formation of the foundation of amateur sports.

From the 1880s to the 1910s, an interesting dispute over the interpretation of the significance of sports arose. School baseball club activities were often suppressed by the authorities of secondary schools (under the old system of education), due to concerns that too much enthusiasm toward baseball may cause students to neglect studies, to be obsessed with winning, to engage in too much exercise or to behave rudely. In 1911, the Tokyo *Asahi* newspaper invited distinguished and intellectual people from various fields to argue for the 'evil influence of baseball' campaign. For instance, Inazō Nitobe, who was the principal of the Daiichi High School at that time and introduced Japanese culture to Western countries in his book *Bushidō* (Bushido, the Soul of Japan),[11] criticised baseball itself as a sport and complained about the tendency among baseball players to neglect studies. Nitobe wrote:

> The game of baseball is, to give it a harder name, a game of pickpocket. In this game, you always have to watch in all directions and heighten your sensitivity in order to deceive or trap the opponent's players or to steal a base... The most alarming thing is that not only private but also government schools may go easy on players in grading their exam papers.[12]

Michiakira Nagai, a professor at the Tokyo Higher Normal School, was another critic of baseball who criticised the tendency for baseball to place the highest priority on winning, as follows:

> In spiritual aspects, the overemphasis on winning and losing in Japanese baseball these days has resulted in various harmful effects. Players clap and heckle the opponent's players in offensive manners, say nasty things about them, or do nasty things that would interfere with them... The overemphasis on winning and losing results in a tendency that only a small number of so-called specialists practice the sport while others simply watch them play, until finally professionals appear and show their play in exchange for admission fees. The emergence of specialists and professionals represents significant corruption from the viewpoint of the original purpose of physical exercises: to train the body and mind of young students.[13]

The opinion of educators at that time was that the purpose of physical activities at school, including physical education and sports, was only to foster sound young people able to serve the nation, and that becoming specialists or professionals in sports was an intolerable corruption. Thus these educators' cautious attitudes toward imported sports arose particularly from ethical concerns. They feared that excessive enthusiasm toward sports among developing teenagers may cause them to neglect studies, become characteristically corrupt, and be tainted by commercialism. To value enjoyment as the primary objective of sports was considered appalling.

In response to these criticisms, Isoo Abe, a professor at Waseda University, and Shunrō Oshikawa, a writer who was also a Waseda graduate, made counter-arguments in support of baseball.[14] This dispute was never resolved, but was ended by reconfirming the significance of baseball for moral improvement. While the amusing and enjoyable aspects of imported sports games had been discovered at schools, the significance of sports in terms of moral education, such as the affection for one's school and sense of solidarity promoted during games, or the training of body and mind through continuous practice, had already been established during the stage of acceptance of these sports. During this period greater emphasis was placed on the benefits of training than on sports as entertainment. Furthermore, the moral improvement aspects of sports, which represent the stoic values inherent in Japanese culture, were further emphasised. This seems to have determined the nature of Japanese sports culture to some extent. In other imported sports too, students' sports activities were supported by the self-improvement philosophy, which valued sustained effort, honesty and diligence. This led to the Japanisation of imported sports, characterised by morality and deep sincerity in approach. This conflict in values between the educational and entertaining aspects of sports culture continued to appear often in the development of Japanese sports culture, as an issue common to all sports. In the process of accepting foreign sports as a form of foreign culture, this seems to have been an inevitable dispute over the interpretation of the significance of sports.

A dozen years after the 'evil influence of baseball' campaign, sports had rapidly spread to the general public. Sports stadiums were built in the 1920s, among them: the Kōshien Stadium (1924), the Meiji Jingū Stadium (1926), and the Hanazono Rugby Stadium (1929). Various other sports facilities were also constructed, including indoor and outdoor swimming pools. These new facilities presented novel spaces for sports activities to the general public. In addition, a new spectator culture associated with mass media emerged, as seen in various sports competitions sponsored by newspaper companies and the start of live broadcasting of sports events on NHK radio. This culminated in an unprecedented sports boom during the 1920s and early 1930s. A large number of spectators jammed into stadiums to watch games of the Tokyo Six University Baseball League Tournament or the Zenkoku Chūtō Gakkō Yūshō Yakyū Taikai (National Middle School Baseball Championship Tournament – the predecessor of today's National High School Baseball Championship held at the Kōshien Stadium). Students' sports other than baseball also grew popular, due partly to active promotional measures taken by the national government.

However, foreign sports were increasingly restricted by the Japanese government under the wartime regime after the Manchurian Incident of 1931. In 1932, the Ministry of Education issued the notification *Yakyū no Tōsei narabini Shikō ni kansuru Ken* (Restrictions on Baseball and Implementation Thereof) (commonly known as the Order Concerning the Control and Management of Baseball), which required institutions organising baseball games not only to report the plans that they made, but also to get permission from the Ministry. In 1943, students' sports competitions were totally banned. School physical education started to encourage martial arts in place of sports. In 1939, judo and kendo became quasi-curricular activities for boys in and above grade five at ordinary primary school. The first Olympics in the 'Orient' had been scheduled to be held in Tokyo in 1940, but the plan was cancelled due to the worsening situation in the international community.

After the Pacific War broke out in 1941, the wartime general mobilisation regime increasingly excluded entertaining elements from people's life, including deprivation of the freedom to enjoy sports. Because English was the language of the enemy, English sports terminology was forcibly translated into Japanese. Not surprisingly, the measures taken by the Japanese government to restrict sports were fiercely opposed by students and other people involved in sports. However, it was impossible to reject government intervention in sports organisations in the general trends of the time. The dominant spirit of nationalism encouraged a return to traditional Japanese physical culture; school physical education was required to nurture patriotism and help students physically develop to serve the Emperor. During this period, Japanese sports culture declined temporarily and physical exercises became a synonym for military training. The sports culture had to wait for revitalisation until the postwar restoration and peace. Until then, Japanese people were left hungry for sports as unrestricted, joyful activity.

Sport as culture

Japan's defeat in the Second World War left a fresh scar and great pain on both the national territory and people's hearts. As Japan recovered from the scorched land and the traumatic defeat, sports furnished cheerful topics of conversation in people's daily life. They were actively re-introduced to school physical education amid the conversion of prewar education to postwar democratic education. Japan was not invited to the 1948 London Olympics due to disqualification as a party to the war, but formally returned to the Olympic Games from the 1952 Helsinki Olympics. Sports served to bring joy and energy to the Japanese people in a postwar climate, providing a symbol of peace and freedom and of Japan's return to the international community. The period of rapid economic growth that followed saw the Tokyo Olympics in 1964, which renewed people's interest in sports culture as well as bringing about improvements to infrastructure, such as the construction of express highways and the opening of the Shinkansen (bullet train). In the meantime, the relationship between mass media and sports became even closer with the advent of a new tool, television. While the popularity of spectator sports shifted from students' baseball in prewar times to professional baseball after the war, High School Baseball games at the Kōshien Stadium remained popular, as was the case with the grand sumo tournaments, ōzumō, which enjoyed the same popularity as before the war. Television provided a new mode of spectatorship to the general public by allowing people to watch sports games at home, far away from the venue of competition. Television also promoted the popularity of professional baseball and wrestling.

In the competitive aspects of sports practice, the nurturing of amateur elite athletes – possible future Olympic athletes – was left to non-professional corporate sports teams, which expect athletes to serve as poster children for their affiliated business corporations, while complying ostensibly with the rules of non-commercial and amateur sports. At the same time, *bukatsu*, or extracurricular sports activities at school, created a large population of teenagers involved in sports and students' sports formed the pool from which high-level athletes were carefully selected.

In its postwar revival, Japanese sports culture retained noticeable traces of the moral, spiritual aspects that had been attached to sports prior to the war, in both elite amateur sports and students' sports. This represents a very distinct characteristic of Japanese sports practice in comparative terms.

For instance, Tobita Suishū (a newspaper journalist who was called the 'father of students' baseball' and wielded a powerful pen commenting on games or presenting unique theories on baseball both before and after the war), made some memorable remarks, such as: *ikkyū nyūkon* (putting all one has in every pitch), *kaida senshin* (a clean hit purifies the hitter's spirit), and *yakyū mushidō* (baseball is a selfless sport). Students' baseball was required not only to teach physical skills to students but also to be worthwhile as an all-round education system that teaches students to internalise rules and to develop an indomitable spirit. This seems to have made Japanese baseball very different from its American counterpart, whose spirit of play encourages students to enjoy the game, while being highly competitive. When this passionate, guts-oriented side of sports, represented particularly by baseball, was emphasised to the maximum, the uniquely Japanese concept of 'sports *konjō shugi*' or *supokon* – literally, a philosophy emphasising fighting spirit and guts in sports – was established. This concept featured in sports stories published in comic books and was broadcast on animated television programs.

These moral, spiritual aspects were emphasised in other students' sports as well. The kind of cooperation that is based on mutual trust among independent individuals was not given much weight in Japanese sports ethics, which tended to deny individualism to the point of extolling selflessness. This doctrine was actually one of the values emphasised in *bukatsu* activities and was regarded as the key reason behind the educational value of sports activities. Through *bukatsu* sports activities, Japanese teenagers are repeatedly taught, to the level of internalisation, to set goals and never give up, the importance of the process of expending effort to achieve goals, and the value of solidarity with fellow players. This is known from the fact that many Japanese people refer to their *bukatsu* as one of the most memorable activities in their school years and remember it as a character building time, more than just a time for developing a habit of playing, and love for, sports.

The code of conduct for traditional Japanese martial arts, which requires players to show their respect for their opponents by bowing both at the beginning and end of the match, was incorporated into students' and amateur sports. At the beginning and end of a High School Baseball game, the players of both teams line up face-to-face and bow to each other. However, the vertical relationship between seniors and juniors at school, which has been preserved as a traditional Japanese social norm, can at times develop into a ruler/ruled relationship and may emerge in *bukatsu* as violence, harassment, bullying and physical punishment, creating a far from cheerful atmosphere associated with sports. This has often been at issue as an 'evil' influence of students' sports.

When sports culture was introduced from Western countries to Japan during the Meiji period, the concepts of socialising and of leisure were not emphasised. This omission seems to have prevented Japan from developing a European-style club culture, which would promote socialisation through sports activities and encourage people to develop the habit of enjoying sports as pleasures of everyday life. However, as outlined above, recent years have seen a change in the purpose of Japanese people's sports practice. Sports participants used to place highest priority on winning, and to practise competition-oriented sports for the sake of their state, school or team. Now they practise sports increasingly for themselves, for the primary purpose of enjoyment.

One turning point toward this change was the establishment of the professional soccer league, the J League, in 1993. One of the changes in the Japanese sports world brought by the launch of the J League was the sports culture promotion scheme based on unique community-based clubs modelled after *sports schule* existing in large numbers in Germany. The J League attempts to create an environment where all people, from children to adults, have access to a variety of sports.

The fact that Japanese youth sports have been supported by school *bukatsu* activities has a down side, in that players must face changes in their coach and coaching system each time they enter a higher level school. The J League has created a mechanism in which players are trained under an integrated system operated by J League club teams. This has produced footballers who have grown up with a club team system, which differs from school *bukatsu* activities, and have become successful game players. Some of them have transferred to leading European club teams and play active roles there. Thus, a new wave of support for soccer, which had been a rather minor sport in Japan before the establishment of the J League, has not only improved the level of technical skill but also produced a supporter culture comprising supporters who do not just watch games passively but are willing to be involved in the sport actively on their own initiative. This has begun to influence other sports.

Another new trend emerging in the past 25 years, is an obvious increase in the number of women practising sports on a regular basis. One example of this would be an increase in the number of 'running women'. When a jogging boom hit Japan around 1980, there was a sudden increase in the number of female joggers, clad in T-shirts and shorts and seen mainly in urban areas. It was an epoch-making event in Japanese sports culture when these women began to enjoy the sport as a means of realistic self-fulfilment to improve their life as well as to promote health in a manner suitable to their abilities. After women's marathon was included in the Olympics, an increasing number of women have participated in this sport. Japanese female athletes have made spectacular achievements in international marathon events. Female athletes have also begun to participate in judo, wrestling, baseball, soccer and other sports that had previously been considered men's sports in Japan. The emergence of 'running women' was a visual indication, before anything else, that many Japanese women who had been forbidden from asserting themselves and had been socially required to be *'yamato nadeshiko'* (an ideal Japanese woman with perfect femininity) under the traditional patriarchy, have now acquired a means to identify or express themselves through sports. Thus a new approach to sport is evident in Japan, where the highest priority is no longer placed on winning and where men are no longer dominant.

Conclusion

Today's Japanese sports culture exists in the context of two waves of social change; one is falling birthrates and the other is globalisation. As of 2006, the total fertility rate in Japan was 1.32, according to statistics published by the Ministry of Health, Labour and Welfare. Japan's birthrates have been continuously on the decline for the past dozen years. Meanwhile, Japanese children now play video games enthusiastically at home and less often play physical games outdoors, which has brought about rapid alienation from sports and decline of their physical strength. In the world of competitive sports, the competition now begins in recruiting talented children from the declining child population. These circumstances seem both to require a redefinition of the meaning of sports practice and to demand improvement of the environment for sports practice. These efforts are required not only to discover potential high-level athletes, but so that children can discover enjoyment and excitement in participating in games or competitions, while acquiring not just physical strength and motor skills but communication abilities.

Globalisation has also brought about significant changes to judo as a traditional Japanese culture of physical exercise. Japanese judo has become a competitive sport by following international standard rules, including the adoption of coloured judo uniforms, a scoring system, and the introduction of matches divided by weight group. Judo was once supposed to be Japan's own forte, but these days the rise of foreign judo wrestlers has been remarkable in international competitions, including the Olympics. This trend has extended to sumo, where foreign wrestlers from such countries as Mongolia, Russia and Bulgaria have begun to surpass Japanese wrestlers in both number and wrestling skill. As of September 2007, both *higashi* (east) and *nishi* (west) *yokozuna* wrestlers, the highest ranked *ōzumō* wrestlers, are Mongolian.

After these rapid changes in the circumstances surrounding Japanese sports, an increasing number of today's Japanese athletes are less aggressive in their pursuit of sporting excellence and positively acknowledge the joys of sports. In addition, Japanese athletes have begun to play active roles in European top leagues and American major leagues, represented by soccer player Shunsuke Nakamura and the baseball players Ichirō and Hideki Matsui. These sporting success stories provide idols for boys and girls to admire and role models for their sports practice, contributing to the increasing number of sports players and fans in Japan. The Japanese sports culture seems to have reached a new turning point to create a new sports culture.

Notes

1. Sasagawa Sports Foundation (2006: 63–4).
2. Sasagawa Sports Foundation (2006).

3. Sasagawa Sports Foundation (2006: 27).
4. Sasagawa Sports Foundation (2006: 27).
5. Sasagawa Sports Foundation (2006: 28).
6. Sasagawa Sports Foundation (2006: 31).
7. Sasagawa Sports Foundation (2006: 35).
8. Sasagawa Sports Foundation (2006: 35–6).
9. One of the slogans adopted by the Meiji government to promote its modernisation policies.
10. See Hagiwara (2005: 11–53).
11. Nitobe (1900).
12. Nitobe (1911: 6).
13. Nagai (1911: 6).
14. See Satoshi Shimizu (1998); Yokota (1991).

Further reading

Abe, Ikuo, Yasuharu Kiyohara and Ken Nakajima (1992), 'Fascism, sport and society in Japan', *International Journal of the History of Sport*, 9(1), pp. 1–28.

Maguire, J (2006), *Japan, Sport and Society: Tradition and Change in a Globalizing World*, London: Routledge.

Guttmann, Allen and Lee Thompson (2001), *Japanese Sports: A History*, Honolulu: University of Hawai'i Press.

18

Globalisation and cultural nationalism

Introduction

This chapter examines the relationship between two important but often vaguely defined ideas: globalisation and cultural nationalism. 'Globalisation' is often used to refer to forces that expand beyond borders, whereas 'cultural nationalism' tends to denote forces that stress a coherent identity, either homogeneous or heterogeneous, within national borders. The respective dynamism of both globalisation and cultural nationalism mean that they cannot remain essentially antagonistic forever. They impact upon, react to and influence each other. Globalisation features both forces of homogenisation on a global scale and forces of indigenisation across borders: it flattens the earth and also digs into the earth, inviting resistance by crushing individuality and yet overcoming resistance by indigenising itself into a localised group. It therefore promotes cosmopolitanism at the same time as it solicits cultural nationalist responses. In a similar vein, cultural nationalism contains both forces of domestic parochialism and transnational universalism: it features both inward-looking exceptionalism and outward-looking transcendence. Due to its chequered 20th century history, cultural nationalism not only looks back in anger at itself, its memory and its identity, but it now looks forward, across borders, with compassion toward those similarly situated. Globalisation and cultural nationalism deserve mutual examination.

Globalisation is not an easy concept to unpack. For the present discussion, it is defined as the uneven compression and expansion of time and space in a selectively discriminating way. Advances in communication and transport technologies are a key driving force underpinning globalisation. Richard O'Brien[1] uses the phrase 'the end of geography' to note that, through globalisation, space and time are greatly compressed, ending the tyranny of distance. Through advances in computer technology, financial services have become fast, easy and cost-efficient. Between 1985 and 1986, for the first time in human history, the amount of currency trade surpassed the amount of goods and services. Since 1986, currency trade has been more or less 50 to 100 times as large as that of goods and services worldwide. Thomas Friedman characterises globalisation as a flattening force of the earth.[2] McDonald's and Starbucks are everywhere. Breakfast served in hotels increasingly tastes the same no matter where you are. But, at the same time, globalisation is a most discriminating force. It highlights competitiveness. Profitability and efficiency are discriminatingly favoured, whereas non-profitable and non-efficient enterprise is marginalised. All matters being equal, individuals without good command of English and good computer skills earn much less in a globalised world than those equipped with such skills. Firms with direct access to well-connected and well-serviced airports do much better than those without such airports. Business flourishes wherever financial professionals form organisational clusters.

A key aspect of globalisation is that it is often subversive of much-vaunted organic national unity. In a sense, globalisation undermines the self-contained unity and standing of nation-states. It subverts conventional ways and means of getting things done within time-tested national territorial boundaries. Cultural nationalism arises today in situations where national boundaries and unity are confronted by globalisation's penetration and/or subversion. Cultural nationalism responds through defensively and aggressively making use of what remains: national memory and identity. That is why for Jean-Marie Guehennot globalisation means *la fin de la democratie*.[3] Globalisation fragments the citizenry and diminishes democracy within national boundaries. This is very serious, especially when capital resources fly fast and large around the globe with the sole aim of gaining further profits without due consideration to the 'nonsense' of the national boundary. Globalisation fragments national economies.

The Toyota motor car that you or your neighbour drives is designed mostly in Tokyo, but it is manufactured everywhere in the world. Parts are manufactured in Japan, China and Brazil. The cars are assembled in Hanoi, Memphis and Rio de Janeiro, and are sold globally. As recently as two decades ago, Japanese car makers thought that their manufacturing should remain in Japan for a number of reasons: (1) Japan's national industrial infrastructure – electric power, transport, communications and parts – worked well; (2) The quality of well-trained labour was high despite high wages in Japan; (3) Language posed a formidable barrier to the Japanese once assembly plants were located, for instance, in Chennai, India. Since then, domestic labour shortages have led Japanese leaders to think that even if their ethnic and cultural origins are different, highly specialised professionals may be brought into the Japanese labour market. Soon after they thought Brazilian Japanese may supply good quality labour for assembly factories – hence a flood of Brazilian Japanese migrating to Ōta, Gumma and Hamamatsu, Shizuoka, to name two destinations. But this influx was not sufficient to meet demand, and now more than 10 000 Indian professionals work in Tokyo in the areas of IT and financial services. Many of them live in Nishiurayasu, a town 30 minutes away from the Tokyo central station. Every morning at the Nishiurayasu station thousands of Indian commuters flood its platforms. This gives you a particular feeling of where you are, especially as other neighbouring foreign nationals are not as easily distinguishable from Japanese as those from South Asia.

The Japanese have one of the longest life-expectancies in the world. Many Japanese in their 70s, 80s and 90s live in collective houses where their care is provided by doctors, nurses and physiotherapists. A shortage of personnel in these facilities poses a similar problem to the labour shortage mentioned above. Recent legislation has permitted well-trained Filipino nurses to be employed by these facilities. Wages are paid to those Filipino workers at Official Development Assistance Scheme rates. The workers come to Japan on a rotational basis (three to five years) on a professional visa after being professionally and linguistically trained in the Philippines. Japanese language acquisition is essential for aged-care work. Yet language acquisition is not easy, and workers expect a similar level of income as they would earn in other countries for the skills they possess without learning a new foreign language. As a result, they often go to one of the Gulf countries where English is used, rather than Japan where English is not widely employed.

In East Asian societies, the daily experience of globalisation has changed the pattern of food production and consumption. Soba noodles, a potent symbol of normative cultural tradition for the Japanese people, are now manufactured in China. Shrimp tempura, another iconic dish, comes from Indonesia. Dried and cut seaweed comes from Korea. Wasabi comes from Izu, Shizuoka. Soy beans for soy sauce production are now grown in the United States. If you are what you eat, the sovereign body of the most benign Japanese national is now increasingly globalised through the every-day consumption of internationally manufactured national dishes. Having provided a definition of globalisation and a few glimpses of its impacts upon

Japanese society, I now turn to the subject of the chapter itself, globalisation and cultural nationalism.

In what follows I examine how British cotton cloth, parliamentary monarchy and stock-based capitalism – all representing the global diffusion of new technologies and institutions – have undergone twists and turns in their accommodation within Japanese society. Here, cultural nationalism might have intervened in a globalising process. I then turn to cultural nationalism as witnessed in East Asian international relations in recent years, focusing on how the three East Asian government leaders cajole, placate and/or suppress cultural nationalism to manage the relentless tide of globalisation and its impact on their international relations. Finally, I examine whether attitudes toward and experiences of globalisation corrode the three Japanese cultural values of trust, networking and mindfulness, using the 2007 AsiaBarometer Survey data.[4] The results of this research show that trust and mindfulness tend to be negatively related to the everyday experiences of globalisation, while networks are positively related to them. Conclusions are then drawn from these three comparative approaches.

Globalisation and cultural nationalism

Globalisation is multidimensional. It entails a range of phenomena that contribute to the uneven conflation of local difference. Critics of globalisation point to the disjunction between its financial and economic dimensions and its global climatic and environmental impacts. Cultural nationalism is no less salient in the debates surrounding the total value of globalisation.[5] Since many aspects of human life are steadily – and seemingly irreversibly – globalised one after another, cultural nationalism could become a last bastion of anti-globalisation protest. Cultural nationalism involves the yearning for an imagined community. It involves cohesion and solidarity in terms of shared memories and architectures of what constitutes a self-defined people's destiny, when globalising forces jeopardise a present way of life. Just as the nation-state started from a construction of imagined communities, so the nation-state must defend itself through its citizens' steadfast subscription to maintaining imagined communities. When the material bases of the nation-state seem to be undermined day by day through globalisation, the ideational and emotional bases of its existence must be defended at any cost. In this sense cultural nationalism is a force that is defensive in its aim but aggressive in its manifestation. Since globalisation itself waxes and wanes in tandem with the speed and diffusion of new technologies and attitudes, the scope and kinds of cultural nationalism differ from one case to another.

The term 'globalisation' is often simply translated into Japanese phonetically as *gurōbarizeishon* without further indicating its meaning. An alternative term, *gurōbaruka* translates the last part of globalisation non-phonetically, using *ka* (transformation) as a suffix, with the first part *gurōbaru* (global) being retained. It is not surprising that *gurōbarizeishon* is the more popular Japanese translation, as Japanese is prone to using foreign words without attempting transliteration or interpretation, a point that Hugh Clarke analyses in chapter 3. It is important to note, however, that Japanese speakers have historically been quite selective in absorbing foreign ideas, institutions and technologies. The partial and selective adoption of legal and political institutions of Sui and Tang China is one good example. Another may be the massive import of Western ideas, institutions and technologies after the Meiji Restoration of 1868, accompanied by the vigorous indigenisation of these innovations on Japanese soil.

Japanese examples of cultural nationalism

Japan has retained a distinctive mode of emulating and accommodating exogenous ideas, institutions and technologies without significantly compromising their ideas or the emotions of the Japanese nation. Why and how the Japanese nation has kept its cultural identity sufficiently intact despite all the vicissitudes it has experienced throughout the modern century is a matter for serious consideration. Three concrete examples help explore this question: the onslaught of British cloth in the Japanese market, the adoption of a constitutional parliamentary monarchy, and the administration of capitalism and stock-based companies.

Cotton cloth

British cotton was first introduced to Japan under an 1856 commercial treaty.[6] Since the treaty did not have provisions to give tariff autonomy to Japan – commercial treaties with Western powers generally did not in any case – Japan was placed in a very disadvantageous position. Tariff autonomy was conferred by Western powers only in 1911. Between 1856 and 1911 Japan imposed no tariff on any imported goods. Why, then, was Japan not only able to retain its traditional cotton industry in the face of a deluge of Western goods, but to further build its own industrial foundations?

British cotton cloth came to Japan offering machine-made uniformity of products and reasonable prices. Japanese cotton cloth was not uniform as it was manufactured by hand, not by machine, without a modicum of quality control. The Japanese cloth was not necessarily cheap either. Yet, unlike in India, where cotton cloth suffered greatly under British trade arrangements, Japanese cotton cloth did not disappear from its domestic market. Mohandas Gandhi preached weaving cotton by hand on traditional Indian cotton looms in recognition of the fact that only a nation with a local industrial base can envisage independence. Only with endogenous industrial bases built in the late 19th century and the early 20th century was Japan able to industrialise its cotton production by World War I, in response to mass imports of tariff-free British cotton cloth from the mid-19th century.

The most widely accepted view as to why this occurred is that the Japanese people were so accustomed to the traditional cotton cloth that they did not like or purchase its British counterpart. Machine-woven British cottons were generally lighter than hand-woven Japanese fabrics. Japanese liked rather thick cotton cloth which retained its strength even when soaked by rainfall. Like judo uniforms, this cloth was so thick and hard that people washed it not by hand but with wooden sticks. Does this social practice represent cultural nationalism? Perhaps: although an important point of difference between the two countries is that India was a British colony while Japan has never been subjugated to colonial status.

One can further see the cultural adaptability of Japan's domestic market in the face of changing external circumstances when one is reminded that Toyota Automobile's predecessor was a cotton cloth manufacturer. The Toyoda family shifted its production from manual labour to mechanisation in the face of British imports. Then, when the domestic cotton cloth industry itself finally became uneconomic in the 1950s and 1960s, the Toyota company shifted its manufacturing focus from cotton cloth to the production of automobiles. Since then, of course, Toyota has achieved significant global success.[7]

Constitutional monarchy

Turning to the second example, to assert that the adoption of a constitutional parliamentary monarchy is an instance of cultural nationalism may be an exaggeration. But clearly the endogenous path of creating a small number of bureaucratic institutions from the existing 300-odd domain bureaucracies was no straightforward emulation of Western institutions. I argue that it makes sense to interpret it as an assertion of cultural nationalism.

The Meiji Restoration of 1868 introduced the emulation of Western institutions into Japan. The Restoration usurped power from the Tokugawa family, establishing the imperial regime in which an Emperor reigned supreme. The Five Promises of the Meiji Emperor dictated that all public issues must be addressed and resolved through public discussion. Hence, a national parliamentary monarchy was adopted. Two key features of this constitutional change have made Japan's parliamentary monarchy internationally distinctive. First, each bureaucratic agency of the Japanese state adopted an independent business model, as if each were in competition with its fellow institutions.[8] The Japanese Metropolitan Police adopted a French organisational model, the Imperial Navy implemented a British model, and the Imperial Army adopted a Prussian one. Second, the Imperial Diet followed the British model of two houses – one elected, the other appointed – existing side by side and in which the plenary session was given weight, and committee sessions were not as important.

The new bureaucratic agencies replaced approximately 300 autonomous domains that had existed during the Tokugawa period (1603–1867). Since Japan's traditional class distinctions – warriors, peasants, artisans and merchants – were abolished immediately after the Restoration, virtually all the warriors (representing the service class) lost their jobs. Until a meritocratic civil service examination system was adopted some 30 years later, each bureaucratic agency recruited according to the principles of convenience and cronyism, that is, favouring those with similar class backgrounds. The initial adoption of a Western model in early bureaucratic agencies combined with their recruitment system consolidated a very decentralised system of central government.[9] Although the central government was meant to be strong, it was internally fragmented, with rival government agencies competing with each other. They not only employed their own bureaucrats independently but also controlled their spheres of jurisdiction tightly, enjoying semi-sovereign status and answerable only to the Emperor. The Meiji regime was not fundamentally different from the Tokugawa regime in that power was split up at the highest level of the central government. Whether this represents cultural nationalism or not is a moot point. It does, however, represent the strength of endogenous development in Japan and points to the self-assertion of its cultural nationalism.

Capitalism and stock companies

A third form of distinct Japanese cultural nationalism has recently arisen where local, anti-globalisation protests of one kind or another have criticised neoclassical or market fundamentalism. The protestors' fundamental tenet is that human beings should be placed at the core of capitalism, especially at the centre of stock companies. This argument is widely known as *jimponshugi* (humanity first-ism) which asserts that human beings should be regarded as being fundamental in running capitalism[10]. According to this position, neither business executives and managers nor stockholders should dominate the administration of companies. The market should not be given exclusive control over the ways in which companies are managed. Arguing against international market capitalism, *jimponshugi* asserts that company managers and employees, who enable a company to live its own life, should together have the sovereignty of their companies as respectable stockholders.

It is not too difficult to comprehend why such *jimponshugi* is imbued with cultural nationalism. Its advocates maintain that it reflects the Japanese corporate governance style and differs from Western corporate philosophy, in which company executives pay primary attention to stockholders' interests. Calling for solidarity, unity and organic wholeness of all employers and employees within each company, *jimponshugi* proponents contend that this value orientation represents Japan's corporate culture and can make a unique international contribution – an argument promoting 'national culture' against the tide of global market capitalism.

East Asian cultural nationalism

Japan

In modern Japan, cultural nationalism has been directed against China and Korea and, latently, against the US. This resonates deep within Japan's historical construction of identity and modernity.[11] The coerced opening of the country and ports by the US Navy in 1853 is an obvious historical departure point. Instead of tenaciously subscribing to a long adhered-to policy of closing the country, the Tokugawa Shogunate decided to open the country to the world and to modernise. This led to the establishment of diplomatic relationships with major Western powers in 1853, and subsequently to unequal trade and tariff regimes in 1856. In this 'opening' of Japan, the nation had to accommodate two important factors that were highly contested at home, and that finally had to be digested, if somewhat bitterly, by the Japanese people. These were extraterritoriality and the lack of tariff autonomy. Opposition to extraterritoriality resulted in the assassination of Western diplomats within Japan in early post-treaty years. The lack of tariff autonomy was removed only in 1911. Thus Japan experienced more than half a century of 'free trade' regimes during its earliest stages of industrialisation. The bitterness of this erosion of national economic and political sovereignty was played down, because it was seen as the price that must be paid for enlightenment, innovation, wealth, and a strong army: catching up with the West had the highest priority at that time. Nation-wide improvements in nutrition, sanitation, irrigation and literacy occurred during the Tokugawa era (1603–1867), paving the way for the Meiji leaders to make advances in their subsequent modernisation endeavours.[12] The imposed free trade regime exposed Japan to external competition and consequently enabled the country to become industrialised by the eve of the First World War.[13]

Thanks to the Meiji Restoration of 1868, in which the goal of parliamentary monarchy was proclaimed, Japan also moved steadily and steadfastly toward democracy during this period. In the 1880s and 90s the birth of political parties and local assembly elections and the promulgation of the Imperial Constitution first took place; the first House of Representatives election was held. The opening of the Imperial Diet followed this. In the 1910s and 20s parliamentary democracy further consolidated, with a two-party system and male universal suffrage. In the 1930s the advance of social democratic forces in the House of Representatives was achieved. It appeared as though Japan were treading its Westernising path correctly and was fast becoming the first non-Western nation-state.

But in the 1930s and 40s, Japan suddenly turned from that democratising path to a militant one. Japan's defeat in the Pacific War liquidated the military cliques that had brought about calamities not only to the nation but also to Japan's neighbouring states. By 1952, as an independent state, Japan returned to the path of democratisation and industrialisation. Since then, it has trod the most peaceful, prosperous and democratic course in the non-Western world. This is a mainstream view of modern Japanese history, that dominates the current domestic cultural-nationalist discourse, and is roughly in accord with the view expressed by such American academics of modernisation theory as WW Rostow and Edwin Reischauer, who acted as important policymakers in the Kennedy Administration.[14]

Korea

After 1953, a post-liberation Korean Peninsula evolved along two altogether difficult and divided paths: the Soviet Union held the northern half while the US occupied the southern half. After independence was granted from these respective powers, the Democratic People's Republic of Korea (DPRK, colloquially, 'North Korea') pursued an 'autonomous policy line' while the Republic of Korea (ROK or 'South Korea') followed an 'associated developmental policy line'.[15]

The ROKs 'associated' approach to development signifies its close financial, technological, economic and political ties with Japan, under the more global umbrella of US hegemony. This has on occasion generated domestic ideological discomfort within the ROK. For South Koreans, Japan has come to represent two negative symbols. First, it was a former Imperial colonist. This was a deep insult to Koreans, who ranked Japan lowest on the Sinicised Confucian ladder in East Asia, with Choson Korea at the top, and Qing China, ruled by 'uncivilised' Jurchens (Manchus), in the middle. Jurchens and Japanese were not fully Confucianised – therefore civilised – nations in the Korean view.[16] Second, South Korean military leaders have often been regarded as being overly pro-Japanese. Therefore they had to act in a more anti-Japanese fashion than would have been the case otherwise. Furthermore, the ROK's democratisation and developmental achievements have seeded further domestic anti-Japanese nationalism. Democratisation has enabled left-wing forces to take power. Developmental success has brought about deep ties with Japan. The Asian financial crisis brought the ROK temporarily under the control of the International Monetary Fund, which led to the further enhancement of foreign capital in the Korean economy. All these factors have intermittently generated anti-Japanese sentiment.

China

China has a history of being humiliated, exploited and disrespected by foreign powers. Since the Opium War of 1842, Westerners led by Britain coerced Qing China and Republican China alike to open their ports, markets, and country to Western trade and culture, rendering China a semi-colony. China's pride as a civilised country endowed with all kinds of materials and knowledge was shattered, and it ceased to be master of its own land and destiny. Japan was one of the principal aggressors. After liberation from Japanese occupation and Kuomintang rule, China opted for a one-sided policy line against the US. This, coupled with the strongly self-reliant developmental policy line, effectively sealed China off from the world economy until the late 1970s. Deng Xiaoping's rise to power in 1978 triggered complex forces in the Japan-China equation.[17] From a departure point of world-standard underdevelopment, Chinese development exploded.

First, China suffered massive dependence on foreign capital and technology. Chinese workers were kept at low wage levels, as a policy line of exporting massive amounts of manufactured products abroad at an exchange rate exceedingly favourable to Chinese exports was maintained. During this period, Chinese society remained in a constant turmoil of disruption and dislocation due to the absence of vigorous improvements to: (1) domestic financial services; (2) levels of industrial and social infrastructure commensurate with the speed of annual economic growth rates; and (3) levels of social policy and the social safety net. Improvements in any or all or these areas would have helped alleviate the high costs of adjustments in the process of labour demand and supply in a two-digit growth per annum economy. This is fertile ground for domestic anti-globalisation protest. Second, China being an authoritarian society, anti-party and anti-government voices are not well received by the governmental hierarchy. When a signal to act eventuates, discontent tends to erupt. Whether this originates from local officials' misconduct or from highly ranked leaders' mistakes does not matter very much. Furthermore, discontents can be manipulated and mobilised in many directions, whether anti-party or anti-globalisation. Third, as development deepens, the links between China and Japan intensify simply because China is significantly dependent on Japan for infrastructural technology and product components, while Japan is mutually reliant on China for its cheap and abundant labour and favourable conditions. This deepening interdependence is irreversible, especially since the lifting of economic sanctions against China in 1991–92 accelerated China's march to global power. In Maoist parlance, deepening internal contradictions in China prompts leaders to occasionally divert the attention of the discontented towards anti-foreign and anti-Japanese directions, particularly when Japanese discontent rises in tandem with the growing dominance of China and Korea.[18]

Since 1991, Japan's 15-year recession has coincided with China's economic renewal. This has led many Japanese business firms to shift production into China. This action has escalated the effects of this transnational phenomenon. When faced with large scale restructuring and redundancies at home, a sizable portion of the Japanese public has become apprehensive of China's rise. Discontent has spilled over within Japan.

In the wake of the terrorist acts of 11 September 2001, the Japanese government opted to support the US-led 'War on Terror'.[19] In the lead-up to spring 2003, and for some time thereafter, the Tokyo market channelled money into the large-scale purchase of US Treasury bonds. (However, it should be noted that purchasers were largely non-government, and that Chinese purchases far surpassed Japanese in this regard.) Japan's Self Defense Forces sent support ships into the Indian Ocean to refuel US and UK fighter aircraft in their initial fighting in Afghanistan. To support post-war peace reconstruction, Japan sent its Self Defense Force troops into Samawa, Iraq, after the declaration of victory by the US. After the withdrawal of troops from Samawa, Japanese aircraft were stationed in Kuwait, shipping materials, vehicles, food and medicine into Baghdad. The transparent cruelty of the War on Terror and the difficulty of gaining victory in Afghanistan and Iraq have led many Japanese to rethink the nature of the nation's alliance with the US. Yet at the same time they also feel that the US-led alliance is a destiny of a sort from which one cannot so easily disengage. This has generated ambivalent anti-Americanism amongst many Japanese.[20] In order not to fuel further anti-Americanism, past Japanese Prime Minister Junichirō Koizumi moved swiftly, paying a visit to the Yasukuni shrine, purportedly as a private citizen, with the sole purpose of soothing the souls of the war dead. This act was probably intended to placate an increasingly vocal extreme right wing at home, which criticised the Japanese government for leaning too closely to the US and for not being tough enough against China and Korea. But the act backfired in China and Korea. In 2005, large- and small-scale anti-Japanese demonstrations broke out in both China and Korea. Both these governments issued harsh statements against the Japanese government. Prime Minister Koizumi rejected all criticism, saying that he was open to any kind of meeting with Chinese and Korean leaders anywhere and anytime, but that interference in internal affairs by China and Korea was inappropriate. These interactions resulted in a stalemate on the issue, which was only resolved by his successor, Prime Minister Shinzō Abe, through his visits to China and Korea upon his ascension to power in October 2006.

The region

The span of this discussion so far includes many good examples of the dynamic interaction between globalisation and cultural nationalism. Globalisation has taken hold frighteningly fast in East Asia, as these economies are very dynamic. Domestic economies are rapidly becoming closely inter-linked regionally and with the rest of the world. Whereas the European combined economy took more than 50 years to achieve an intra-regional trade figure of 60 per cent, the East Asian economy surpassed the 50 per cent level in a mere 15 years.[21] At the same time, dislocation at home has become more rampant, especially since the start of the 'anti-terrorist' war led by the US. Naturally, East Asian leaders have wanted to enhance regional economic links only when domestic discontent and dissent are managed reasonably well. Otherwise they have had to cajole, placate, and suppress domestic dissent. Cultural nationalism is a last resort under these circumstances, reminding the domestic populace of the historical memories of humiliation, anger, pride and self-esteem.

Globalisation and cultural values

We have dealt with cultural nationalism as confronted by the tide of globalisation. But, in daily life, rather more mundane changes in cultural values are visible. Individuals uphold cultural values related either to the homogenising forces of globalisation or to the indigenising forces of culture. The AsiaBarometer Survey aims in part to learn how the daily experiences of globalisation might influence the changes in East Asian cultural values. Results of our empirical investigations are provisional, as this is one of the very few empirical examinations testing such relationships.[22] This chapter focuses on the following three values as representative of East Asian cultural values of past times: (1) generally, people can be trusted; (2) if a person who needs a government permit is told, 'Just be patient and wait', he or she instead ventures to use connections to obtain the permit; and (3) mindfulness is a significant quality that children are encouraged to learn at home. The survey, using two-level logit regression models, determined that these values are each regressing via the daily experiences of globalisation.[23] Responses from the survey's East Asian participants show us how the values and daily experiences of globalisation may be positively or negatively related. The daily experiences of globalisation have four variables: (1) support for globalisation; (2) digital connectivity across borders; (3) personal contacts across borders; and (4) English language fluency. On the first variable, in measuring respondents' support for globalisation, the survey asked them to express their views verbally on the benefits or disadvantages of globalisation. The reasoning that underlies the relationship between the experiences of globalisation and the East Asian cultural values that we are testing here are as follows:

1. Attitudes toward globalisation reverberate either positively or negatively with these cultural values.
2. Globalisation generates exposure to a variety of cultures. This is bound to increase distrust, suspicion or dissonance – at least in the short term.

Therefore, the increase in daily experiences of globalisation is counter to the cultural value that 'people can be trusted'.

3. Globalisation calls for broad connectedness and makes parochial connections less useful. Therefore an increase in globalised daily experiences is negative to cultural values such as 'use connections to obtain a permit'.

4. Globalisation promotes competitiveness, strength and sustainability along with connections, negotiation and trans-cultural traffic. This increase in daily globalised experiences is negative to the cultural value of 'be mindful of other persons'.

Initial empirical results point to the following: first, pro-globalisation attitudes are negatively correlated to the three investigated cultural values outlined above. Second, digital connectivity consolidates the three cultural values; after all, all kinds of connectivity may be harmonious whether they are digitally mediated or not. Third, personal contacts with those abroad erode the three cultural values. Fourth, English language fluency undermines two of the three cultural values: trust and mindfulness. It is still useful, perhaps in some centres necessary, to employ connections when seeking a permit from government. All in all, however, it appears that the daily experience of globalisation overall stands in the way of the preservation of these selected cultural values.

Conclusion

Globalisation and cultural nationalism are seemingly antithetical. However, we have observed in this chapter that both globalisation and cultural nationalism contain forces running in opposite directions. Globalisation enables the homogenisation and self-affirming indigeneity of local groups. In order for globalisation to penetrate locally, it needs to accommodate local forces and structures. In a similar vein, cultural nationalism enables inward-looking resistance and outward-looking transcendence. Cultural nationalism's strength for local coherence comes from a self-transcendence across borders toward a broader and more universal appeal to causes such as justice, peace, equality and compassion.[24] More specifically, we have observed that in select aspects, Japanese cultural nationalism allows the selective absorption of the global diffusion of foreign ideas, institutions and technologies in a facile and nonchalant fashion, but does not let these penetrate society easily. Japanese culture's deep traditions normally stand in the way of globalisation's penetrating processes. In East Asia, the galloping speed of interdependence forged by globalisation often brings about a collision of neighbours. Cultural nationalism stands salient in this context.

To sum up, while globalisation diffuses into Japanese society and triggers cultural nationalism in the process of adaptation, the results of these processes seem to suggest that Japanese society tends to be accommodative of foreign ideas, technologies and institutions to a great extent but that their direct penetration tends to be moderated by the tenacity of endogenising forces coming from Japanese cultural nationalism. At the dawn of the 21st century, Japan's nationalism has not exploded externally in aggressive military action nor has it imploded internally to face the relentless tide of globalisation violently. It is a sign of maturity and adaptability of Japanese nationalism today that it is expressed mainly in cultural terms.

Notes

1. O'Brien (1992).
2. Friedman (1999); Guehennot (2000). See also Tessa Morris-Suzuki's imaginative works on Japan and globalisation (1998; 2000; 2004).
3. Morris-Suzuki (1998; 2004). See also Inoguchi (2007f: 240–258).
4. The AsiaBarometer Survey is an annual survey conducted by Takashi Inoguchi and his team since 2003, focusing on the daily lives of ordinary people. See www.asiabarometer.org. See especially Inoguchi and Fujii (2008) and Inoguchi (2007g). BBC, CNN and Chicago Council of Global Affairs have posed similar questions to the AsiaBarometer Survey.
5. Hsiao and Wan (2007).
6. Kawakatsu (2006).
7. Liker (2003).
8. Inoguchi (2007c: 266–89).
9. Inoguchi (2005a; 2005b).
10. Itami (2002).
11. Pyle (2007); Samuels (2007).
12. Hanley (1999).
13. Sugihara (2005).
14. Rostow (1991).
15. Song (2003); Eberstadt (2007).
16. Bell and Hahm (2003).
17. MacFarquhar (1997).
18. Inoguchi (2005a: 49–50).
19. Inoguchi (2003).
20. Inoguchi (2007g).
21. Inoguchi (2007g).
22. See Acemoglu and Robinson (2006) and Inoguchi (2007d).

23. Inoguchi, Mikami and Fujii (2007).
24. The argument for the positive path cultural nationalism might be able to tread is fully advanced in Ōsawa (2007).

Further reading

Acemoglu, Daron and James A Robinson (2006), *Economic Origins of Democracy and Dictatorship*, Cambridge: Cambridge University Press.
Guehennot, Jean-Marie (2000), *The End of the Nation-State*, St Paul: University of Minnesota.
Inoguchi, Takashi (2005), *Japanese Politics: An Introduction*, Melbourne: Trans Pacific Press.

19

Exporting Japan's culture: From management style to manga

Thinking about Japan's cultural exports

For well over a century Japan has been exporting aspects of its culture. Toward the end of the 19th century, World Fairs in Paris and elsewhere offered Japan an early opportunity to take that which was 'Japanesque' to the Western world. The first half of the 20th century saw Japanese culture – especially the Japanese language, various technologies and ideas about architecture, archaeology, infrastructure and how to run government – disseminated throughout the Korean Peninsula, Taiwan and large parts of China. In the early years following the Second World War, overseas interest in Japan's martial arts and, not unrelated, in Zen Buddhism emerged and came to have a marked impact abroad on philosophy, poetry, film and the arts.

A half century later, Brown[1] noted that anime's global popularity had resulted in Japan having an added presence in global markets, one which is as much cultural as it is economic. Over 25 years earlier Vogel's[2] volume on learning from Japan came to symbolise a new way of thinking about Japan. In drawing attention to Japan's across-the-board successes in creating a society of highly motivated citizens, Vogel argued that Americans should take a proactive interest in reversing the commonly accepted pattern for culture to flow 'from the West to the rest'. He argued that many Western societies, particularly America, might do well to adopt social institutions and to learn cultural habits of the mind from Japan. This perspective gave way to the idea of 'reverse convergence' – the idea that, after a century of modernisation premised on 'catching up' with the West, further global convergence might occur 'in reverse' as the Western world adopted Japanese ways.

The learn-from-Japan campaign in the 1980s focused mainly on management techniques, and the number of English language articles and books about Japanese-style management rose sharply. During that decade many firms sent senior managers on fact-finding missions to the Japan Productivity Centre and other organisations in Japan to learn the secrets of Japan's superior economic performance. However, when Japan's economic bubble burst in the early 1990s amidst much hype about the next century being 'the Japanese Century', this interest seemed to vanish as suddenly as it had emerged in the late 1970s and early 1980s. Cynically, one might reflect on this period and conclude that the interest was not in Japanese culture, but only in institutions that were seen to have an instrumental value in running corporations overseas. While arguing that much of the trade in Japanese-style management techniques focused on structures underpinning Japanese manufacturing, this chapter also considers some of the more lasting changes in the way work organisation has been conceived outside Japan. In doing so it briefly considers why the interest in Japanese-style management waned so remarkably in the early to mid-1990s. To gain a fuller understanding of that phenomenon, the second part of the chapter reflects on the export of popular culture which began to become conspicuous in the mid-1990s, grew immensely over the next decade, and shows no signs of abating more than five years into the 21st century.

This chapter addresses a simple question: Why has the export of Japanese-style management declined while the export of Japanese popular culture has flourished? Clues to answering this question might be found in Kassalow's[3] prognosis for the future of Japanese-style management shortly after the learn-from-Japan boom had been launched. In his survey of the rise and fall of various models of industrial relations over a period of about 100 years, Kassalow suggested that any given society's ways of conducting and thinking about life would become a standard for other societies only if: (1) that society's national economy generated surpluses over an extended period of time; (2) there was consensus among members of the exporting society that their model was a good one; and (3) leaders in the originating society were willing and wanting to export it.

Although Kassalow was skeptical as to whether the second two conditions had been met, the first was well met at the time in terms of Japan's mammoth balance of payments surpluses and improved standard of living. When enthusiastically endorsing Japan's success in generating surplus, many pundits simply assumed that the other two conditions were also met. Observers both inside and outside Japan encouraged Japanese leaders to be more confident in transferring the model so that the third condition would also inevitably be met. A more measured analysis suggests that the second factor was always far from being met, rendering the third problematic. In the paragraphs below, the process of exporting Japanese-style management is briefly reviewed before attention is shifted to consider the state of the trade in popular culture.

The export of Japanese-style management

Many Japanese management practices came to be a source of interest overseas in the late 1970s. As Japan's balance of payments surplus set new records, the interest in understanding and transferring those practices abroad seemed to grow exponentially. Studies by the OECD[4], Dore[5], Ouchi[6] and Athos and Pascale[7] highlighted 'the positives' associated with images of what the Japanese model might be. Three practices in particular were seen as forming the core features of industrial relations in Japan: lifetime employment, seniority wages and enterprise unionism.

Lifetime employment: Literally translated as 'end-of-life employment', *shūshin koyō* might better be rendered as 'long-term employment'. Some have argued that this feature grew out of the sense of reciprocal loyalty associated with the overlord-retainer relationship among *samurai*, Japan's bureaucratic tradition in state-run enterprises, the interests of management in retaining skilled employees to operate new technologies, and the need felt by many ordinary Japanese men after Japan's defeat in the Pacific War to reorient their strong sense of identity, which had previously revolved around the nation state. More realistic observers note, however, that labour turnover has been significant in postwar Japan, although lower than in many other industrialised economies such as the United States or Australia. More significant in terms of gaining society-wide consensus, segmentation of the labour market has been reflected, for example, in the fact that turnover has been lower in Japan's large firms than in its smaller ones. In other words, the experience of working in Japan has by no means been the same for all Japanese. In this regard, many have argued that the importance of lifetime employment for many Japanese has rested in the idea of job security. Some Japanese enjoyed that high degree of security and others a much lower degree.

Enterprise unions: 'Enterprise union' (*kigyōbetsu kumiai*) refers to a form of union organisation characterised by a tight definition of who is eligible for membership: the regular employee of a given enterprise. When

the interest in Japan's economic prowess surfaced in the 1970s, this form
of organisation was brought forward as a key feature of Japan's industrial
relations. Enterprise unionism was often confused with company unionism, an approach to employee relations whereby the union is co-opted by
management to foster and maintain a compliant labour force subservient to
the needs of management.[8] The Japanese have a term (with negative connotations) to describe this kind of unionism – the 'goyō kumiai', literally a
union at your (i.e. management's) service. Obviously, management abroad
saw those aspects associated with company unionism as a means of obtaining greater commitment or input from their labour force, and attached
importance to the contribution of business unionism to building corporate
culture. In Australia, which was seeking to move away from a complex system that centralised the determination of working conditions (stimulated
partly by the criticisms being openly aired in the late 1980s by Japanese
managers of Japanese firms that were investing, or planning to invest, in
Australia), enterprise bargaining was seen as a means of making that move
by focusing attention on the consolidation of negotiations at the firm level,
thereby replacing a system whereby management at a single firm often had
to negotiate with three or more industrial unions.

   Seniority wages: *Nenkō joretsu chingin seido* (literally 'age-merit ordered
wage system') is commonly rendered in English as the 'seniority wage system'. It continues to be used to describe a variety of payment schemes
which link age and merit to the wages received by Japanese employees in many established firms. Some have emphasised its importance as
an effective strategy for retaining skilled labour that is in short supply,
thus protecting the firm's investment in training staff in new technologies and in the organisation's administrative procedures. Others, including
Hazama,[9] have emphasised the extent to which the system was an extension
of a peculiarly Japanese approach to paternalistic management, although
such explanations are pressed to account for variations in its application.
Kaneko[10] noted that Japan's wartime government sought to implement an
age-based system in certain critical industries in order to stop the rampant
job-shifting which accompanied inflationary conditions during the early
1940s.

   It was, however, in the immediate postwar years that the *nenkō* system became fully institutionalised. Koike[11] argued that Japanese firms had
elected to hire a small number of outstanding high school graduates and then
invest in their careers as highly skilled blue-collar workers. For Koike this
was the critical difference in Japan that bound that category of employee to

the firm. It explained how rational workers would make market-conforming decisions to work long hours of overtime and to seriously commit to quality control schemes and other procedures that contributed to the overall success of their firms.

Other features – Japanese-style management

Loosely used, the term 'Japanese-style management' also embraces a range of other human resources management practices predicated upon the three core structures introduced in the preceding section. While their implementation varies from firm to firm, they are seen as integral to the vocabulary associated with a common corporate culture in Japan, and include extensive bottom-up consultation (e.g. *nemawashi*, the tying up of 'loose ends' through careful consultation prior to a decision being made), the memo system known as *ringi seido*, quality control circles, internal labour markets, joint labour-management consultations and production systems highly integrated through complex webs of tiered subcontracting.

Kassalow's three criteria

In the 1980s, the debate concerning the exportability of Japanese-style management went in two directions: one focused on the cultural proclivities commonly associated with work organisation in Japan and the other focused in a more instrumental fashion on the structures themselves. One legacy of the first thrust was a large body of literature about corporate culture. As Japanese investment in North America and Europe grew it came under increasing scrutiny and by the mid-1990s a solid literature had emerged examining how Japanese-style management was being implemented outside Japan.

Returning to Kassalow's first proposition, the substantial growth rates of the 1960s, 70s and 80s were not realised in the 1990s. The shine associated with the overall performance of Japan's national economy had tarnished, as is evident in the figures presented in Table 19.1. Although the economy continued to maintain its huge balance of payments surpluses (ironically the first measure that had attracted foreign interest in Japan), the economy itself was truly in recession by 1993. This soon had an impact on employment practices as deregulation of the labour market signalled the growth of casual employment and lower levels of employment security. In terms of Kassalow's second proposition about consensus, another irony might be identified in the evolution of the union movement. Characterised by ideological cleavage in the 1960s and 70s, with strong left-wing opposition to the

Table 19.1 *Some indicators of change, 1986–2000*

Year	Economic growth rate (%) in nominal terms	in real terms	Annual change in wages (%)	Balance of payments surplus (in 100 trillion yen)	Total monthly hours of work
1986	4.7	3.0	4.3	142	175.2
1987	4.4	4.5	3.6	422	175.9
1988	7.2	6.5	5.6	101	175.9
1989	7.3	5.3	7.1	87	174.0
1990	7.9	5.3	8.4	65	172.0
1991	6.2	3.1	7.9	91	168.6
1992	2.6	0.9	3.3	142	165.2
1993	1.0	1.4	2.2	147	16.0
1994	1.1	1.0	1.9	133	159.2
1995	1.2	1.6	1.8	104	159.2
1996	2.6	3.5	1.6	72	159.9
1997	2.2	1.8	2.7	114	157.6
1998	−1.2	−1.1	−1.0	157	155.9
1999	−0.8	0.7	−1.7	121	153.3
2000	0.3	2.4	−0.9	125	154.4

Sources: Ministry of Health, Labour and Welfare, Japan (2002: 16–21) and Mouer and Kawanishi (2005: 78).

conservative government's strategies for development and management's efforts to rationalise production processes, the union movement unified in the late 1980s and markedly toned down its Marxist militancy against organised management. Although hours of work had begun to drop and figures showed that housing and public facilities had improved immensely during the 1980s as overseas travel became fairly common, the 1990s brought a growing awareness that income differentials were becoming more pronounced and that social class was reproducing itself. The short-lived government of Murakami (June 1994–January 1996), following the defeat of the Liberal Democratic Party for the first time since 1955, was seen as weak and indecisive, its shortcomings underlined abroad by media coverage given to its clumsiness in dealing with the aftermath of the Kobe earthquake in January 1995. Some of the unpleasant tensions created by having a growing number of foreign workers, legal and illegal, also received attention abroad. Each of these instances pointed to ways in which the illusion of consensus in Japan came to be challenged in the 1990s.

Turning to Kassalow's third criteria – the willingness of those involved in Japan to export Japanese-style management – the picture is less clear. With the flow of Japanese investment overseas went Japanese ways of doing things. For large firms this involved the dispatch of senior management teams from the parent firm in Japan and tight financial control from the head office. Although expatriate staff worked under the assumption of seniority wages and promotions in line with deep career structures, promotion (and remuneration) for local employees was limited. While this may have fit in with local assumptions among blue-collar operatives, many in supervisory and lower/middle management positions felt the weight of an ethnic ceiling, a barrier often justified and readily obvious in terms of the need for high levels of Japanese language proficiency. In many areas, however, Japanese firms sought to fit into local practices while advancing rational arguments to local partners and their political leaders that enterprise unionism, quality control measures and just-in-time arrangements made good economic sense. The spread of such practices abroad was evident in Australia during the late 1980s and early 1990s. Part of Australia's economic restructuring included a shift to enterprise bargaining, away from centralised approaches to determining working conditions that required manager to undergo time-consuming, legalistic and otherwise cumbersome rounds of negotiations with a range of unions.

Other factors affecting the export of Japanese-style management
Other powerful factors have also been at work both domestically and globally, one being the spread of English as an international language. Although Japanese have often been criticised for 'Japlish' and for low scores on TOEFL (Test of English as a Foreign Language) and other measures of English language competency, the reality is that the government has funded English language education and the levels have improved remarkably over the past 10 to 15 years. In recent times the possibility of recognising English officially or unofficially as a second language in Japan has been vigorously debated, and in many corporations promotion to middle management has come to require some standard of English language competency. The importation of English words into Japanese continues unabated. These changes are further spurred by inflows of non-Japanese people and ideas from abroad into Japan, a process that might loosely be labelled 'Japan's multicultural-isation'. One outcome is that the realm of 'uniquely' Japanese culture is diminished in relative terms. Also significant is the greater extent to which non-Japanese come to know and to understand Japanese society – especially

work practices. The result is that much that seemed culturally exotic becomes more familiar in cultural terms. There may then be a further extension which accepts that structures may be different but questions whether Japanese culture itself, especially its values, is as different as it is made out to be. In other words, a good deal of what used to be perceived as cultural difference is reduced to structural difference, what Cole once referred to as 'functional equivalents',[12] to achieve similarly conceived economic values. At best it is difficult to assess values as being similar or different when structures are seen to shape and even coerce behaviour. In the more broadly couched Asian values debate, arguments assuming the efficacy of value-laden rhetoric as a determinant of behaviour have had trouble overcoming that difficulty. Accordingly, with regard to the culture of work, the sense of difference and the perception that something unique from Japanese culture has been exported has declined. Here one is reminded that the Japanese export of quality control circles was actually recycling ideas imported from the American WE Deming in the 1950s. As mentioned above, much of what was once thought to be peculiarly Japanese has become standard practice abroad and is no longer thought of as being Japanese. The global exchange of ideas in the corporate world makes it increasingly difficult to delineate what is and is not 'purely' Japanese.

For some time into the future the jury will be out on Kassalow's second criteria: Have the Japanese attained the good life? On the one hand, the achievement of a high material standard of living, migration into Japan and its maturation as a civil society all lead to an affirmative answer among most Japanese. On the other hand, regimented discipline in many work places, difficulties in responding to the various welfare challenges presented by an ageing and more affluent population, reports of exploitation among overseas trainees coming to learn Japanese work practices and technology, and the reassessment of the way work is organised in Japan by Japan's youth mean that the final answers to that question remain problematic.

Finally, returning to Kassalow's first criteria (the performance of the national economy and how it is perceived by others), it is clear that at least in Australia, attention has swiftly shifted over the last five to 10 years from Japan to the emergence of China and India. While their rise to prominence has been seen partly as a threat in terms of the dislocations caused by their competitive exports, supply of cheap labour and the environmental consequences of their rapid development, attention has also been drawn, in ways Japan did not experience, by marketing opportunities and by the sheer dynamics of change. It is unlikely in the near future that the world of work outside Japan will once again become infatuated with Japanese work culture and the other cultural trappings associated with Japanese-style management.

The export of Japan's popular culture

Comic culture and the new wave of manga

Since Tezuka Osamu's *Astro Boy* in the early 1960s, Japan's export of animation has continued to grow. *Astro Boy* was followed by a string of well-known anime, including *Kimba the White Lion* (1966), *Speed Racer* (1967), *Star Blazers* (1979), and *Robotech* (1985). The latest animated version of *Astro Boy* has been screened from 2003 in Japan and other countries such as the US. In 1980–81, animated films comprised 56 per cent of all television exports from Japan; in 1992–93, the figure was 58 per cent.[13] A recent Japanese government report[14] estimated that 60 per cent of all the animation broadcast worldwide is from Japan, and anime generates approximately $4 billion a year in the US alone. The popular anime series *Pokemon* has been broadcast in 68 countries, with the movie version screening in 46 countries and earning approximately $280 million (US).

Taking Australia as an example, at the beginning of the 1990s, interest in comics was at a low point. However, from the mid-1990s that began to change as the popularity of Japanese popular culture overseas began to grow at a rapid pace. In the early 1990s, the few Japanese manga in selected bookstores were suddenly augmented by works such as Takahashi Rumiko's *Ranma 1/2* and Ōtomo Katsuhiro's *Akira* in a somewhat wider range of bookshops. A little over 10 years later, Rampant and Mouer[15] report that bookshops such as Borders at Melbourne Central were filling a number of bookcases with English-language manga; most, though not all, were translations of Japanese originals. Minotaur is a large book shop in Melbourne specialising in comics and other 'counter culture' products that has over seven floor-to-ceiling bookcases filled with English-language manga from publishers ranging from Delray to Tokyopop.

Another gauge of the change over the last decade in Melbourne is in the holdings of libraries. Although some of this shift might be understood in the context of Australia's multiculturalism, a policy to service the needs of ethnic minorities, the local Japanese community is too small to warrant the scale of expenditure on Japanese-language materials. However, the Chinese ethnic community is large, and in Melbourne's eastern suburbs, for example, one library has a large collection of Japanese manga that have been translated into Chinese. It is reported that the interest in manga and other aspects of Japan's popular culture is connected to the interest that local Chinese students and others have in studying the Japanese language in Australia. Because of donations from Japan through a sister-city arrangement (which included an extensive set of *Sazae-san*) one library did have a small collection of Japanese-language manga. The Manga Library at Monash University's Japanese Studies Centre in Melbourne has the only extensive collection of Japanese-language manga in Australia, much of it donated by the families of Japanese business community members before returning to Japan. A number of local public libraries have books on how to create manga or comics, usually located among books on knitting, ceramics and woodworking in the arts and crafts section. At the same time, librarians are now much more alert to the interest of young people in 'graphic novels', and some librarians are even winning a budget line for purchasing such materials in translation (i.e. in English) as adult or young adult fiction.

While many librarians treat Japanese animation and comics in the same way that any such materials are treated, some of their colleagues noted that a subculture is emerging around Japanese works, and that a growing number of fans seem to be attracted to the style and thematic presentations that are said to characterise Japanese manga. The internet has played a major role in the dissemination of manga amongst Australian readers. In this regard, the growing number of 'scanlations' available has played a major role. An increasing number of manga are being scanned into a computer, with the words rendered into English by fans who serve as amateur translators. The manga is then 'republished' (made available freely) in public space on the internet. Although a breach of copyright laws, many companies seem to be turning a blind eye to scanlation for the time being because the practice is spawning a growing fan base for this type of literature.

Explaining the export of Japanese manga and anime

With the 'republishing' of scanlations on line, the export of manga and anime within today's global capitalism is bringing together important production techniques, marketing strategies and cultural practices. A number of scholars[16] have analysed the transnational movement of Japanese popular culture. In dealing with the political and economic dimensions two key propositions are juxtaposed. The first is that the worldwide dissemination of Japanese media marks a new form of cultural imperialism, sometimes referred to as Japan's 'soft power'. The other is that manga and anime's lack of a clearly identifiable 'Japaneseness' in terms of national, racial, or ethnic markers undercuts (or at least complicates) the reconstruction of Japanese national and cultural identity.

While some Japanese cultural products – such as popular music and television dramas – have only achieved popularity in Japan and Asia, anime and manga have a global clientele. Nevertheless, anime has been able to shift between the local and the global in a way that even manga has not. Iwabuchi[17] argues that a key reason for the smooth transnational flow of Japanese cultural goods, like anime, is that the most popular examples – such as *Pokemon* or *Astro Boy* – do not represent a Japanese lifestyle or peculiarly Japanese set of cultural values. This contrasts with the noticeable association between the US and cultural goods, such as Coca Cola or McDonalds, which are popularly linked to values such as freedom, capitalism and youthfulness.

Comparing the export strategies of Japanese audio-visual companies during the 1990s, Iwabuchi[18] identified three methods that Japanese cultural industries use to export cultural goods. Sony's globalisation of the Walkman demonstrates the first method of creating standardised global products that appeal to different domestic markets. Aksoy and Robins suggest that this strategy 'transcends vestigial national differences ... to create standardised global markets, whilst remaining sensitive to the peculiarities of local markets and differentiated consumer segments'.[19] A second process is demonstrated in the way Japan's music industry 'indigenises' or assimilates foreign cultural forms into its domestic culture. Rather than exporting Japanese goods directly to the Asian market, Iwabuchi argues, the Japanese music industry has exported the process of successfully indigenising foreign popular culture to create appealing local versions. This approach is not uniquely Japanese, but can be seen in many other countries where the format of a television show like *Big Brother* is indigenised by using local contestants and cultural markers. The third process, referred to by the Japanese term '*mu-kokuseki*' (literally meaning 'the absence of nationality'), is used by Iwabuchi[20] and Ueno[21] to indicate the process of removing the Japanese cultural presence from anime and computer game characters.

Before returning to Kassalow's three criteria, the three processes identified by Iwabuchi – globalisation, indigenisation and *mu-kokuseki* – are examined further in the subsections below.

Globalisation: Using the Walkman as a vehicle to explain the cultural studies approach to commodification and globalisation, Du Gay *et al.*[22] claimed that the Walkman represented Japaneseness in terms of miniaturisation, technical sophistication and high quality. Iwabuchi,[23] however, argues that 'Japaneseness' did not explain the Walkman's commercial appeal, instead attributing its global success to its being a standardised global product that was indigenised by local marketing campaigns to appeal to different domestic markets. He maintained that it 'does not evoke images or ideas of a Japanese lifestyle, even if consumers know it is made in Japan and appreciate "Japanese-ness" in terms of its sophisticated technology' and stresses that any image of Japan was a surface level association that did *not* convey a deeper Japanese lifestyle or cultural presence.

Indigenisation: Sony Entertainment Music and other Japanese music industries conducted talent quests in Asia in the early 1990s. Iwabuchi notes that the strategy for developing a pop idol system in Asia did not involve Japanese cultural industries exporting Japanese musicians or pop music, but saw them distributing a 'process whereby local contestants and audiences can appropriate and consume products of foreign origin'.[24] Iwabuchi[25] claimed that a dynamic process of indigenisation within Asian media centres had flowed from Japan's own experience with indigenising foreign cultures. Karaoke is another example of how Japanese interests developed and exported the know-how that allows foreign songs to be reproduced with local flavour while also enhancing dissemination of local products.

In 2001 the Japan Foundation's Asia Centre opened an exhibition in Tokyo titled '*Asia in Comics: Where are we going?*' The original artwork of 11 comic artists in East Asia (including Japan) was featured. In his exhibition catalogue essay Hosogaya Atsushi[26] praised the importance of Japan's manga industry in influencing Asian artists and indicated that one aim of the exhibition has been to raise awareness in Japan of the continuities and differences in comic art in the region. He argued that it was because Japan's manga industry provided schools for training foreign artists that it had the influence over global popular culture it does today. Rather than locating the significance of Japan's success to its strong export and consumption of manga, Hosogaya located it in capturing the hearts and minds of Asian comic book creators who come to Japan and study the Japanese method of visual art and design. However, he also acknowledged the risk that Japan might be marginalised by other Asian comic book industries, owing to its failure to realise the independence and modernity of the industry elsewhere in Asia. He mentioned the Manga Summits that have been held in Japanese and overseas locations since 1996 as a space bringing together artists and industry personnel – a space where the possibilities and difficulties facing exporters of Japanese cultural goods are thrown into high relief. He warns that the general public in Japan has little knowledge of Asian comics. As examples, he mentioned a lack of awareness regarding the restrictions on expression in Seoul, challenges of educating public comic artists in Taipei and difficulties facing the integration of new media in Hong Kong. These concerns over the low level of broad public awareness of important social and industrial issues facing Asia offer a sobering balance to the enthusiasm surrounding the benefits to Japan of its current popular culture success.

De-nationalisation: One line of arguments explaining the phenomenal international success of anime revolves around notions of hybridity: the creation of forms that can be 'domesticated' into any local market. Because of this transnationalism, anime can be appropriated by the imagination of global audiences, specifically through using their particular perspectives and fantasies. There are two key characteristics of anime's transnationalism: its textual malleability and its financing, production, and distribution by national, multinational and transnational organisations.

Anime such as *Astro Boy* and *Pokemon* 'speak' in the different national languages of the markets into which they are dubbed.[27] Visually the malleability of the characters' bodies makes it easy for them to 'speak' different languages without the jarring incongruity of live-action cinema. Moreover, their 'cartoon' features (big eyes and exaggerated body proportions that often mix a number of racial, cultural, and gender characteristics) give many anime characters racially or ethnically indeterminate features.

Japanese animators can easily soften, erase, or replace a character's Japaneseness. Oshii Mamoru goes a step further, suggesting that animators like himself unconsciously prefer to model attractive characters on ideal Western bodies rather than 'realistic' Japanese ones.[28] Consequently, many characters in Japanese anime may appear non-Japanese with blonde hair (*Sailor Moon*), large eyes (*Pokemon*), and fantasy uniforms (*Dragon Ball Z*). This can also be seen in computer games developed in Japan. Mario, in the popular computer game *Super Mario Brothers*, has an Italian name and appearance. For analysts like Iwabuchi,[29] cultural erasure is a crucial factor explaining the international success of manga and anime, and as his research shows, it has become the dominant mantra within the Japanese anime industry.

It is significant that during the 1960s, US television stations broadcast many of these anime in the same year as Japan, suggesting that a strong relationship had emerged between the Japanese producers and US distributors. Western companies and markets have become increasingly important in assisting the globalisation of anime. During the 1980s, French and Japanese animation companies co-produced a number of successful television animation series, including *Ulysses 31* (*Ulyssé 31* / *Uchu Densetsu Ulyssés XXXI*) (1981) and *The Mysterious Cities of Gold* (*Les Mystérieuses Cités d'Or* / *Taiyo No Ko Esteban*) (1982).

From the 1990s, Western (principally US-based) companies increased their financing and worldwide distribution of anime. The anime, *Ghost in the Shell* (1995), was partially financed by the US-based anime distributor, Manga Entertainment, and was screened simultaneously in Japan, the US and the UK. In 1996, Buena Vista International (Disney's worldwide distribution company) undertook the worldwide distribution of Hayao Miyazaki's theatrical anime *Princess Mononoke*, and gained the worldwide rights to distribute other anime from the Tokuma Shoten media group (parent company of Studio Ghibli, which produces Miyazaki's anime).[30] In November 1999, Warner Brothers released *Pokemon the Movie: Mewtwo Strikes Back* to 3043 theatres in the US, making it the highest grossing anime in the US, and generating a total box office taking of $85 744 662 (US).[31] Hollywood movie companies have acquired the rights to a number of anime; Twentieth Century Fox has the rights to a live-action version of *Dragon Ball*, Warner Brothers has the rights to *Akira* and Sony Pictures Entertainment plans to make a computer-graphic movie of *Astro Boy*.

The increasing co-financing of anime from transnational and multinational companies – such as Buena Vista International or Manga Entertainment – reveals a tightly woven network of multinational investment in anime. The sale of anime's licensing and distribution rights to foreign distributors plays an increasingly significant role in Japan's anime industry.

The domestication and transnationalism of anime reveal the commercial forces that finance and distribute anime. One result of the influence of these commercial forces is a preference for *mu-kokuseki* anime that can become standardised global icons, like *Astro Boy* or *Pokemon*. These anime can be promoted by marketing campaigns and easily appropriated by audiences to become an appealing product in any domestic market. Through this process, anime is placed within the familiar, everyday television environment and becomes another globally recognised brand claiming its market share.

Kassalow's three criteria

The export of Japanese manga and anime would seem to meet the first two of Kassalow's three criteria introduced in the first section of this chapter. Most observers would acknowledge that the industry is healthy in Japan and is likely to grow further in the future (even with an eye frequently on foreign market demands from the very initial creative stages in the case of many products). They would also acknowledge that such cultural products are widely consumed without controversy as different products are customised for specific age cohorts, gender-based groupings, differing socio-economic statuses and those with various leisure-time activities. As outlined above, producers are not only willing but anxious to export these cultural forms.

At the same time, Japanese television programs and popular music have gained a large following in many parts of Asia, and local Asian companies create a pull factor as they strive to promote and distribute these Japanese cultural products. But is this really Japanese culture? Iwabuchi[32] argues that many Japanese cultural industries still prefer to export well-recognised products that conform to a non-Japanese view of Japanese culture. When explaining the reluctance of Japanese cultural industries to export distinctively Japanese products, he first notes that two images of Japan coexist in the West: a traditional and particularistic Japan and a more contemporary Japan that is a faceless economic superpower of hi-tech sophistication. Iwabuchi posits that neither image offers the type of engagement and appropriation found in the notions of freedom, beauty and youthfulness that many associate with 'American' goods. Rather, assuming that foreigners cannot *become* Japanese by imitating traditional Japanese cultural forms (such as the tea ceremony, Zen Buddhism, *kabuki*, or skills in *karate*), the unique cultural essence of Japanese culture is protected and kept at home rather than being exported abroad.

Conclusion

What remains in Japan's cultural exports that is truly 'Japanese culture' as distinct from that which is universally utilitarian or in service of foreign images of Japan? Perhaps it is the belief or a confidence, however naively positioned, that other Asian countries can learn from Japan's knowledge of indigenising foreign popular culture. In saying this one can perhaps point to a broader principle or perspective that is being exported – the view that it is time for a new cultural world order to be instigated, one in which Asia will have an increasingly important role to play. Through hybridity – a process whereby distinctive Japanese aesthetics and Western cultural forms and values coexist and are appreciated by Japanese and Western audiences alike – Japanese style management, along with manga and anime, may ironically be reinvigorated as part of a global approach to the indigenisation of foreign cultures.

Disney comics and animation were widely distributed and screened in Japan during and after its postwar occupation by the US[33] and consequently heavily influenced many elements of the manga style, such as the large eyes and cute features of characters like *Astro Boy*. These characters gave new life to American notions of social organisation, teamwork and corporate culture as derived from manuals for the American armed forces immediately following the Second World War. Tezuka Osamu, one of the earliest and most famous pioneers of manga, openly acknowledged the strong influence of US animators such as Walt Disney and Max Fleisher on his work.[34] In his foreword to Schodt's book, Tezuka wrote: 'The Japanese comics industry first began to show signs of heating up... after World War II. Western comics were imported by the bushelful, and had a tremendous impact'.[35] In a similar manner, the management guide books of Peter Drucker provided food for thought for the management gurus in Japan who are intent on propelling forward Japanese thinking about how firms should organise work in the last three decades of the 20th century.

Japanese-style management and Japanese popular culture are both being reproduced overseas. As with quality control circles, ideas from abroad have been reproduced and packaged in Japan before being recycled for export back to their countries of origin with what initially appears to be a uniquely Japanese flavour. However, like stones being rolled along in the torrent, the sharp edges and bulges that make these exports peculiarly Japanese are worn away and what was once Japanese becomes part of the global currency. Will the presence of Japanese cars and manga abroad, not just as consumer goods but as production processes, soon denude Japanese cultural exports of their Japaneseness? While this may occur, the debate among aficionados of Japanese manga concerning the authenticity of Japanese products is likely to continue at least for a while longer. In the meantime, Japanese concerned about the future of their culture as a distinct culture will be challenged to come up with yet new forms of hybridity. Such is likely to be the challenge to all cultures as the structures of global capitalism reformulate in the years ahead.

Notes

1. Brown (2006: 6–7).
2. Vogel (1979).
3. Kassalow (1983).
4. Organization of Economic Cooperation and Development (1973, 1976).

5. Dore (1974).
6. Ouchi (1981).
7. Athos and Pascale (1981).
8. Galenson and Odaka (1976).
9. Hazama (1971).
10. Yoshio Kaneko (1980).
11. Koike (1989).
12. Cole (1972).
13. Kawatake and Hara in Iwabuchi (1998: 168).
14. Ministry of Economy, Trade and Industry (2003).
15. Rampant and Mouer (2006).
16. See, for example, Kenji Sato (1997), Iwabuchi (1998, 2002b), Ueno (1999), Allison (2000a).
17. Iwabuchi (1998; 2002b).
18. Iwabuchi (1998; 2002a; 2002b).
19. Aksoy and Robins (1992: 18).
20. Iwabuchi (1998; 2002b).
21. Ueno (1999).
22. Du Gay, Hall, Janes and Mackay (1997).
23. Iwabuchi (1998: 167–8).
24. Iwabuchi (1998: 170–3).
25. Iwabuchi (1998).
26. Atsushi Hosogaya (2001).
27. Stronach (1989: 144).
28. Oshii, Itō and Ueno (1996).
29. Iwabuchi (1998).
30. Pollack (1996).
31. Box Office Mojo (2003).
32. Iwabuchi (1998: 169–71).
33. Kosei Ono (1983).
34. Schodt (1983: 63).
35. Tezuka (1983: 11).

Further reading

Bailey, David, Dan Coffey and Philip Tomlinson (eds) (2007), *Crisis in Japan: State and Industrial Economy*, Cheltenham, UK: Edward Elgar.

Iwabuchi, Koichi (ed.) (2004), *Feeling Asian Modernities: Transnational Consumption of Japanese TV Drama*, Hong Kong: Hong Kong University Press.

Watanabe, Yasushi and David L McConnell (2008), *Soft Power Superpowers: Cultural and National Assets of Japan and the United States*, Armonk, New York: ME Sharpe.

Consolidated list of references

In the notes and bibliography, the Western name order convention is used: given name then surname. Only the main author's name is reversed (surname, given name) to enable alphabeticisation by surname.

2005 SSM Chōsa Kenkyūkai (2005 Social Stratification and Mobility Research Group) (2008), *2005 SSM Chōsa Shirīzu* (*2005 SSM Research Series*), 15 vols, Sendai: 2005 SSM Chōsa Kenkyūkai (based in the Faculty of Arts and Letters at Tohoku University).

Abe, Ikuo, Yasuharu Kiyohara and Ken Nakajima (1992), 'Fascism, sport and society in Japan', *International Journal of the History of Sport*, 9(1), pp. 1–28.

Abe, Kazushige (2001), *Nipponia Nippon*, (2004 reprint) Tokyo: Shinchōsha.

— (2005), *Gurando Fināre* (*The Grand Finale*), Tokyo: Kōdansha Bunko.

Acemonglu, Daron and James A Robinson (2006), *Economic Origins of Democracy and Dictatorship*, Cambridge UK: Cambridge University Press.

Aksoy, Asu and Kevin Robins (1992), 'Hollywood for the 21st century: Global competition for critical mass in image markets', *Cambridge Journal of Economics*, 16(1), pp. 1–22.

Allison, Anne (1996), *Permitted and Prohibited Desires: Mothers, Comics, and Censorship in Japan*, Boulder: Westview Press.

— (2000a), 'A challenge to Hollywood? Japanese character goods hit the US', *Japanese Studies*, 20(1), pp. 67–88.

— (2000b), 'Sailor Moon: Japanese superheroes for global girls', in Timothy J Craig (ed.), *Japan Pop! Inside the World of Japanese Popular Culture*, Armonk: ME Sharpe, pp. 259–78.

— (2006), *Millennial Monsters: Japanese Toys and the Global Imagination*, Berkeley: University of California Press.

Almond, Gabriel and Sidney Verba (1963), *The Civic Culture*, Princeton: Princeton University Press.

Amanuma, Kaoru (2007), *Dankai Sedai no Dōjidai Shi* (*A History of the Generation Born Immediately After the War*), Tokyo: Yoshikawa Kōbunkan.

Anderson, Benedict (1983), *Imagined Communities: Reflections on the Origin and Spread of Nationalism*, London: Verso.

Anderson, Perry (1975), *Lineages of Absolutism*, London: Verso.

Aoki, Hideo (2006), *Japan's Underclass: Day Laborers and the Homeless*. Melbourne: Trans Pacific Press.

Aoki, Tamotsu (2004), 'Toward multilayered strength in the "cool" culture', *Gaiko Forum*, 4(2), pp. 8–16.

Aoyagi, Hiroshi (2000), 'Pop idols and the Asian identity', in Timothy J Craig (ed.), *Japan Pop! Inside the World of Japanese Popular Culture*, Armonk: ME Sharpe, pp. 309–27.

Aoyama, Nanae (2007), *Hitori Biyori (A Perfect Day for Being Alone)*, Tokyo: Kawade Shobō Shinsha.

Apple, Michael (1979), *Ideology and Curriculum*, New York: Routledge.

Arai, Masato (1993), '*Kyōin no shokugyō-teki shakaika* (Occupational socialisation of teachers)', in Takahiro Kihara, Takanori Mutō, Kazunori Kumagai and Hidenori Fujita (eds), *Gakkō Bunka no Shakaigaku (Sociology of School Culture)*, Tokyo: Fukumura Shuppan, pp. 194–212.

Arai, Paula Kane Robinson (1999), *Women Living Zen: Japanese Sōtō Buddhist Nuns*, New York: Oxford University Press.

Aramaki, Shōroku (1990), *Gakkō Bunka: Sono Genryū to Kadai* (School Culture: Its Origins and Challenges), Tokyo: Fukutake Shoten.

Aruga, Kizaemon (1954), 'The family in Japan', *Marriage and Family Living* 16(4), pp. 362–68.

Athos, Anthony G and Richard Tanner Pascale (1981), *The Art of Japanese Management*, New York: Simon and Schuster.

Babcock, Barbara A (1978), 'Introduction' in Barbara A Babcock (ed.), *The Reversible World: Symbolic Inversion in Art and Society*, Ithaca: Cornell University Press, pp. 11–36.

Bachnik, Jane and Charles Quinn (eds) (1994), *Situated Meaning: Inside and Outside in Japanese Self, Society, and Language*, Princeton: Princeton University Press.

Bailey, David, Dan Coffey and Philip Tomlinson (eds) (2007), *Crisis in Japan: State and Industrial Economy*, Cheltenham, UK: Edward Elgar.

Balint, Michael (1992), *The Basic Fault: Therapeutic Aspects of Regression*, Evanston: Northwestern University Press.

Bartholomew, James R (1978), 'Japanese modernization and the imperial universities, 1876–1920', *The Journal of Asian Studies*, 37(2), February, pp. 251–71.

Batson, Andrew (2004), 'China's choke-hold over Asia', *Far Eastern Economic Review*, 8 July, pp. 28–33.

Beck, Ulrich and Elisabeth Beck-Gernsheim (2002), *Individualization: Institutionalized Individualism and its Social and Political Consequences*, London: Sage.

Befu, Harumi (1989), 'The *Emic-Etic* distinction and its significance for Japanese studies', in Yoshio Sugimoto and Ross Mouer (eds), *Constructs for Understanding Japan*, London: Kegan Paul International, pp 323–43.

— (1992), 'Framework of analysis', in Harumi Befu and Josef Kreiner (eds), *Othernesses of Japan: Historical and Cultural Influences on Japanese Studies in Ten Countries*, München: Iudicium, pp. 15–35.

— (2000), 'Globalization as human dispersal: From the perspective of Japan', in JS Eades, Tom Gill and Harumi Befu (eds), *Globalization and Social Change in Contemporary Japan*, Melbourne: Trans Pacific Press, pp. 17–40.

— (2001), *Hegemony of Homogeneity: An Anthropological Analysis of Nihonjinron*, Melbourne: Trans Pacific Press.

Bell, Daniel A and Chaibong Hahm (2003), *Confucianism for the Modern World*, Cambridge UK: Cambridge University Press.

Bellah, Robert (2003), 'Japan's cultural identity: Some reflections on the work of Watsuji Tetsurō', in Robert Bellah, *Imagining Japan: The Japanese Tradition and Its Modern Interpretation*, Berkeley: University of California Press.

Belson, Ken (2007), 'Silent hands behind the iPhone', *The New York Times*, 18 July, pp. C1, C8.

Ben-Ari, Eyal (2003), 'The Japanese in Singapore: The dynamics of an expatriate community', in Roger Goodman, Ceri Peach, Ayumi Takenaka and Paul White (eds), *Global Japan: The Experience of Japan's New Immigrants and Overseas Communities*, London: RoutledgeCurzon, pp. 116–30.

Benedict, Ruth (1946), *The Chrysanthemum and the Sword: Patterns of Japanese Culture*, Boston: Houghton Mifflin.

Bernstein, Gail (1972), *Haruko's World: A Japanese Farm Woman and Her Community*, Stanford: Stanford University Press.

Berque, Augustin (1996), 'The Japanese thought of milieu (*Fūdo*): From peculiarism to the quest of the paradigm', in Josef Kreiner and Hans Dieter Ölschleger (eds), *Japanese Culture and Society: Models of Interpretation*, Munich: Iudicium.

Bestor, Theodore C (2004), *Tsukiji: The Fish Market at the Center of the World*, Berkeley: University of California Press.

Blondel, Jean and Takashi Inoguchi (2006), *Political Cultures in Asia and Europe: Citizens, States and Societal Values*, London: Routledge.

Bourdieu, Pierre (1984), *La Distinction*, Cambridge MA: Harvard University Press. Translated by Richard Nice (1984) as *Distinction: a Social Critique of the Judgment of Taste*, Cambridge MA: Harvard University Press.

Box Office Mojo (2003), 'Anime', May, online at: http://www.boxofficemojo.com/genres/anime.htm.

Brinton, Mary C (1993), *Women and the Economic Miracle*, Berkeley: University of California Press.

Brown, Steven T (2006), *Cinema Anime: Critical Engagements with Japanese Animation*, New York: Palgrave Macmillan.

Buckley, Sandra (1991), '"Penguin in Bondage": A graphic tale of Japanese comic books', in C Penley and A Ross (eds), *Technoculture*, Minneapolis: University of Minnesota Press, pp. 163–95.

Buraku Kaihō to Jinken Seisaku Kakuritsu Yōkyū Chūō Jikkō Iinkai (Central Executive Committee to Demand the Establishment of a Buraku Liberation and Human Rights Policy) (ed.) (2006), *Zenkoku no Aitsugu Ssabetsu Jiken (The Successive Incidents of Discrimination across Japan)*, Osaka: Buraku Liberation Publishing House.

Buraku Liberation and Human Rights Research Institute (BLHRRI) (ed.) (1998), *Buraku Problem in Japan*, Osaka: Buraku Liberation Publishing House.

— (ed.) (2001), *Buraku Mondai to Jinken Jiten (Encyclopedia of Buraku and Human Rights Issues)*, Osaka: Buraku Liberation Publishing House.

Buraku Liberation Research Institute (BLRI) (ed.) (1986), *Buraku Mondai Jiten (Encyclopedia of Buraku Issues)*, Osaka: Buraku Liberation Publishing House.

Burgess, Christopher (2003), '(Re)Constructing identities: Permanent migrants as potential agents of social change in a globalizing Japan', PhD thesis submitted to Monash University, Melbourne.

Burke, Peter (1993), *History and Social Theory*, Ithaca: Cornell University Press.

Buruma, Ian (1985), *A Japanese Mirror: Heroes and Villains of Japanese Culture*, Harmondsworth: Penguin.

Cabinet Office, Economic and Social Research Institute, Japan (ed.), (2003), *Kakei Shōhi no Dōkō (Trends in Household Consumption)*, Tokyo: Kokuritsu Insatsukyoku.

Cabinet Office, Quality-of-Life Policy Bureau, Japan (2007), *Kokumin Seikatsu Hakusho: Tsunagari ga Kizuku Yutaka na Kokumin Seikatsu Heisei 19 Nenban (2007 White Paper on the National Lifestyle: A Comfortable Way of Life for the Japanese People, Founded on Personal Relationships)*, online at: http://www5.cao.go.jp/seikatsu/whitepaper/h19/10_pdf/01_honpen/pdf/07sh_0102_2.pdf.

Callon, Scott (1995), *Divided Sun: MITI and the Breakdown of Japanese High-Tech Industrial Policy 1975–1993*, Stanford: Stanford University Press.

Carroll, Tessa (1997), *From Script to Speech: Language Policy in Japan in the 1980s and 1990s*, Oxford: Oxford University Press.

—— (2001), *Language Planning and Language Change in Japan*, Richmond: Curzon.

Caruana, Lou (2000), 'Japanese WAP saps capital', *The Australian*, 25 July, p. 25.

Casegard, Carl (2007), *Shock and Naturalization in Contemporary Japanese Literature*, Folkestone: Global Oriental.

Cashmore, Ellis (ed.) (1996), *Dictionary of Race and Ethnic Relations*, 4th edition, London: Routledge.

Castells, Manuel, Mireia Fernández-Ardèvol, Jack Linchuan Qui and Araba Sey (2007), *Mobile Communication and Society: A Global Perspective*, Cambridge MA: MIT Press.

Chan-Tiberghien, Jennifer (2004), *Gender and Human Rights Politics in Japan: Global Norms and Domestic Networks*, Stanford: Stanford University Press.

Chapman, David (2008), *Zainichi Korean Identity and Ethnicity*, London: Routledge.

Chiavacci, David (2008), 'From class struggle to general middle-class society to divided society: Models of inequality in postwar Japan', *Social Science Japan Journal*, 11(1), pp. 5–27.

Chung, Daekyun (2001), *Zainichi Kankokujin no Shūen (The End of Korean Japanese)*, Tokyo: Bungei Shunjū.

Clarke, Peter B (ed.) (2000), *Japanese New Religions in Global Perspective*, Richmond: Curzon.

Coaldrake, William (1989), 'The architecture of reality: Trends in Japanese housing 1985–1989', *The Japanese Architect*, 390, October, pp. 61–6.

Cole, Robert (1972), 'Permanent employment in Japan: Facts and fantasies', *Industrial and Labor Relations Review*, 26(1), pp. 615–30.

Consalvo, Mia (2006), 'Console video games and global corporations', *New Media and Society*, 8(1), pp. 117–37.

Cornell, Andrew (2001), 'Second best and suffering', *The Australian Financial Review*, 7 June, p. 60.

Covell, Stephen G (2005), *Japanese Temple Buddhism*, Honolulu: University of Hawai'i Press.

Covell, Stephen G and Mark Rowe (2004), 'Editors' introduction: Traditional Buddhism in contemporary Japan', *Japanese Journal of Religious Studies*, 31(2), pp. 245–54.

Cox, Rupert (2007), 'Wagamama technology', in Rein Raud (ed.), *Japan and Asian Modernities*, London: Kegan Paul, pp. 203–15.

Cutts, Robert (1997), *An Empire of Schools*, Armonk: ME Sharp.

Cwiertka, Katarzyna (2005), 'From ethnic to hip: Circuits of Japanese cuisine in Europe', *Food and Foodways*, 13(4), pp. 241–72.

— (2006), *Modern Japanese Cuisine: Food, Power and National Identity*, London: Reaktion Books.

Dale, Peter N (1981), *The Myth of Japanese Uniqueness*, London: Croom Helm.

Darling, Darnan (1987), 'Grown men in Japan still read comics and have fantasies', *Wall Street Journal*, 21 July.

Davis, Winston (1992), *Japanese Religion and Society: Paradigms of Structure and Change*, Albany: State University of New York Press.

Dazai, Osamu (1948), *Ningen Shikkaku* (Disqualified as human being), Tokyo: Shinchōsha. Translated by Donald Keene (1981) as *No Longer Human*, Charles E Tuttle.

De Vos, George and Hiroshi Wagatsuma (1972), *Japan's Invisible Race: Caste in Culture and Personality*, revised edition, Los Angeles: University of California Press.

DeChicchis, Joseph (1995), 'The current state of the Ainu language', in John Maher and Kōko Yashiro (eds), *Multilingual Japan*, Clevedon: Multilingual Matters, pp. 103–24.

Denoon, Donald, Gavan McCormack, Mark Hudson and Tessa Morris-Suzuki (eds) (2001), *Multicultural Japan: Paleolithic to Postmodern*, Cambridge UK: Cambridge University Press.

Dethlefs, Noriko and Brian Martin (2006), 'Japanese technology policy for aged care', *Science and Public Policy*, 33(1), February, pp. 47–57.

DigitalEve Japan (2007), 'Media kit', online at: http://www.digitalevejapan.org/about_us/media_kit.

Dixon, MR (1997), *The Rise and Fall of Languages*, Cambridge UK: Cambridge University Press.

Doi, Takayoshi (1998), '*Gakkō bunka to asupirēshon: Dōwachiku ni kyojū suru jidō, seito no chō taketsu mondai ni kansuru ichi kōsatsu* (School culture and aspirations: A study of *buraku* children's absenteeism)', *Shakaigaku Jānaru*, (*Sociology Journal*), 23, pp. 125–50.

Doi, Takeo (1973), *The Anatomy of Dependence* (translated by John Bester), Tokyo: Kodansha International.

— (1979), '*Amae*: A key concept for understanding Japanese personality structure', in Takeo Doi (ed.), *Seishin Igaku to Seishin Bunseki* (*Psychiatry and Psychoanalysis*), Tokyo: Kōbundō.

Dore, Ronald (1958), *City Life in Japan*, Berkeley: University of California Press.

— (1974), *British Factory/Japanese Factory: The Origins of National Diversity in Industrial Relations*, Berkeley: University of California Press.

Dower, John (1986), *War without Mercy*, New York: Pantheon.

Du Gay, Paul, Stuart Hall, Linda Janes and Hugh Mackay (1997), *Doing Cultural Studies: The Story of the Sony Walkman*, London: Sage.

Duke, Benjamin (1986), *The Japanese School: Lessons for Industrialized America*, New York: Praeger.

Duland, Reiko (2007), *Ichidomo Shokuminchini Natta Kotoganai Nihon* (*Japan Never Colonized*), Tokyo: Kōdansha.

Durkheim, Emile (1984), *The Division of Labor* (translated by WD Halls), New York: Free Press.

Earhart, H Byron (1982), *Japanese Religion: Unity and Diversity*, 3rd edition, The Religious Life of Man Series, Belmont CA: Wadsworth Publishing Company.

Easton, David (1979), *A Systems Analysis of Political Life*, Chicago: University of Chicago Press.

Eberstadt, Nicholas (2007), *The North Korean Economy between Crisis and Catastrophe*, New York: Transaction Publishers.

Economic Planning Agency, Japan (2000), *Nisennen-Ban Kokumin Keikatsu Hakusho (The 2000 White Paper on the Life Styles of the Populace)*, Tokyo: Ōkura-shō Insatsu Kyoku.

Elliott, Stuart (2007), 'A year for quick hits and fast flops as campaigns broke new ground', *The New York Times*, 17 December, p. C8.

Ellwood, Robert (2007), *Japanese Religion – the Ebook*, Providence, UT: Journal of Buddhist Ethics Online Books, online at: http://www.jbeonlinebooks.org/eBooks/japanese/.

Endō, Hiromi (2002), '"*Sapōtokō*" ni okeru gakkō bunka: "*Gakkō bunka*" naru mono no tokusei kaimei no zentei to shite (The school culture of a "support school": An attempt to identify features of "school culture")', *Kyōikugaku Kenkyū Shūroku* (Studies in Pedagogy), 26, pp. 25–35.

— (2004), '*Kōtō gakkō kyōiku no danryokuka to gakkō bunka* (Flexibility of senior secondary education and school culture)', *Kyōikugaku Kenkyū Shūroku* (Studies in Pedagogy), 28, pp. 1–11.

Etō, Jun (1967), *Seijuku to Soshitsu: Haha no Hōkai (Maturity and Loss: The Collapse of the Mother)*, Tokyo: Kōdansha Bunko.

Fackler, Martin (2007a), 'A Japanese export: Talent; technologists see brighter prospects in other parts of Asia', *The New York Times*, 24 May, pp. C1, C5.

— (2007b), 'In Japan, rural economies wane as cities thrive', *The New York Times*, 5 December, online at: http://www.nytimes.com/2007/12/05/business/worldbusiness/05gap.html.

— (2007c), 'Japan nuclear-site damage worse than reported', *The New York Times*, 19 July, p. A8.

— (2007d), 'Japan shuts nuclear plant after leak', *The New York Times*, 18 July, p. A9.

Films-for-the-Humanities-and-Sciences (2003), 'Japanese education in crisis', videorecording, Princeton: Films for the Humanities and Science, 20 minutes.

Foulk, Emi (2007), 'For many senior citizens, high-tech has its limits', *The Japan Times*, 26 September, p. 3.

Fridell, Wilbur (1973), *Japanese Shrine Mergers 1906–1912*, Tokyo: Sophia University Press.

Friedman, Thomas (1999), *The Lexus and the Olive Tree*, New York: Anchor Books.

Fromm, Eric (1980), *Greatness and Limitations of Freud's Thought*, New York: Harper & Row.

Fuess, Harald (2004), *Divorce in Japan: Family, Gender, and the State, 1600–2000*, Stanford: Stanford University Press.

Fuess, SM (2006), *Working Hours in Japan: Who is Time-Privileged?* Bonn: Institute for the Study of Labor (IZA) (IZA Discussion Paper No. 2195).

Fujii, Yoshihiko (2005), *Keieisha Kakusa: Kaisha Ga Wākingu Pūra O Jochō Suru (The Management Differential: How Companies Are Promoting the Working Poor)* Tokyo: PHP Kenkyūjo.

Fujimoto, Takeshi (1963), *Rōdō Jikan (Working Hours)*, Tokyo: Iwanami Shoten.

Fujita, Hidenori (2000), *Shimin Shakai to Kyōiku: Shinjidai no Kyōiku Kaikaku Shian* (*Civil Society and Education: A Proposal for Education Reforms in the New Era*), Yokohama: Seo Shobō.

Fukuchi, Makoto (2006), *Kyōiku Kakusa Zetsubō Shakai* (*Unequal Educations and the Society Where Hope Is Lost*), Tokyo: Yōsensha.

Fukuoka, Yasunori (1993), *Zainichi Kankoku-Chōsenjin: Wakai Sedai no Aidentiti* (*Japanese Koreans: The Identity of the Younger Generation*), Tokyo: Chūō Kōronsha.

— (2000), *Lives of Young Koreans in Japan*, Melbourne: Trans Pacific Press.

Fukuzawa, Rebecca and Gerald LeTendre (2001), *Intense Years: How Japanese Adolescents Balance School, Family and Friends*, New York: RoutledgeFalmer.

Funabashi, Kuniko (1995), 'Pornographic culture and sexual violence', in Atsuko Kameda and Kumiko Fujimura-Fanselow (eds), *Japanese Women: New Feminist Perspectives on the Past, Present and Future*, New York: The Feminist Press.

Funabashi, Yōichi (2000), *Aete Eigo Koyogo Ron* (*A Humble Proposal to Have English as One of the Official Languages*), Tokyo: Bungei Shunjū.

Galenson, Walter and Konnosuke Odaka (1976), 'The Japanese labor market', in Hugh Patrick and Henry Rosovsky (eds), *Asia's New Giant*, Washington DC: The Brookings Institute, pp. 587–672.

Galliano, Luciana (2002), *Yōgaku: Japanese Music in the Twentieth Century*, Lanham: The Scarecrow Press.

Garon, Sheldon (1997), *Molding Japanese Minds: The State in Everyday Life*, Princeton: Princeton University Press.

Gelb, Joyce (2003), *Gender Policies in Japan and the United States*, New York: Palgrave Macmillan.

Geraci, Robert M (2006), 'Spiritual robots: Religion and our scientific view of the natural world', *Theology and Science*, 4(3), pp. 229–46.

Gill, Tom (1998), 'Transformational magic: some Japanese super-heroes and monsters', in DP Martinez (ed.), *The Worlds of Japanese Popular Culture: Gender, Shifting Boundaries and Global Cultures*, Cambridge UK: Cambridge University Press, pp. 33–55.

— (2003), 'When pillars evaporate: Structuring masculinity on the Japanese margins', in James E Roberson and Nobue Suzuki (eds), *Men and Masculinities in Contemporary Japan: Dislocating the Salaryman Doxa*, London: RoutledgeCurzon.

Gilley, Bruce, Chester Dawson and Dan Biers (2000), 'Internet warrior on the defensive', *Far Eastern Economic Review*, 16 November, pp. 54–60.

Gilligan, Carol (1982), *In a Different Voice: Psychological Theory and Women's Development*, Cambridge MA: Harvard University Press.

Goldthorpe, John H, David Lockwood, Frank Bechhofer and Jennifer Platt (1968), *The Affluent Worker: Industrial Attitudes and Behaviour*, Cambridge UK: Cambridge University Press.

— (1969), *The Affluent Worker in the Class Structure*, Cambridge UK: Cambridge University Press.

Goodenough, Ward (1968), 'Componential analysis', *International Encyclopedia of the Social Sciences*, vol. 3, New York: Macmillan and Free Press, pp. 186–92.

— (1970), *Description and Comparison in Cultural Anthropology*, Chicago: Aldine Publishing.

Goodman, Roger (1990), *Japan's 'International Youth': The Emergence of a New Class of School Children*, Oxford: Clarendon Press.

— (2003), 'The changing perception and status of Japan's returnee children (*kikokushijo*)', in Roger Goodman (ed.), *Global Japan: The Experience of Japan's New Immigrants and Overseas Communities*, London: RoutledgeCurzon, pp. 177–94.

Goossen, Theodore (1997), *Oxford Book of Japanese Short Stories*, Oxford: Oxford University Press.

Gordon, Andrew (2005), 'Managing the Japanese household: The New Life Movement in postwar Japan', in Barbara Molony and Kathleen Uno (eds), *Gendering Modern Japanese History*, Cambridge MA: Harvard University Asia Center.

Gordon, June A (2008), *Japan's Outcaste Youth: Education for Liberation*, Boulder CO: Paradigm Publishers.

Gottlieb, Nanette (1994), 'Language and politics: The reversal of post-war script reform policy in Japan', *The Journal of Asian Studies*, 55(4), pp. 1175–98.

— (1995), *Kanji Politics: Language Policy and Japanese Script*, London and New York: Kegan Paul International.

— (2005), *Language and Society in Japan*, Cambridge UK: Cambridge University Press.

Grapard, Allan G (1984), 'Japan's ignored cultural revolution: The separation of Shinto and Buddhist divinities in the Meiji and a case study: Tōnomine', *History of Religions*, 23(3), pp. 240–65.

Guehennot, Jean-Marie (2000), *The End of the Nation-State*, St. Paul: University of Minnesota Press.

Guttmann, Allen (1996), *Games and Empires, Modern Sports and Cultural Imperialism*, New York: Columbia University Press.

Guttmann, Allen and Lee Thompson (2001), *Japanese Sports: A History*, Honolulu: University of Hawai'i Press.

Hadfield, Peter (1988), 'More strip than comic', *Punch*, 5 August, pp. 36–7.

Hagiwara, Miyoko (2005), '*Burūma tōjō izen – Ashi to ihuku no kankei kara* (Before the introduction of bloomers – examining the connection of legs and clothes)' in Ichirō Takahashi, Miyoko Hagiwara, Masako Taniguchi, Michiko Kakemizu and Satomi Tsunoda (eds), *Burūma No Shakaishi: Joshitaiiku Eno Manazashi* (*Social History of Bloomers: An Approach to Female Physical Education*), Tokyo: Seikyūsha, pp. 11–53.

Hall, Edward (1966), *The Hidden Dimension*, New York: Doubleday.

Halsey, Albert H (1995), *Change in British Society: From 1900 to the Present Day*, Oxford and New York: Oxford University Press.

Hamabata, Matthews Masayuki (1990), *Crested Kimono: Power and Love in the Japanese Business Family*, Ithaca: Cornell University Press.

Hamada, Hideo and Yukiko Ōkuma (2002), '*Shakai hoshō shakai fukushi* (Social security and social welfare)', in Asahi Gendai Yōgo *CHIEZŌ 2002* (*The 2002 Asahi Treasury of Knowledge concerning Key Words*), edited by the Asahi Shimbun Jiten Henshū Bu, Tokyo: Asahi Shimbunsha.

Hamada, Tomoko (1997), 'Absent fathers, feminized sons, selfish mothers and disobedient daughters: Revisiting the Japanese *ie* household', *JPRI Working Paper*, 33, May, online at: http://www.jpri.org/publications/workingpapers/wp33.html.

Hamaguchi, Esyun (1985) 'A contextual model of the Japanese: Toward a methodological innovation in Japanese studies', *Journal of Japanese Studies*, 11(2), pp. 289–321.

— (1988), '"*Nihonrashisa*" *no saihakken* (*Rediscovering "Japaneseness"*)', revised edition, Tokyo: Kōdansha.

Hani, Yoko (2007), 'Cellphone bards hit bestseller lists', *The Japan Times*, 23 September, online at: http://search.japantimes.co.jp/cgi-bin/fl20070923x4.html.

Hanihara, Kazurō (1995), *Nihonjin No Naritachi (Formation of the Japanese people)*, Kyoto: Jinbun Shoin.

Hanley, Susan (1999), *Everyday Things in Premodern Japan*, Princeton: Princeton University Press.

Hara, Junsuke and Kazuo Seiyama (2006), *Inequality amid Affluence: Social Stratification in Japan*, Melbourne: Trans Pacific Press.

Hardacre, Helen (1984), *Lay Buddhism in Contemporary Japan: Reiyūkai Kyōdan*, Princeton: Princeton University Press.

— (1986), *Kurozumikyō and the New Religions of Japan*, Princeton: Princeton University Press.

— (1997), *Marketing the Menacing Fetus in Japan*, Berkeley: University of California Press.

Hargreaves, Andy (1994), *Changing Teachers, Changing Times*, London: Cassell.

Harloe, Michael (1995), *The People's Home? Social Rented Housing in Europe and America*, Oxford: Blackwell Publishers.

Harris, Marvin (1968), *The Rise of Anthropological Theory*, New York: Harper & Row.

Hasegawa, Hiroshi (1996), '*Seito bunka: Nihon ni okeru sono yōtai to henyō* (Student culture: Status quo and changes in Japan),' in Teruhisa Horio, Yasuteru Okudaira, Takahiko Tanaka, Hiroshi Sanuki, Noriyuki Shiomi, Masao Ōta, Sonoko Yokoyu, Toshiaki Sudō, Yoshiyuki Kudomi and Yōichi Urano (eds), *Gakkō Bunka To Iu Jiba (The Magnetic Field Called School Culture)*, Tokyo: Kashiwa Shobō, pp. 73–116.

Hashimoto, Katsuhiko (2007), *Dankai no Shozō (A Portrait of the First Postwar Generation)*, Tokyo: NHK Books.

Hashimoto, Kenji (2003), *Class Structure in Contemporary Japan*. Melbourne: Trans Pacific Press.

Hashimoto, Takehiko (2002), 'Introduction', in Shigehisa Kuriyama and Takehiko Hashimoto (eds), 'The birth of tardiness: The formation of time consciousness in modern Japan', *Japan Review*, special issue, 14, pp. 5–9.

Hattori, Yuichi (2006), 'Social withdrawal in Japanese youth: A case study of thirty-five hikikomori clients', *Journal of Trauma Practice*, 4(3–4), pp. 180–201.

Hayano, Toshiaki (2006) '*Steppu famirī to hōseido* (Stepfamilies and the legal system in Japan)', in Shinji Nozawa, Naoko Ibaraki and Toshiki Hayano (eds), *Q&A Suteppu Famirī No Kiso Chishiki (An Introduction to Step Families: Questions and Answers)*, Tokyo: Akashi Shoten.

Hayashi, Chikio (2001), *Nihonjin no Kokuminsei Kenkyū (Study of Japanese National Character)*, Tokyo: Nansōsha.

Hayashi, Shingo (2005), *Shinobiyoru Neo-kaikyū Shakai (Creeping Class Society)*, Tokyo: Heibonsha.

Hazama, Hiroshi (1971), *Nihonteki Keiei: Shūdanshugi no Kōzai (Japanese-style Management: The Merits and Demerits of Japan's Strong Group-Oriented Ethos)*, Tokyo: Nihon Keizai Shimbunsha.

Headland, Thomas N, Kenneth L Pike, and Marvin Harris (eds) (1990), *Emics and Etics: The Insider/Outsider Debate*, Newbury Park: Sage.

Hei Konsarutingu Gurūpu (Hei Consulting Group) (2007), *Gurōbaru Jinji: Kadai to Genjitsu (Global Management: Issues and Realities)*, Tokyo: Nihon Keidanren Shuppan.

Hendry, Joy and Massimo Raveri (eds) (2002), *Japan at Play: The Ludic and the Logic of Power*, London: Routledge.

Hida, Daijirō, Hiroaki Mimizuka, Hideo Iwaki and Takehiko Kariya (2000), *Kōkōsei Bunka to Shinro Keisei no Henyō (Changes in Senior High School Culture and Post-school Paths)*, Tokyo: Gakuji Shuppan.

Hinokidani, Mieko (2007), 'Housing, family and gender', in Yosuke Hirayama and Richard Ronald (eds), *Housing and Social Transition in Japan*, London: Routledge, pp. 114–39.

Hirayama, Yosuke (2007), 'Reshaping the housing system: Home ownership as a catalyst for social transformation', in Yosuke Hirayama and Richard Ronald (eds), *Housing and Social Transition in Japan*, London: Routledge, pp. 15–46.

Hirayama, Yosuke and Richard Ronald (eds) (2007), *Housing and Social Transition in Japan*, London: Routledge.

Hjorth, Larissa (2005), 'Odours of mobility: Mobile phones and Japanese cute culture in the Asia-Pacific', *Journal of Intercultural Studies*, 26(1–2), February–May, pp. 39–55.

Honda, Yuki (2004), '"Nīto" ni hitsuyō nano wa ishiki keihatsu yorimo chansu (What the NEET generation needs is a chance, not a new outlook)', in Bungei Shunjū (ed.), *Nihon no Ronsō (Japan's Debates)*, Tokyo: Bungei Shunjū, pp. 628–31.

Horio, Teruhisa (1988), *Educational Thought and Ideology in Modern Japan*, Tokyo: University of Tokyo Press.

Hosogaya, Atsushi (2001), 'Comic exchanges between Asia and Japan: past and future', 'Asia in comics' exhibition, *Where Are We Going*, Tokyo: The Japan Foundation Asia Center, pp. 50–1.

Howe, Rachel (2007), 'Japanese women online', May, online at: http://www.international-business-research.com/JapaneseWomenOnline.html.

Hsiao, Michael and Po-san Wan (2007), 'The experiences of cultural globalizations in Asia-Pacific', *Japanese Journal of Political Science*, 8(3), November.

Ihara, Ryoji (2007), *Toyota's Assembly Line: A View from the Factory Floor*. Melbourne: Trans Pacific Press.

Ii, Nohiro (2003), '"Kyōiku konnankō" kara mieru Nihon shakai to kokusai rikai kyōiku no yakuwari: "tozetsu" to mukiau gakkō bunka no naka de (Japanese society and the roles of international understanding education seen from a "difficult school"', *Kokusairikai (International Understanding)*, 34, pp. 136–57.

Ikeda, Hiroshi (1985), 'Hisabetsu buraku ni okeru kyōiku to bunka: Gyoson buraku ni okeru seinen no raifu sutairu ni kansuru esunogurafī (Education and culture in a buraku community: An ethnography of youth lifestyles in a fishing village)', *Osaka Daigaku Ningen Kagakubu Kiyō (Osaka University Faculty of Human Science Research Bulletin)*, 11, pp. 241–71.

Ikegami, Eiko (1995), *The Taming of the Samurai: Honorific Individualism and the Making of Modern Japan*, Cambridge MA: Harvard University Press.

— (2005), *Bonds of Civility: Aesthetic Networks and the Political Origins of Japanese Culture*, Cambridge UK: Cambridge University Press.

Imamura, Anne E (1996), *Re-imaging Japanese Women*, Berkeley: University of California Press.

Imazu, Kōjirō (2000), 'Gakkō no kyōdō bunka: Nihon to ōbei no hikaku (Collaborative culture in schools: A comparison between Japan and the West)', in Hidenori Fujita and Kōkichi Shimizu (eds), *Hendō Shakai no Naka no Kyōiku Chishiki Kenryoku*

Mondai Toshiteno Kyōiku Kaikau Kyōshi Gakkō Bunka (Educational Reform, Teachers and School Culture Seen as Problems of Education, Knowledge and Power in a Changing Society), Tokyo: Shinyōsha, pp. 300–21.

Inagaki, Tadahiko, and Yoshiyuki Kudomi (1994), *Nihon no Kyōshi Bunka (Teachers' Culture in Japan)*, Tokyo: University of Tokyo Press.

Inglehart, Ronald (1993), *The Silent Revolution in Europe*, Princeton: Princeton University Press.

Inkster, Ian (2000), 'Introduction: Culture and technology in Japan', in Ian Inkster and Fumihiko Satofuka (eds), *Culture and Technology in Modern Japan*, London: IB Tauris, pp. 1–21.

Inkster, Ian and Fumihiko Satofuka (eds) (2000), *Culture and Technology in Modern Japan*, London: IB Tauris.

Inoguchi, Takashi (1997), '*Tanegashima Tokitaka kara Plaza gōi made* (From Lord Tokitaka of Tanegashima to the Plaza Agreement of 1985)', *Gakushüin Kaihō, Kōenkai Tokushūgō*, November, pp. 104–14.

— (1999), 'Japan's medieval legacy', *Asian Affairs*, 9, pp. 19–28.

— (2003), 'The Japanese decision', *Open Democracy*, 7 August, online at: http://www.opendemocracy.net/democracy-iraqi_war/article_1416.jsp.

— (2004), *Kokumin Ishiki to Globalism (National Consciousness and Globalism)*, Tokyo: NTT Shuppan.

— (2005a), *Japanese Politics: An Introduction*, Melbourne: Trans Pacific Press.

— (2005b), '*Cong Riben de jiaodu toushi Zhongguo de minzuzhuyi* (Looking into Chinese nationalism from a Japanese angle)', *Shijie Jingji Yu Zhengzhi (World Economics and Politics)*, 11, pp. 49–50.

— (2006), 'Social capital in East Asia: Comparative political culture in Confucian societies', Asian Development Bank workshop at the University of Sydney, 14–15 December.

— (2007a), 'Can Fukuda handle stress left by Abe?' *The Straits Times*, 27 September.

— (2007b), 'Culture and democracy: Reflections on the Japanese experiences', *Political Science in Asia*, 2(2), pp. 1–19.

— (2007c), 'Federalism and quasi-federal tradition in Japan', in Baogang He, Brian Galligan and Takashi Inoguchi (eds), *Federalism in Asia*, London: Edward Elgar, pp. 266–89.

— (2007d), 'The AsiaBarometer Survey Questionnaire of 2006', *Japanese Journal of Political Science*, 8(3), pp. 427–53.

— (2007e), 'The ghost of absolutism or lack thereof: Elizabeth and Nobunaga in the late sixteenth century as seen in the framework of democracy and power', Seminar organised by the Anglo-Japanese Daiwa Foundation and the Japan Society, One Birdcage Walk, Westminster, London, 22 November.

— (2007f), 'Clash of values across civilizations', in Russel Dalton and Hans-Dieter Klingemann (eds), *The Oxford Handbook of Political Behavior*, Oxford: Oxford University Press, pp. 240–58.

— (2007g), 'The place of the United States in the triangle of Japan, China and India', Afrasian Centre for Peace and Development Studies, Ryukoku University, *Workshop Paper Series*, 22.

Inoguchi, Takashi and Ian Marsh (eds) (2008), *Globalization, Public Opinion, and the State,* London: Routledge.

Inoguchi, Takashi and Jean Blondel (2008), *Citizens and the State: Attitudes in Western Europe and East and Southeast Asia,* London: Routledge.

Inoguchi, Takashi and Seiji Fujii (2008), 'The AsiaBarometer: Its aim, its scope and its development', in Valerie Møller, Denis Huschka and Alex C Michalos (eds), *Barometers of Quality of Life around the Globe: How Are We Doing?*, Social Indicators Research Book Series, Netherlands: Springer, pp. 187–232.

Inoguchi, Takashi, Satoru Mikami and Seiji Fujii (2007), 'Social capital in East Asia: Comparative political culture in Confucian societies', *Japanese Journal of Political Science*, 8(3), November, pp. 409–26.

Inoue, Hisashi (2002), *Kokugo Gannen (National Language Year One)*, Tokyo: Chūkō Bunko.

Inoue, Kiyoshi (1950), '*Buraku kaihō riron to burakushi no kadai (Buraku* liberation theory and the subject of *buraku* history)', in Buraku Mondai Kenkyūsho (Buraku Problem Research Institute) (ed.), *Buraku Mondai (The Buraku Problems)*, 18, pp. 2–10.

Inoue, Nobutaka (ed.) (1991), *New Religions*, Contemporary Papers on Japanese Religion, 2, Tokyo: Institute for Japanese Culture and Classics, Kokugakuin University.

Inoue, Yoshikazu and Taku Yasuda (2002), '*Erīto chūtōgakkō bunka no ruikei bunseki* (An analysis of categories of elite secondary school culture)', *Soshioroji (Sociology)*, 4, pp. 73–89.

Internet World Stats (2007), 'Japan: Internet usage stats and marketing report', August, online at: http://www.internetworldstats.com/asia.jp.htm.

Inui, Akio (2002), ' "*Sengo Nihon-gata seinenki*" to sono kaitai saihen (Postwar Japan and the maturation of youth: Restructuring the post-schooling trajectory)', *Portiku*, 3, pp. 88–107.

Ishige, Naomichi (1991), 'Change and transformation in table setting: Home dining in modern Japan', *Bulletin of the National Museum of Ethnology*, 16, Special issue edited by Naomichi Ishige and Tadashi Inoue.

— (2001a), *The History and Culture of Japanese Food*, London: Kegan Paul International.

— (2001b), '*Nijuseiki Nihon no shoku* (Twentieth century diet in Japan)', in Nihon Seikatsu Gakkai (ed.), *Seikatsu-gaku (Lifology)*, vol. 25, Tokyo : Domesu Shuppan, pp. 9–21.

— (2005), *Shokutaku Bunmeiron: Chabudai wa Doko e Kieta (Table Civilization Theory: Where Has the Chabudai Gone?)*, Tokyo: Chūō Kōronsha.

— (2007), '*Bouddhism, Shintoism et consommation de viande animale au Japon*', in Jean-Pierre Poulain (ed.), *L'Homme, le Mangeur, l'Animal*, Paris: Les Cahiers de l'Ocha, vol. 12, pp. 80–92.

Ishii, Kenji (1997), *Dēta Bukku: Gendai Nihonjin no Shūkyō – Sengo Gojūnen no Shūkyō Ishiki to Shūkyō Kōdō (Data Book: Religions of the Contemporary Japanese – Religious Consciousness and Religious Behavior for the Last Fifty Years)*, Tokyo: Shinyōsha.

Itami, Noriyuki (2002), *Jimponshugi Kigyō (Human Capital Enterprises)*, Tokyo: Nihon Keizai Shimbunsha.

Itō Kinen Zaidan (Itō Foundation) (ed.) (1990), *Nihon Shokuniku Bunkashi* (A Cultural History of Meat Eating in Japan), Tokyo: Itō Kinen Zaidan.

Ito, Kinko (1995), 'Sexism in Japanese weekly comic magazines for men', in JA Lent (ed.), *Asian Popular Culture*, Boulder: Westview Press.

— (2005), 'A history of Manga in the context of Japanese culture and society', *Journal of Popular Culture*, 38(3), pp. 456–75.

Itō, Shigeki (2002), 'Seinen bunka to gakkō no 90 nendai (Youth culture and schools in the 1990s)', Kyōiku Shakaigaku Kenkyū (The Journal of Educational Sociology), 70, pp. 89–104.

Ito, Takatoshi (1992), The Japanese Economy, Cambridge MA: MIT Press.

Itō, Tetsuji (2004), Shinrigakusha ga Kangaeta 'Kokoro no Nōto' Gyaku Katsuyōhō (A Psychologist's Contrarian Method for Using 'Kokoro no Nōto [the Heart and Mind Notebook]'), Tokyo: Kōbunken.

Itō, Yasuhiro (1994), 'Kyōshi bunka gakkō bunka no nichibei hikaku (A comparative study of teachers' culture and school culture in Japan and the US)', in T Inagaki and Y Kudomi (eds), Nihon no Kyōshi Bunka (Teachers' Culture in Japan), Tokyo: Tokyo Daigaku Shuppankai, pp. 140–56.

Ivy, Marilyn (1995), Discourses of the Vanishing: Modernity, Phantasm, Japan, Chicago: University of Chicago Press.

Iwabuchi, Koichi (1998), 'Marketing "Japan": Japanese cultural presence under a global gaze', Japanese Studies, 18(2), pp. 165–80.

— (2002a), '"Soft" nationalism and narcissism: Japanese popular culture goes global', Asian Studies Review, 26(4), pp. 447–68.

— (2002b), Recentering Globalization: Popular Culture and Japanese Transnationalism, Durham: Duke University Press.

Iwabuchi, Koichi (ed.) (2004), Feeling Asian Modernities: Transnational Consumption of Japanese TV Drama, Hong Kong: Hong Kong University Press.

Iwai, Katsuto and Masashi Miura (2007), Shihonshugi to Shiminshugi (Capitalism and Citizen-Firstism), Tokyo: Shinyōsha.

Iwamoto, M. (1984), 'Gētobōru kyōgi no hassei to sono fukyū katei (The origin and the dissemination process of gate ball)', Minzokugaku Kenkyū (Ethnological Studies), 49(2), pp. 174–82.

Iwata, Masami (2007), Gendai no hinkon: wākingupua/hōmuresu/seikatsu hogo (Poverty in the Contemporary World: The Working Poor, Homelessness and Livelihood Protection), Tokyo: Cikuma Shobō.

Iwata, Masami and Akihiko Nishizawa (eds) (2008), Poverty and Social Welfare in Japan, Melbourne: Trans Pacific Press.

Izuhara, Misa (2007), 'Turning stock into cash flow: strategies using housing assets in an ageing society', in Yosuke Hirayama and Richard Ronald (eds), Housing and Social Transition in Japan, London: Routledge, pp. 94–113.

Jaffe, Richard (2001), Neither Monk nor Layman: Clerical Marriage in Modern Japanese Buddhism, Princeton: Princeton University Press.

Japan External Trade Organization (JETRO), Japanese Economy Division (2005), 'Industrial report: Japan animation industry trends', Japan Economic Monthly, 15 June.

Japan External Trade Organization (JETRO) (2007), '"Japan Cool" rises in global importance and significance', Focus Newsletter, May, online at: http://www.jetro.org/documents/focus/JETRO_Focus_May2007.pdf.

Japan Institute for Labour Policy and Training (2007), Japanese Working Life Profile 2006/2007 – Labor Statistics, Tokyo: The Japan Institute for Labour Policy and Training.

Japan Labor Bulletin (1991), 'Image of workaholic Japanese clear: Rengosoken's survey on living time for workers of five nations', 30(19), pp. 3–4.

Johnson, Chalmers (1982), MITI and the Japanese Miracle: the Growth of Industrial Policy, 1925–1975, Stanford: Stanford University Press.

Johnson, Frank A (1993), *Dependency and Japanese Socialization: Psychoanalytic and Anthropological Investigations into* Amae, New York: New York University Press.

Johnstone, Bob (1997), 'Japan saps the world's rain forests', *New Scientist*, 114, 2 April, p. 18.

Jones, Maggie (2006), 'Shutting themselves in', *New York Times Magazine*, 155(53460), 15 January, pp. 46–51.

Kabanov, Alexander M (1992), 'Japan through the eyes of modern Soviet scholars', in Harumi Befu and Josef Kreiner (eds), *Othernesses of Japan: Historical and Cultural Influences on Japanese Studies in Ten Countries*, München: Iudicium, pp. 241–58.

Kabashima, Ikuo and Yoshito Takenaka (1988), *Nihon no Ideology (Japanese Ideologies)*, Tokyo: University of Tokyo Press.

Kamata, Satoshi (1982), *Japan in the Passing Lane: An Insider's Shocking Account of Life in a Japanese Auto Factory* (translated by Tatsuru Akimoto, with an introduction by Ronald Dore), New York: Pantheon Books.

Kamei Takeshi, Rokurō Kōno and Eiichi Chino (eds) (1997), *Nihon Rettō no Gengo: Gengogaku Daijiten Serekushon (Languages of the Japanese Archipelago: Selections from the Encyclopedia of Linguistics)*, Tokyo: Sanseidō.

Kanehara, Hitomi (2004), *Hebi ni Piasu (Snakes and Earrings)*, Tokyo: Shūeisha.

— (2005), *Amebic* (Amebic), Tokyo: Shūeisha.

Kaneko, Sachiko (2006), '"Japan's socially withdrawn youths" and time constraints in Japanese society: Management and conceptualization of time in a support group for "hikikomori"', *Time and Society*, 15(2–3), pp. 233–49.

Kaneko, Yoshio (1980), 'The future of the fixed-age retirement system', in Shunsaku Nishikawa (ed.), *The Labor Market in Japan: Selected Readings*, Tokyo: University of Tokyo Press, pp. 104–23.

Kanemoto, Yoshitsugu (1997), 'The housing question in Japan', *Regional Science and Urban Economics*, 27, pp. 613–64

Kantō Bengoshi-kai Rengōkai (Federation of Bar Associations in the Kantō Area) (ed.) (1990), *Gaikokujin Rōdōsha no Shūrō to Jinken (Employment and Human Rights of Foreign Workers)*, Tokyo: Akashi Shoten.

Karatani, Kojin (1993), *Origins of Japanese Literature*, Durham: Duke University Press.

Kariya, Takehiko (1995), *Taishū Kyōiku Shakai No Yukue: Gakureki Shugi To Byōdō Shinwa No Sengo-Shi (The Future of Mass Education Society: A History of Education Credentialism and the Myth of Equality in Postwar Japan)*, Tokyo: Chūō Kōron sha.

— (2001), *Kaisōka Nihon to Kyōiku Kiki: Fubyōdō Saiseisan Kara Iyoku Kakusa Shakai E (Education in Crisis and Stratified Japan: From Inequality Reproduction Society to Incentive Disparity Society)*, Tokyo: Yūshindō.

Kassalow, Everett (1983), 'Japan as an industrial relations model', *Journal of Industrial Relations*, 25(2), pp. 201–9.

Kato, Hidetoshi, Richard Gid Powers and Bruce Stronach (1989), *Handbook of Japanese Popular Culture*, New York: Greenwood Press.

Katō, Norihiro (2004) *Katari no Haikei (Behind the Narratives)*, Tokyo: Shōbunsha

Katsuno, Hirofumi and Christine Yano (2002), 'Face to face: On-line subjectivity in contemporary Japan', *Asian Studies Review*, 26(2), June, pp. 205–31.

Kawakami, Hiromi (1996) *Atarayoki* and *Stepping on a snake* in *Hebi Wo Fumu (Stepping on a Snake)*, (1999 reprint) Tokyo: Bunshun Bunko.

— (2001), *Sensei no Kaban (Teacher's Briefcase)*, (2004 reprint) Tokyo: Bunshun Bunko.

— (2002), *Ryūgū*, (2005 reprint with '*Kaitetsu* (Commentary)' by Saburo Kawamoto) Tokyo: Bunshun Bunko.

— (2005), *Manazuru*, Tokyo: Bungei Shunjū.

Kawakatsu, Heita (2006), *Bunkaryoku: Nihon no Sokojikara* (*Cultural Power: Japan's Underlying Strength*), Tokyo: Wedge Publications.

Kawamura, Nozomu (1989), 'The transition of the household system in Japan's modernization', in Yoshio Sugimoto and Ross Mouer (eds), *Constructs for Understanding Japan*, London: Kegan Paul International.

Kawanishi, Hirosuke (1992), *Enterprise Unionism in Japan*, London: Kegan Paul International.

Kawato, Akio (2008), *Japan and the World*, online at: www.akiokawato.com/ja/cat40/post_139.php.

Kazahaya, Yasoji (1973), *Nihon no Shakai Seisakushi*, (*A History of Social Policy in Japan*), 2 vols, Tokyo: Aoki Bunko.

Ketelaar, James Edward (1990), *Of Heretics and Martyrs in Meiji Japan: Buddhism and Its Persecution*, Princeton: Princeton University Press.

Kihara, Takahiro, Takanori Mutō, Kazunori Kumagai, and Hidenori Fujita (eds) (1993), *Gakkō Bunka no Shakaigaku* (*Sociology of School Culture*), Tokyo: Fukumura Shuppan.

Kimura, Bin (1972), *Hito to Hito no Aida: Seishin Byōrigakuteki Nihonron* (*Between Person and Person: A Psychopathological View of Japan*), Tokyo: Kōbudō.

Kinsella, Sharon (1996) 'Change in the social status, form and content of adult manga, 1986–1996', *Japan Forum*, 8(1), pp. 103–12.

— (1998) 'Japanese subculture in the 1990s: *Otaku* and the amateur *manga* movement', *The Journal of Japanese Studies*, 24(2), pp. 289–316.

— (2000a), *Adult Manga: Culture and Power in Contemporary Japanese Society*, Richmond: Curzon.

— (2000b), 'The movement against manga', in *Adult Manga: Culture and Power in Contemporary Japanese Society*, Richmond: Curzon, pp. 139–61.

Kisala, Robert (1999), *Prophets of Peace: Pacifism and Cultural Identity in Japan's New Religions*, Honolulu: University of Hawai'i Press.

Koike, Kazuo (1989), 'Some conditions for QC circles: Long-term perspectives in the behaviour of individuals', in Yoshio Sugimoto and Ross Mouer (eds), *Constructs for Understanding Japan*, London: Kegan Paul International, pp. 94–129.

Koizumi, Kenkichiro (2002), 'In search of Wakon: The cultural dynamics of the rise of manufacturing technology in postwar Japan', *Technology and Culture*, 43, pp. 29–49.

Komai, Hiroshi (2001), *Foreign Migrants in Contemporary Japan* (translated by Jens Wilkinson), Melbourne: Trans Pacific Press.

Kosugi, Reiko (2007), *Escape from Work: Freelancing Youth and the Challenge to Corporate Japan* (translated by Ross Mouer), Melbourne: Trans Pacific Press.

Kudō, Tadatsugu (2005), '*Mijuku na nīto wo otana ni sodatete ageru: Waga "wakamono jiritsu juku" no chōsen* (Raising the immature NEET to be adults: The challenge to institute a training program for our youth)', in Bungei Shunjū (ed.), *Nihon no Ronsō* (Japan's Debates), Tokyo: Bungei Shunjū, pp. 632–35.

Kudomi, Yoshiyuki (1988), *Kyōin Bunka No Shakaigaku-Teki Kenkyū* (*A Sociological Study of Teachers' Culture*), Tokyo: Taga Shuppan.

Kuki, Shūzō (1930), *Iki no Kōzō* (*The Structure of Iki*), Tokyo: Iwanami Shoten.

Kunii, Irene M (2000), 'Japan's net builders', *Business Week*, Asian edition, 6 March, pp. 18–22.

Kuwahara, Motoko (2001), 'Japanese women in science and technology', *Minerva*, 39, pp. 203–16.

Kuwayama, Takami (2001), 'The discourse of *Ie* (family) in Japan's cultural identity and nationalism: A critique', *Japanese Review of Cultural Anthropology*, (2), pp. 3–37.

— (2004), *Native Anthropology: The Japanese Challenge to Western Academic Hegemony*, Melbourne: Trans Pacific Press.

— (2005), 'Native discourse in the academic world system: Kunio Yanagita's project of global folkloristics reconsidered', in Jan van Bremen, Eyal Ben-Ari and Syed Farid Alatas (eds), *Asian Anthropology*, London: Routledge.

Kyūka Seido no Arikata to Keizai Shakai e no Eikyō ni Kansuru Chōsa Kenkyū Iinkai (Research Committee on the Leave System and its impact on Japan's Economy and Society) (2002), *Kyūka Kaikaku Wa 'Koronbusu no Tamago': 12-Chō en no Keizai Hakyū Kōka to 150 Man Nin no Kōyō Sōshutsu (Vacation Reform is Columbus's Egg: Economic Ripple Effects of 12 Trillion Yen for the Creation of 1.5 Million Jobs)*. Tokyo: Jiyū Jikan Dezain Kyōkai (Free Time Design Association).

Lacy, P (1996), 'Training for collaboration', *British Journal of Inservice Education*, 22(1), pp. 67–80.

Lambert, Priscilla A (2007), 'The political economy of postwar family policy in Japan: Economic imperatives and electoral incentives', *Journal of Japanese Studies*, 33(1), pp. 1–28.

Lasswell, Harold (1990), *Politics: Who Gets What, When, How*, New York: Peter Smith Publishing.

Ledden, Sean and Fred Fejes (1987), 'Female gender role patterns in Japanese comic magazines', *Journal of Popular Culture*, 21(1), pp. 155–76.

Lee, O-Young (1984), *The Compact Culture: The Japanese Tradition of 'Smaller Is Better'*, Tokyo: Kodansha International.

Leheny, David (2003), *The Rules of Play: National Identity and the Shaping of Japanese Leisure*, Ithaca: Cornell University Press.

Lent, John A (1989), 'Japanese comics', in Hidetoshi Kato, Richard Gid Powers and Bruce Stronach (eds), *Handbook of Japanese Popular Culture*, New York: Greenwood Press, pp. 221–42.

Lenz, Ilse (2001), 'Technology and gender in Japan', in Arne Holzhausen (ed.), *Can Japan Globalize? Studies on Japan's Changing Political Economy and the Process of Globalization in Honour of Sung-Jo Park*, Heidelberg, Germany: Physica-Verlag, pp. 213–28.

LeTendre, Gerald (1994), 'Guiding them on: Teaching hierarchy, and social organization in Japanese middle schools', *Journal of Japanese Studies*, 20, pp. 37–59.

— (2000), *Learning to be Adolescent: Growing up in US and Japanese Middle Schools*, New Haven: Yale University Press.

Levi, Antonia (1997), 'Using Japanese animation to teach Japanese religion', *Education About Asia*, 2(1), pp. 26–9.

Lewis, Catherine C (1995), *Educating Hearts and Minds: Reflections on Japanese Preschool and Elementary Education*, Cambridge UK: Cambridge University Press.

Lie, John (2004), *Multiethnic Japan*, Cambridge MA: Harvard University Press.

Liker, Jeffrey (2003), *The Toyota Way*, New York: McGraw-Hill.

Linhart, Sepp (1984), 'Some observations on the development of "typical" Japanese attitudes towards working hours and leisure', in Gordon Daniels (ed.), *Europe Interprets Japan*, Tenterden: Paul Norbury Publications, pp. 207–14.

— (1989), '*Die Anwendbarkeit des Freizeitbegriffs auf Japan* (The usability of the notion of 'leisure' when dealing with Japan)', Leviathan, *Zeitschrift für Sozialwissenschaft (Journal for the Social Sciences)*, 17(2), pp. 204–15.

— (2000), '*Auf der Suche nach der verlorenen Zeit: Anmerkungen zum Verhältnis von Arbeit und Freizeit in Japan* (In search of lost time: Some considerations about the relation between work and leisure in Japan)', in M Kim, K Park and A Schirmer (eds), *Eins und Doppelt: Festschrift für Sang-Kyong Lee*, Frankfurt am Main: Peter Lang Verlag, pp. 127–52.

Linhart, Sepp and Sabine Frühstück (eds) (1998), *The Culture of Japan as Seen Through its Leisure*, Albany: State University of New York Press.

Lochner, KA, I Kawachi, RT Brennan and SL Buka (2003), 'Social capital and neighborhood mortality rates in Chicago', *Social Science and Medicine*, 56(8), pp. 797–805.

Lock, Margaret (2002), *Twice Dead: Organ Transplants and the Reinvention of Death*, Berkeley: University of California Press.

Louie, John (1996), 'Earthquake effects in Kobe, Japan', online at: http://www.seismo.unr.edu/ftp/pub/louie/class/100/effects-kobe.html

Loveday, Leo (1996), *Language Contact in Japan: a Socio-Linguistic History*, New York: Clarendon Press.

Loveday, Leo and Satomi Chiba (1986), 'Aspects of the development toward a visual culture in respect of comics: Japan', in Alphons Silbermann and Hans-Dieter Dyroff (eds), *Comics and Visual Culture: Research Studies from Ten Countries*, München: KG Saur, pp. 158–83.

MacFarquhar, Roderick (ed.) (1997), *The Politics of China: The Eras of Mao and Deng*, 2nd edition, Cambridge UK: Cambridge University Press.

Machida, Kō (2003), *Fukumi-warai (Pregnant smile)* in *Gongen no Odoriko (The Dancer of Gongen)*, (2006 reprint) Tokyo: Kōdansha.

Machimura, Takashi (2003), 'Living in a transitional community within a multi-ethnic city: Making a localized "Japan" in Los Angeles', in Roger Goodman, Ceri Peach, Ayumi Takenaka and Paul White (eds), *Global Japan: The Experience of Japan's New Immigrants and Overseas Communities*, London: RoutledgeCurzon, pp. 147–56.

Maguire, J (2006), *Japan, Sport and Society: Tradition and Change in a Globalizing World*, London: Routledge.

Maher, John C and Kyōko Yashiro (eds) (1995), *Multilingual Japan*, Clevedon: Multilingual Matters.

Mann, Michael (1986), *The Sources of Social Power: Volume 1, A History of Power from the Beginning to AD 1760*, Cambridge UK: Cambridge University Press.

Manzenreiter, W and E Ben-Ari (2004), 'Leisure and consumer culture', in Josef. Kreiner, Ulrich Möhwald and Hans-Dieter Ölschleger (eds), *Modern Japanese Society*, Leiden: Brill, pp. 489–524.

Marra, Robert J (1996), 'Social relations as capital: The story of Yuriko', in Anne E Imamura (ed.), *Re-Imaging Japanese Women*, Berkeley: University of California Press, pp. 104–16.

Masui, Keiji (ed.) (1980), *Dēta, Ongaku, Nippon (Data, Music, Japan)*, Tokyo: Min-on Ongaku Shiryōkan.

Matsuda, Tetsuo (2007), 'Literature in Japan today: Publishing trends for 2006', *Japanese Book News*, 51.

Matsui, Yayori (1987), *Women's Asia*, London: Zed Books.

Matsumoto, Yukio (2007), '*Nazeka, Shigoto Ga Hayai Hito' No Jikan Kanri Jutsu (The Techniques of Managing Time Used by Those Who Are 'Fast at Work')*, Tokyo: Asukī.

McAllister, Ian (2007), 'The personalization of politics', in Hans-Dieter Klingemann and Russell A. Dalton (eds), *The Oxford Handbook of Political Behavior*, Oxford: Oxford University Press, pp. 571–88.

McCarter, Charles and Chad Kime (1996), 'Dreaming in black and white: An interview with Fred Schodt', *EX* (1)3, online at: http://www.ex.org/1.3/07-schodt1.html.

McGray, Douglas (2002), 'Japan's gross national cool', *Foreign Policy*, 44(11), May–June, pp. 44–54.

McKay, Hugh (2002), *Media Mania: Why Our Fear of Modern Media is Misplaced*, Sydney: University of New South Wales Press.

McLelland, Mark (2000), *Male Homosexuality in Modern Japan: Cultural Myths and Social Realities*, Richmond: Curzon.

McRoberts, Kenneth (2001), *Catalonia: Nation Building without a State*, Oxford: Oxford University Press.

McVeigh, Brian (2000), *Wearing Ideology: State, Schooling and Self-presentation in Japan*, Oxford: Berg.

Mead, George Herbert (1934), *Mind, Self, and Society: From the Standpoint of a Social Behaviorist*, Chicago: University of Chicago Press.

Meguro, Yoriko (2005), '*Jendā shisutemu to shōshika* (The gender system and declining birthrate)', in Yoriko Meguro and Hachirō Nishioka (eds), *Shōshika no Jendā Bunseki (Gender Analysis of the Declining Birthrate)*, Tokyo: Keisō Shobō, pp. 11–26.

Mika (2007), *Koizora (Deep Love)*, Tokyo: Sutaatsu Shuppan.

Miller, Roy Andrew (1971), *Japanese and the Other Altaic Languages*, Chicago: University of Chicago Press.

— (1977), *The Japanese Language in Contemporary Japan*, Washington DC: American Enterprise Institute for Public Policy Research.

— (1982), *Japan's Modern Myth: The Language and Beyond*, New York: Weatherhill.

Ministry of Economy, Trade and Industry, Commerce and Information Policy Bureau, Media and Content Industry Division, Japan (2003), *Animation Sangyō no Genjō to Kadai (The Animation Industry's Present Condition and Problems)*.

Ministry of Education, Japan (ed.) (2002), *Kokoro no Nōto: Shōgaku 5–6 Nen (The 'Heart and Mind Notebook': Primary School Levels 5 and 6)*, Tokyo: Gyōkyōiku Tosho.

Ministry of Education, Japan (2006), '*Nihongo shidō ga hitsuyōna gaikokujin jidō seito no ukeire jōkyōnado ni kansuru chōsa (Heisei 18 nendo) no kekka* (The results of the 2006 survey of foreign students who require Japanese as a Second Language instruction)', online at: http://www.mext.go.jp/b_menu/houdou/19/08/07062955/001.htm#ao1, viewed 17 October 2008.

Ministry of Foreign Affairs, Consular Bureau, Policy Division, Japan (2007), *Kaigai Zairyū Hōjin-Sū Tōkei: Heisei 19-Nen Sokuhō-Ban (Statistics of Japanese Corporations Overseas: Preliminary Report 2007)*, Tokyo: Gyōkyōiku Tosho.

Ministry of Health, Labour and Welfare, Minister's Secretariat, Statistics and Information Department, Japan (ed.) (2002), *Rōdō Tōkei Yōran Heisei 13 Nendo* (*Handbook of Labour Statistics 2001*), Tokyo: Ministry of Finance, pp. 16–21.

Ministry of Justice, Immigration Bureau, Japan (2007), 'Hōmushō nyūkoku kanri kyoku (Immigration Bureau of the Ministry of Justice),' online at: http://www.immi-moj.go.jp/toukei/index.html.

Ministry of Land, Infrastructure and Transport, Japan (2006), *Jūtaku Keizai Dēta Shū* (*Economic Data on Housing*), Tokyo: Jūtaku Sangyō Shimbunsha.

Ministry of Public Management, Home Affairs, Posts and Telecommunications, Japan (2001), *Jōhō Tsūshin Hakusho: Jōhō Tsūshin Ni Kansuru Genjō Hakusho* (*The White Paper on the Communication of Information: A Report on the Transmission of Information*), Tokyo: Ministry of Public Management, Home Affairs, Posts and Telecommunications.

Ministry of Public Management, Home Affairs, Posts and Telecommunications, Statistics Bureau, Japan (2004), *Shakai Seikatsu Tōkei Shiryō Jinkō Setai Koin Rikon* (*Social Life Statistical Index: Population, Household, Marriage and Divorce*).

— (ed.) (2006), *Japan Statistical Yearbook 2007*, Tokyo: Japan Statistical Association and Mainichi Shimbunsha.

Ministry of Welfare, Japan (1998), *Kōsei Hakusho Shoshi Shakai Wo Kangaeru* (*Welfare White Paper Considering the Low Birthrate Society*).

Misaki, Aki (2005a), *Tonarimachi Sensō* (*War with the Town Next Door*), online at: http://www.shueisha.co.jp/rookie/.

— (2005b), *Tonarimachi Sensō* (*War with the Town Next Door*), Tokyo: Shūeisha.

Miura, Atsushi (2007), *Kakusa ga Iden Suru! Kodomo no Karyūka wo Fusegu ni wa* (*The Reproduction of Inequality: How to Prevent the Dumbing Down of Our Children*), Tokyo: Takarajimasha.

Miyazaki, Ayumi (1993), 'Jendā sabukaruchā no dainamikusu (Dynamics of gender-based sub-cultures)', *Kyōiku Shakaigaku Kenkyū* (*The Journal of Educational Sociology*), 52, pp. 157–77.

Molony, Barbara and Kathleen Uno (eds) (2005), *Gendering Modern Japanese History*, Cambridge MA: Harvard University Asia Center.

Morishima, Michio (1982), *Why Has Japan Succeeded: Western Technology and the Japanese Ethos*, Cambridge UK: Cambridge University Press.

Morris, Ivan (1964), *The World of the Shining Prince: Court Life in Ancient Japan*, New York: Alfred A Knopf.

Morris-Suzuki, Tessa (1998), *Re-inventing Japan: Time, Space, Nation*, New York: ME Sharpe.

— (2000), 'Anti-area studies', *Communal/Plural*, 8(1), pp. 9–23.

— (2004), *Gurobarizshon no Bunka Seiji* (*Cultural Politics of Globalization*), Tokyo: Heibonsha, 2004.

Morton, Leith (2003), *Modern Japanese Culture: The Insider View*, Melbourne: Oxford University Press.

Mouer, Ross (1983), '"Orientalism" as knowledge: Lessons for Japanologists?,' *Keio Journal of Politics*, 4, pp. 11–31.

— (2008) 'Globalization and multiculturalism in Japan', in Russell Smyth and Marika Vicziany (eds), *Business in Asia*, Melbourne: Monash University Press, pp. 29–51.

Mouer, Ross and Hirosuke Kawanishi (2005), *A Sociology of Work in Japan*, Cambridge UK: Cambridge University Press.

Mouer, Ross and Yoshio Sugimoto (1986), *Images of Japanese Society*, London: Kegan Paul International.

— (1995), 'Nihonjinron at the end of the twentieth century: A multicultural perspective', in Yoshio Sugimoto and Johann Arnason (eds), *Japanese Encounters with Post-modernity*, London: Kegan Paul International, pp. 237–69.

— (2003), 'Civil society in Japan', in David Schak and Wayne Hudson (eds), *Civil Society in Asia*, Aldershot: Ashgate, pp. 209–24.

Mowery, David C and Nathan Rosenberg (1989), *Technology and the Pursuit of Economic Growth*, Cambridge UK: Cambridge University Press.

Murakami, Ryū (2001), *Saigo no Kazoku* (*The Last Family: Out of Home*), (2003 reprint) Tokyo: Gentōsha Bunko.

Murakami, Yasusuke (1982), 'The age of the new middle mass politics: The case of Japan', *The Journal of Japanese Studies*, 8, pp. 29–72.

Murakami, Yoshio (2004), *Tokyo to no 'Kyōikukaikaku': Ishihara Tosei De Ima Naniga Okotteiruka* (*'Educational Reform' in Tokyo: What Is Occurring under the Ishihara Government?*), Tokyo: Iwanami Shoten.

Murayama, Shichirō (1977), 'Nihongo no seiritsu (The establishment of the Japanese language)', in Akira Matsumura (ed.), *Kōza Kokugoshi: 1. Kokugoshi Sōron* (*Series on the History of the Japanese Language, vol. 1, Overview*), Tokyo: Taishūkan Shoten.

Nagai, Michiakira (1911) 'Evil influence of baseball', *Asahi Shimbun*, 4 September, p. 6.

Nagata, Takashi (1996), *Ryūkyū de Umareta Kyōtsūgo* (*A Common Language Born in the Ryukyus*), Tokyo: Ōfū

Naitō, Asao (2006), 'Yankī to gariben nomi: Imada hinkon ni aegu chihō no gakkō bunka (*Only Yankees and nerds: Poor school cultures in rural schools*)', *Chūō Kōron*, 161(6), pp. 112–19.

Nakamura, Ken (director) and Etsuko Izumi (writer) (1989), *Japanese Technology, A Tradition of Craftsmanship*, videorecording, Tokyo: Shin-ei Armz.

Nakane, Chie (1967a), *Kinship and Economic Organization in Rural Japan*, New York: The Humanities Press.

— (1967b), *Tateshakai no Ningen Kankei: Tan'itsu Shakai no Riron* (*Human Relationships in a Vertical Society: A Theory on Unitary Society*), Tokyo: Kōdansha.

— (1970), *Japanese Society*, Berkeley: University of California Press.

Nakayama, Ichiro (1975), *Industrialization and Labor-Management Relations in Japan* (translated by Ross Mouer), Tokyo: Japan Institute of Labor.

Namiki, N (1975), 'A vision of Japan's industrial structure', in G Fodella (ed.), *Social Structures and Economic Dynamics in Japan up to 1980*, Milano: Universita Bocconi, pp. 223–38.

Napier, Susan Jolliffe (2001), *Anime from Akira to Princess Mononoke: Experiencing Contemporary Japanese Animation*, New York: Palgrave.

National Agency for Enterprise and Housing, Denmark (2004), *Housing Statistics in the European Union 2003*, Copenhagen, July, online at: http://www.ebst.dk/file/2256/housing_statistics.2003.pdf

Newitz, A (1995), 'Magic girls and atomic bomb sperm: Japanese animation in America', *Film Quarterly*, 49(1), pp. 2–15.

NHK Hōsō Bunka Kenkyūsho Yoron Chōsa-bu (NHK Broadcasting Culture Research Institute, Public Opinion Department) (2008), *Nihonjin no Sukinamono: Dēta de Yomu Shikō to Kachikan (What Japanese Like: What Data Reveal about Japanese Taste and Value Orientations)*, Tokyo: Nippon Hōsō Shuppan-kai.

NHK Hōsō Yoron Chōsa Kenkyūjo (NHK Broadcasting Public Opinion Research Institute) (1982), *Gendaijin to Ongaku (Contemporary People and Music)*, Tokyo: Nippon Hōsō Shuppan Kyōkai.

Nihon Daijiten Kankōkai (ed.) (1976), *Nihon kokugo daijiten* (Comprehensive dictionary of the Japanese language), 20 vols, Tokyo: Shōgakkan.

Nihon Record Kyōkai (Recording Industry Association of Japan) (2007), online at: http://www.riaj.or.jp/release/2007/pr070223.html and http://www.riaj.or.jp/data/money/index.html.

Nikkeiren (The Japan Federation of Employers' Associations) (1995), *Shinjidai no 'Nihon-teki Keiei': Chōsen Subeki Hōko to Sono Gutaisaku ('Japanese-style Management' for a New Era: The Challenge and Some New Strategies)*, Tokyo: Nikkeiren.

Nishikawa, Yūko (1999), 'The modern family and changing forms of dwellings in Japan: Male-centered houses, female-centered houses, and gender-neutral rooms', in Haruko Wakita, Anne Bouchy and Chizuko Ueno (eds), *Gender and Japanese History*, vol. 2, Osaka: Osaka University Press, pp. 477–507.

Nishimura, Kyōtarō (1980), *Shūchakueki Satsujin Jiken (Death at Ueno Station)*, Tokyo: Kōbunsha.

Nishiyama, Uzō (1989), *Sumai Kōkongaku: Gendai Nihon Jūtakushi (The 'Now-ology' of Dwellings: The History of Housing in Modern Japan)*, Tokyo: Shōkokusha.

Nitobe, Inazo (1900), *Bushidō: The Soul of Japan*, (2002 edition) New York: Kodansha America.

— (1911), 'Evil influence of baseball', *Asahai Shimbun*, 29 August, p. 6.

Nitschke, Gunter (1994), 'The manga city', in A Ueda (ed.), *The Electric Geisha: Exploring Japan's Popular Culture*, Tokyo: Kodansha International.

Noda, S (2006), 'Legal issues on long-term leave: Conflicting structure of leave benefits', *Japan Labor Review*, 3(3), pp. 55–73.

Noguchi, Michihiko (2000), *Buraku Mondai no Paradaimu Tenkan* (A Paradigm Shift in the *Buraku* Problem), Tokyo: Akashi Shoten.

Nolte, Sharon H and Sally Ann Hastings (1991), 'The Meiji state's policy toward women, 1890–1910' in Gail Lee Bernstein (ed.), *Recreating Japanese Women, 1600–1945*, Berkeley: University of California Press.

Norgen, Tiana (2001), *Abortion before Birth Control: The Politics of Reproduction in Postwar Japan*, Princeton: Princeton University Press.

Nozawa, Shinji (2006), '*Suteppu famirī wo meguru shakai jōkyō* (Stepfamilies in contemporary Japan: An overview)', in Shinji Nozawa, Naoko Ibaraki and Toshiaki Hayano (eds), *Q&A Suteppu Famirī no Kiso Chishiki (An Introduction to Stepfamilies: Questions and Answers)*, Tokyo: Akashi Shoten.

Nukaga, Misako (2003), 'Japanese education in an era of internationalization: A case study of an emerging multicultural coexistence model', *International Journal of Japanese Sociology*, 12, pp. 79–94.

Nurkse, Ragnar (1953), *Problems of Capital Formation in Underdeveloped Countries*, New York: Oxford University Press.

Nye, Joseph S, Jr (2004), 'The soft power of Japan', *Gaiko Forum*, 4(2), pp. 3–7.

O'Brien, Richard (1992), *Global Financial Integration: The End of Geography*, London: Pinter.

Ochi, Kevin Clone (2007), *Eigo Ritchhi Eigo Pua: Ingurisshu Kakusa Shakai (English Rich English Poor: The Unequal Society in Terms of English Ability)*, Tokyo: Kōbunsha.

Ochiai, Emiko (2006), '*Kazokushugi seiaku no kiketsu to shite no chōtei shusshō ritsu: Kazoku sapōto nettowāku saihensei no shippai* (Lowest low fertility as a result of Japanese familism: A failure in the reorganization of family support networks)', in Kita Kyūshū Shiritsu Danjo Kyōdō Sankaku Sentā Mūbu (ed.), *Jendā Hakusho 4: Josei to Shoshika (White Paper 4: Women and the Declining Birthrate)*, Tokyo: Akashi Shoten, pp. 37–55.

Ogawa, Hiroshi (1998), 'The effects of karaoke on music in Japan', in Toru Mitsui and Shuhei Hosokawa (eds), *Karaoke around the World*, London: Routledge, pp. 45–53.

Ogawa, Tsuneko (1995), *Sokoku Yo: 'Chūgoku Zanryū Fujin' no Han Seiki (My Fatherland! Half a Century of 'Women Left in China')*, Tokyo: Iwanami Shoten.

Oguma, Eiji (2002), *A Genealogy of 'Japanese' Self-images*, Melbourne: Trans Pacific Press.

Ogura, Kazuya (2006), 'Contemporary working time in Japan: Legal system and reality', *Japan Labor Review*, 3(3), pp. 5–22.

Oh, Junhi (1998), '*Gakkō bunka no danzetsu, sōshutsu no seijishakaigaku* (Political sociology of school culture discontinuity and creation)', *Shakaigaku Jānaru (Tsukuba Journal of Sociology)* 23, pp. 199–227.

Ohmae, Kenichi (1999), *The Borderless World: Power and Strategy in the Interlinked World*, revised edn, New York: HarperCollins.

Ōishi, Toshikazu (1997), *Eigo Teikoku Shugi Ron: Eigo Shihai o do suru ka (Arguments about English Language Imperialism: What Can be Done about the Way English Controls the World?)* Tokyo: Kindai Bungei Sha.

Ōizumi, Eiji (2007), 'Transformations in housing construction and finance', in Yosuke Hirayama and Richard Ronald (eds), *Housing and Social Transition in Japan*, London: Routledge, pp. 47–72.

Okada, Tetsu (2000), *Tonkatsu no Tanjō (The Birth of Deep-Fried Pork Cutlets)*, Tokyo: Kōdansha.

Okano, Kaori (1993), *School to Work Transition in Japan: An Ethnographic Study*, Clevedon: Multilingual Matters.

—— (2006a), 'The global-local interface in multicultural education policies in Japan', *Comparative Education*, 42, pp. 473–91.

—— (2006b), 'The impact of immigrants on long-lasting ethnic minorities in Japanese schools: Globalization from below', *Language and Education*, 20, pp. 338–54.

—— (in press), 'Education reforms in Japan: Neo-liberal, neo-conservative, and "progressive education" directions', in Dave Hill (ed.), *The Rich World and the Impoverishment of Education: Diminishing Democracy, Equity and Workers' Rights*, New York: Routledge.

Okano, Kaori and Motonori Tsuchiya (1999), *Education in Contemporary Japan: Inequality and Diversity*, Cambridge UK: Cambridge University Press.

Okimoto, Daniel I (1989), *Between MITI and the Market: Japanese Industrial Policy for High Technology*, Stanford: Stanford University Press.

Okinawaken Kikakubu Tōkeika (Statistics Division, Department of Planning, Okinawa Prefectural Government), (2007) 'Okinawa ken (Okinawa prefecture),' online at: http://www.pref.okinawa.jp/toukeika/.

Ōkōchi, Kazuo (1970), *Shakai Seisaku no Yonjūnen (Forty Years with Social Policy)*, Tokyo: University of Tokyo Press.

Okuda, Hitoshi (2002), '*Posuto "Tokusohō" jidai no shuppatsuten: Dēta kara kangaeru kekkon sabetsu mondai* (The point of departure in the post-"Special Measures Law" era: Data-based understanding of the marriage discrimination problems)', *Hyūman Raitsu (Human Rights)*, no. 166, pp. 4–17.

Okuyama, Masurō (ed.) (1974), *Gendai Ryūkōgo Jiten (Dictionary of Contemporary Words in Fashion)*, Tokyo: Tōkyōdō Shuppan.

Ōno, Hiroki (1998), '*Gakkō bunka no esunogurafi: Kōkō kōchō no rīdākōdō no bunseki o chūshin to shite* (An ethnography of school culture: A focus on the leadership of senior high school principals)', *Nihon Kyōikugyōseigakkai Nenpō (Annual Review of Japan Educational Administration Society)*, 24, pp. 72–86.

Ono, Kosei (1983), 'Disney and the Japanese', *Look Japan*, pp. 6–12.

Ōno, Susumu (1974), *Nihongo o Sakanoboru (Backtracking Japanese Language)*, Tokyo: Iwanami Shoten.

Onosaka, Junko R (2003), 'Challenging society through the information grid: Japanese women's activism on the net' in Nanette Gottlieb and Mark McLelland (eds), *Japanese Cybercultures*, London: Routledge, pp. 95–108.

Organization of Economic Cooperation and Development (1973), *Manpower Policy in Japan*, Paris: OECD.

— (1976), *The Development of Industrial Relations in Japan: Some Implications of the Japanese Experience*, Paris: OECD.

Ōsawa, Masachi (2007), *Nashonarizumu no Yurai (The Origins of Nationalism)*, Tokyo: Kōdansha.

Oshii, Mamoru, Kazunori Itō and Toshiya Ueno (1996), '*Eiga to wa jitsu wa animeshon datta* (Film was actually a form of animation)', *Yuriika*, August, pp. 50–81.

Otomo, Rio (2007), 'A girl with her writing machine', in Tomoko Aoyama and Barbara Hartley (eds), *Girls Reading Girls*, online at: http://rotomo.net/.

Ōtsuka, Hisao, Takeyoshi Kawashima, and Takeo Doi (1976), '*Amae' to Shakai Kagaku ('Amae' and the Social Sciences)*, Tokyo: Kōbundō.

Ouchi, William G (1981), *Theory Z: How American Business Can Meet the Japanese Challenge*, Reading: Addison-Wesley.

Parry, Richard Lloyd (2007), 'Japan's phone books novel but not literary', *The Australian*, 7 December, online at: http://www.theaustralian.news.com.au/story/0,25197,22882858-2703,00.html.

Parsons, Anne (1969), *Belief, Magic and Anomie: Essays in Psychological Anthropology*, New York: Free Press.

Partner, Simon (1999), *Assembled in Japan: Electrical Goods and the Making of the Japanese Consumer*, Berkeley: University of California Press.

— (2001), 'Taming the wilderness: The lifestyle improvement movement in rural Japan', *Monumenta Nipponica*, 56(4), pp. 487–520.

Pawasarat, Catherine (2002), 'Group seeks to close digital gender divide', *The Japan Times*, 17 January, online at: http://search.japantimes.co.jp/print/nc20020117a1.html.

Peak, Lois (1991), *Learning to Go to School in Japan*, Berkeley: University of California Press.

Pempel, TJ (1998), *Regime Shift: Comparative Dynamics of the Japanese Political Economy*, Ithaca: Cornell University Press.

Perkins, Dorothy (1999), *Encyclopedia of China*, Chicago: Fitzroy Dearborn Publishers.

Pilling, David (2007), 'Shinzo Abe sounds contrite note', *Financial Times*, 20 September.

Pink, Daniel H (2007), 'Japan, ink: Inside the manga industrial complex', *Wired*, 15, 11 November.

Poitras, Gilles (1999), *The Anime Companion: What's Japanese in Japanese animation?* Berkeley: Stone Bridge Press.

Pollack, Andrew (1996), 'Disney in pact for films of top animator in Japan', *The New York Times*, p. 1 and p. 19.

Price, Michelle (1996), 'Femininity: An ethnography of subcultures in a women's university in Japan', unpublished Honours thesis, Department of Asian Studies, La Trobe University.

Prost, Antoine (1991), 'Public and private spheres in France', in Antoine Prost and Gerard Vincent (eds), *A History of Private Life (Volume 5): Riddles of Identity in Modern Times*, Cambridge MA: Harvard University Press, pp. 1–144.

Putnam, Robert (1994), *Making Democracy Work: The Civic Tradition in Modern Italy*, Princeton: Princeton University Press.

Pye, Lucian W (1982), *Asian Power and Politics*, Cambridge MA: Harvard University Press.

Pyle, Kenneth (2007), *Japan Rising*, New York: Public Affairs Press.

Rampant, James and Ross Mouer (2006), *Comic Culture and the New Wave of Manga in Australia*, Kyoto International Manga Museum.

Ravetz, Alison (1995), *The Place of Home: English Domestic Environments, 1914–2000*, London: E and FN Spon.

Ray, Rebecca and John Schmitt (2007), *No-vacation Nation*, Washington: Center for Economic and Policy Research.

Raymo, James M and Miho Iwasawa (2005), 'Marriage market mismatches in Japan: An alternative view of the relationship between women's education and marriage', *American Sociological Review*, 20, October, pp. 801–22.

Reader, Ian (1991), *Religion in Contemporary Japan*, Honolulu: University of Hawai'i Press.

Reader, Ian and George Tanabe (1998), *Practically Religious: Worldly Benefits and the Common Religion of Japan*, Honolulu: University of Hawai'i Press.

Rebick, Marcus (2005), *The Japanese Employment System: Adapting to a New Economic Environment*, New York: Oxford University Press.

— (2006), 'Changes in the workplace and their impact on the family', in Marcus Rebick and Ayumi Takenaka (eds), *The Changing Japanese Family*, London: Routledge.

Rebick, Marcus and Ayumi Takenaka (eds), (2006), *The Changing Japanese Family*, London: Routledge.

Reischauer, Edwin (1978), *The Japanese*, Cambridge MA: The Belknap Press of Harvard University Press.

— (1991), *Japan: The Case of a Nation*, 4th edition, New York: Knopf.

Rich, Roland (2007), *Pacific Asia in Quest of Democracy*, Boulder: Lynne Rienner.

Richardson, Bradley (1974), *The Political Culture of Japan*, Berkeley: University of California Press.

Riesman, David, with Nathan Glazer and Reuel Denney (1950), *The Lonely Crowd: A Study of the Changing American Character*, New Haven: Yale University Press.

Rindfuss, Ronald R, Larry L Bumpass, Minja Kim Choe and Noriko O Tsuya (2004), 'Social networks and family change in Japan', *American Sociological Review*, 69, December, pp. 856–7.

Rizzolatti, Giacomo and MA Arbib (1998), 'Language within our grasp', *Trend in Neuro-science*, 21, pp. 188–94.

Roberts, Glenda S (1994), *Staying on the Line: Blue-Collar Women in Contemporary Japan*, Honolulu: University of Hawai'i Press.

Rohlen, Thomas (1983), *Japan's High Schools*, Berkeley: University of California Press.

Rosenbluth, Frances McCall (ed.) (2007), *The Political Economy of Japan's Low Fertility*, Stanford: Stanford University Press.

Rostow, WW (1959), *The Stages of Economic Growth: A Non-Communist Manifesto*, Cambridge UK: Cambridge University Press.

Rowe, Mark (2003), 'Grave changes: Scattering ashes in contemporary Japan', *Japanese Journal of Religious Studies*, 30(1–2), pp. 112–13.

— (2006) 'Death by association: Identity, burial, and the transformation of contemporary Japanese Buddhism', unpublished PhD thesis, Princeton University, technically published with UMI.

Rybczynski, Witold (1986), *Home: A Short History of an Idea*, New York: Viking Penguin.

Saijō, Tadashi (1978), *Chūgokujin Toshite Sodatta Watashi: Kaihō-go no Harubin De (I Grew Up as a Chinese: In Harbin after the Liberation)*, Tokyo: Chūō Kōronsha.

— (1980), *Futatsu no Sokoku o Motsu Watashi: Harubin Kara Kaette 15-Nen (I Have Two Motherlands: Fifteen Years Since Returning from Harbin)*, Tokyo: Chūō Kōronsha.

Saitō, Takashi (2001), *Koe ni Dashite Yomitai Nihongo (Japanese to Be Read Aloud)*, Tokyo: Sōshisha.

Sakai, Chie (2003), 'Japanese community in Hong Kong in the 1990s: The diversity of strategies and intentions', in Roger Goodman, Ceri Peach, Ayumi Takenaka and Paul White (eds), *Global Japan: The Experience of Japan's New Immigrants and Overseas Communities*, London: RoutledgeCurzon, pp. 131–46.

Samuels, Richard (2007), *Securing Japan*, Ithaca: Cornell University Press.

Sand, Jordan (2003), *House and Home in Modern Japan: Architecture, Domestic Space and Bourgeois Culture, 1880–1930*, Cambridge MA: Harvard University Asia Center.

Sasagawa Sports Foundation (2006), *Sports Hakusho: Sports no Kachi no Aratana Hakken (Sports White Paper: Rediscovery of the Values of Sports)*.

Sato, Iwao (2007), 'Welfare regime theories and the Japanese housing system', in Yosuke Hirayama and Richard Ronald (eds), *Housing and Social Transition in Japan*, London: Routledge, pp. 73–93.

Sato, Kenji (1997), 'More animated than life: A critical overview of Japanese animated films', *Japan Echo*, 24(5), pp. 50–3.

Sato, Manabu (1992), 'Japan', in Howard B Leavitt (ed.), *Issues and Problems of Teacher Education: An International Handbook*, Westport: Greenwood Press, pp. 155–68.

Sato, Nancy (2004), *Inside Japanese Classrooms: the Heart of Education*, New York: RoutledgeFarmer.

Satō, Takamitsu (2003), *Nihon no 'Kōzō Kaikaku': Ima, dō Kangaeru Beki ka (Structural Reform: How Should We Evaluate the Present Situation?)*, Tokyo: Iwanami Shoten.

Satō, Toshiaki (2000), *Fubyōdō Sahaki Nihon: Sayonara Sōchūryū (Japan, the Inegalitarian Society: The End of Japan's Middle Class)*, Tokyo: Chūō Kōronsha.

Schodt, Frederik L (1983), *Manga! Manga!: The World of Japanese Comics*, Tokyo: Kodan-sha International.

— (1996), *Dreamland Japan: Writings on Modern Manga*, Berkeley: Stone Bridge Press.

Schwartz, Frank J and Susan J Pharr (eds) (2003), *The State of Civil Society in Japan.* Cambridge UK: Cambridge University Press.

Seeley, Christopher (2000), *A History of Writing in Japan*, Honolulu: University of Hawai'i Press.

Sekine, Naoki (2007), 'The music business in Asia', in Arthur Bernstein, Naoki Sekine and Dick Weissman (eds), *The Global Music Industry*, New York: Routledge, pp. 199–263.

Seifert, Wolfgang (2007), 'Seikatsu/seikatsusha', in George Ritzer (ed.), *The Blackwell Encyclopedia of Sociology*, vol. viii, pp. 4150–53.

Sender, Henny (2000), 'Unknown frontier', *Far Eastern Economic Review*, 13 January, p. 36.

Sharf, Robert H (1995), 'Sanbōkyōdan: Zen and the way of the New Religions', *Japanese Journal of Religious Studies*, 22(3–4), pp. 417–58.

Sheffield, Meg (1990), *Going to School in Japan*, videorecording, UK: Open University.

Shibata, Michiko (1972), *Hisabetsu Buraku no Denshō to Bunka: Shinshū no Buraku Korō Kiki Gaki* (*Oral Tradition and Culture of the Discriminated Buraku Communities: Writing the Oral Memories of the Elderly in Shinshū's Buraku Community*), Tokyo: San-ichi Shobō.

Shibatani, Masayoshi (1990), *The Languages of Japan*, Cambridge UK: Cambridge University Press.

Shigematsu-Murphy, Stephen (2002), *Amerajian no Kodomo Tachi: Shirarezaru Mainoriti Mondai* (*Amerasian Children: Unknown Minority Problems*), Tokyo: Shūeisha.

Shimahara, Nobuo, and Akira Sakai (1992) 'Teacher internship and the culture of teaching in Japan', *British Journal of Sociology of Education*, 13(2), pp. 147–62.

— (1995), *Learning to Teach in Two Cultures*, New York: Garland.

Shimazaki, Tōson (1965), *Ie* (*Domestic life*), in *Gendai Bungaku Taikei*, 9, Tokyo: Chikuma Shobō (1st edition: vol. 1, (1910) Yomiuri Shimbun; vol. 2, (1911) Chūō Kōron).

Shimazono, Susumu (2004), *From Salvation to Spirituality: Popular Religious Movements in Modern Japan*, Melbourne: Trans Pacific Press.

Shimazono, Susumu and Yoshio Tsuroka (eds) (2004), *'Shūkyō' Saikō* (*Re-examining 'Religion'*), Tokyo: Perikansha.

Shimizu, Isao (1991), *Manga no Rekishi* (*The History of Manga*), Tokyo: Iwanami Shoten.

Shimizu, Kōkichi (2002), *Gakkō Bunka no Hikaku Shakaigaku: Nihon to Igirisu no Chūtō Kyōiku* (*A Comparative Sociology of School Culture: Secondary Schools in Japan and England*), Tokyo: University of Tokyo Press.

— (2005), *Gakuryoku o Sodateru* (*Nurturing Academic Capacity*), Tokyo: Iwanami Shinsho.

Shimizu, Kōkichi (ed.) (1998), *'Nyūkamā mondai kara mita gakkō bunka no henkaku* (School culture change as seen through new migrants' problems)', *Kyōiku Tenbō* (*Education Outlook*), 44, pp. 26–37.

Shimizu, Kōkichi and Kōzō Tokuda (1991), *Yomigaere Kōritsu Chūgaku* (*Reinvigorating Public Middle Schools*), Tokyo: Yūshindō.

Shimizu, Kōkichi and Mutsumi Shimizu (eds) (2001), *Newcomer to Kyōiku* (*Newcomers and Education*), Tokyo: Akashi Shoten.

Shimizu, Satoshi (1998), *Kōshien Yakyū no Archeology* (*The Archeology of Kōshien Baseball*), Tokyo: Shinhyōron.

Shirahata, Yōzaburō (1996), *Karaoke Anime Ga Sekai O Meguru: 'Nihon Bunka' Ga Umu Atarashii Seikatsu* (*Karaoke and Anime around the World: Japanese Culture Gives Rise to New Lifestyle*), Tokyo: PHP Kenkyūsho.

Skelton, Russell (1996), 'Japan goes to Asia, where it's cheaper', *The Sydney Morning Herald*, 27 July, p. 34.

Small, Christopher (1987), *Music of the Common Tongue*, London: John Calder.

Smith, Jacob (2004), 'I can see tomorrow in your dance: A study of dance, dance revolution and music video games', *Journal of Popular Music Studies*, 16(1), pp. 58–84.

Smith, Jonathan Z (1998) 'Religion, religions, religious', in Mark C Taylor (ed.), *Critical Terms for Religious Studies*, Chicago: University of Chicago Press, pp. 269–84.

Society for the Study of Japonisme (1980), *Japonisme in Art: An International Symposium*, Tokyo: Committee for the Year 2001.

Song, Byung-Wak (2003), *The Rise of Korea*, Oxford: Oxford University Press.

Spencer, Jane (2007), 'China could blame West for its emissions as battle looms over who should pay', *The Australian*, 13 November, p. 26.

Standish, Isolde (1998), 'Akira, postmodernism and resistance', in DP Martinez (ed.), *The Worlds of Japanese Popular Culture: Gender, Shifting Boundaries and Global Cultures*, Cambridge UK: Cambridge University Press, pp. 56–74.

Steinhoff, Patricia G (1994), 'A cultural approach to the family in Japan and the United States', in Lee-Jay Cho and Motoo Yada (eds), *Tradition and Change in the Asian Family*, Honolulu: East West Center, pp. 29–44.

Stevens, Carolyn S (2008), *Japanese Popular Music: Culture, Authenticity and Power*, London: Routledge.

Stevenson, Harold W and James W Stigler (1992), *The Learning Gap: Why Our Schools Are Failing and What We Can Learn from Japanese and Chinese Education*, New York: Simon and Schuster.

Stevenson, Reed (2000), 'Mobile web in Japan's pocket', *The Australian*, 18 April, p. 7.

Stronach, Bruce (1989), 'Japanese television', in Hidetoshi Kato, Richard Gid Powers and Bruce Stronach (eds), *Handbook of Japanese Popular Culture*, New York: Greenwood Press, pp. 127–65.

Subramanian, SV and I Kawachi (2006), 'Bonding versus bridging social capital and their associations with self-rated health: A multilevel analysis of 40 US communities', *Journal of Epidemiol Community Health*, 60(2), pp. 116–22.

Subramanian, SV, DJ Kim and I Kawachi (2002), 'Social trust and self-rated health in US communities: A multivariate analysis', *Journal of Urban Health*, 79(4), Supplement I, pp. 21–34.

Sugawara Nobuo (1997), '*Ikei no nen* (Feelings of awe)', *Asahi Shimbun*, 27 May, evening edition, p. 9.

Sugihara, Kaoru (2005), *Japan, China and the Growth of the Asian International Economy: 1850–1949*, Oxford: Oxford University Press.

Sugimoto, Yoshio (1975), 'Structural sources of popular revolts and the Tobaku Movement at the time of the Meijji Restoration', *Journal of Asian Studies*, 34(4), August, pp. 875–89.

— (1996), '*Nihon bunka to iu shinwa* (The myth of Japanese culture)', in Shun Inoue, Chizuko Ueno, Masachi Ōsawa, Munesuke Mita and Shunya Yoshimi (eds), *Gendai Shakaigaku 23: Nihon Bunka no Shakaigaku* (*Contemporary Japanese Sociology Series, Volume 23: Sociology of Japanese Culture*), Tokyo: Iwanami Shoten, pp. 7–37.

— (1999), 'Making sense of *Nihonjinron*', *Thesis Eleven*, 57, pp. 81–96.

— (2003), *An Introduction to Japanese Society*, 2nd edition, Cambridge UK: Cambridge University Press.

— (2006), 'Nation and nationalism in contemporary Japan', in Gerard Delanty and Krishan Kumar (eds), *The Sage Handbook of Nations and Nationalism*, London: Sage Publications, pp. 473–87.

— (2008), 'Tsurumi Shunsuke: Voice of the voiceless', in Gloria Davies, JV D'Cruz and Nathan Hollier (eds), *Profiles in Courage: Political Actors and Ideas in Contemporary Asia*, North Melbourne: Australian Scholarly Press, pp. 30–42.

Sugimoto, Yoshio and Ross Mouer (1989), 'Cross-currents in the study of Japanese study', in Yoshio Sugimoto and Ross Mouer (eds), *Constructs for Understanding Japan*, London: Kegan Paul International, pp. 1–35.

— (1995) Nihonjinron *no Hōteishiki* (*The Structure of* Niihonjinron), Tokyo: Chikuma Shobō.

Sugishita, Tsuneo (2001), *NPO•NGO Gaido* (*Guide to NPOs and NGOs*), Tokyo: Jiyū Kokuminsha.

Sullivan, Harry Stack (1970), 'Self as concept and illusion', in Gregory Stone and Harvey Farberman (eds), *Social Psychology through Symbolic Interaction*, Waltham: Xerox College Publishing, pp. 386–94.

Sumita, Shōji (1983), *Gendai Jūtaku no Chihōsei* (*Regional Characteristics in Modern Housing*), Tokyo: Keisō Shobō.

Suzuki, Mamiya (2007), *Kakusa Shakai de Nihon Wa Katsu* (*Inequality and a Better Japan*), Tokyo: Kōfuku no Kagaku Shuppan.

Suzuki, Sadami (2005), *Nihon no Bunka Nashonarizumu* (*Japan's Cultural Nationalism*), Tokyo: Heibonsha.

Suzuki, Satoshi (2002), *Sedai Saikuru to Gakkō Bunka: Otona to Kodomo no Deai no Tameni* (*Generational Cycles and School Culture: Adults Meeting Children*), Tokyo: Nihon Editāsukūru Shuppanbu.

Tachibanaki, Toshiaki (1998), *Nihon no Keizai Kakusa* (*Economic Inequality in Japan*), Tokyo: Iwanami Shoten.

— (2005) *Confronting Income Inequality in Japan: A Comparative Analysis of Causes, Consequences and Reform*, Cambridge MA: MIT Press.

— (2006), *Kakusa Shakai: Nani ga Mondai Nanoka* (*The Unequal Society: Sources of the Problem*), Tokyo: Iwanami Shoten.

Tai, Eika (2005), '"*Wareware Nihonjin*" "*junsui na Nihonjin*" soshite "*uchinaru ekkyō*" ("We, the Japanese", "pure Japanese" and "internal border-crossing")', *Journal of Human Rights*, 5, pp. 55–69.

Takeda, Yūko and Reiko Kinoshita (eds), (2007) *Chizu de Miru Nihon no Josei* (*Gender Atlas of Japan*), Tokyo: Akashi Sho ten.

Takeuchi, Kiyoshi (1993), '*Seito bunka no shakaigaku* (Sociology of student culture)', in Takahiro Kihara, Takanori Mutō, Kazunori Kumagai and Hidenori Fujita (eds), *Gakkō Bunka no Shakaigaku* (*Sociology of School Culture*), Tokyo: Fukumura Shuppan, pp. 107–22.

Takeuchi, Yō (1995), *Nihon no Merit tokurashī* (*Japan's Meritocracy*), Tokyo: University of Tokyo Press.

Tamai, Kingo (2001), '*Nenkin* (Pensions)', in Kingo Tamai and Maki Ōmori (eds), *Shakai Seisaku o Manabu Hito no Tame Ni* (*For Those Wanting to Know about Social Security in Japan*), 3rd edition, Kyoto: Sekai Shisōsha, pp. 96–121.

Tamura, Suzuko (2000), *Ainu Language*, Tokyo: Sanseidō.

Tatsuno, Sheridan M. (1990), *Created in Japan: From Imitators to World-Class Innovators*, New York: Harper Business.

Tawada, Yōko (2002), *Yogisha no Yakō Ressha (The Night Train of the Suspect)*. Tokyo: Seidosha.

— (2003), *Ekusofonī: Bogo no Soto Ni Deru Tabi (Exophony: A Journey out of the Mother Tongue)*, Tokyo: Iwanami Shoten.

Terada, Nobuhiko (2006), *Gakkō Bunka o Takameru Kikaseru Hanashi, Yomaseru Hanashi (Principals' Speeches to Foster School Culture)*, Tokyo: Gakuji Shuppan.

Tezuka, Osamu (1983), 'Foreword', in Frederik L Schodt, *Manga! Manga! The World of Japanese Comics*, Tokyo: Kodansha International, pp. 10–11.

Thakur, Ramesh and Takashi Inoguchi (2003), 'Is Japan to mainland Asia what Britain is to Europe?', *The Japan Times*, 9 November.

Thorn, Matt (2001), 'Shōjo manga: Something for the girls', online at: http://www.matt-thorn.com /shoujo_manga /japan_quarterly /index.html.

— (2005), 'A History of Manga', online at: http://www.matt-thorn.com/mangagaku/history.html.

Tōkei Sūri Kenkyūjo Kokuminsei Chōsa Iinkai (Institute of Statistical and Mathematical Research, National Character Research Committee) (1961), *Nihonjin no Kokuminsei (National Character of Japanese)*, Tokyo: Shiseidō.

— (1970), *Dai 2 Nihonjin no Kokuminsei (National Character of Japanese, 2nd edition)*, Tokyo: Shiseidō.

— (1975), *Dai 3 Nihonjin no Kokuminsei (National Character of Japanese, 3rd edition)*, Tokyo: Shiseidō.

— (1982a), *Dai 4 Nihonjin no Kokuminsei (National Character of Japanese, 4th edition)*, Tokyo: Idemitsu Shoten.

— (1982b), *Dai 5 Nihonjin no Kokuminsei: Sengo Showaki Sōshū (National Character of Japanese – Postwar Showa Era Special)*, Tokyo: Idemitsu Shoten.

Tokuda, Yasuharu and Takashi Inoguchi (forthcoming), 'Influence of income on health status and healthcare utilisation in working adults: An illustration of health among the working poor in Japan', *Japanese Journal of Political Science*.

Tokuda, Yasuharu, Seiji Fujii and Takashi Inoguchi (2007), 'Association between individual's concerns about human rights issues and poor health in Asian people: The AsiaBarometer Survey', Tokyo: St Luke's Life Science Institute, St Luke's International Hospital, unpublished manuscript.

Trifiletti, Rossana (2006), 'Different paths to welfare: Family transformations, the production of welfare, and future prospects for social care in Italy and Japan', in Marcus Rebick and Ayumi Takenaka (eds), *The Changing Japanese Family*, London: Routledge, pp. 177–203.

Tsukada, Mamoru (1998), *Juken Taisei to Kyōshi no Raifu Kōsu (The Entrance Examination System and Teachers' Life Courses)*, Tokyo: Taga Shuppan.

Tsuneyoshi, Ryoko (2001), *The Japanese Model of Schooling: Comparisons with the United States*, New York: RoutledgeFalmer.

— (2004), 'The "new" foreigners and the social reconstruction of difference: The cultural diversification of Japanese education', *Comparative Education*, 40, pp. 55–81.

Tsunoda, Ryusaku, Wm Theodore deBary and Donald Keene (1964), *Sources of Japanese Tradition*, Volume II, New York: Columbia University Press.

Tsushima, Michihito, Shigeru Nishiyama, Susumu Shimazono and Hiroko Shiramizu (1979), 'The vitalistic conception of salvation in Japanese new religions: An aspect of modern religious consciousness', *Japanese Journal of Religious Studies*, 6(1–2), pp. 139–61.

Twine, Nanette (1991), *Language and the Modern State: The Reform of Written Japanese*, London: Routledge.

Tyler, Stephen (1969), *Cognitive Anthropology*, New York: Holt, Rinehart and Winston.

Uemura, Yukio (2003), *The Ryukyuan Language* (translated by Wayne Lawrence), Osaka: ELPR Osaka Gakuin University.

Ueno, Toshiya (1999), 'Techno-orientalism and media-tribalism: On Japanese animation and rave culture', *Third Text*, 47, Summer, pp. 95–106.

Ueyama, Shunpei, Kōmei Sasaki and Sasuke Nakao (1976), *Shōyō Jurin Bunka: Higashi Ajia Bunka no Genryū (Culture of the Shiny Leaves Forest: Origins of East Asian Culture)*, Tokyo: Chūō Kōronsha.

Unger, J Marshall (1996), *Literacy and Script Reform in Occupation Japan: Reading between the Lines*, New York: Oxford University Press.

Urabe, Shinichi (1999), *'Shōhi bunka seinen: Gakkō bunka no shūhen-bu ni sonzaisuru seitotachi no sekai* (Youth in consumer culture: The world of students at the periphery of school culture)', *Kyōiku (Education)*, 49, pp. 78–86.

Usui, Chikako (2005), 'Japan's frozen future: Why are women withholding investment in work and family?', in Amy McCreedy Thernstrom (ed.), *Japanese Women: Lineage and Legacies*, Washington DC: Woodrow Wilson International Center for Scholars, pp. 57–68.

Usui, Hiroshi (2001), *Amerika no Gakkō Bunka, Nihon no Gakkō Bunka: Manabi no Comyunitī no Sōzō (School Culture in America and Japan: Creating Learning Communities)*, Tokyo: Kaneko Shobō.

Van Bremen, J (1996), 'A spell in Japan in the world of play with Johan Huizinga', B Frellesvig and CM Hermansen (eds), *Florilegium Japonicum*, Studies presented to Olof G Lidin on the occasion of his 70th birthday, Copenhagen: Akademisk Forlag, pp. 79–92.

Van Sant, John E (2004), 'Sakuma Shozan's Hegelian vision for Japan', *Asian Philosophy*, 14(3), November, pp. 277–92.

Varian, Hal R (2007), 'An iPod has global value. Ask the (many) countries that make it', *The New York Times*, 28 June, p. C3.

Vlastos, Stephen (ed.) (1998), *Mirror of Modernity: Invented Traditions of Modern Japan*, Berkeley: University of California Press.

Vogel, Ezra (1979), *Japan as Number One: Lessons for America*, Cambridge MA: Harvard University Press.

von Baelz, Erwin OE (1974), *Awakening Japan: The Diary of a German Doctor*, Bloomington: Indiana University Press.

Wade, Bonnie C (2005), *Music in Japan*, New York: Oxford University Press.

Walker, James (1988), *Louts and Legends: Male Youth Culture in an Inner-city School*, Sydney: Allen & Unwin.

Walthall, Anne (1991), 'The life cycle of farm women in Tokugawa Japan', in Gail Lee Bernstein (ed.), *Recreating Japanese Women, 1600–1945*, Berkeley: University of California Press.

Waswo, Ann (2002), *Housing in Postwar Japan: A Social History*, London: Routledge-Curzon.

Watabe, Jun (1998), '*Sekai no seitoshidō: yawarakai gakkō bunka* (Student guidance in the world: Soft school culture)', *Gekkan Seito Shidō (Monthly Journal of Student Guidance)*, 28, pp. 40–3.

Watanabe, Yasushi, and David L McConnell (2008), *Soft Power Superpowers: Cultural and National Assets of Japan and the United States*, Armonk, New York: ME Sharpe.

Watanuki, Joji (1979), 'Materialist versus postmaterialist orientations in Japan', *Research Paper No. 11*, Tokyo: Institute of International Relations, Sophia University.

Watsuji, Tetsurō (1935), *Fūdo: Ningengakuteki Kōsatsu (Climate: A Humanistic Consideration)*, Tokyo: Iwanami Shoten.

— (1971), *Culture and Climate: A Philosophical Study* (translated by Geoffrey Bownas), Tokyo: Hokuseidō Press.

Watts, Jonathan (2002), 'Public health experts concerned about "Hikikomori"', *The Lancet*, 359, 30 March, p. 1131.

Weber, Max (1958), *The Protestant Ethic and the Spirit of Capitalism* (translated by Talcott Parsons), New York: Charles Scribner's Sons.

Weiner, Michael (ed.) (1997), *Japan's Minorities: The Illusion of Homogeneity*, London: Routledge.

White, Merry (1993), *The Material Child: Coming of Age in Japan and America*, New York: Free Press.

— (2002), *Perfectly Japanese: Making Families in an Era of Upheaval*, Berkeley and Los Angeles: University of California Press.

White, Paul (2003), 'The Japanese in London: From transience to settlement?', Roger Goodman, Ceri Peach, Ayumi Takenaka and Paul White (eds), *Global Japan: The Experience of Japan's New Immigrants and Overseas Communities*, London: RoutledgeCurzon, pp. 79–97.

Willis, Paul (1977), *Learning to Labour*, Hampshire: Gower.

Wu, Wan Hong (2004), *Chūgoku Zanryū Nihonjin no Kenkyū: Ijū Hyōryū Teichaku no Kokusai Kankeiron (Study on the Japanese Left in China: Moving, Drifting, Settling)*, Tokyo: Nihon Tosho Sentā.

Yabuno, Yuzō (1995), *Rōkaru-inishiateibu: Kokkyō wo koeru kokoromi (Local Initiatives that Cross National Borders)* Tokyo: Chūō Kōronsha.

Yaguchi, Kunio and Yōsuke Ōga (eds) (1999), *Manga no Jidai (The Manga Age)*, Tokyo: Museum of Contemporary Art.

Yamada, Masahiro (1999), *Parasaito Shinguru no Jidai (The Age of the Parasite Singles)*, Tokyo: Chikuma Shobō.

— (2000), '*Furītā nihyakuman-nin ni ashita wa nai sa* (The two million floating casuals have no economic future)', *Bungei Shunjū*, July, pp. 1989–204.

— (2006), 'The real story behind Japan's marriage crisis', *Japan Echo*, 33(1), pp. 20–24.

— (2007), *Shōshi shakai Nihon: Mou hitotsu no kakusa no yukue* (Low birthrate society: Moving toward a new differentiation), Tokyo: Iwanami Shoten.

Yamamura, Fumiko (1981), *Chichi Yo Haha Yo Waga Sokoku Yo: Chūgoku Zanryū Koji no Tegami (Father! Mother! My fatherland! Letters from Orphaned Children in China)*, Tokyo: Asahi Shimbunsha.

Yamazaki, Masakazu (1972), *Ōgai: Tatakau Kachō (Ōgai: The Combatant Head of the House)*, Tokyo: Kawade Shobō Shinsha.

Yamazaki, Shinchika (1996), '*Gakkō seido no naka no kyōin bunka* (Teachers' culture in the school system)', in Teruhisa Horio, Yasutoru Okudaira, Takahiko Tanaka, Hiroshi Sanuki, Noriyuki Shiomi, Masao Ōta, Sonoko Yokoyu, Toshiaki Sudō, Yoshiyuki

Kudomi and Yōichi Urano (eds), *Gakkō Bunka to Iu Jiba* (*A Magnetic Field Called School Culture*), Tokyo: Kashiwa Shobō, pp. 117–50.

Yano, Christine R (2002), *Tears of Longing: Nostalgia and the Nation in Japanese Popular Song*, Cambridge MA: Harvard University Asia Center.

Yatabe, Kazuhiko (2001), 'Objects, city and wondering: The invisibility of the Japanese in France', in Harumi Befu and Sylvie Guichard-Anguis (eds), *Globalizing Japan*, London: Routledge, pp. 25–40.

Yinger, J Milton (1982), *Counterculture: The Promise and Peril of a World Turned Upside Down*, New York: The Free Press.

Yoder, Robert S (2004), *Youth Deviance in Japan: Class Reproduction of Non-Conformity*, Melbourne: Trans Pacific Press

Yokota, Junya (1991), *Nekketsuji Oshikawa Shūrō* (*Passionate Person: Shūrō Oshikawa*), Tokyo: San'ichi Shobō.

Yomiuri Shimbun (2002), *Nihon no Yoron* (*Public Opinion in Japan*), Tokyo: Yomiuri Shimbunsha.

Yoneyama, Shoko (1999), *The Japanese High School: Silence and Resistance*, London: Routledge.

Yoneyama, Toshinao (1985), 'Nihon bunka no chiikisei o megutte (On regional variations within Japanese culture)', *Minzokugaku Kenkyū* (*Japanese Journal of Ethnology*), 49 (4), pp. 388–94.

Yoshimi, Shunya (1999), '"Made in Japan": The cultural politics of "home electrification" in postwar Japan', *Media, Culture and Society*, 21, pp. 149–71.

— (2003), 'Television and nationalism: Historical change in the national domestic TV formation of postwar Japan', *European Journal of Cultural Studies*, 6, pp. 459–87.

Yoshimoto, Banana (1998), *Kicchin*, Tokyo: Kadokawa Bunko. Translated by Megan Backus (1988) as *Kitchen*, New York: Grove Press.

Yoshino, Ryōzō (2007), *Higashi Ajia Kokuminsei Hikaku* (*A Comparison among East Asian National Characters*), Tokyo: Benseidō.

Young-Bruehl, Elisabeth and Faith Bethelard (2000), *Cherishment: A Psychology of the Heart*, New York: Free Press.

Yū, Miri (1997), *Kazoku Shinema* (*Family Cinema*), Tokyo: Kōdansha.

— (1998), *Gōrudo Rasshu* (*Gold Rush*), Tokyo: Shinchōsha.

Yū, Sawako (1993), 'Kyōshi no shokugyō pāsonaritī (Occupational personalities of teachers)', in Takahiro Kihara, Takanori Mutō, Kazunori Kumagai and Hidenori Fujita (eds), *Gakkō Bunka no Shakaigaku* (*Sociology of School Culture*), Tokyo: Fukumura Shuppan, pp. 176–93.

Zielenziger, Michael (2006) *Shutting Out the Sun: How Japan Created Its Own Lost Generation*, New York: Nan A Talese.

Index